Dynamics of Local Governance in China during the Reform Era

CHALLENGES FACING CHINESE POLITICAL DEVELOPMENT

Series Editor: Sujian Guo, Ph.D.
San Francisco State University

In an attempt to reflect the rapidly changing political environment of the People's Republic of China, editor Sujian Guo has assembled a book series to present specialized areas of research in current Chinese political studies. Incorporating theoretical, empirical, and policy research on contemporary Chinese politics both domestically and internationally, this series contemplates the Chinese past, present, and future by utilizing interdisciplinary perspectives to approach issues related to Chinese politics, economy, culture, social development, reform, the military, legal system, and foreign relations. Aimed at bringing a greater understanding of the current Chinese political climate to Western audiences, this series is focused on the emerging voices of Chinese scholars and their perspectives on the ever-changing Chinese diaspora.

Recent titles in the series are:

Challenges Facing Chinese Political Development, edited by Sujian Guo and Baogang Guo

New Dimensions of Chinese Foreign Policy, edited by Sujian Guo and Shiping Hua

The Dragon's Hidden Wings: How China Rises with Its Soft Power, by Sheng Ding

"Harmonious World" and China's New Foreign Policy, by Sujian Guo and Jean-Marc F. Blanchard

China in Search of a Harmonious Society, edited by Sujian Guo and Baogang Guo

Greater China in an Era of Globalization, edited by Sujian Guo and Baogang Guo

Toward Better Governance in China, edited by Baogang Guo and Dennis Hickey

Dynamics of Local Governance in China during the Reform Era

Edited by Tse-Kang Leng and Yun-han Chu

LEXINGTON BOOKS

A division of

ROWMAN & LITTLEFIELD PUBLISHERS, INC.

Lanham • Boulder • New York • Toronto • Plymouth, UK

Published by Lexington Books
A division of Rowman & Littlefield Publishers, Inc.
A wholly owned subsidiary of The Rowman & Littlefield Publishing Group, Inc.
4501 Forbes Boulevard, Suite 200, Lanham, Maryland 20706
http://www.lexingtonbooks.com

Estover Road, Plymouth PL6 7PY, United Kingdom

British Library Cataloguing in Publication Information Available

Library of Congress Cataloging-in-Publication Data

Dynamics of local governance in China during the reform era / edited by Tse-Kang Leng and Yun-han Chu.
p. cm. — (Challenges facing Chinese political development)
Includes index.
ISBN 978-0-7391-2688-2 (cloth : alk. paper) — ISBN 978-0-7391-4409-1 (electronic)
1. Local government—China. 2. China—Economic conditions—1976–2000.
3. China—Economic conditions—2000– 4. China—Politics and government—1976–2002. 5. China—Politics and government—2002– I. Leng, Tse-Kang. II. Zhu, Yunhan
JS7353.A2D96 2010
320.80951—dc22 2009036003

∞™ The paper used in this publication meets the minimum requirements of American National Standard for Information Sciences—Permanence of Paper for Printed Library Materials, ANSI/NISO Z39.48-1992.

Printed in the United States of America

Contents

Introduction

Yun-han Chu and Tse-Kang Leng

There have been significant developments in political institutions and local governance in both rural and urban China during the past decade or more. In rural China, economic reforms have reintroduced private farming and created multiple forms of enterprise ownership. The accompanying diversification of the rural economy has given rise to a variety of new social forces. In urban China, economic reforms have broken up the work units, redefined the relationship between citizens and the state, and created new social stratification as well as diverse economic interests.

These developments have thrown up many significant issues for empirical as well as theoretical analysis for social scientists and policy makers. Economic reform was accompanied by new political institutions at grassroots level to cope with the acute challenge of local governance. Since the early 1990s, tens of thousands of villages in rural China have held local-government elections. New forms of participation and expression have also steadily grown in the urban setting. These new phenomena need thorough discussion on the continuity and change of reforms. There also has been a revival of both indigenous and Western religions as well as a mushrooming of nonprofit organizations and civic groups. On the other hand, the "take off" in the rural as well as urban areas deserves further elaboration and theoretical innovation. All these developments provide a good opportunity to investigate the impact of institutional, behavioral, and attitudinal changes on the scope and level of public goods provision, local political economy, and the overall state-society relationship.

The main theme of this volume is to explore various forms of local governance and political change in China in the era of reform. Special emphases will be put on issues of cultural and institutional shifts, bottom-up dynamics of political changes, and new roles of the local government to cope with rapid economic and social changes in the era of reform. Local governance includes the diverse objectives of vibrant, living, working, and environmentally preserved self-governing communities. Good local governance is not just about providing a range of local services, but also about preserving the life, safety, and rights protection of residents, creating space for democratic participation and civic dialogue, supporting market-led and environmentally sustainable local development, and facilitating outcomes that enrich the quality of life of residents.[1] Thus, a synthesis of the conceptual literature suggests that the modern role of a local government is to deal with market failures as well as government failures. This role requires a local government to operate as a purchaser of local services, a facilitator of networks of government providers and entities beyond government, and a gatekeeper and overseer of state and national governments in areas of shared rule. Local government also needs to play a mediator's role among various entities and networks to foster greater synergy and harness the untapped energies of the broader community for improving the quality of life of residents.[2]

On the other hand, the importance of local government and governance could be demonstrated by the so-called de facto federalism, because it satisfies the following conditions:

1. A hierarchical political system in which the activities of government are divided between the provinces and the center in such a way that each level of government has some activities on which it makes final decisions.
2. Intergovernmental decentralization is institutionalized to such a degree that it is increasingly becoming difficult, if not impossible, for the national government to unilaterally impose its discretion on the provinces and alter the distribution of authority between governments.
3. Provinces have primary responsibility over the economy and, to some extent, politics and governance within their jurisdictions.[3]

Furthermore, the de facto federalism is accompanied by the rise of localities as the major forces of economic take-off in the past two decades. China's local state is a developmental state of its own kind. No longer passive agents of the central government, China's local governments are responsible for local prosperity. Local governments are empowered to carry out development by means of realignment of revenue distribution between the central offers and localities, leading to autonomous local governments that are highly motivated to maximize revenues in order to support local growth. China's local governments have become economic interest groups with their own policy agenda, and thus the local developmental state.[4] Dynamics of local development could also go beyond the administrative boundaries. Typical cases of cross-boundary governance could be demonstrated in the case between Hong Kong and the Pearl River Delta region.

Existing literatures on local governance argue that some radical strategies to centralize administrative and fiscal power, as political expediency in the short run, might not enhance the effectiveness of governance, but possibly demoralize local cadres and further destroy regional competition in the long run. In the long run, good governance will be the outcome of a decentralized administrative and fiscal system that includes a sound intergovernmental fiscal arrangement of wider local political participation and competition under free elections (supported by information revealed through yardstick comparison) and, ultimately, of stronger factor mobility cross-regions.[5]

Moreover, the "good governance" of economic performance in China relies on the reform of institutional change in the political realm, especially on the issues of cultural shift and elite mobility. This new stimulus is also embedded in the framework of globalization. The point is that in the intense competitive environment caused by globalization, local government still plays an important role, and the transformation of its governance pattern is gradual and deeply affected by the original system. What in fact causes the development of conflict among local governments in the Yangtze River Delta is not administrative division itself, but the hidden irrational system. The conflict of administration division actually reflects the fact that China's political system reform lags behind its economic system reform. Both systems must be reformed in such a way as to solve the problems caused by the disjuncture of reforms.[6]

Political participation in various forms also challenges the existing framework of local governance in China. While political innovation is much riskier than economic changes, competition also exists in this area. Localities can be willing to act as trial sites for experimentation because of the potential for recognition and benefits from higher levels of party leadership. If experimentation is successful, local leaders might be promoted more quickly. Participation is thought to generate ownership and agency, which contribute to social sustainability, community building, and a harmonious society. Experiments with various forms of public and stakeholder participation will lead to social learning and better understanding of the dynamics of the public participation process. Successful experiments may lead to a change in the current practice of relative non-participation. Local and regional stakeholders and the public will be better informed on plans, programs, and policies, as well as on projects.[7] This would suggest, as Saich and Yang argue, that we might need more local institutional innovation that tries to walk the fine line of broadening civic participation while retaining Leninist organizational control.[8]

As a reaction to numerous protests by farmers and land-owners against expropriation, absence of compensation, and preferential treatment of project developers by local politicians, China's central government is cautiously exploring the relationship between governance and public participation. Meaningful public participation will only come about when there is trust and equity; therefore, public participation should be institutionalized, and authorities should prove to be committed by being responsive and accountable.[9]

The emergence of Chinese non-governmental organizations (NGOs) implies the rise of a public sphere and new forms of state-society interaction. Generally, the participation of registered social organizations in the policy process takes the form of invited consultation and comments on policy changes, including drafting and amendments of relevant regulations and laws. Participation typically is initiated from above rather than from below. However, governance processes in China increasingly are fragmented, localized, and untidy, despite continuing attempts by the central party state to exercise macro control. The restructuring of state organizations in the late 1990s has reduced the capacity of officials to monitor social organizations, while local officials are willing to be lax about the implementation of regulations where the activities of non-registered groups benefit local development.[10]

For instance, the situation of Chinese environmental NGOs reflects the general tendencies of Chinese civil society and other nongovernmental organizations. As McBeath and Leng indicate, Chinese environmentalism has three main features: its broad development, the lack of confrontation with the national government, and its gradual evolution.[11] A core issue to Chinese NGOs is their degree of autonomy. A few influential organizations remain under the control of the government and the communist party in terms of financial and personnel resources and decision-making. At the same time, seemingly independent organizations have emerged in large numbers, especially at the local level. Then there are the "quasi governmental, quasi people" (*banguan banmin*), or "governmental as well as people" (*Yiguan yimin*) organizations. These do not depend entirely on the government for their income and have more freedom in decision-making. On the whole, Chinese NGOs gradually are moving out from under governmental control. Social organizations have created new programs, mobilized citizen participation, promoted multiple interests, provided alternatives for professional and social services, and practiced democratic procedures.[12]

This edited volume reflects the multiple facets of local governance and democracy in China. The following chapters also go beyond the traditional wisdom of analyzing rural development, local participation, rise of grassroots dynamics, and impetus of development in China.

In chapter 1, Jean Oi and Kaoru Shimizu divide the industrialization path into five main types to distinguish the composition of agriculture and industry in the reform era by their data collected in the 1980s and 1990s. Their most important finding is that industrialization also can leave villagers with the largest decrease in incomes. For the purposes of this chapter, the important issue is not which fees went up, but in which villages would one find peasant burdens going up. The standard assumption in the literature is that there is a link between *sources* of income and peasant burdens in China's villages after the decollectivization of agriculture.

Oi and Shimizu also suggest that the link between the path of development and peasant burdens is far from linear. Sources of revenue may determine village access to profits and the size of profits. However, industrialization does not lead necessarily to wealth or a decrease in peasant burdens; the costs may outweigh the benefits if the effort to industrialize ultimately fails.

Shaoguang Wang and Jianyu He argue in chapter 2 that while it is important to study the extent to which associations are autonomous from the party-state, approaching China with a strictly "civil society" lens may run the risk of treating the reality in a Procrustean manner. In the prospect of "social capital," the key question here is not whether associations are autonomous from state control, but to what extent people are associated with one another in some structured forms. Whereas the civil society approach emphasizes associations' "external" effects on the wide polity (e.g., providing a counterweight to the state), the social capital approach focuses on their "internal" effects on individual members' ways of thinking and behaviors.

Wang and He's chapter attempts to map out the whole picture of associational life in China, top-down or bottom-up, voluntary or involuntary, and formal or informal. Association here is broadly defined as social space in which individuals with a common interest are tied to each other through formal and informal group membership. The authors argue that studies on China's civil society often focus on "social organizations" and "private nonenterprise units," assuming that they cover the entire associational landscapes in China. Wang and He estimate that the number of social organizations that operate without official registration could be as many as 30,000–50,000 in the nation. Reforms in the last quarter of a century have further weakened their political roles and strengthened their functional roles.

In chapter 3, Richard Madsen analyzes the relation between the religion and rural self-government. Madsen argues that tensions are most stark when religious leaders interact with state officials at the national level. In many rural contexts, however, both religion and politics are deeply embedded in local community. The tensions do not go away when religious leaders and government officials are both embedded in local society, but they are blurred. Different degrees of this blurring are conducive to different forms of religious leadership, different substantive forms of religious belief, and different patterns of cooperation and conflict between religious leaders and the government.

Madsen has suggested three different models of religious social organization: a socially embedded model, a socially transcendent model, and a hierarchically nested model. During the reform era, religion has become an important social force in rural China. It is a force arising from the bottom-up in the face of varying degrees of government opposition ranging from ineffectual disapproval to vigorous suppression. Because these religious networks are separated from reinforcing social ties of family and kinship and from political patron-client ties, they provide few points of leverage to leaders who would like to subject them to unifying discipline.

In contrast, as demonstrated in chapter 4, Anne Thurston's interest in associational China has three dimensions. First, China's growing number of associations—NGOs and government-organized nongovernmental organizations (GONGOs) especially—are worthy of study in their own right. Second, many leaders of these new associations are what David Bornstein calls "social entrepreneurs"—"people with new ideas to address major problems who are relentless in the pursuit of their visions. She argues some of these social entrepreneurs are offering the Chinese people alternative models of leadership. Third, she is interested in what the nature and existence of these organizations tell us about the development of civil society in China and its potentially democratizing effects.

Thurston makes a sizable description of civil society in China through three cases—the China Youth Development Foundation's Project Hope, Sanchuan Development, and the Snowland Service Group—to assess their leadership, capacity to fulfill their missions, and whether and how they are contributing to the development of civil society. Furthermore, Thurston indicates the three organizations described in this study have three qualities in common. First, none of the organizations would have come into being without the vision of its founder. Second, the founder of each is what David Bornstein would call a "social entrepreneur." Third, each of these organizations is having a transformative effect on the communities within its sphere of influence. The new social entrepreneurship represented by these three men is not a trivial phenomenon. That the Chinese government allows such social entrepreneurs to operate and thrive is a significant change, but the social entrepreneurship, however, does not necessarily translate into civil society. In uncivil societies, integrity comes to be regarded as deviant, as it is so often in China today.

Yun-han Chu's chapter focuses on analyzing and exploring whether China's political culture, in particular its civic culture, will eventually undergo some profound transformation as a consequence of the far-reaching and rapid economic, social, and institutional changes occurring in China. This chapter adopts the concept of civic culture and, using empirical data from China including both individual-level and village-level data, identifies the key socioeconomic structural and institutional factors that drive change in political culture.

Chu's findings in the research show that the increase of democratic orientation in rural China has a lot to do with the implementation of village-level democracy and the process of socioeconomic modernization, but not much with the decline of Traditionalism. Chu's research lends strong support to both the modernization argument and institutionalist claim while, in a rather unexpected way, turning the culturalist on its head. The findings also lend support to the argument that China's political culture, in particular its civic culture, will eventually undergo some profound transformation as a consequence of the far-reaching and rapid economic, social, and institutional changes occurring in China.

Jay Chen's analyses, as elaborated in chapter 6, employ data from a 2002 China Survey, which has 3,183 urban and rural individual samples and includes measures at both the individual and contextual levels. In the aspect of individual-level measure, the concept of "capital," including human, social, and kinship capital, is the major independent variable, while the extent of a village's economic development and liberalization is also considered as village-level measures of institutional environment.

Chen further points out the existing dual career paths for rural elite positions and that political and educational credentials are screened differently for entry into cadre posts and entrepreneur positions. The results correlate with previous researches on the viewpoint that party membership is the fundamental determinant for village leaders, and that educational credentials are paramount for cadre and entrepreneur positions. In addition, the data shows that state socialist practices are still alive, which means that the effect of political capital increases notably when it is combined with social, kinship, and human capital. These aspects are closely related, especially for a Chinese villager pursuing a cadre post today. Chen stresses that post-reform rural China cannot be understood simply in a one-dimensional aspect, not only because political, social, and kinship capital would not matter the same with human capital, but also because some particular institutional arrangements have played a role in dynamic stratification mechanisms.

In chapter 7, Susan Whiting tries to explore the changing role of the courts in Chinese political economy and analyze the contracting practices and choice of dispute resolution mechanisms on the part of Chinese firms. Based on the results of analysis of a representative sample of seventy-six purchase and sales contracts, implemented through face-to-face interviews with seventy-six enterprise managers conducted in Nanjing and Shanghai between 2002 and 2004, her study seeks to evaluate the extent to which a well-functioning legal system—as opposed to political and/or cultural substitutes—provides the basis for securing intertemporal transactions and economic growth.

Whiting argues that the absence of a basis in law was the problem that still hindered the development for the nonstate economy prior to the early 1990s. The records show that private enterprises are induced to enter into legally enforceable contracts and employ resources to the courts in the late 1990s. With concrete data analysis, Whiting suggests that when firms do encounter disputes, there are few effective substitutes for an institution, such as the courts, in dispute resolution. Litigation of contract disputes is rarely the first resort. Other factors, such as the judges' qualifications, judgments and their enforcement, and private coercion, would also have impact on the firms' attitude toward the legal system. As Whiting indicates, the courts appear to play a role in contract disputes because they are seen as authoritative, but not necessarily fair or just. The understanding about the concept "rule of law" is related to the goal of regime maintenance, which seems to be more important than dispute solving. That is, if contract disputes do become politically sensitive, the "rule of law" does not always hold sway.

Shu Keng's work in chapter 8 utilizes the Kunshan township in Jiangsu Province as an example to broaden our understanding of the diverse roles of the state in market transition in general and in China's post-Mao reforms in particular. The primary focus in his chapter is the interaction between the local state and Taiwanese investors (Taishang) in Kunshan—through which we hope to grasp the dynamic roles of the state.

Keng discusses the role change of state in China's market transition, including the state-society relations and the government-business relations. The dynamic state-society relationships, according to Keng, can be best observed through observing government-business relations at the local level. The reasoning is two-fold. First, to be able to understand Chinese state and society, the best strategy is to focus on their interface with the locality—where state and society meet and cadres and entrepreneurs (standing for state and society) interact. Second, local cadres usually embody the interests of the old party-state, while business entrepreneurs are themselves emerging groups in marketization or even globalization. Then the author analyses theories of market transition, such as the "market convergence thesis" and the "institutional path-dependency perspective." Keng points out the drawbacks and wants to challenge such oversimplified interpretation of China's transition in particular and the nature of capitalist transformation in general.

Last but not least, Peter Cheung's chapter describes a special form of local governance, which is called "One Country, Two Systems." Exploring the cross-boundary interaction between Hong Kong and Mainland China after 1997, Cheung concludes six main cross-boundary developments between

Hong Kong and south China. First, governments in Hong Kong and the mainland have to respond to the community demands for further facilitation of traffic and demographic movements and to cope with the various problems arising from such interactions. Second, the scope of intergovernmental interactions has expanded to encompass a much wider agenda, including social, environmental, and public health issues. Third, while other localities in south China expected Hong Kong to take the lead in pursuing closer economic and social integration, Hong Kong still encountered considerable difficulties in such an endeavour. Fourth, with greater state involvement in managing cross-boundary affairs, cross-boundary issues have also become highly politicized matters on the policy agenda. Fifth, Beijing was increasingly asked by the Hong Kong Special Administrative Region (HKSAR) government (and perhaps by Guangdong as well) to play a role in balancing the different interests and governments in south China. Sixth, there are still many challenges, such as the need for Hong Kong and Guangdong to work closely together to solve cross-boundary problems, like infrastructure development, environment, or public health issues, that will demand great political and administrative skills from the top echelons of the HKSAR government.

This collection touches on all of the most fascinating aspects of the evolution of political institution and local governance in the context of China's rapid socioeconomic transformation. Today, the CCP regime is wrestling with the daunting task of retaining the party's hegemonic presence in the society with dwindling capacity for ideological persuasion and social control, co-opting the newly emerging social forces that came with a rapidly expanding private economy, accommodating the growing popular demand for political representation and participation, and coping with the political consequences of economic opening-up. Together, these chapters provide an illuminating intellectual framework and empirical evidence for a critical understanding of how the regime is coping with these daunting challenges, just as a realignment of the state-society relationship is being unfolded.

NOTES

1. Anwar Shah, and Furhawn Shah, 2007, "Citizen-centred Local Governance: Strategies to combat democratic deficits," *Development*, Vol. 50, No. 1, p. 73.
2. Anwar Shah, and Furhawn Shah, 2007, "Citizen-centred Local Governance: Strategies to combat democratic deficits," *Development*, Vol. 50, No. 1, p. 79.
3. Yongnian Zheng, 2006, "Explaining the Sources of de facto Federalism in Reform China: Intergovernmental Decentralization, Globalization, and Central-Local Relations," *Japanese Journal of Political Science*, Vol. 7, No. 2, p. 107.

4. Jieming Zhu, 2004, "Local Developmental State and Order in China's Urban Development during Transition," *International Journal of Urban Regional Research*, Vol. 28, No. 2, p. 424.

5. Mingxing Liu, Binwen Song, and Ra Tao, 2006, "Perspective on Local Governance Reform in China," *China & World Economy*, Vol. 14, No. 2, p. 30.

6. Jingxiang Zhang, and Fulong Wu, 2006, "China's Changing Economic Governance: Administrative Annexation and the Reorganization of Local Governments in the Yangtze River Delta," *Regional Studies*, Vol. 40, No. 1, p. 18.

7. Bert Enserink, and Joop Koppenjan, 2007, "Public participation in China: sustainable urbanization and governance," *Management of Environmental Quality*, Vol. 18, No. 4, p. 469.

8. Tony Saich, and Xuedong Yang, 2003, "Innovation in China's Local Governance: 'Open Recommendation and Selection,'" *Pacific Affairs*, Vol. 76, No. 2, p. 205–208.

9. Enserink, and Koppenjan, Ibid.

10. Jude Howell, 2003, "New Directions in Civil Society: Organizing around Marginalized Interests," in Jude Howell ed. *Governance in China*, Lanham, Md: Rowman & Littlefield Publishers, p. 163.

11. Gerald McBeath, and Tse-Kang Leng, 2006, *Governance of Biodiversity Conservation in China and Taiwan*, London: Edward Elgar.

12. Qiusha Ma, 2002, "Defining Chinese Nongovernmental Organizations." *Voluntas: International Journal of Voluntary and Nonprofit Organizations*, Vol. 13, No. 2, pp. 113–130.

Chapter One

The Uncertain Outcomes of Rural Industrialization: A Reassessment

Jean C. Oi and Kaoru Shimizu

INTRODUCTION

Until recently, much of the scholarship on rural China has tended to portray two distinct pictures: that of the impoverished, struggling peasants and that of the successful, industrialized countryside with profitable township and village enterprises (TVEs). The former is the site of poverty and increasing peasant demonstrations, where peasants pursue rightful resistance or outright use of violence to seek redress against corrupt cadres and increasing peasant burdens.[1] The latter is where villages have successfully developed enterprises via what Oi has termed "local state corporatism," where local officials spearheaded development.[2] In these localities burdens are relatively light, thanks to increases in village income derived from collectively owned enterprises.[3]

These two distinct pictures, however, only describe the two extremes of the spectrum: villages that failed to prosper and those that flourished. What of all of the villages in between? Did all villages that embarked on the road to industrialization succeed? Did today's struggling villages always face such hardships? What about villages in transition from agriculture to industry? Seldom have we asked what happens to villages on the road to industrialization. Do they stay on that path? What is the change over time? Paths of development are complex and not always linear.

A major source of this complexity in China's rural economic landscape is the diverse and changing fate of TVEs. When TVEs flourished in the 1980s, the profitable ones were the source of wealth and subsidies for villagers. However, we also know that some successful TVEs of the 1980s saw hard times by the 1990s, leaving villages with rusting factories and heavy debt.[4] This raises the possibility that villages that never attempted to industrialize may have found themselves in better economic condition than ones that attempted to industrialize but failed and, thereby, accrued heavy debt in the process.[5] Contrary to earlier assumptions, it may be the case that financially troubled villages include those that did not industrialize *and* those that attempted to industrialize but failed.

This study endeavors to put the varied snapshots of China onto one canvas, to examine the costs and benefits of the industrialization process as well as to see what happens if industrialization is never attempted. While in the early 1980s, rural village profiles were by and large similar in their dependence on agriculture, over time there is divergence in development patterns. What have been the structures of growth and what are their fiscal and political consequences? These are some of the questions addressed in this chapter.

THE UNCERTAIN ROAD OF INDUSTRIALIZATION: VARIATION AND CHANGE IN RURAL CHINA

The shift away from agriculture toward industrialization is one major indicator of economic development worldwide. In developing countries, household agriculture remains largely inefficient, with minimum mechanization and small returns on labor hours. As economies develop, the means of production gradually turn to industry, and agriculture becomes an increasingly smaller part of the economy. The assumption is that once villages move into industry, the economic situation will improve. While much more research needs to be done, the case of China suggests that the outcome of industrialization is far from certain.

In the early 1980s, soon after the rural reforms began, most villages in China depended largely on agriculture as their source of income. In the decade that followed, the Chinese rural economy went through rapid structural change. Overall, there is a dramatic decrease in average agricultural output and an increase in average industrial output, as one would expect.

Past work has highlighted the rapid growth of rural industry, the "rural China takes off" story, where villages and townships have successfully industrialized.[6] This industrialization became the source of jobs that took up the slack from agriculture and increased rural incomes in the 1980s. By some accounts, more than 200 million people escaped poverty, and per capita grain availability reached levels comparable to those in developed countries. Rich villages paid surcharges and taxes out of collective income and provided subsidies for education as well as for inputs for those who remained in agriculture to grow the grain for the village.[7]

We have long known that the economic boom was unevenly distributed. In general, areas along the eastern coast and near big urban centers, such as

Wuxi and Shanghai, enjoyed rapid growth; however, those in the interior, particularly in the central and western most provinces, remained poor. Many of these poor villages remain dependent on agriculture and the peasants shoulder heavy burdens. Some of these villages are in remote areas of rural China with poor access to major transportation routes, such as those in mountainous areas with infertile land.[8]

While variation over space has long been known, less attention has been paid to change over time in villages. By the late 1980s into the early 1990s, problems in rural industry were evident. Recent evidence suggests that a large number of villages today are suffering from large debt dating from the collapse of their township and village enterprises. It is one of the most often cited causes of debt in today's villages.[9] It is this change and variance in the development of rural industry over time that necessitates a more complex and temporal examination of the different paths taken in China's countryside. These different paths have economic as well as political consequences.

To provide a more complete understanding of the development process over time, this paper will delineate the divergent paths taken by rural Chinese villages between 1984 and 1995. It will examine existing theories and assumptions about paths of development and their consequences for peasant incomes and burdens. Rather than assume that once villages start on the road to industrialization they will continue on that path, we trace the actual experience of villages over time. We find large variation in the type of development paths taken and in the turns villages take along the way. While on average and in absolute terms there has been economic growth, many villages have also seen economic conditions worsen as time progressed. They include villages that never attempted to industrialize and stayed dependent on agriculture with continued low incomes, but they also include villages that "failed at industrialization"—those that invested resources and time into efforts to industrialize, only to be left relatively worse off over time.

THE RESEARCH

The research for this study draws on a nationwide survey conducted in China's countryside. The survey, which was implemented in 1996, is unusual in that it collected data on various aspects of China's rural political economy for an eleven-year period when the countryside experienced significant change. Information was collected from villages for three points in time: 1984, 1988, and 1995, which covers the period right after decollectivization and the take off of rural industrialization, to the late 1980s when the problems in the industrialization process began, until the first half of the 1990s when rural industry was clearly in trouble and a move toward privatization from collective ownership was underway.

The survey was implemented in twenty-five provinces and municipalities. These can be further divided into those in the coastal regions (Beijing, Tianjin, Hebei, Hainan, Liaoning, Jiangsu, Zhejiang, Fujian, Shandong, Guangdong, and Guangxi) and inland regions (Shanxi, Neimengu, Jilin, Heilongjiang, Anhui, Jiangxi, Henan, Hubei, Hunan, Sichuan, Shaanxi, Gansu, Yunnan, and Ningxia). Within these provinces and municipalities, we surveyed 200 villages in 104 counties. See map below.

Our sample design stratified the survey population by two characteristics, first by geographical region, which carried many socioeconomic differences, and second, within region, by county economic status. We used implicit stratification to give us the same proportion of rich and poor counties in the sample as in the population. Townships and villages were then drawn from these counties based on similar economic variables. At the village level we surveyed both officials and a sample of villagers.

Map 1.1

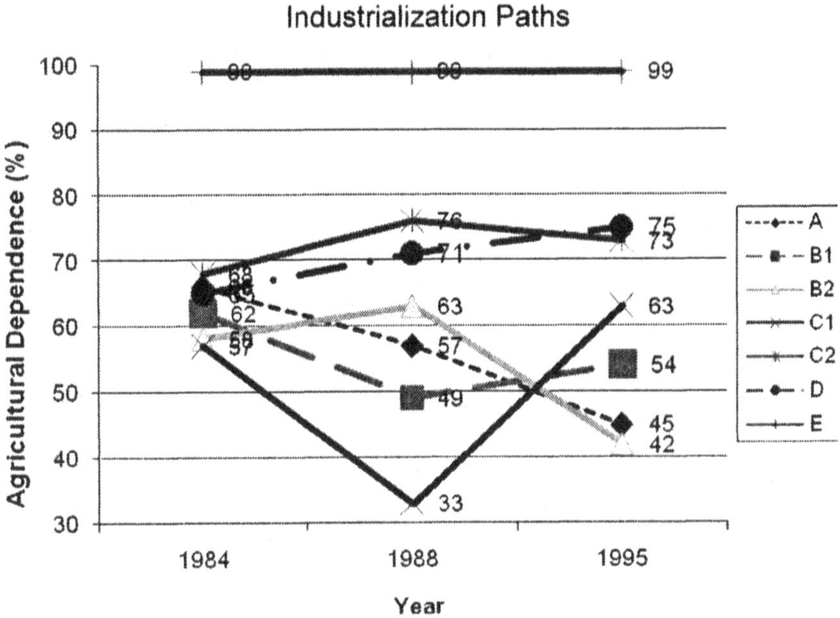

Figure 1.1

PATHS OF RURAL ECONOMIC CHANGE

As a first step in examining the divergent paths of economic transformation in rural China, we first coded and sorted our villages based on changes in the source of income over three points in time: 1984, 1988, and 1995.[10] The outcome of this exercise showed that a majority of villages in the survey went through either a consistent decrease in their reliance on agriculture as the means of production, Tier A (thirty-one villages, 29 percent of sample), or had their source of production remain the same, that is, steadily relying on agriculture, Tier D (thirty-three villages, 30 percent of sample). However, outside of these steady, linear trends, for more than 40 percent of villages in our sample, there are some important variations where villages followed a nonlinear path as shown in the following sections. The following graph and table provide details of these different paths. Because we have three points in time, we are able to examine trends within and over the entire eleven-year period. It should be clear from figure 1.1 that looking only at end points is quite deceptive.

Tracing the experience of villages that by 1995 relied primarily on industry, that is, those where output was from nonagricultural sources was close to 50 percent of collective village income, we find three distinct paths.[11]

Table 1.1. Industrialization Coding Scheme

Seven Tier Development Path	Path Description	*Change in Agricultural Dependence* 1984–1988	1988–1995	1984–1995
A	Early and Sustained Industrialization	↘	↘	↘
B1	Early Stalled Industrialization	↘	↗	↘
B2	Delayed and Rapid Industrialization	↗	↘	↘
C1	Early Take-off with Crash	↘	↗	↗
C2	Delayed and Slow Industrialization	↗	↘	↗
D	Agricultural	→	→	→
E	Steady Return to Agriculture	↗	↗	↗

Note: I. The baseline of measurement is the 1984 data.
II. Agricultural dependence is defined as the proportion of village income from agriculture.
III. For villages in group D, agricultural dependence in 1984, 1988, and 1995 remain continuously close to 100 percent.

Only a portion of the villages that began the industrialization process early (by 1984) continued to steadily pursue industry, decreasing their percentage of output from agriculture over the entire eleven-year period (from 1984 to 1995). These villages we grouped into Tier A. We label this path *Early and Sustained Industrialization.*

Early and Sustained Industrialization

While most studies implicitly assume that villages remain on a steady path once they start on the road to industrialization, only about one-third of the villages in our sample followed this path. If one only had data on level of industrialization in 1995, one would likely also assume this was the only path to industrialization. However, as figure 1.1, which is based on our more fine-grained analysis of what happened in earlier years on the road to industrialization, shows, there are two other distinct paths that can also leave villages primarily industrial.

Early Stalled Industrialization

Villages in Tiers B1 began the industrialization process early like villages in Tier A and early on managed to decrease their output from agriculture. In fact, one sees that those in Tier B did so more than villages in Tier A in the early period (1984 to 1988). However, unlike those in A, these villages then stopped moving forward on the path of increasing industrialization. Instead, they gradually returned to a path that increased the percentage of output from agriculture, although that shift is not dramatic. This suggests that these villages may have experienced some difficulty or simply decided, for reasons that we are not able to discern from our data, that enough industrialization had been attained and no further movement should be made in that direction. We label Tier B1 *Early Stalled Industrialization.*

Delayed and Rapid Industrialization

Tier B2 led villages to delay industrialization. In fact, villages on this path in the early years increased reliance on agriculture until 1988. However, these villages then turned sharply down the path of industrialization, rapidly taking off after 1988, becoming by 1995 the most industrialized of all the villages. This path we label *Delayed and Rapid Industrialization.*

Thus, overall, all villages in the A and B categories attained industrialization, but only those in Tier A pursued a linear path toward industrialization. Villages in Tiers B1 and B2 experienced an uneven and nonlinear move toward industrialization.

In contrast, disaggregating the progression and changes over time in different villages, we see that even though some villages decreased their dependence on agriculture during one of the intervals of 1984 to 1988 or 1988 to 1995, some never managed the transition to where industry was dominant. Some villages found themselves in 1995 still primarily relying on agriculture, and some even had an overall increase in percentage of output from agriculture. Again, just looking at the statistics in 1995 would not have revealed the villages' earlier attempts to shift the structure of the economy.

Early Take-off with Crash

Villages that took C1 experienced industrialization likes those in Tiers A and B1. However, industrialization on this path not only occurred early like B1, but it was very rapid. Unfortunately, those on this very early and rapid road to industrialization came to a halt. Moreover, after the halt there was a sharp turn back to agriculture. While our data do not tell us the exact circumstances, it would appear that villages that took the path of C1 took off early and fast on the road of industrialization, but then crashed and burned by 1995. Examples of failed industrialization are well known, but that term generally is used to refer to villages that never took off; seldom do we consider failure after a successful take off and period of growth. C1 villages exhibited a sharp decrease in the percentage of output from agriculture between 1984 and 1988 and then a sharp U-turn that returned villages to an even greater dependence on agriculture than in the beginning of the eleven-year period. C1 we label *Early Take-off with Crash.*

Delayed and Slow Industrialization

C2 was a more conservative path where villages had little industrialization in 1984, but instead turned more to agriculture when others were turning to industry. These villages eventually do try to pursue industrialization, but it is a delayed and timid attempt. However, in C2 both the shifts to agriculture and industrialization are minimal. This path is labeled *Delayed and Slow Industrialization.*

Agricultural

For those villages that are primarily agricultural in 1995, when we look into their past, we find two paths that differ from those described so far. Those villages in Tier D basically are those that exhibited little change of any sort. We find no significant change in the composition of their outputs over time, with a large majority remaining close to 100 percent reliant on agriculture for the entire time period examined. This path we simply label *Agricultural.*

Steady Return to Agriculture

Those in E seem to have attempted some industrialization and enjoyed some success, but then relatively early decided to remain primarily agricultural. Villages that took this path, E, like those in C2, at approximately the same time that many other villages were trying to move toward more income from industry, went in the opposite direction and steadily increased their dependence on agriculture. Path E we label *Steady Return to Agriculture.*

This typology of pathways of development allows us to appreciate the changing conditions in the same villages over time. Contrary to what one might expect given the existing literature on development in general and reform in China in particular, five of the seven pathways took villages *away* from industrialization at least part of the time—Tiers B1, B2, C1, C2, and E. Let us now examine the economic well-being of these villages and the burdens that the villages and their peasants had to shoulder over time.

INCOME AND PATHS OF DEVELOPMENT

Having delineated the various paths of development, we turn to address the question of whether a particular path makes a difference to the rural political economy of a village. What impact did these paths have on a village's income? Equally, if not more importantly, what impact did these paths have on the income of individual peasants in these different types of villages?

As figure 1.2 shows, only one of the seven paths led to increased per capita village income over the eleven-year period. Based on earlier studies, one might think it would be Path A. However, our data shows that those that took Path A, *Steady and Sustained Industrialization,* had relatively high income for a period of time, with a dip in 1988. After that, controlling for inflation, per capita village income never made it back up to the 1984 level. Most surprisingly, again controlling for inflation, it was those villages that steadily moved toward increased reliance on agriculture (Path E) after some early industrialization, that experienced the greatest percent increase in per capita income over time. We didn't expect this, given the emphasis that is traditionally placed on industrialization as a measure of development.[12] Granted, peasant income in Tier E villages are still among the lowest of all villages, there is also a dip between 1984 and 1988, but by 1995 the *percentage* increase from 1984 to 1995 is the highest among all the paths. Obviously, this is not the path to wealth, but it did yield an increase in income over time.[13] The fate of those villages that did nothing but rely on agriculture, that is, those that never attempted to industrialize (Path D), show that only keeping to the path

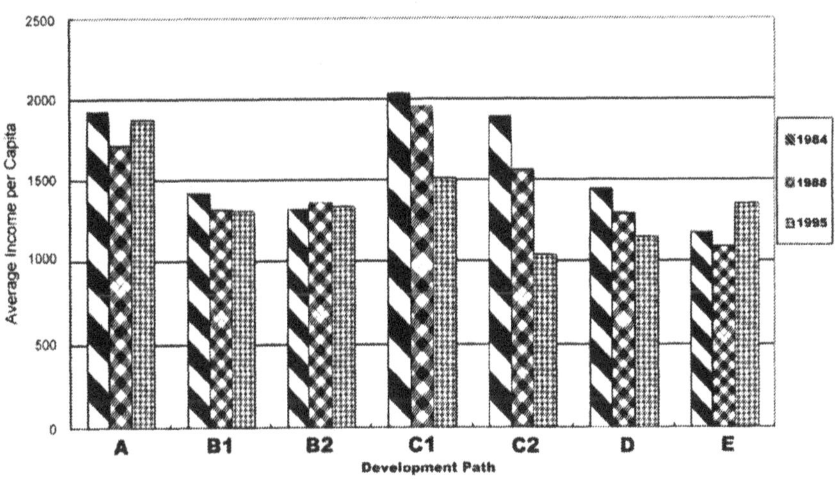

Figure 1.2

of agriculture did, as most studies have concluded, leave villagers with low and declining incomes, although the drops were not sharp.

Perhaps our most important finding is that industrialization can also leave villagers with the largest decrease in incomes. The consequences of villages following Path C1 suggest that those who followed a path of rapid industrialization and then suddenly stopped find themselves in trouble. We assume that the halt in industrialization was most likely caused by failure or trouble. In 1984, villages in C1 were among the most industrialized, although the difference was not great from those in B2. What distinguishes C1 is the extremely aggressive industrialization process that resulted in almost 70 percent of village income coming from industry by 1988, considerably more than those in B1, the next most industrialized, at approximately 50 percent. In 1988, incomes in villages on the C1 path were the highest among the surveyed villages. However, already by 1988, we see incomes declining, only to go down even further and more steeply between 1988 and 1995. Again, we are not here referring to absolute levels of income—villages that industrialized early, even those that had problems, such as C1, still have fairly high incomes in 1995. The point is that the assumption that rural industrialization would continually lead to higher incomes is not borne out. Our findings show that while increases did take place, they did not necessarily continue over time. We find a decline by 1995 in average per capita income, at least in villages like those in C1, after a substantial and successful start to industrialization.

The path that led to worse consequences for average per capita village income is C2, *Delayed and Slow Industrialization.* This is a conservative path—waiting until 1988 to start turning to industrialization and then only successfully decreasing their dependence on agriculture slightly. Ironically, these C2 villages were doing quite well in 1984, coming in third in terms of average per capita income. However, as they move toward more agriculture during the 1984 to 1988 period, incomes declined, probably because the price of agricultural output was quite low during that period. But then incomes went down even lower when villages attempted to industrialize, moving away from agriculture starting in 1988. This is not surprising because that was the beginning of the retrenchment in rural industry, when credit was scarce and the market was softening. Thus, they tried to enter the market at the worst time. These villages thus seemed to be the real losers, with little luck moving more toward agriculture or toward industrialization. It is quite likely that both C1 and C2 are cases of failed industrialization that significantly and negatively affected village income. For example, villages in B1 also moved back a bit to agriculture, but the change in income was much less dramatic, suggesting that the industry they had continued to run, perhaps not as lucratively, was in a relatively stable situation.

To summarize this section of our discussion, looking only at rates of change, not absolute levels of income, our findings suggest that attempting to decrease agricultural dependence and failing can have a more detrimental effect on income than simply never attempting to diversify and industrialize at all. But average per capita village income only shows part of the costs of industrialization. So far we have simply divided total village collective income by population. As the following section will show, different paths of development also affected peasant burdens.

PEASANT BURDENS AND PATHS OF DEVELOPMENT

Fees and taxes on rural households have come to be known as peasant burdens. These include taxes as well as the surcharges and corvee labor on top of the regular, standardized taxes levied by the central state.[14] The two main sources of peasant burdens are *tiliu* (village-retained fees) and *tongchou* (township unified fees). Central state directives ordered the sum total of *tiliu* and *tongchou* not to exceed 5 percent of peasant incomes.[15] In practice, these varied from village to village. The question is whether these burdens, like income, were similarly affected by different paths of development.

On top of *tongchou* and *tiliu*, other taxes and fees that peasants must pay include the agricultural tax, agricultural special tax, contract fee (*chengbao fei*), administrative fees, and corvee labor. Because the agricultural tax historically has been nominal, the literature to date has focused almost exclusively on the surcharges that are kept by the township (*tongchou*) and village (*tiliu*). However, as we will show below, these fees and taxes showed significant variation, which suggests that they also have become subject to manipulation as localities attempted to extract more revenue from peasants. Therefore, in our definition and examination of peasant burdens we will use the entire range of levies (see table 1.2 below).

Table 1.2. Major Types of Peasant Burdens

Central State	*Township*	*Village*
Agricultural Tax	*Tongchou*	*Tiliu*
Special Products Tax	*Ad Hoc* Fees	Collective Land Contract Fee (*Chengbao Fei*)
Quota Grain Sales to State	Fines	Labor Quotas
	Collective Fundraising	Collective Fundraising

Rising peasant burdens lie at the root of peasant discontent and protests. The state's concern about the instability that these were generating among the rural populace was the impetus for the 2002 *feigaishui* policy that finally abolished these surcharges and fees in an attempt to stop the increases.[16]

Our survey data confirms total peasant burdens going up throughout the surveyed period. In almost all cases we found that the amount of the various *tiliu* and *tongchou* exceeded the legally prescribed limit of 5 percent of peasant income. However, the aggregate numbers mask important variations. Disaggregating peasant burdens into its various components, one finds some significant patterns of change in the various fees and taxes. Elsewhere, Oi has shown that some types of peasant burdens *decreased* or at least did not increase.[17] For example, *tiliu* and *tongchou*, the two fees most often associated with peasant burdens, went down by 1995 from the late 1980s, for the nation as a whole. However, taxes and other fees that were previously nominal went up during this same period. Most prominent were increases in the agricultural tax and contract fees.

EXPLAINING VARIATION IN PEASANT BURDENS

For the purposes of this chapter, the important issue is not which fees went up but in which villages one finds peasant burdens going up. The standard assumption in the literature is that there is a link between *sources* of income and peasant burdens in China's villages after the decollectivization of agriculture. It has generally been assumed that villages that relied only on agriculture would assess the highest burdens on their peasants. This is because after the decollectivization of agriculture, the rights of the residual were transferred from the collective to the household, leaving the village authority with no rights to any income from the sale of the agricultural harvest. Consequently, those villages with no nonagricultural sources of income, that is, village-owned industry, had few reliable sources of revenue. The only revenue village authorities were allowed to collect was the *tiliu*, the village management fee, along with the *tongchou*, which went to the townships. Thus, it was thought, villages with other sources of income, that is, rural industry, were less likely to need to squeeze peasants for these fees. Alternatively, those villages that had no other sources of income were dependent on the *tiliu* for their expenditures and thus likely to try to maximize the exactions. We have numerous examples of rich, industrialized villages that paid the *tiliu*, and sometimes the taxes, for their peasants; we also have examples where peasants in the poor village are left to pay everything on their own, leaving them even poorer.[18]

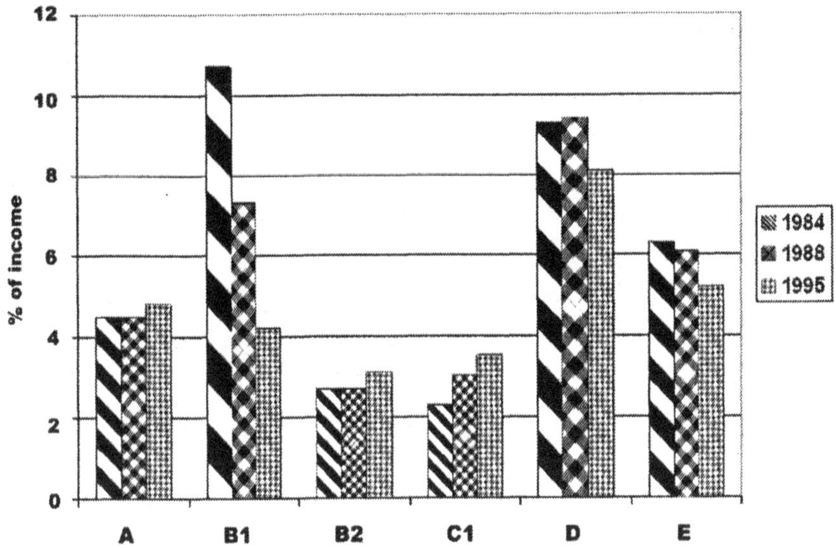

Figure 1.3

We thus expected to find that the paths of development that relied steadily on agriculture or that led villages to depend more on agriculture would leave villagers with more burdens relative to their income. Combined with the decreasing value of agricultural products, peasants in these villages would have less real income now than they did at the beginning of the reform period. Hence, as a percentage of per capita income, peasants in these villages would shoulder heavy burdens. Furthermore, individually, these peasants would likely shoulder significant, absolute amounts of burdens (i.e., taxes and fees) because the collective income in these villages could not rely on income from TVEs. However, as the following graphs show, our assumptions about the relationship between sources of income and peasant burdens only partially held up once we tested it against our data.

As we expected, the burdens in villages that remained consistently agricultural through time (Path D) were high, with only a slight decrease by 1995. They are among the highest by 1988. To our surprise, however, the pathway that resulted in the highest peasant burdens in any time period, 1984, was B1, *Early Stalled Industrialization.* Remember that B1 villages attempted to industrialize relatively early but then returned to agriculture. This likely meant that the village as a collective had little capital of its own during the initial spurt of industrialization and probably needed to borrow funds to mount the industrialization drive. A common source of funds in that period was funds raised from the peasant households in the village. Our findings about villages

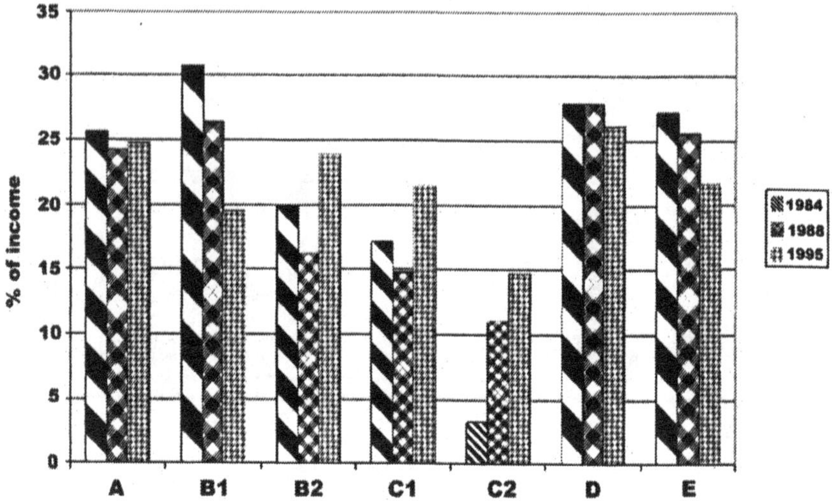

Figure 1.4

following this B1 path show that peasants were burdened with having to turn over more to the village, not only when there was no industry and thus little collective income, but also in cases where the village was rapidly industrializing and thus in need of more capital. The plausibility of this investment logic is borne out by the fact that peasant burdens steadily go down once the path of development turns and returns to agriculture, suggesting that the industrialization effort had stabilized, industries established were producing profits, and a decision had been made to halt expansion, and thus less capital was needed. Similarly those on the pathway that moved increasingly toward agriculture, Path E, saw peasant burdens go down steadily. This decrease suggests that there was no great debt incurred from the early industrialization, in contrast to C1 (see below), nor was there any further great need for capital.

A similar logic seems also to be at work when one looks at the change in peasant burdens in B2, *Delayed and Rapid Industrialization.* It is only when the path of development veers toward rapid industrialization and thus the need for capital increases that peasant burdens shoot up. In the period up to 1988, moving more toward agriculture, there would have been less need for village authorities to seek significantly higher surcharges; there is, in fact, a decrease from the 1984 period. C2 may be a similar situation, although it is unclear why peasant burdens were so much lower in these villages than any others in 1984. However, by 1988, we see that the peasant burdens are increasing—in the first instance because these are largely agricultural villages, but then in the second instance, in 1995, when there seems to have been movement toward some attempt at industrialization.

The change in peasant burdens in C1 villages, the rapid take-off-then-crash scenario, illustrates what is likely the other cause of peasant burdens, debt from failed attempts at industrialization. This is different from the cases described above where the increased levies were likely for investment and the trend toward industrialization was going up. Path C1 led to early, rapid industrialization that yielded high income (the highest in 1984 as figure 1.2 shows) and among the lowest peasant burdens for the same period. This is the scenario that early studies described of highly industrialized, rich villages that had little need to burden their peasants—enough income had already been generated from the previous success at industrialization. The amount of peasant burden goes even lower by 1988, further suggesting that profits were accumulating up to that point; income was slightly less than 1984 but not by much. However, the story changes dramatically after 1988, no doubt because of the impact of the retrenchment described above and perhaps other problems particular to these villages that we do not know. The figures on income and burdens suggest that the industrialization effort crashed, incomes dropped substantially, and peasant burdens increased substantially. We suspect that these increased surcharges went to pay for the village debt accumulated from the previous rapid industrialization process.[19]

TIME AND STAGES IN THE INDUSTRIALIZATION PROCESS

The inconclusive and unexpected findings on the relationship between sources of income and peasant burdens can be better understood if, when thinking about paths of development, one specifically takes into account both change over time and phase of industrialization. A village's phase of industrialization is crucial to understanding variation in peasant burdens. Had a village already reached a high plateau of development where it was able to enjoy the profits and no longer in need of large amounts of capital for further development such as C1? Or was a village still in the midst of rapid and concerted efforts to develop and thus in great need of more capital, in spite of substantial development of village enterprises such as those taking Path B1? Or is this a case where the villages have suffered some sort of economic crisis and the industrialization process has come to a crashing halt, leaving the village with large debt, as was likely the case in C1 between 1988 and 1995? Only after we factored in both the time and the phase of development could we make sense of our data on peasant burdens.

Deconstructing the process of industrialization shows that in villages where rapid industrialization was continuing, peasant burdens remained high, even as incomes were going up. It is only when a village has accumulated enough profits and no longer needs to raise additional funds to pursue a strategy of rapid industrialization that peasant burdens start to go down. Path A is sustained industrialization, but it is relatively gradual and not as dramatic as what C1 experienced between 1984 and 1988. We hypothesize that over the eleven-year period we are studying, C1 continually pursued faster industrialization and thus continually needed to collect high *tiliu*. The hypothesis that we would find lower peasant burdens in industrialized villages wrongly extrapolated from the most industrialized, richest villages to those still climbing up the ladder of industrialization.

Also relevant is the time period over which development took place. For example, we found that the still rapidly industrializing villages increased rather than decreased *tiliu* between 1988 and 1995, when most other villages were cutting *tiliu* (see below). Part of the explanation is that the late 1980s, when the central government instituted retrenchment measures to cool down the economy and froze credit from the banks, was a depressed period for village and township enterprises. Thus, it is not surprising that those who had not started their industrialization earlier had difficulty, for example, those on Paths C2 and B2. Path B2 also did not take off until then but its drive is much more intense and the turn to industry is much more aggressive. Our data is insufficient for detailed analysis, but we speculate that the more industrialized base of Path B2 villages—these villages in 1988 already had approximately 40 percent industrial economies—aided their rapid post-1988 growth.

Following the 1988 retrenchment, villages that had embarked upon a rapid development plan relatively late had to seek funds from all possible sources, including village households. The early industrializers already had an economic cushion when the retrenchment began in 1988 and, thus, were better prepared for the subsequent scarcity of funds. Moreover, as better established villages with commensurate lower credit risk, the early industrializers were better able to borrow from outside the village. In this manner, the early industrializers faced less need to squeeze funds from households.

Finally, it is important to clarify the difference between villages that remained dependent on agriculture and those that failed in industrialization. Villages that remained dependent on agriculture most likely suffered as a result of declining prices of agricultural goods, especially relative to nonagricultural goods. Their incomes remained relatively low. However, their ability to retain their means of production meant that major production costs were relatively stable, thus avoiding the need to enter into debt. Conversely, villages that attempted but failed in industrialization expended large amounts of effort and resources in the effort to industrialize. These resources were collected by local governments through fund-raising campaigns directed at local villagers and were used to build and operate the ultimately unsuccessful TVEs. These unsuccessful TVEs thus consumed large portions of village collective incomes and eventually resulted in collective debt.

POLITICAL VERSUS ECONOMIC PRESSURES

While economic need is an important variable in explaining the variation in peasant burdens in villages that took different paths to development, we must not forget that these villages also operated within a still strong state. Political context always must be taken into account. As Oi has detailed elsewhere, the state issued directives for all villages to cut *tiliu* and *tongchou* long before the *feigaishui* policy in 2002.[20] The question is thus how the economic and political pressures interacted in different types of villages.

Villages with different economic resources reacted differently to the increasing directives to cut *tiliu and tongchou.* Data from figure 1.3 supports the economic argument that the most industrialized and thus, most likely, the wealthiest villages implemented the largest cuts in *tiliu and tongchou,* even in the 1988 to 1995 period when economic conditions were poor. These highly industrialized, rich villages could afford to comply with the state's directives to cut peasant burdens.

Evidence of political pressures creating results counter to those suggested by our economic argument is the finding that the majority of villages either did not increase or cut *tiliu* and *tongchou* in the 1988 to 1995 period. It was precisely during this period that the state stepped up its political efforts to limit *tiliu* and *tongchou.* This suggests that political pressure from the center to limit these two surcharges did have an impact. This decrease in charges was also found in those villages most dependent on agriculture, presumably those villages with the greatest stake in maintaining or increasing a high level of *tiliu.*[21] Rather than having a purely economic or political rationale at work, it appears that villages had to weigh the two types of pressures and act on the one most pressing.

It is also interesting to note that villages that took Path A increased rather than cut *tiliu* and *tongchou* (figure 1.3). One explanation is related to the above logic that villages on a path of sustained industrialization required similarly sustained investment and expansion capital, raised through *tiliu* and *tongchou.* These villages also likely felt more politically secure because they were not the target of the directives to cut *tiliu*—the state was primarily concerned with the much poorer agricultural villages. A similar logic was probably at work in the Path B2 villages, those that embarked upon rapid industrialization around 1988. However, rather than being related to lesser political pressure, the increase in *tiliu* and *tongchou* seen in Path C1 is most likely related to the economic crash experienced by these villages. Path C1 villages needed to increase funds through all possible means, including *tiliu* and *tongchou.*

A further factor that must be considered when analyzing ostensibly politically compliant villages is that some cuts of *tiliu* were offset by other levies. *Tiliu* was only one of several village fees (table 1.1) and, when all peasant burdens were summed, constitutes only a portion of total peasant burden (figure 1.4). One common avenue that local officials used to compensate for decreased *tiliu* and *tongchou* fees was increased land rent prices. From 1984 to 1995 there were no specific regulations on how much villages could charge for fees such as land rent, which was not a central government focus, and, consequently, local cadres in all types of villages had more leeway to increase these land fees.

Land rents were especially attractive to those villages that were dependent on agriculture because it was a viable way to increase revenues without any collective investment. Land rents were likely also increasingly attractive to those villages with industry who witnessed declining incomes in the late 1980s and early 1990s. The percentage increase in land rent per *mu* is greatest in the tier of villages that were most dependent on industry.[22]

THE UNPREDICTABILITY OF DEVELOPMENT

Taken together, our findings suggest that the level of industrialization alone is not a sufficient predictor of peasant burdens or economic well-being. There are many paths of development open to villages. The path of agriculture results in predictably high peasant burdens due to the villages' inability to generate more productive sources of income. On the other hand, industrialization may lead to wealth but it may also lead to higher debt and burdens. Our findings amply illustrate the fate of those villages that attempt, but fail, to industrialize. The generalization that peasant burdens decrease in concert with village industrialization *only* holds after a village reaches a point of development where profits are sufficient to repay initial investments, meet current costs, and fund expansion plans. Rather than immediately decreasing peasant burdens, the industrialization process in Chinese villages, at least at some point in each village's development history, depended on increased peasant burdens.

Our findings thus broaden our understanding of the cause of rural poverty—an understanding previously incorrectly focused exclusively on agriculture-based poverty. Staying dependent on agriculture does not necessarily lead to an increase in peasant burdens, while unsuccessful attempts to industrialize can saddle villages with crippling debt. Thus, the key point that emerges from our study is that burdens are not determined by the industry/agriculture ratio in the composition of the economy. In some cases, continued dependence on agriculture may be an alternative, more stable path to "development." Only those that have successfully industrialized can decrease peasant burdens. The worst-case scenarios are villages that try to take off and then flop (Path C1). By attempting to industrialize, then reverting back to agriculture, peasants shoulder a "double" burden, some of which are still being felt today.[23] Debt from failed TVE development is widespread as recent studies have begun to document.

While the determinants of development remain unclear, our findings suggest that the link between the path of development chosen and peasant burdens is far from linear. The case of China's TVEs shows that rural industrialization does not lead necessarily either to wealth or to a decrease in peasant burdens; the costs may outweigh the benefits if the effort to industrialize ultimately fails. Moreover, our data show that even successfully industrializing villages may have heavy burdens. Villages must "take off" *and* stay in flight; otherwise, the burdens will be greater than if they had not "taken off" at all.

NOTES

1. Albert Park, Scott Rozelle, Christine Wong, and Changqing Ren, 1996, "Distributional Consequences of Reforming Local Public Finance in China," *China Quarterly*, No. 147, pp. 751–779; Tom Bernstein, and Xiaobo Lu, 2003, *Taxation without Representation in Contemporary Rural China*, Cambridge University Press; Kevin O'Brien, 1996, "Rightful Resistance," *World Politics*, Vol. 49, No. 1, pp. 31–55; and other articles by Kevin O'Brien and Liangjiang Li.

2. Jean C. Oi, 1999, *Rural China Takes Off: Institutional Foundations of Economic Reform*, University of California Press; also Susan Whiting, 2001, *Power and Wealth in Rural China: The Political Economy of Institutional Change*, Cambridge University Press.

3. This does not include those villages where there was a predominance of private firms. In those cases, the village as a collective was often still poor, even as individual entrepreneurs became rich. The right to the profits from those enterprises belonged to the individual, not the village.

4. Jean C. Oi, 1999, *Rural China Takes Off: Institutional Foundations of Economic Reform*, University of California Press; and Jean C. Oi, and Zhao Shukai, 2007, "Fiscal Crisis in China's Townships: Causes and Consequences," in Merle Goldman and Elizabeth Perry, (eds.), *Grassroots Political Reform in Contemporary China*, Cambridge, Mass.: Harvard University Press, pp. 75–97.

5. There are signs of this in studies such as Sally Sargeson and Jian Zhang, 1999, "Reassessing the Role of the Local State: A Case Study of Local Government Interventions in Property Rights Reform in a Hangzhou District," *The China Journal*, No. 42, pp. 77–99.

6. Jean C. Oi, 1999, *Rural China Takes Off: Institutional Foundations of Economic Reform*, Berkeley: University of California Press.

7. For a detailed discussion of this process see Jean C. Oi, 1999, *Rural China Takes Off: Institutional Foundations of Economic Reform*, Berkeley: University of California Press.

8. The plight of these types of villages is detailed in Tom Bernstein and Xiaobo Lu, 2003, *Taxation without Representation in Contemporary Rural China*, Cambridge University Press. This is not to say that there was no change in the nonindustrializing areas. Recent studies show that even the poorest of rural villages have seen significant economic improvements over the past twenty years. More villages have electricity and running water, and even the poorest villages are showing signs of modernization. See Scott Rozelle, Jikun Huang, and Linxiu Zhang, 2002, "Emerging Markets, Evolving Institutions, and the New Opportunities for Growth in China's Rural Economy," *China Economic Review*, No. 123, pp. 1–8.

9. See Jean C. Oi and Zhao Shukai, 2007, "Fiscal Crisis in China's Townships: Causes and Consequences," in Merle Goldman and Elizabeth Perry, (eds.), *Grassroots Political Reform in Contemporary China*, Cambridge, Mass.: Harvard University Press, pp. 75–97.

10. For this paper we only used the data from 107 villages because these had complete data on all three years: 1984, 1988, and 1995. These villages were sorted into seven tiers based on their percentage of total output from agricultural production over time.

11. We include in this those in Tier B1, which is slightly less than 50 percent.

12. At this point we are not sure why this is the case. Explanations for these observed trends require further research. Given the low price of grain, this increase may be explained by a switch to cash crops. Alternatively, another possible explanation may be that this masks income gained from remittances sent back from family members working outside of the village as migrant workers. Such alternative paths to improving average income and economic well-being are outside the scope of this current work but need further exploration.

13. We are not able at this point to say why this was the case. It may have something to do with the type of agriculture they were pursuing, that is perhaps cash crops. Perhaps it was also the case that the short-lived foray into industry provided some sort of necessary base.

14. China is a unitary system where localities have no right to levy taxes. The surcharges are levied and kept by the localities but the ceilings on this amount are in theory set by the center. But as we will see, this rule is not always followed.

15. *Nongmin Fudan 200 Wen.*

16. For or a more detailed discussion of the various attempts to reduce peasant burdens, see Jean C. Oi, 2004, "Old Problems for New Leaders: Institutional Disjunctions in Rural," in Yun-Han Chu, Chihcheng Lo, and Ramon Myers, (eds.), *The New Chinese Leadership: Challenges and Opportunities after the 16th Party Congress*, Cambridge: Cambridge University Press, pp. 141–155.

17. Jean C. Oi, 2004, "Old Problems for New Leaders: Institutional Disjunctions in Rural," in Yun-Han Chu, Chihcheng Lo, and Ramon Myers, (eds.), *The New*

Chinese Leadership: Challenges and Opportunities after the 16th Party Congress, Cambridge: Cambridge University Press, pp. 141–155.

18. See, for example, Jean C. Oi, 1999, *Rural China Takes Off: Institutional Foundations of Economic Reform*, Berkeley: University of California Press; and Tom Bernstein, and Xiaobo Lu, 2003, *Taxation without Representation in Contemporary Rural China*, Cambridge: Cambridge University Press.

19. The information from these villages does not list any debt, so we do not know for sure what the problems were.

20. Jean C. Oi, 2004, "Old Problems for New Leaders: Institutional Disjunctions in Rural," in Yun-Han Chu, Chihcheng Lo, and Ramon Myers, (eds.), *The New Chinese Leadership: Challenges and Opportunities after the 16th Party Congress*, Cambridge: Cambridge University Press, pp. 141–155.

21. The *tongchou* was also collected by the village but that amount went to the township.

22. This pattern also is reaffirmed if one divides villages according to the macro regions. Villages in the Zhongnan area, which include the most highly industrialized areas of the countryside, showed the highest percent increase in land rents in the 1988-to-1995 period, precisely the period when village enterprises began their decline. Bernstein and Lu, citing State Council agricultural economist Lu Mai, conclude that industrialized villages had to increase taxes to maintain their level of expenditures. It was not stated which taxes increased. No mention was made of land rents. Bernstein and Lu, *Peasant Taxation*, Chapter 3.

23. Jean C. Oi, and Zhao Shukai, 2007, "Fiscal Crisis in China's Townships: Causes and Consequences," in Merle Goldman and Elizabeth Perry, (eds.), *Grassroots Political Reform in Contemporary China*, Cambridge, Mass.: Harvard University Press, pp. 75–97.

Chapter Two

Associational Revolution in China: Mapping the Landscapes

Shaoguang Wang and Jianyu He

INTRODUCTION

In recent years, political and scholarly interest in associational life has increased noticeably, because "a striking upsurge is under way around the global in organized voluntary activity and the creation of private, nonprofit or non-governmental organizations."[1] However, little is known about associational life in China, the world's most populous country with an estimated population of 1.3 billion. If we are indeed in the midst of a "global associational revolution" as Salamon proclaims, it is quite important and timely to ask whether China is part of the revolution.[2]

Some outside commentators often assume that associational life is repressed and therefore insignificant under the communist rule.[3] In fact, the situation in China does not appear to be very different from the above-mentioned worldwide trend. After thirty years of omnipresent government control, the Chinese state began in the late 1970s to step back from its effort to program totally all of social life. As the economy and society become more pluralistic and as the people enjoy more freedom than ever before, it is only natural for Chinese to pursue a more active associational life. Now a significant number and wide range of associations are in operation in the country. The problem is that, except for few aggregated numbers, we know very little about this aspect of modern Chinese society. For this reason, improving the base of knowledge about Chinese associational life in a systematic fashion is a matter of great academic interest. The purpose of this study is to do just that—contributing to our understanding of associational landscapes in China.[4]

RATIONALE

Since the early 1990s, the expanding social space between the individual and the state has attracted growing interest from China specialists. The focus of the field has been on so-called "civic associations." Some studies examine specific types of membership organizations, such as trade unions,[5] business and professional associations,[6] student associations,[7] leisure groups,[8] or foundations.[9] Others focus on associations located in certain towns and cities.[10] Still others deal with civil associations in general.[11] Those studies are often informative and insightful. Together, they provide a broad yet diverse picture about associational life in contemporary China.

Rich as it is, however, with few recent exceptions,[12] the literature suffers from three drawbacks.

Approach

The central theoretical concern of the literature has been whether the growth of civic associations is indicative of the emergence of "civil society" in China. Some specialists conclude that elements of civil society are already present in such associations, and that civil society may emerge more fully in the future.[13] Others disagree. In their view, those associations can best be explained as examples of corporatism.[14] Still others point out that there may be "a possible continuum" of associational experiences stretching from those completely dominated by the state at one extreme to those relatively autonomous at the other.[15] The civil society approach focuses its attention almost exclusively on trying to ascertain whether associations represent the emergence of a civil society that can challenge the party-state. While it is important to study the extent to which associations are autonomous from the party-state, approaching China with a strictly "civil society" lens may run the risk of treating the reality in a Procrustean manner. No wonder that many studies end up with a disappointing conclusion that there is little resemblance between Chinese and Western experiences. Perry is right that a simple state-society dichotomy is of little help in explaining associational life in China.[16] To study the space between the state and the market, we should not force the world to fit our concepts. Rather, we should adjust our concepts to fit the real world.

Coverage

Perhaps due to the influence of the civil society approach, much of the research has focused on civic associations, especially on what have come to be known as nongovernmental organizations (NGOs), not on associations in general. The concept of NGOs, while quite useful for some purposes, embraces a very limited range of associations. It excludes most associations that exist in today's China. Moreover, the concept of NGOs often functions as an ideological screen used to differentiate "good" associations from "bad" ones along lines that are often not entirely clear.[17] Thus, studies on NGOs may at best supplement, but certainly cannot substitute, studies on associations.

Data

Most studies are case studies in nature, covering either certain types of associations or associations in certain local communities. As Pei comments, they may have enabled us to examine individual "trees," but overlooked the "forest."[18] Moreover, most of the previous research has been either published before the mid-1990s[19] or was based upon data collected before the mid-1990s.[20] As snapshots of particular times and places, they are of course valuable. But China is a country where "the situation changes so fast that updates are needed almost before the ink is dry."[21] It is necessary to provide up-to-date information on the rapidly changing associational landscapes in China.

This chapter intends to provide a quantitative assessment of the density and diversity of associational life in China. Informed by another prevailing concept in social sciences in the last decade or so—social capital— the key question here is not whether associations are autonomous from state control, but to what extent people are associated with one another in some structured forms. The concept of social capital refers to "resources embedded in social networks accessed and used by actors for action."[22] Associational activity is a cornerstone of the theory of social capital. Various associations, formal or informal, constitute durable networks of interpersonal relationships that provide their members with such capital. For this reason, the degree of associational life is often used as a surrogate measure of social capital.[23]

Social capital is not only individual goods but also collective goods.[24] In addition to enabling individuals to gain access to information, favors, status, wealth, power, reputation, and the like, it may also contribute to the creation and maintenance of democracy, albeit indirectly. Through fostering the exchange of information, the norms of reciprocity, and interpersonal trust, for instance, social capital may help facilitate spontaneous cooperation, thus "overcoming dilemmas of collective action and the self-defeating opportunism that they spawn."[25] Thus, a society with a relatively high level of social capital stock does not have to rely as heavily on the use of force by the state to induce cooperation as those with lower levels of social capital stock.[26] Perhaps equally important, as a particular form of social capital, membership in associations may instill habits of compromise and tolerance, and cultivate organizational and communications skills, which in turn may increase people's motivation and capacity to take part in politics and also their sense of political efficacy and competence.[27] Because associations may breed a democratic ethic among their members, they are often viewed as the school for democratic citizenship.

Whereas the civil society approach emphasizes associations' "external" effects on the wide polity (e.g., providing a counterweight to the state), the social capital approach focuses on their "internal" effects on individual members' ways of thinking and behaviors.[28] Both types of effects may be necessary for the emergence, consolidation, effectiveness, and stability of democratic government, but the conditions for them to occur are quite different. External effects are unlikely to happen unless associations are somewhat political and relatively autonomous from state control. However, internal effects do not require that manifest purpose of the association be political. That is why Tocqueville praises various kinds of associations, "religious, moral, serious, futile, very general and very limited, immensely large and very minute" as virtuous organizations.[29] In fact, as Tocqueville insists, civil associations are more crucial than political associations to a democratic society. "If the inhabitants of democratic countries had neither the right nor the taste for uniting for political objects, their independence would run great risks, but they could keep both their wealth and their knowledge for a long time," Tocqueville argues. "But if they did not learn some habits of acting together in the affairs of daily life, civilization itself would be in peril."[30] SidneyVerba, Key Lehman Schlozman, and Henry E. Brady echo that thought, "Both the motivation and the capacity to take part in politics have their roots in the fundamental non-political institutions."[31] Putnam put it more vividly, "Taking part in a choral society or a bird-watching club can teach self-discipline and an appreciation for the joys of successful collaboration."[32] There are many more studies demonstrating that participation in nonpolitical organizations can stimulate political involvement and interest.[33]

Similarly, it can be argued that for associations to generate social capital or some of the above-mentioned "internal" effects, they do not have to be formal, voluntary, or fully autonomous from state control. According to Pierre Bourdieu,[34] social capital is rooted in "a durable network of more or less institutionalized relationships of mutual acquaintance and recognition—or in other words, to membership in a group." As long as an association forms such a network, the ensuing dense interpersonal relationships would constitute a valuable asset that may benefit its own members as well as the society at large, whether the association is a formal, voluntary nongovernmental organization or not. Studies in the United States and the United Kingdom, for instance, have found that social networks, both formal and informal, reduced crime.[35] Claus

Offe and Susanne Fuchs observe that among informal groups in Germany, "This informality does not preclude a strong preparedness on the part of those attached to provide help and to share resources with other (recognized) members."[36] Likewise, a study of involuntary organizations in England questions the current emphasis on voluntary organizations when examining social capital. The formal institutions active within England's smaller communities in the fourteenth to the seventeenth centuries were found to have generated considerable social capital (including both internal and external returns), regardless of whether participation in them was obligatory or voluntary. The emphasis upon the voluntary nature of organizations by political scientists in their study of social capital therefore is deemed unnecessary.[37] For similar reasons, it may also be premature to exclude the possibility that associations incorporated or coopted by the state can produce useful social returns just as effectively as can groups that are independent from the state. Foster is right when he points out that, "Associations do not invariably seek autonomy from the state. Viewing associations as fundamentally 'civic' in nature, embodying a societal interest in freedom from state domination, obscures the more basic fact that associations are organizations created to accomplish particular goals."[38]

In sum, the analytic framework that undergirds the civil society approach is unduly restrictive. Consequently, many interesting and important parts of the associational universe are dismissed as unworthy of attention. In contrast, the social capital approach is more inclusive, allowing the fullest possible array of associations to be included in our study. Applying this approach, the article attempts to map out the whole picture of associational life in China, top-down or bottom-up, voluntary or involuntary, and formal or informal. *Association* here is broadly defined as social space in which individuals with a common interest are tied to each other through formal and informal group membership.[39]

Measuring the density and diversity of associational life may appear to be a modest objective, but in fact, it is a Herculean task. The study of associations in China has long been handicapped by the absence of a central source of information on the subject. As in most other countries, the Chinese government rarely gathers statistical data on associations, and even if some of its agencies do, they often collect information only in their respective jurisdictions. Thus, even at the most basic level of quantification, information is abysmally inadequate and fragmented. Since no single information source on associations is available, we have made great efforts in assembling data from a large assortment of sources. The picture emerged from the data presented below make it unambiguously evident that a veritable associational revolution is indeed underway in China, which may well prove to be as momentous a feature of contemporary China as the rise of a market economy.

		Nature	
		Voluntary	**Involuntary**
Makeup	**Formal**	Organizations under the Jurisdiction of the Ministry of Civil Affairs	Quasigovernmental Organizations
	Informal	Grassroots Groups Virtual Groups	Traditional Kinship

Figure 2.1

For the sake of convenience, we build a simple typology of associative forms of social life based upon the combination of two dimensions: nature can be voluntary or involuntary, and makeup can be formal or informal (figure 2.1).

THE BENCHMARK

In order to demonstrate that the above-mentioned "associational revolution" is real, not illusory, we need to place the recent development in a historical perspective. A brief history of associations in China therefore is presented here.

In traditional China, primary associations of family and kinship were abundant, membership in most of which were non-voluntary. Qiangxue Society—a reformist group founded by Kang Youwei in Beijing in September 1895—was thought to be the first modern secondary or civic association in the country. This group existed for barely five months before the Qing government outlawed it in January 1896. Ironically, the ban of Qiangxue Society spurred even greater interest in starting reform-oriented learned societies among the literati. The following two years witnessed the first wave of association formation in the modern history of China, with sixty-three such groups established in the period.[40]

In the first decade of the twentieth century, voluntary groups began to proliferate. A study identifies 733 membership associations that came into being between 1899 and 1909, including 85 reformist groups, 65 revolutionary, 265 commercial, 103 educational, 65 academic, 50 diplomatic, 17 cultural, and 83 others.[41] Of course, the number of associations at any particular moment during these years were much smaller than 733, because early groups tended to be fragile or short-lived.

In 1911, the Qing dynasty was overthrown and replaced by the Republic of China, the first republic in Asia. The political change catalyzed another wave of associational development. Within a year or so, nearly 700 political organizations emerged across the country.[42] Soon after, business associations began to burgeon. While only 57 chambers of commerce were identified in 1912,[43] the number jumped to 1,242 in 1915.[44] After the death of Yuan Shikai in 1916, the subsequent political chaos and tangled warfare between regional warlords temporarily hampered associational activity. However, following the May Fourth Movement of 1919, China saw the beginning of yet another upsurge of associational building. Hundreds of youth groups, learned societies, literary clubs, mutual aid co-ops, and so on sprang up in major cities, especially among university students and professors, between 1920 and 1923.[45]

In order to mobilize political support against their common enemies—warlords and local bullies—both the Nationalist Party (KMT) and newly established Communist Party made painstaking efforts to set up trade unions and peasants' associations in the mid-1920s. Around the time when the two parties split in 1927, there were about 700 trade unions with over 2 million members[46] and 22,000 peasants' associations with 9,153,093 members.[47] Afterward, the two parties separately controlled their own workers' and peasants' organizations. There is no record on the communist side, but the Nanjing government claimed to have 33,000 grassroots peasants' associations with 34,681,000 members in 1938.[48]

From 1937 to 1945, China was at war with Japan. Large parts of China's territory fell under Japanese occupation. The KMT government then moved its capital to an inland city, Chongqing. In 1942, it stipulated "Organic Law of People's Groups during the War Time," which required associations to register with the government. A total 17,250 organizations did in the same year. Two years later in 1944, the number reached 26,126. Of course, organizations existing in areas under Japanese control were excluded.[49] No one knew the real number for the whole country. The Japanese surrendered in 1945, but soon after China fell into a 3.5-year-long civil war, during which the government lost track of the number of operating associations. The war ended in 1949 with a victory of the Communist forces. The KMT forces fled to Taiwan.

In the early years of the People's Republic, the national governments did not seem to have kept records of the total number of associations in the whole country, but some local governments did. As table 2.1 indicates, in four provinces (Jiangxi, Fujian, Guangdong, and Liaoning) and three metropolises (Shanghai, Tianjin, and Nanjing) for which information was available, no general pattern was discernible during the period. In some places, the number of associations plunged substantially from the previous peak (Jiangxi and Guangdong); in others, the decline was quite minor (Shanghai and Tianjin); and yet in the rest, the number swelled (Fujian, Liaoning, and Nanjing).

Table 2.1. Registered Associations in Selected Places, 1912–1990

	Jiangxi	*Fujian*	*Gansu*	*Guandong*	*Liaoing*	*Shanghai*	*Tianjin*	*Nanjing*	*Shaoing*
1912							100		
1928							142		
1934								1123	
1935								1142	
1936									15
1937		2403							
1941		2988							
1942		2225							
1943								97	
1944		3273	1572	1416			212		
1945			2087						
1946	4536	4385	2479	4090	388				
1947			2740						27
1948		5143				1320	492	379	
1949			2794			1336	350	278	

1951				504	485			1116	
1952		9231				904	377		
1953	1210								
1954								1474	
1956						590			
1981						633			
1985						2256			
1987				7000					
1988						4299			
1989					10000	4290			80
1990	8172	13200	11403				4803		

Sources: *Jiangxi Minzheng Zhi* [Records of Jiangxi Civil Affairs], 1993, Huangshan Publishing House; *Fujian Shengzhi-Minzheng Zhi* [Fujian Records-Civil Affairs], 1997, Beijing: Fangzhi Publishing House; *Gansu Shengzhi-Minzheng Zhi* [Gansu Records-Civil Affairs], 1994, Lanzhou: Gansu Peoples' Publishing House; *Guangdong Shengzhi-Minzheng Zhi* [Guangdong Records-Civil Affairs], 1993, Guangzhou: Guangdong Peoples' Publishing House; *Liaoning Sheng Minzheng Zhi* [Records of Liaoning Civil Affairs], 1996, Liaoning Peoples' Publishing House; *Shanghai Minzheng Zhi* [Records of Shanghai Civil Affairs], 2000, Shanghai: Shanghai Academy of Social Science Publishing House; Ma and Liu, Yili Ma and Hanbang Liu, 1993, *Shanghai Shehui Tuanti Gailan* [A General Introduction to Social Organizations in Shanghai], Shanghai: Shanghai People's Publishing House; *Tianjin Tongzhi-Minzheng Zhi* [All Records of Tianjin-Civil Affairs], 2001, Tianjin Academy of Social Science Publishing House; *Nanjing Minzheng Zhi* [Records of Nanjing Civil Affairs], 1994, Shenzhen: Haitian Publishing House; *Jiangsu Shengzhi-Minzheng Zhi* [Jiangsu Records-Civil Affairs], 2002, Beijing: Fangzhi Publishing House; *Shaoxing Minzheng Zhi* [Records of Shaoxing Civil Affairs], 1998, Beijing: Fangzhi Publishing House.

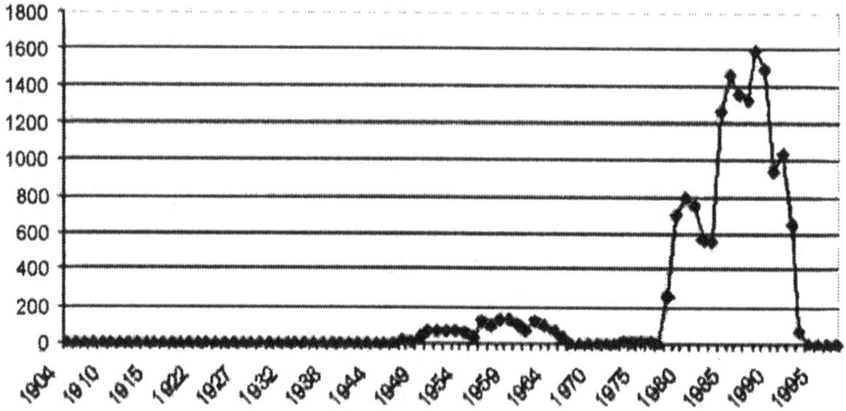

Figure 2.2

After 1956, there was no longer any single government ministry that took the sole responsibility for the administration of associational affairs. Instead, all party/state agencies (including Ministry of Culture, State Sports Commission, State Science and Technology Commission, Chinese Academy of Sciences, and, above all, the Party's Department of Propaganda) were involved, with each in charge of certain types of organizations. No centralized registration was required. This situation did not change until 1989.[50] Thus, systematic statistics on associations were simply nonexistent for more than thirty years. To the best of our knowledge, there were about 100 nation-level associations and 6,000 local associations in 1965.[51] After China embarked on reforms, Chinese associations underwent a post-reform renaissance in the 1980s. Based on a dataset that contains information from 16,379 existing associations, figure 2.2 plots the frequencies of their respective founding years. Clearly, never before had China seen such a high level of association building. When the Ministry of Civil Affairs assumed the duty of overseeing associational affairs in 1989, it estimated that there were altogether 1,600 national and 200,000 local organizations. In the nine places included in table 2.1, the number of registered associations in 1989–1990 all surpassed the previous record year.

ORGANIZATIONS UNDER THE JURISDICTION OF MCA

"Registered groups" refer to those that have registered with the Minister of Civil Affairs (MCA) and its subsidiaries throughout the country. Those fall into two broad categories: "social organizations" and "private nonenterprise units."

Social Organizations

In 1989, the State Council promulgated the Regulation on the Registration and Administration of Associations, which entrusted the MCA with the sole authority of registration. With some exceptions, all civic associations were required to register with the MCA and its local bureaus. To do so, an association had to find a party-state agency that was willing to be its official sponsor first. Otherwise, it would have to dissolve itself. The system of dual regulations was designed for the party-state to control the development of the registered associations. In the highly electric political environment after the Tiananmen, thousands of associations failed to obtain appropriate sponsorship. Consequently, the total number of registered associations dropped from around 200,000 in 1989 to barely 110,000 in 1991.

As figure 2.3 shows, associational activism quickly resumed in the first half of the 1990s. By 1996, the number of registered associations reached 186,666, a level only slightly lower than the peak of 1989. However, the rapid growth of associations was seen by the government as a serious challenge to its ability to manage associational affairs. In particular, the emergence of such semi-religious organizations as Falungong greatly worried the government. With hierarchical structure and top-to-bottom control, such organizations could pose a threat to the regime. In 1999, such concern turned into a reality when more than 10,000 Falungong practitioners surrounded Zhongnanhai, the compound in central Beijing housing the core government and CCP leaders and their families. To remove potential time bombs, the government became stricter in conducting annual inspections over associations. Those failing the

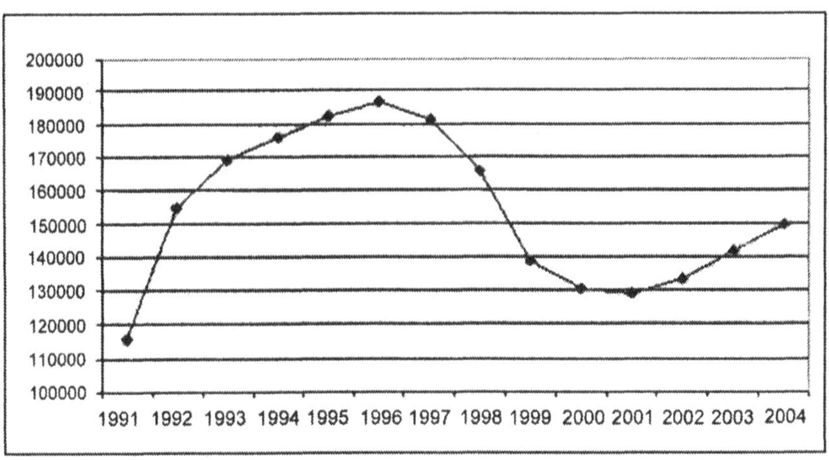

Figure 2.3

inspections were forced to shut down. In 1998, the State Council amended the Regulation on the Registration and Administration of Associations, which increased the threshold of the initial funds and required sponsoring agencies to take full responsibility for the conducts of related associations. Those measures resulted in another slump of the number of registered associations between 1996 and 2001. Afterward, the falling trend was reversed. By the end of 2004, China had around 150,000 registered associations.

What kinds of associations were most vulnerable to the above-mentioned policy changes? The government seems to have favored some types of associations over others. Officially, MCA divides associations into five large categories: academic associations (*xueshu*), trade associations (*hangye*), professional associations (*zhuanye*), federations (*lianhe*), and foundations (*jijinhui*). Data from the MCA Statistical Yearbook shows that the government tends to be more supportive of the first two categories, which together accounted for nearly 60 percent of the total number of registered associations in 2003 (figure 2.4).

From the very beginning of the reform era, the role of science and technology in modernization has been emphasized. Many academic associations that had been disbanded during the Cultural Revolution resumed their activities after 1978. The number of academic associations has not fluctuated as much as other types of associations when the state intervened. At the end of 2003, in the area of natural science and technology alone, there were 3,781 academic

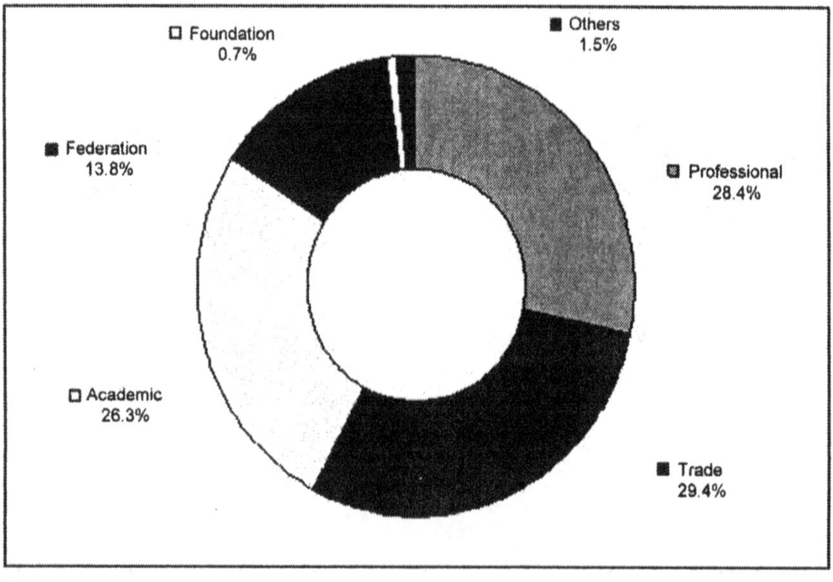

Figure 2.4

associations at the national and provincial levels, with a membership of 7.9 million (table 2.2).

Trade association is a product of marketization and denationalization. The pre-reform system of planned economy left no space for trade associations to function. As government agencies increasingly withdrew from microman-agement of state-owned enterprises and more and more nonstate enterprises came into being, the state realized that trade associations could play such important roles as facilitating information exchange and conducting self-regulation among their member firms. For this reason, the government has gone out of its way to promote the development of trade associations in the recent years. In 2000, for instance, nearly 40 percent of the newly registered associations were trade associations. The ratio increased to 45 percent in the following year. In this sense, the current distributional pattern of registered associations reveals the preference order of the state with regards to different types of associations.

Moreover, figure 2.5 suggests that the administrative level matters: the lower the level, the more vulnerable. After 1994, the number of nation-level, province-level, and prefecture-level associations have fluctuated but within narrow ranges. County-level associations, however, were more sensitive to changing policy environment.

Table 2.2. Academic Associations in Natural Science and Technology: 1987–2003

		Organizations by Level			*Membership by Level*		
	Total	*Nation*	*Province*	*Prefecture*	*Nation*	*Province*	*Prefecture*
1987	—	146	2885	—	1718780	2396037	—
1988	—	146	2828	—	2012312	—	—
1989	—	151	3013	—	2238956	—	—
1990	—	155	3257	—	2305991	3384177	—
1991	—	159	3198	—	2943469	3655743	—
1992	—	163	3107	—	3235631	3592950	—
1993	—	160	3160	—	—	—	—
1994	—	164	3124	—	—	—	—
1995	—	165	3538	—	2734589	2858868	
1996	13369	165	3055	10149	4157297	4071087	4859651
1997	13092	165	3006	9921	4174262	4219741	4703818
1998	—	165	2950	—	—	—	—
1999	—	163	3535	—	—	—	—
2000	12111	168	3470	8473	4570400	4551200	
2001	12023	167	3648	8208	4490000	3710000	
2002		167	3609	—	3940000	3960000	
2003		167	3614		3870000	4000000	

Source: Ministry of Science & Technology, *Zhongguo Keji Tongji Nianjian* [Statistical Yearbook of Science & Technology], Beijing: China Statistical Press, various years.

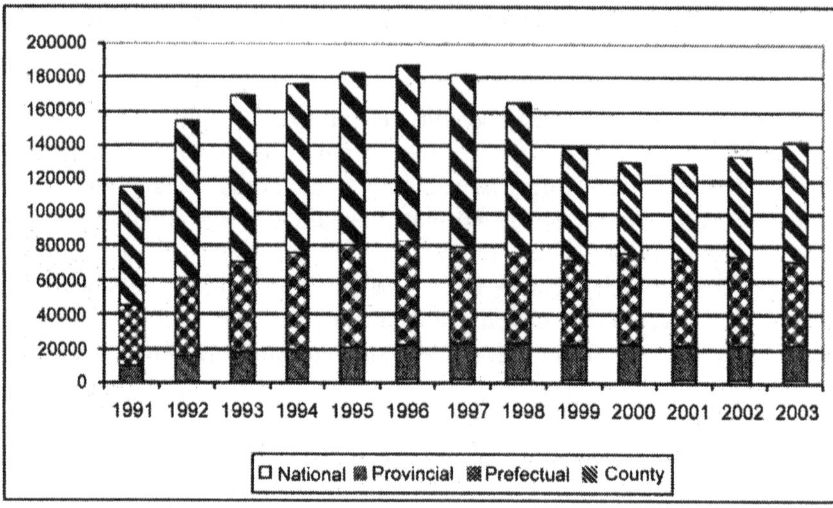

Figure 2.5

Private Nonenterprise Units

Private nonenterprise units are providers of social services whose purposes are not to maximize profits. Examples include private schools, day care centers, facilities for the physically and mentally challenged, retirement homes, and so on. Most of such entities used to be owned by the state or collectives. Now they became privatized in one way or another. In addition, an increasing number of such entities was recently established to meet new demands because of China's rapid socioeconomic transition. They tended to be privately owned from the outset. Whatever their origins, those organizations did not begin their registration with MCA until 1999. In the last five years, the number of registered organizations increased by more than twenty-fold. By the end of 2004, there were altogether 133,000 "private non-enterprise units" (figure 2.6).

What Is Excluded?

Studies on China's civil society often focus on "social organizations" and "private non-enterprise units," assuming that they cover the entire associational landscape in China.[52] In fact, organizations registered with MCA only occupy a small corner of the vast landscape. Most associations in China are actually not registered with MCA. First of all, there are organizations that should register with the Ministry of Civil Affairs but fail to do so. Figure 2.5 shows that more than 40,000 county-level social organizations vanished from

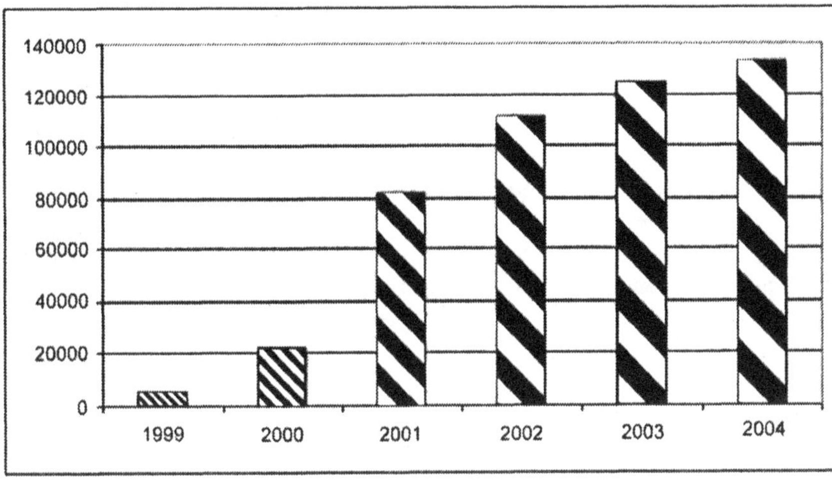

Figure 2.6

MCA's records between 1996 and 2000. That they were no longer registered with MCA did not mean that they no longer existed. Some of them might have disbanded or merged into other organizations, but most might have chosen either to register as commercial entities or simply continue their operation without registration at all. As a matter of fact, many high-profile environment groups in China have never registered with MCA. Because the thresholds for registration are quite high, many newly formed organizations might also not be able to register even if they are willing to do so.[53] We have reasons to estimate that the number of social organizations that operate without official registration could be as many as 30,000–50,000 in the nation.

As for private nonenterprise units, MCA itself estimated that there might in fact be 200,000–300,000 of them currently operating in the country but failing to register.[54]

In addition to the registered and unregistered social organizations and private nonenterprise units, there is huge number of associations that are not required to register with MCA by law. Those include local chapters of the eight categories of "mass organizations" that are represented at the Chinese People's Political Consultative Congress and of twenty-five "social organizations" that are exempt from registrations with MCA (e.g., the China Writers Association or the All-China Journalism Association). Moreover, grassroots associations below the county level, especially those operating within enterprises, government agencies, schools, urban neighborhoods, rural townships and villages, and so on do not have to register with MCA either. The next two sections turn to examining these vast areas of China's associational landscape.

QUASI-GOVERNMENTAL ORGANIZATIONS

Established by the Communist Party before or after 1949 and covering the party's key constituencies (workers, youth, women, scientists and engineers, businesspersons, overseas Chinese, literary and art circles, and so on), mass organizations have been important institutional pillars of China's political system. Designed as two-way transmission belts between the party-state and the masses of people, they are expected to carry out the directives of the party-state and pass them down to the masses on the one hand, and collect the will and opinion of the masses and carry them back to the policy-makers of the party-state on the other. Even before the reform era, "there has been variation over time in the degree of political integration demanded of mass organizations. During periods of political mobilization, mass organizations were highly politicized. During periods of consolidations, they became relatively independent of political demands and more responsive to the expressed needs and interests of their members."[55] Reforms in the last quarter of the century have further weakened their political roles but strengthened their functional roles.[56]

All mass organizations are umbrella organizations, each of which has thousands of branches and subsidiaries and millions of members throughout the country. Table 2.3 presents breakdown information on some mass organizations. Space limit does not allow us to elaborate how we arrive at those num-

Table 2.3. Mass Organizations and Their Grassroots Groups

Mass Organizations	*Grassroots Groups*
Trade Unions	1,713,000
Youth League Branches	2,720,000
Women's Associations	684,000
Science & Technology Associations	50,000
Rural Special Associations	115,658
AST	10,674
WST*	25,611
Returned Overseas Chinese	11,000
Federation of Industry & Commerce	18,481
Self-Employed Association**	30,000
Taiwanese Associations	—
Youth Federation	—
Sub-total	**5,378,424**

Notes:
* Workers' Technical Associations are sponsored by trade unions. For convenience, they are included under the category of science and technology.
** The Administrative Bureau of Industry and Commerce sponsor associations of self-employed and private businesspersons. However, their functions are similar to the Federation of Industry & Commerce.

bers. What follows is the discussion of a couple of cases, which is meant to illustrate how we assembled data from a myriad of sources for such exercises.

All-China Federation of Trade Unions (ACFTU)[57]

Trade unions are supposed to protect the rights and interests of workers, but at the same time, they are used by the party-state to pacify workers or mobilize workers for achieving certain political goals. The dual nature has often led unions to conflict with the party-state.[58] Due to the massive denationalization of the Chinese economy in recent years, unions are in a process of searching for new identities. While it is uncertain about whether they will eventually become true representatives of workers' interests, no one can deny their potentiality of serving as a powerful counterforce against management. Recent restructuring of trade unions seems to hint that such change is highly probable.

As figure 2.7 reveals, the numbers of grassroots trade unions and their membership reached their peaks in the early 1990s. Afterward, both began to fall. This was so because at that time trade unions operated mainly in the state-owned sector, which was experiencing a painful decline in much of the 1990s. The year of 1999 appeared to be a turning point. In the subsequent three years, the number of grassroots unions more than tripled and their membership increased by 50 percent. Both changes were the results of the expansion of unions into the private sector. Interestingly, although the num-

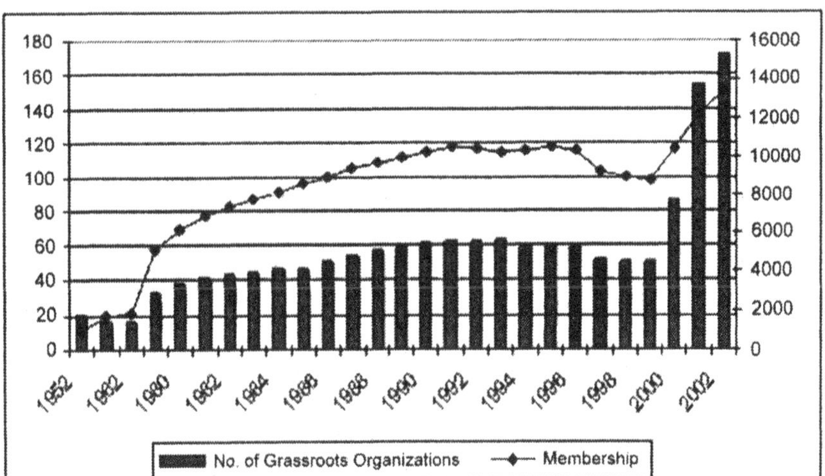

Figure 2.7

ber of grassroots trade unions expanded rapidly after 1999, the number of the full-time staff working for them was still shrinking, an indication that the party-state's control over unions was relaxing. At the end of 2002, there were all together 1,712,528 grassroots trade unions in China with a total membership of 133,977,709.

Chinese Communist Youth League (CCYL)[59]

Chinese Communist Youth League is defined as the vanguard of the youth. To serve as an "assistant and reserve" for the Chinese Communist Party (CCP), the main function of CCYL is to recruit and educate outstanding young men and women. In the 1990s, the CCYL became less attractive to the young people. After the mid-1990s, though the membership was still growing, the number of grassroots branches declined (see table 2.4), a change that might also be related to the shrinkage of the state sector of the economy. In the new century, the CCYL began to establish branches in the private sector, which helped to increase its grassroots branches, but only slightly. At the end

Table 2.4. Development of Youth League (million)

Year	*Membership*	*No. of Staff*	*No. of Branches*
1978	48.54	150200	212.7
1979	/	161600	/
1980	47.74	168034	227.3
1981	46.95	184716	226.5
1982	46.60	200820	227.8
1985	51.82	220511	239.5
1986	56.37	229692	247.7
1987	60.07	225308	249
1988	56.00	208027	256.9
1989	/	209188	/
1990	55.35	220571	260.8
1991	56.48	235235	258.1
1992	56.80	227546	/
1993	58.00	210593	263.9
1994	61.80	215612	264.8
1995	63.76	213891	274.7
1996	65.56	214960	271.2
1997	68.54	213695	276.6
1998	68.71	208876	264.2
1999	68.03	186971	254.9
2000	/	/	/
2001	/	/	/
2002	69.86	183000	272

Source: http://80years.ccyl.org.cn/80year/tdjs/index.htm.

of 2002, there were 2.57 million branches with a total membership of nearly 70 million.

China Association for Science and Technology (CAST)[60]

China Association for Science and Technology is an umbrella mass organization of scientists and engineers. In addition to directly managing near 200 nation-level scientific societies, CAST has around 2,600 local branches at provincial, municipal, and county levels, which in turn oversee 42,000 scientific societies at the corresponding levels. More importantly, below the

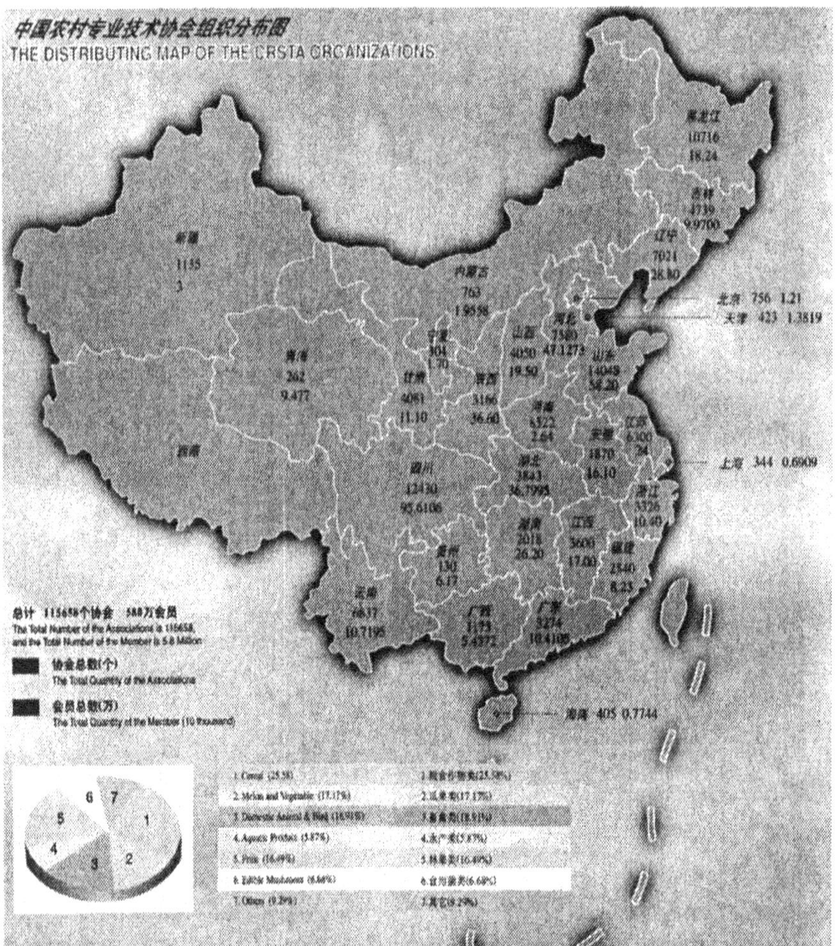

Figure 2.8

Table 2.5. Grassroots Workers' Technical Associations

	Grassroots WTA Nos.	*Membership*	*Full-time Staff*
1991	59,750	3,642,203	39,049
1992	60,154	4,008,042	48,099
1993	61,298	4,339,543	56,426
1994	70,000	4,340,000	—
1996	47,091	327,854	118,203
1997	33,940	3,258,082	65,627
1998	38,000	3,260,000	—
2002	25,611	2,288,960	—

Source: *Zhongguo Gonghui Tongji Nianjian* and *Zhongguo Gonghui Nianjian* (various years).

county level, there exist three vast networks of grassroots associations for science and technology, namely, rural special technique associations (RSTA), associations for science and technology in enterprises (AST), and the workers' technical associations (WTA).

RSTAs emerged after the introduction of household responsibility system in the late 1970s and early 1980s. They were technical and economic cooperative organizations of the farmers who happened to plant the same crops or engage in similar activities. RSTAs have expanded quickly, especially after CAST set up a subsidiary—China Rural Special Technique Association (CRSTA)—to direct RSTAs in 1995. It is reported that 5.8 million farmers joined 115,658 RSTAs by the end of 2001 (figure 2.8).

Also at the end of 2001, there were 10,674 ASTs operating in enterprises. While ASTs are composed of engineers and technicians, WTAs are organizations of workers. WTA was first founded by some model workers in Shenyang in 1961.[61] From then on, the government has made efforts to promote their development, aiming at increasing the participation of workers in technical innovation, cooperation, competition, and transfer. Table 2.5 presents statistics on WTAs for the last decade or so. Apparently, WTAs have contracted since the mid-1990s, which no doubt is a consequence of the denationalization of the Chinese economy. Private enterprises do not seem to have much interest in WTAs at all.

All-China Federation of Industry and Commerce (ACFIC)

Established in 1953, the All-China Federation of Industry and Commerce was an organization representing the interests of industrial and commercial business. Approved by the State Council, now the ACFIC is also known as the China General Chamber of Commerce (CGCC). The adoption of a "new face" is a sign that the organization intends to downplay its "united front" role and shift its emphasis more toward economic and nonstate activities. By the end of 2002, the ACFIC system had a membership of about 1.64 million, comprising enterprises, institutions, and individuals. Members were predominantly small and medium-size enterprises as well as individually owned ventures (*getihu*). The system has an extensive network of local chambers of commerce throughout the country, including 3,059 local chapters at the county level and above, of which 358 local chapters are located in major cities throughout the country, covering 95 percent of the nation's administrative regions. Below the county level, there are some 18,481 chapters at the township community levels, 461 of which were founded in 2001 alone. The relationships among the chambers at various levels are informal and quite loose. The national ACFIC may provide guidance to provincial and local chambers, and the provincial chambers may also provide guidance to their respective local chambers, but the national and provincial chambers do not have formal authority to issue orders to local chambers.[62]

In addition to the ACFIC, private businesspersons may also join either local *getihu* associations or private enterprise associations. Supervised by the State Administration for Industry and Commerce (SAIC) and its local branches, the two organizations have their own networks throughout the country at every administrative level, which are separated from, and compete in, supplying certain services to members with the ACFIC system. Although both appear to have a top-down structure, each local association is actually independent and is administered by its respective local government. There is also considerable variation in the name, structure, size, and activities of different associations depending upon the local conditions and the attitudes of local governments. Since two organizations generally overlap the ACFIC system, it is conservative to estimate that they together have at least 30,000 groups below the county level.[63]

Other Quasigovernmental Organizations

On top of the eight major mass organizations, there are other government-sponsored organizations, each of which has its own nationwide network. Examples include China Family Planning Association (CFPA)[64] and the consumers' associations.[65] Established in 1980, CFPA has since penetrated nearly all provinces, municipalities, counties, and a large portion of urban neighborhoods and rural communities. Those organizations have served as an effective instrument for the government to carry out its birth control policy, especially in the countryside. Besides, they have also been active in the fields of health education and community development. CFPA reportedly has about 1.02 million local branches and 83 million members.[66]

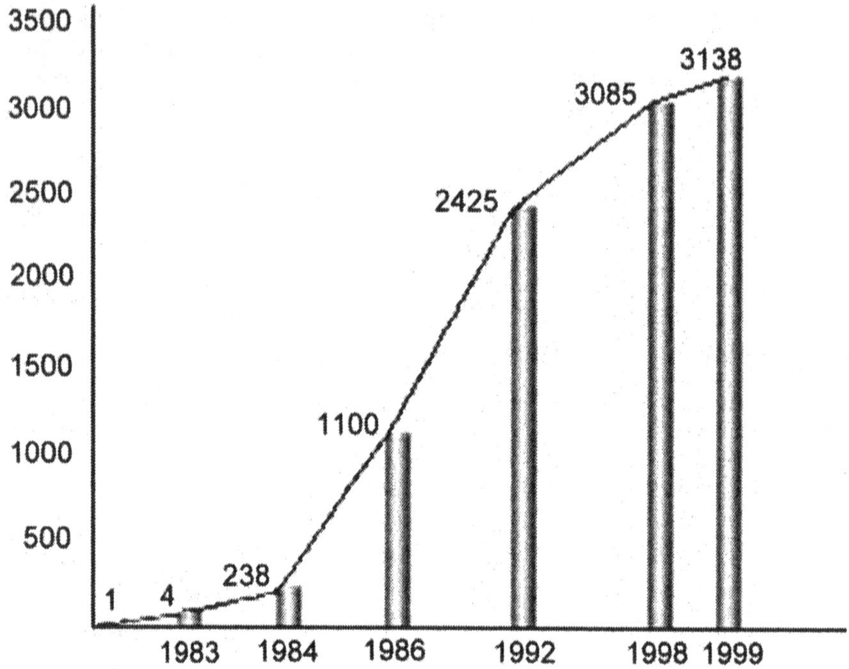

Figure 2.9

The mission of China Consumers' Association is to protect consumer rights and to probe and mediate the consumers' complaints according to the Law on Consumer Rights Protection. After its foundation in the early 1980s, the organization has expanded rapidly. Its local branches now penetrate all corners of the country. As figure 2.9 shows, by 1999, there were already 3,138 chapters at the county level and above. It is reported that consumers' associations at lower levels amounted to 156,000.[67]

Table 2.6 sums up the number of grassroots groups affiliated with six quasi-governmental associations. Together, the fourteen organizations included in

Table 2.6. Other Quasigovernment Associations and Their Grassroots Groups

Other Quasigovernment Associations	*Grassroots Groups*
Family Planning Associations	1,020,000
Consumers' Associations	156,000
Associations of Disabled	40,000
Volunteers' Associations	24,000
Associations of Literature & Arts	45,000
Sports Associations	53,220
Sub-total	**1,338,220**

tables 2.5 and 2.6 encompass some 6.7 million grassroots organizations. The main function of those organizations is to involve people from specific segments of the society in activities in specific areas and make sure that such activities would not spin out of state control. Due to their close connections with the government, they may be more susceptible to state interference than other organizations, and the membership within some (not all) of them may not even be entirely voluntary. Nevertheless, as they play important roles in the economic, social, political, and cultural lives for millions of Chinese, any study of associational life in China would be incomplete if they were to be excluded.

GRASSROOTS AND VIRTUAL ORGANIZATIONS

According to China's "Regulation on the Registration and Administration of Associations," groups operating within government agencies, institutions, enterprises, schools, urban neighborhoods, and rural communities are considered "internal" organizations and not required to register with MCA. MCA and its local bureaus do not even bother to collect information about associations below the county level. For this reason, grassroots associations have largely been ignored by the literature on China's civil society, although they have played an active and increasingly more important role in Chinese associational life. Examples include book discussion clubs, choral societies, hiking clubs, amateur sports clubs, literary circles, religious groups, hobby groups, elderly associations, friendship groups, students' associations, disease support groups, and the like. A report on grassroots associations in Shanghai, for instance, found that there were 4,658 reading groups in 92 work units surveyed in August 1999, including 1,061 groups on social science, 1,600 on science and

Table 2.7. Grassroots Groups

Grassroots Groups	*Number*
College Student Groups	20,700
High School Student Groups	95,000
Community-Based Recreational Groups	50,000
Philately Groups	41,000
Other Hobby Groups	130,000
Senior Citizens' Schools	17,000
The Elderly Associations	70,000
Home-Owners' Associations	15,000
Religious Groups	170,000
Friendship Groups	50,000
BBS and Virtual Associations	700,000
Sub-total	**1,358,700**

technology, 648 on economics and management, 644 on culture and arts, and 705 on hobbies.[68] Most grassroots associations are locally based, significantly autonomous, and volunteer-run. They provide their members with information, stimulation, opportunities for self-expression, social support, fellowship, and mutual aid, and thus have many kinds of significant "internal impact" on their members. In each work unit or community, the number of such grassroots groups may be small, but cumulatively, their total number must be gigantic. It is impossible to ascertain the exact number without a nationwide survey. Table 2.7 presents our conservative estimates about the numbers of eleven types of grassroots groups. Three types are discussed below.

Students' Associations at College Campuses

There were 1,472 universities and colleges in China by the end of 2003. We randomly selected 108 for our investigation. After sampling, we browsed the websites of these schools to look for information on students' associations in each of them. All of these schools provide their lists of students' groups active on their campuses, and some offer detailed information on each of them. These lists may or may not be exhaustive. In any event, we identify altogether 1,519 students' groups among the 108 universities. In other words, each university on average has 14.06 groups.[69] Some universities seem to have more vibrant associational life than others. The number of student groups on each campus ranges from 100 at Harbin Polytechnic University to just 1 at Xinjiang University. Table 2.8 shows that the distribution of different types of student associations in our sample. Apparently, literary and arts groups are most attractive to college students. Using the average derived from our sample, we estimate that there are at least 20,700 (14.06 × 1,472) students' associations on university campuses in China. The same method is also used to estimate the number of students' groups at high schools.

Table 2.8. Types of Students' Associations at 108 Universities

Types	*Number*	*Percentage*
Literary & Arts	647	42.6
Sports & Health	253	16.6
Science & Technology	183	12.0
Social Science	157	10.3
Voluntary Service	146	9.6
Study Groups	100	6.6
Others	33	2.2
Total	**1519**	**100.0**

Source: Our own databank.

Community-Based Groups

China has 5,751 urban residential communities and 20,226 townships.[70] How many community-based recreational groups are there? No one knows. Nevertheless, any tourist to Chinese cities would immediately spot signs of lively recreational activities in group form. Of course, more group activities are not observable to outsiders. Take Ruijin Community in Shanghai as an example. An area of 1.98 square kilometers with the population of 93,000, the community had 465 grassroots associations of 41 types, which involve the participation of more than 6,000 residents (see table 2.9). All these groups were

Table 2.9. Grassroots Associations in the Ruijin Community, Shanghai

Types	*No.*	*Name (including Activities)*	*Group #*	*Membership*
Self-Service	1	Volunteers' Associations and Groups	12	128
	2	Voluntary Patrol Groups	30	5295
	3	Legal Consulting Service Groups	12	65
	4	Health Consulting Groups (Consist of Retired Doctors)	5	30
	5	Sanitation Monitoring Groups	9	133
	6	Medical Service Groups (Including Human Milk Feeding Supporting Groups)	5	77
	7	Psychological Counseling Groups	3	17
	8	Voluntary Groups for Helping Families with Subsistence Difficulties	6	30
	9	Groups for Scientific Baby-Fostering	2	11
Learning and Propganda	10	Senior Citizens' Schools	4	51
	11	Newspaper Reading Groups for the Elders	3	37
	12	Current Affairs Discussion Groups	2	29
	13	Citizenship Schools	2	45
	14	Propaganda Groups	2	31
	15	Young Pioneers Radio Groups	5	52
	16	Young People's Propaganda Groups	3	35
	17	Popular Science Groups	12	164
Caring and Mutual Help	18	Comprehensive Caring Groups for the Weakens	4	27
	19	Army Man's Family-Caring Groups	4	29
	20	Elders-Caring Groups	4	29
	21	Women and Children-Caring Groups	2	15
	22	Youth-Caring Groups	4	29
	23	Associations for Floating Women Workers	2	31

(continued)

Table 2.9. (*continued*)

Types	*No.*	*Name (including Activities)*	*Group #*	*Membership*
	24	Neighboring Mutual Helping Groups	3	28
	25	Other Mutual Helping Groups	2	17
Sports and Health Improving	26	Chinese Gongfu Exercising Groups	13	220
	27	Eighteenth Qigong Groups	11	196
	28	Health Improving Groups	5	105
	29	Long-Life Qigong Groups	6	78
	30	Waist-Drum Groups	2	25
	31	Ruyi Qigong Groups	3	58
	32	Other Sports Groups	4	60
Arts and Hobbies	33	Singing Groups	17	244
	34	Dancing Groups	5	67
	35	Painting and Calligraphy Groups	8	65
	36	Foreign Language Corner	2	26
	37	Braid and Weaving Groups	7	76
	38	Traditional and Beijing Opera Groups	5	55
	39	Cooking Groups	5	60
	40	Miniascape and Ikebana Groups	5	41
	41	Other Arts Groups	4	48

Source: Jizuo Yin (ed.), 2001, *2001 Nian Shanghai Shehui Baogao Shu* [Report on Shanghai Society: 2001] (Shanghai: Shanghai Social Science Publishing House, pp. 246–47).

founded after 1990. Retirees were among the most active participants. Most of the group leaders were either members of the Residential Committee (46 percent) or retirees (46 percent). Moreover, most of the groups were initiated by the Residential Committee, and only a handful of sports clubs were started by individual residents.[71]

This case is by no means representative of the overall situation in China. Most of the country's urban and rural communities may not be as vivacious as the Ruijin Community. Nevertheless, even if we assume that each urban community has five groups and each rural community has only one, the number of community-based groups in the country would reach around 50,000, which is a very conservative estimate.

Associations in Cyberspace

What we have discussed thus far are all associations in real space. Since the mid-1990s, personal computers have penetrated workplaces and homes in urban China. Meanwhile, the growth of the Internet has been equally astounding, with the number of Internet users doubling every twelve months or so (see figure 2.10). According to the "Fifteenth Semiannual Survey Reports on

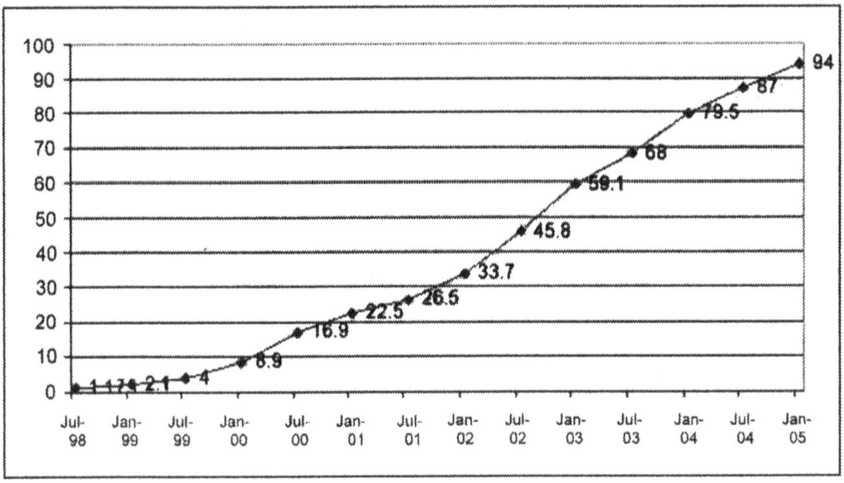

Figure 2.10

the Internet in China" released by the China Internet Network Information Center (CNNIC, www.cnnic.net.cn/download/2005/2005011801.pdf), the number of Internet users reached 94 million by January 2005.

The Internet provides a platform for individuals—through e-mail, chat rooms, news groups, and clubs—to form formal and informal groups "for the purpose of exchanges, including resource transactions and relations reinforcement"[72] regardless of their physical location. How does the Internet affect Chinese associational life? Does it promote the growth of "virtual" associations? This subsection tries to answer these questions by focusing on one particular form of virtual community—the Bulletin Board System.

Interaction between members is both the main cause and function of association. The Bulletin Board System (BBS) on the Internet is a virtual forum that provides a general community structure around which users can gather and interact. Any individuals who frequent a virtual forum or BBS can be considered members of that community, simply by their attendance. The BBS community consists of a variety of boards, each of which focuses on a specific topic, such as current affairs, history, reading, literature, arts, techniques, hobbies, mutual help, and volunteering. Some eminent BBS forums have large numbers of loyal members. For example, set up by *People Daily's Net* in May 1999, *Qiangguo Luntan* (Strengthening China Forum, http://bbs.people.com.cn/bbs/start) is one of the most renowned political forums, with 365,807 membership IDs as of April 6, 2005. On average, about 12,000 messages are posted every day. The highest number of simultaneous online members amounts to 50,000. Also set up in 1999, *Tianya Virtual Club* now

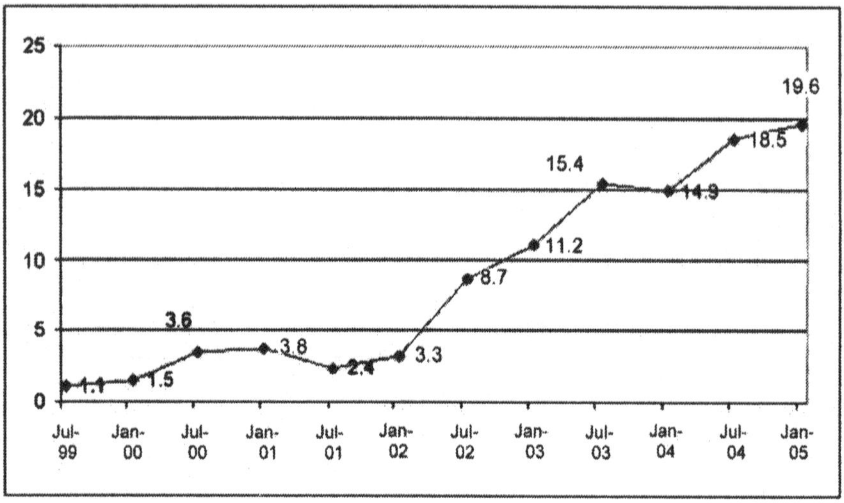

Figure 2.11

has more than 5.1 million registered IDs, among whom 2.3 million are active. *SMTH BBS* (http://www.smth.org), the earliest bulletin board established in China, is one of most famous university-based BBSs. With more than 150,000 member IDs, it always has more than 10,000 members spontaneously online. According to the estimation of its managers, the real membership should be no less than 100,000. *SMTH* offers over 300 boards, covering almost every area of university life.

Calculated from CNNIC's Fifteenth Semiannual Survey, figure 2.11 traces the growth of Chinese BBS users in the last few years. By January 2005, as many as nearly 20 million Chinese were regular BBS users.

How many BBS forums are there in China? There is no systematic statistic available, but it is possible to come up with a rough estimate. There were altogether 668,900 websites in the country by the beginning of 2005. Their operators could divide into seven broad categories: enterprises, commercial, government, education and research, nonprofit organizations, personal, and others. In its 2004 survey, CNNIC reported that 35 percent of education websites, 27.6 percent of personal websites, 19.1 percent of commercial websites, 18.8 percent of government websites, and 12.7 percent of enterprise websites provided BBS service. Altogether, at least 106,349 websites run BBS forums.[73] Assuming that each website operates only one BBS forum, there would be at least 106,349 forums. In fact, however, many commercial websites provide dozens, if not hundreds, of BBS forums. Examples include such popular websites as SINA.com, SOHU.com, and CAT898.com. Xilu.com, a professional provider of virtual communities, is a more telling example, which alone operates some 540,000 forums with more than 10 million registered member IDs! At any moment, more than 10,000 persons visit those forums.[74] Similarly, education and research institution websites also generally offer numerous BBS forums. According to a 2003 CNNIC survey of college websites, for instance, each of them provides on average 17 BBS forums, each of which, in turn, has on average 13,730 registered member IDs.[75] Adding the estimates together, we are confident to conclude that there must be no less than 700,000 BBS forums in China, probably many more.

Each bulletin board functions as a virtual community. To what extent is a virtual community different from a traditional association? Two types of activities are worth noting. First, as opposed to the open forum, closed forums have emerged recently. These forums have clear goals and orientations. Their membership is not open to the public, and a reference from an existing member is always the prerequisite to join the forum. Rights and obligations are always clearly declared and must be obeyed. The closed forum is very much like an association. *Dogn Club* (http://www.dogn.net), a closed forum oriented to the serious-minded communication, is a good example. It is open for browsing, but the membership is under strict control. The club establishes a five-person membership committee to screen applications. One veto from any committee member will deny an application. Now it has only 386 member ID and 12 boards.

League for BBS Masters is another example. Founded in September 2001, it is a confidential forum aimed at building a virtual association for the communication of BBS masters. The precondition for its membership is that the applicant has to be a master of large-sized BBS. Internal referee is required for anyone who intends to apply for membership. Second, virtual associational life can be transformed from the cyberspace into formal or informal associations in the real world. Get-togethers of net-mates are now quite common for the BBS users. Some members of a tourist BBS may travel together; sports lovers may play ball every weekend; and reading groups may meet to debate on some issues. *Guantian Teahouse,* a board in *Tianya Club* (http://www.tianyaclub.com), is a virtual tea bar for those who are interested in political debate, and it attracts many prominent scholars and writers from both liberal and new-left camps. Despite their conflicting ideological orientations, net-mates of the BBS organize lectures at different cities from time to time. As table 2.10 shows, during the summer of 2003, fourteen gatherings were held by the net-mates of *Guantian* in nine cities. Constitutionalism, citizenship, and democratizations were hot topics at the gatherings.

No doubt, the Internet has greatly expanded the social space for Chinese associational life.

Table 2.10. Recent Gatherings of Guantian Teahouse Board in Tianya Club

Date	*City*	*Topics*	*# of Participants*
2003-6-28	Hangzhou, Zhejiang	Lecture on the Economic Sociological Explanation of China's Reform	
2003-6-29	Hangzhou, Zhejiang	Environmental Protecting Hiking	
2003-7-11	Beijing	Dinner Talk on Constitutionalism	About 20 persons
2003-7-13	Guangzhou, Guangdong	Lecture on News Reform	
2003-7-19	Guangzhou, Guangdong	Climbing	20 persons
2003-7-26	Xi'an, Shaanxi	Internet, Citizenship, and Democratization	7 persons
2003-7-26	Beijing	Lecture on Rule by Law, Given by Dr. Yu Jianrong, a Famous Scholar in the Field of Rural Politics	About 50 persons
2003-8-2	Chengdu, Sichuan	Constitutional Reform	
2003-8-6	Wenzhou, Zhejing	Confucianism and Culture and Development of Wenzhou	
2003-8-9	Wuhan, Hubei		
2003-8-10	Beijing	Lecture Given by Dr. Liu Junning, a Political Scientist	80 persons
2003-8-26	Shanghai	Chinese Culture and Democracy, Internet, and Public Opinion	About 20 persons
2003-8-27	Ji'nan, Shandong	Huang Jing's Case (A Well-Known Dating Rape Case of the Year)	About 30 persons
2003-9-3	Xi'an, Shaanxi	History, Democratization, Labor	

SUMMARY

This chapter provides a quantitative assessment of the density and diversity of associational life in China. Table 2.11 summarizes our findings presented in the preceding sections. Clearly, were our attention to be focused on what Chinese call "social organizations" or worse yet on those social organizations that are financially, functionally, and politically autonomous from the state, we would miss large parts of China's associational landscapes.

Table 2.11. The Total Estimated Number of Associations in China

Category	*Number*
Registered Social Organizations	150,000
Registered Private Nonprofit	133,000
Unregistered Social Organizations	40,000
Unregistered Private Nonprofit	250,000
Eight Mass Organizations	5,378,424
Other Quasigovernment Associations	1,358,700
Grassroots Groups	1,358,700
Total	**8,648,344**

The findings about the number of operating associations run parallel with those about the participation rate of associational life. The 1990 World Value Survey, for instance, found that 27.6 percent of Chinese had active membership in one or more associations (table 2.12). Commissioned by UNDP, our own 2001 survey confirmed the results of the World Value Survey (table 2.13). Therefore, it is hardly an exaggeration for us to conclude, "Yes, China is indeed part of the global association revolution."

Of course, the organizations listed in table 2.11 differ greatly from one another in their origins, natures, internal structures, sources of financing, membership profiles, relationships with the state, and so on, even though they all help form durable networks of more or less institutionalized relationships among their members. Therefore, mapping out the landscape is at best the first step to studying the associational revolution in China. Many more questions need to be scrutinized before we can fully grasp the significance of the revolution. What factors have contributed to China's recent associational revolution? Why has the associational space in China been populated more by certain types of organizations than others? How are different types of association organized

Table 2.12. Active Membership in Any Associations Except Political Party

No. of Associations that Interviewee Participated	*Frequency*	*Percent*
0	1810	72.4
1	468	18.7
2	149	6.0
3	57	2.3
4	13	0.5
5	2	0.1
6	1	0.0
Total	**2500**	**100**

Source: World Value Survey (1990).

Table 2.13. Have You Participated in Associational Activities?

Answer	*Frequency*	*Percent*
Yes	422	23.9
No	1345	76.1
Total	**1767**	**100**

Source: Our own databank.

internally? What kinds of people are most likely to join associations? Are all associations alike with respect to both the amount and the sort of social capital "produced"? Is the membership of a particular associational sector more likely to score highly on certain dimensions of social capital than on others? To what extent is the social capital generated by these organizations of benefit not only to their own members but also to the society as a whole? What kinds of social capital are different categories of associations likely to produce, bonding or bridging? What types of associations are more capable of fostering cooperation, civic engagement, tolerance, trust, and the norms of reciprocity? Does participation in nonpolitical or involuntary organizations help stimulate political involvement and interest? Is associational life really the school for democratic citizenship? How conducive is associational life to the formation of civic and democratic virtues? Do association members tend to act as better citizens than non-members do? Those questions will guide our future research.

NOTES

1. Lester M. Salamon, 1994, "The Rise of the Nonprofit Sector", *Foreign Affairs*, Vol. 73, No. 4.
2. See Lester M. Salamon, 1994, "The Rise of the Nonprofit Sector", *Foreign Affairs*, Vol.73, No. 4.
3. Jessica T. Mathews, 1997, "Power Shift", *Foreign Affairs*, Vol. 76, No. 1.
4. This study excludes associations of Chinese abroad as well as associations of foreigners in China because they constitute at best a tiny fraction of the associational universe in the country. An online directory of international NGOs operating in China is available at http://www.chinadevelopmentbrief.com/dingo/index.asp.
5. Anita Chan, 1993, "Revolution or Corporatism? Workers and Trade Unions in Post-Mao China," *Australian Journal of Chinese Affairs*, No. 29; Elizabeth J. Perry, 1994, "Labor's Battle for Political Space: The Role of Worker Associations in Contemporary China," in Deborah S. Davis, Richard Kraus, Barry Naughton, and Elizabeth J. Perry (eds.), *Urban Spaces in Contemporary China: The Potential for Autonomy and Community in Post-Mao China*, Cambridge: Cambridge University Press.

6. See Margaret M. Pearson, 1994, "The Janus Face of Business Associations in China: Socialist Corporatism in Foreign Enterprises," *Australian Journal of Chinese Affairs*, No. 31; Jonathan Unger, and Anita Chan, 1995, "China, Corporatism, and the East Asian Model," *Australian Journal of Chinese Affairs*, No. 33; and Jonathan Unger, 1996, "Bridges: Private Business, the Chinese Government and the Rise of New Associations," *China Quarterly*, No. 147.

7. Jeffrey N. Wasserstrom, and Xinyong Liu, 1994, "Student Associations and Mass Movements," in Deborah S. Davis, Richard Kraus, Barry Naughton, and Elizabeth J. Perry (eds.), *Urban Spaces in Contemporary China: The Potential for Autonomy and Community in Post-Mao China*, Cambridge: Cambridge University Press.

8. Shaoguang Wang, 1994, "The Politics of Private Time: Changing Leisure Patterns in Urban China," in Deborah S. Davis, Richard Kraus, Barry Naughton, and Elizabeth J. Perry (eds.), *Urban Spaces in Contemporary China: The Potential for Autonomy and Community in Post-Mao China*, Cambridge: Cambridge University Press; Nancy N. Chen, 1994, "Urban Spaces and Experiences of Qigong," in Deborah S. Davis, Richard Kraus, Barry Naughton, and Elizabeth J. Perry (eds.), *Urban Spaces in Contemporary China: The Potential for Autonomy and Community in Post-Mao China*, Cambridge: Cambridge University Press.

9. Ye Zhang, 1995, "Foundations in China: A Survey Report," in Tadashi Yamamoto (ed.), *Emerging Civil Society in the Asia Pacific Community: Nongovernmental Underpinnings of Emerging Asia Pacific Regional Community*, Tokyo: Japan Center for International Exchange.

10. See Gordon White, 1993, "Prospects for Civil Society in China: A Case Study of Xiaoshan City," *Australian Journal of Chinese Affairs*, No. 29; Ying Wang, Bingyao Sun, and Xiaoye Zhe, 1993, *Shehui Zhongjianceng* [Intermediate Sphere in Society: Reforms and Chinese Social Organizations], Beijing: China Development Press; Viviene Shue, 1994, "State Power and Social Organization in China," in Joel S. Migdal, Atul Kohli, and Vivienne Shue (eds.), *State Power and Social Forces: Domination and Transformation in the Third World*, Cambridge: Cambridge University Press; Gordon White, Jude Howell, and Xiaoyuan Shang, 1996, *In Search of Civil Society: Market Reform and Social Change in Contemporary China*, Oxford: Clarendon Press; and Kin-man Chan, 1999, "Intermediate Organizations and Civil Society: The Case of Guangzhou," in Chong Chor Lau and Geng Xiao (eds.), *China Review 1999*, Hong Kong: Chinese University Press.

11. Susan H. Whiting, 1991, "The Politics of NGO Development in China," *Voluntas*, Vol. 2, No. 2; Junhai Zhang, 1992, "The Voluntary Sector in the People's Republic of China: An Overview and New Challenges," in Kathleen D. McCarthy, Virginia A. Hodgkinson, and Russy D. Sumariwalla (eds.), *The Nonprofit Sector in the Global Community: Voices From Many Nations*, San Francisco: Jossey-Bass Publishers; Martin King Whyte, 1992, "Urban China: A Civil Society in the Making?" in Arthur L. Rosenbaum (ed.), *State and Society in China: The Consequences of Reform*, Boulder, Colo.: Westview; National Committee on U.S.-China Relations, 1994, *The Rise of Non-Governmental Organizations in China: Implications for Americans*, Report #8; Jude Howell, 1994, "Striking a New Balance: New Social Organizations in Post-Mao China," *Capital and Class*, Issue 54; Ye Zhang, 1995, "Chinese NGOs:

A Survey Report," in Tadashi Yamamoto (ed.), *Emerging Civil Society in the Asia Pacific Community: Nongovernmental Underpinnings of Emerging Asia Pacific Regional Community*, Tokyo: Japan Center for International Exchange; B. Michael Frolic, 1997, "State-Led Civil Society," in Timothy Brook and B. Michael Frolic (eds.), *Civil Society in China*, Armonk: M. E. Sharpe; Minxin Pei, 1998, "Chinese Intermediate Associations: An Empirical Analysis," *Modern China*, Vol. 24, No. 3; and Kin-man Chan and Haixiong Qiu, 1998, "Small Government, Big Society: Social Organizations and Civil Society in China," *China Area Studies Series*, No. 8.

12. Yuanzhu Ding (ed.), 1999, *Zhiyuan Jingshen zai zhongguo* [Volunteerism in China], Beijing: UNDP; Shaoguang Wang, 2000, "Money and Autonomy: Dilemma Faced by the Nonprofit Sector," unpublished manuscript, Hong Kong: The Chinese University of Hong Kong; Nick Young, and Anthony Woo, 2000, *An Introduction to the Nonprofit Sector in China*, Kent: Charities Aid Foundation.

13. Martin King Whyte, 1992, "Urban China: A Civil Society in the Making?," in Arthur L. Rosenbaum (ed.), *State and Society in China: The Consequences of Reform*, Boulder, Colo.: Westview; Gordon White, 1993, "Prospects for Civil Society in China: A Case Study of Xiaoshan City," *Australian Journal of Chinese Affairs*, No. 29.

14. Anita Chan, 1993, "Revolution or Corporatism? Workers and Trade Unions in Post-Mao China," *Australian Journal of Chinese Affairs*, No. 29; Margaret M. Pearson, 1994, "The Janus Face of Business Associations in China: Socialist Corporatism in Foreign Enterprises," *Australian Journal of Chinese Affairs*, No. 31; Jonathan Unger, and Anita Chan, 1995, "China, Corporatism, and the East Asian Model," *Australian Journal of Chinese Affairs*, No. 33; Jonathan Unger, 1996, "Bridges: Private Business, the Chinese Government and the Rise of New Associations," *China Quarterly*, No. 147.

15. Viviene Shue, 1994, "State Power and Social Organization in China," in Joel S. Migdal, Atul Kohli, and Vivienne Shue (eds.), *State Power and Social Forces: Domination and Transformation in the Third World*, Cambridge: Cambridge University Press.

16. See Elizabeth J. Perry, 1994, "Labor's Battle for Political Space: The Role of Worker Associations in Contemporary China," in Deborah S. Davis, Richard Kraus, Barry Naughton, and Elizabeth J. Perry (eds.), *Urban Spaces in Contemporary China: The Potential for Autonomy and Community in Post-Mao China*, Cambridge: Cambridge University Press.

17. Lester M. Salamon, and Helmut K. Anheier, 1997, "The Third World's Third Sector in Comparative Perspective," A Working Paper of the Johns Hopkins Comparative Nonprofit Sector Project.

18. See Minxin Pei, 1998, "Chinese Intermediate Associations: An Empirical Analysis," *Modern China*, Vol. 24, No. 3.

19. See, for instance, Susan H. Whiting, 1991, "The Politics of NGO Development in China," *Voluntas*, Vol. 2, No. 2; Martin King Whyte, 1992, "Urban China: A Civil Society in the Making?," in Arthur L. Rosenbaum (ed.), *State and Society in China: The Consequences of Reform*, Boulder, Colo.: Westview; Junhai Zhang, 1992, "The Voluntary Sector in the People's Republic of China: An Overview and

New Challenges," in Kathleen D. McCarthy, Virginia A. Hodgkinson, and Russy D. Sumariwalla (eds.), *The Nonprofit Sector in the Global Community: Voices From Many Nations*, San Francisco: Jossey-Bass Publishers; Anita Chan, 1993, "Revolution or Corporatism? Workers and Trade Unions in Post-Mao China," *Australian Journal of Chinese Affairs*, No. 29; Jude Howell, 1994, "Striking a New Balance: New Social Organizations in Post-Mao China," *Capital and Class*, Issue 54; National Committee on U.S.-China Relations, 1994, *The Rise of Non-Governmental Organizations in China: Implications for Americans*, Report #8; Ying Wang, Bingyao Sun, and Xiaoye Zhe, 1993, *Shehui Zhongjianceng* [Intermediate Sphere in Society: Reforms and Chinese Social Organizations], Beijing: China Development Press; Gordon White, 1993, "Prospects for Civil Society in China: A Case Study of Xiaoshan City," *Australian Journal of Chinese Affairs*, No. 29; Nancy N. Chen, 1994, "Urban Spaces and Experiences of Qigong," in Deborah S. Davis, Richard Kraus, Barry Naughton, and Elizabeth J. Perry (eds.), *Urban Spaces in Contemporary China: The Potential for Autonomy and Community in Post-Mao China,* Cambridge: Cambridge University Press; Margaret M. Pearson, 1994, "The Janus Face of Business Associations in China: Socialist Corporatism in Foreign Enterprises," *Australian Journal of Chinese Affairs*, No. 31; Elizabeth J. Perry, 1994, "Labor's Battle for Political Space: The Role of Worker Associations in Contemporary China," in Deborah S. Davis, Richard Kraus, Barry Naughton, and Elizabeth J. Perry (eds.), *Urban Spaces in Contemporary China: The Potential for Autonomy and Community in Post-Mao China,* Cambridge: Cambridge University Press; Viviene Shue, 1994, "State Power and Social Organization in China," in Joel S. Migdal, Atul Kohli, and Vivienne Shue (eds.), *State Power and Social Forces: Domination and Transformation in the Third World*, Cambridge: Cambridge University Press; Shaoguang Wang, 1994, "The Politics of Private Time: Changing Leisure Patterns in Urban China," in Deborah S. Davis, Richard Kraus, Barry Naughton, and Elizabeth J. Perry (eds.), *Urban Spaces in Contemporary China: The Potential for Autonomy and Community in Post-Mao China*, Cambridge: Cambridge University Press; Jeffrey N. Wasserstrom, and Xinyong Liu, 1994, "Student Associations and Mass Movements," in Deborah S. Davis, Richard Kraus, Barry Naughton, and Elizabeth J. Perry (eds.), *Urban Spaces in Contemporary China: The Potential for Autonomy and Community in Post-Mao China*, Cambridge: Cambridge University Press; Jonathan Unger, and Anita Chan, 1995, "China, Corporatism, and the East Asian Model," *Australian Journal of Chinese Affairs,* No. 33; Ye Zhang, 1995, "Chinese NGOs: A Survey Report," in Tadashi Yamamoto (ed.), *Emerging Civil Society in the Asia Pacific Community: Nongovernmental Underpinnings of Emerging Asia Pacific Regional Community*, Tokyo: Japan Center for International Exchange; and Ye Zhang, 1995, "Foundations in China: A Survey Report," in Tadashi Yamamoto (ed.), *Emerging Civil Society in the Asia Pacific Community: Nongovernmental Underpinnings of Emerging Asia Pacific Regional Community*, Tokyo: Japan Center for International Exchange.

20. See Jonathan Unger, 1996, "Bridges: Private Business, the Chinese Government and the Rise of New Associations," *China Quarterly*, No. 147; Gordon White, Jude Howell, and Xiaoyuan Shang, 1996, *In Search of Civil Society: Market Reform and Social Change in Contemporary China*, Oxford: Clarendon Press; B. Michael

Frolic, 1997, "State-Led Civil Society," in Timothy Brook and B. Michael Frolic (eds.), *Civil Society in China*, Armonk: M. E. Sharpe; and Minxin Pei, 1998, "Chinese Intermediate Associations: An Empirical Analysis," *Modern China*, Vol. 24, No. 3.

21. Nick Young, and Anthony Woo, 2000, *An Introduction to the Nonprofit Sector in China*, Kent: Charities Aid Foundation, p.5.

22. Nan Lin, 2001, *Social Capital: A Theory of Social Structure and Action*, New York: Cambridge University Press, p.25.

23. See Pierre Bourdieu, 1986, "The Forms of Capital," in J. G. Richardson (ed.), *Handbook of Theory and Research for the Sociology of Education*, Westport, Conn.: Greenwood Press; James S. Coleman, 1990, *Foundations of Social Theory*, Cambridge, Mass.: Harvard University Press, pp. 302–304; Robert D. Putnam, 1993, *Making Democracy Work: Civic Traditions in Modern Italy*, Princeton, N.J.: Princeton University Press, pp.173–176.

24. Nan Lin, 2001, *Social Capital: A Theory of Social Structure and Action*, New York: Cambridge University Press, p.26.

25. Robert D. Putnam, 1993, *Making Democracy Work: Civic Traditions in Modern Italy*, Princeton, N.J.: Princeton University Press, p. 167.

26. Robert D. Putnam, 1993, *Making Democracy Work: Civic Traditions in Modern Italy*, Princeton, N.J.: Princeton University Press, pp. 163–185.

27. Sidney Verba, Key Lehman Schlozman, and Henry E. Brady, 1995, *Voice and Equality: Civic Voluntarism in American Politics*, Cambridge, Mass.: Harvard University Press.

28. Robert D. Putnam, 1993, *Making Democracy Work: Civic Traditions in Modern Italy*, Princeton, N.J.: Princeton University Press, pp. 89–90.

29. Alexis De Tocqueville, 1969, *Democracy in America*, Lawrence. NY: Anchor Book, pp. 513–514.

30. Alexis De Tocqueville, 1969, *Democracy in America*, Lawrence, NY: Anchor Book, p. 514.

31. Sidney Verba, Key Lehman Schlozman, and Henry E. Brady, 1995, *Voice and Equality: Civic Voluntarism in American Politics*, Cambridge, Mass.: Harvard University Press, p. 3.

32. Robert D. Putnam, 1993, *Making Democracy Work: Civic Traditions in Modern Italy*, Princeton, N.J.: Princeton University Press, p. 90.

33. B. Erickson, and T. A. Nosanchuck, 1990, "How an Apolitical Association Politicizes," *Canadian Review of Sociology and Anthropology*, Vol. 27, No. 2; M. Olson, 1972, "Social Participation and Voting Turnout," *American Sociological Review*, Vol. 37, No. 3; D. Rogers, K. Barb, and G. Bultena, 1975, "Voluntary Association Membership and Political Participation: An Exploration of the Mobilization Hypothesis," *Sociological Quarterly*, Vol. 16, No. 3.

34. Pierre Bourdieu, 1986, "The Forms of Capital," in J. G. Richardson (ed.), *Handbook of Theory and Research for the Sociology of Education*, Westport, Conn.: Greenwood Press, p. 248.

35. Robert D. Putnam, and Kristin A. Goss, 2002, "Introduction," in Robert D. Putnam (ed.), *Democracies in Flux: The Evolution of Social Capital in Contemporary Society*, Oxford: Oxford University Press, p. 6.

36. Claus Offe, and Susanne Fuchs, 2002, "Decline of Social Capital: The German Case," in Robert D. Putnam (ed.), *Democracies in Flux: The Evolution of Social Capital in Contemporary Society*, Oxford: Oxford University Press, p. 242.

37. Marjorie K. McIntosh, 2001, "The Diversity of Social Capital in English Communities, 1300-1640 (with a Glance at Modern Nigeria)," in Robert I. Rotberg (ed.), *Patterns of Social Capital: Stability and Change in Historical Perspective*, Cambridge: Cambridge University Press.

38. Marjorie K. McIntosh, 2001, "The Diversity of Social Capital in English Communities, 1300–1640 (with a Glance at Modern Nigeria)," in Robert I. Rotberg (ed.), *Patterns of Social Capital: Stability and Change in Historical Perspective*, Cambridge: Cambridge University Press, p. 94.

39. Although "guanxi" may also generate social capital, it differs from "association" in that, as a sort of "particularistic ties," see J. Bruce Jacobs, 1979, "A Preliminary Model of Particularistic Ties in Chinese Political Alliances: KanCh'ing and Kuanhsi in a Rural Taiwanese Township," *China Quarterly*, Vol. 78, pp. 237–273; the former contains strong instrumental or/and sentimental elements while the latter does not. See Thomas Gold, Doug Guthrie, and David Wank, 2002, "An Introduction to the Study of Guanxi," in Thomas Gold, Doug Guthrie, and David Wank (eds.), *Social Connections in China: Institutions, Culture, and the Changing Nature of Guanxi*, Cambridge: Cambridge University Press, pp. 3–20.

40. Yufa Zhang, 1971, *Qingji de Lixian Tuanti* [Constitutional Association in Qing Dynasty], Taipei: Modern History Institution of Academia Sinica, pp. 126–130.

41. Yufa Zhang, 1971, *Minguo Chunian de Zhengdang* [Political Parties in the Early Years of the Republic of China], Taipei: Modern History Institution of Academia Sinica, pp. 90–148.

42. Yufa Zhang, 1975, *Qingji de Geming Tuanti* [Revolutional Association in Qing Dynasty], Taipei: Modern History Institution of Academia Sinica, p. 33; Shuhuai Wang, 1984, *Zhongguo Xiandaihua de Quyu Yanjiu: Jiangsu* [Regional Analysis on China's Modernization: Jiangsu Province], Taipei: Modern History Institution of Academia Sinica, p. 541.

43. Ying Zhu, 1991, *Xinhai Geming Shiqi Xinshi Shangren Shetuan Yanjiu* [Research on New Businessmen during the Period of the Revolution of 1911], Beijing: Remin University of China, p. 55.

44. Editing Board (EB), 1975, *Minguo Banian Zhongguo Nianjian* [China Yearbook in 1917], Taipei: Tianyi Publishing House, p. 117.

45. Shigang Wang ,and Xiusong Li, 1994, *Zhongguo Shetuan Shi* [Associational History in China], Hefei: Anhui Peoples' Publishing House, pp. 358, 372.

46. Jianqing Liu, 1998, *Zhonghua Wenhua Tongzhi-Shetuan Zhi* [All Records of Chinese Culture-Associations], Shanghai: Shanghai Peoples' Publishing House, p. 343.

47. Dept. of International Politics of Peking University (DIPPKU), 1985, *Zhongguo Jinxiandai Shi Tongji Ziliao Xuanbian* [Selective of Statistics in Modern and Contemporary History of China], Zhengzhou: Henan Peoples' Publishing House, p. 170.

48. The Second Historical Dossier House of China (TSHDHC), 1994, *Zhongguo Minguo Shi Dang'an Ziliao Huibian* [Collection of the Dossiers of the Republic of China], Nanjing: Jiangsu Ancient Books Publishing House, pp. 86, 497.

49. Jianqing Liu, 1998, *Zhonghua Wenhua Tongzhi-Shetuan Zhi* [All Records of Chinese Culture-Associations], Shanghai: Shanghai Peoples' Publishing House, p. 423–424.

50. Yili Ma and Hanbang Liu, 1993, *Shanghai Shehui Tuanti Gailan* [A General Introduction to Social Organizations in Shanghai], Shanghai: Shanghai People's Publishing House, pp. 10–11.

51. Zhongze Wu and Jinluo Chen, 1996, *Shetuan Guanli Gongzuo* [Administration of Social Organizations], Beijing: China Society Publishing House, pp. 4–7.

52. Nick Young and Anthony Woo, 2000, *An Introduction to the Nonprofit Sector in China*, Kent: Charities Aid Foundation.

53. A former official from Shanghai municipal bureau of civil affairs told us that, after retirement, she worked for a nongovernmental organization, but her organization was forced to operate without registration, because the requirement of initial funds for social organizations was set too high.

54. Yong Zhao, 2003, "Minban Fei Qiye Danwei Shuliang Fenxi" [Analysis on the amount of Private Non-enterprises Units], Online Paper, see http://www.mca.gov.cn/artical/content/WGJ_TJFX/20031229122655.htm.

55. Allon Fisher, 1974, "Associational Life in the People's Republic of China," in David Horton Smith (ed.), *Voluntary Action Research: 1974—The Nature of Voluntary Action around the World*, Toronto: Lexington Books, pp. 11–12.

56. With a membership of 68 million, the Chinese Communist Party (CCP) may also offer its members opportunities to accumulate social capital. This study excludes the CCP because the party and the state are almost inseparable in China.

57. All China Federation of Trade Unions' website, http://www.acftu.org.

58. For the detailed description of the conflicts between All-China Federation of Trade Unions and the party-state, see Harper (1969) and Zhang (2003).

59. Chinese Communist Youth League's website, http://www.ccyl.org.cn.

60. China Association for Science and Technology's website http://www.cflac.org.cn.

61. For administrative purpose, WTAs are under the jurisdiction of the All China Federation of Trade Unions.

62. ADB, 2003, *The Development of Private Enterprise in the People's Republic of China*, Manila: Asian Development Bank, p. 44.

63. ADB, 2003, *The Development of Private Enterprise in the People's Republic of China*, Manila: Asian Development Bank, p. 46.

64. China Family Planning Association's website is http://www.chinafpa.org.cn.

65. The website of China Consumers' Association is http://www.cca.org.cn.

66. http://www.chinafpa.org.cn/xhjs01.asp.

67. http://www.cca.org.cn/aboutus/6-gzcj1.htm.

68. Jizuo Yin (ed.), 2001, *2001 Nian Shanghai Shehui Baogao Shu* [Report on Shanghai Society: 2001], Shanghai: Shanghai Social Science Publishing House, p. 244.

69. A survey conducted in Shanghai largely confirms this estimate. There were 712 associations in 56 universities in Shanghai in 2000. The average was about twelve. The distribution of those associations was also similar with our online survey

with 57 percent of groups active in the areas of literary and arts and sports (School Department of Shanghai Youth League (SDSYL), 2001, "Shanghai Xuesheng Shetuan de Xianzhuang Fenxi yu Yanjiu" [Analysis and Research on Current Situation of Students' Associations in Shanghai], *Thoughts, Theory, and Education*, Vol. 11).

70. State Statistical Bureau, 2004, *China Statistical Abstract 2004*, Beijing: China Statistical Press, p. 2.

71. Jizuo Yin (ed.), 2001, *2001 Nian Shanghai Shehui Baogao Shu* [Report on Shanghai Society: 2001], Shanghai: Shanghai Social Science Publishing House.

72. Nan Lin, 2001, *Social Capital: A Theory of Social Structure and Action*, New York: Cambridge University Press, p. 212.

73. http://www.cnnic.net.cn/download/2005/2005041401.pdf. The BBS forums on enterprises websites were mostly oriented toward their customers or staff, and related to its products or services. Most of them have little influence in the public.

74. http://ad.xilu.com/.

75. http://www.cn-bbs.org.

Chapter Three

Religious Organizations and Local Self-rule in Rural China

Richard Madsen

INTRODUCTION

Religion is one of the important new social forces in rural China. According to the government's own, certainly underestimated, figures, there are 100,000 religious practitioners in China today. But if we consider religion to include any form of evocation of supernatural powers—and therefore include traditional folk practices such as fortune telling, geomancy, and burning incense to the gods or ancestors at life-cycle rituals or seasonal festivals—then, according to Peter Ng of the Chinese University of Hong Kong, as much as 95 percent of the population could be considered religious to some degree.[1] Although there are certainly important religious movements among urban residents (Falungong was one of the most important of these), religious belief and practice are most prominent among rural people.

After having been severely repressed during the Maoist era, rural religious organizations are demonstrating a remarkable ability to mobilize believers and to influence local economic, social, and political life.[2] This religious ferment takes many different forms: revivals of traditional practices, adoption of new practices, and various combinations of the two. Rural religious organizations are vehicles for grassroots self-governance and can be competitors with Party control. Sometimes the competition is a relatively friendly one—the religious organizations reach an amicable modus vivendi with local political officials—and sometimes it is hostile. In any case, religious organizations have the potential to affect local governance. When there are local elections, religious leaders can either run for office themselves or influence their followers to vote for certain candidates. If the competition between the religious organization and the local Party is hostile, the Party obviously must find a way to get the organization out of the political process. Even if the competition with the Party is amicable, the participation of religious organizations can increase the complexity of political contention and lead to unanticipated outcomes.

To help us think in an orderly way about the rather bewildering variety of rural religious forms and to explore the implications of these forms for local governance, I will outline several models of rural religious development. These are based on actual cases, but the cases are used as the basis for ideal types, whose value may come from their usefulness in developing analytical frameworks rather than from their ability to fully reflect all of the complexities of the phenomena from which they were derived.

GENERAL POLITICAL CONTEXT: STATE OPPOSITION TO RELIGION

A fundamental challenge to all forms of religious organization in China is the state's opposition to religion in principle. This does not at all mean that it is committed to suppressing all forms of religion in practice. China is like the mirror opposite of a state with an established religion. Secular liberal states, like the United States, are officially neutral with regard to religion, as long as religion stays within the private sphere. Theocratic states in principle legitimate themselves through support of a particular religion. In contrast to a secular liberal state like the United States, which is officially neutral with regard to religion, as long as religion stays within the private sphere, states with an established religion use a particular religious denomination (like the Church of England in the UK) to symbolize the core aspirations of the state as a whole. Primary state rituals are held in the established religion's cathedrals; a certain primacy may be given to the established religion in official versions of national history. But depending on historical and political circumstances, a state with an established religion may tolerate a wide variety of religious beliefs and associations, and adherents to these may well outnumber adherents of the established religion. The Chinese state is not a liberal state, officially neutral toward religion. It is based on an established atheism. It uses the ideology and rituals of Marxism and scientific progress to symbolize its core aspirations, and it gives dialectical materialism a primacy in its official versions of national history, even though in practice it can tolerate a wide variety of religious belief.

Even when religious organizations flourish within a state with an atheist establishment, they have to be on the defensive. They can have no guarantee that the government will be indifferent to them. Their worldviews are always at least partially at variance with the government's legitimating ideology. Their leaders face particular tensions. If they do not develop a cooperative relationship with the government, they may suffer various personal difficulties, as well as being unable to deliver protection and benefits to their religious community. But if they become too closely identified with the government, they can lose credibility in the minds of ordinary practitioners.[3]

These tensions are most stark when religious leaders interact with state officials at the national level. In many rural contexts, however, both religion and politics are deeply embedded in local community. The tensions do not go away when religious leaders and government officials are both embedded in local society but they are blurred. Different degrees of this blurring are conducive to different forms of religious leadership, different substantive forms of religious beliefs, and different patterns of cooperation and conflict between religious leaders and the government.

SOCIALLY EMBEDDED RELIGION: A COMMUNITY TEMPLE

The first model of rural religious organization is one with a long history behind it. Before the twentieth century, most rural folk religion was inextricably intertwined with economic, political, and social life within local communities. As Kristofer Schipper puts it,

> Before modern iconoclasm held sway, religion was in evidence everywhere in China: each house had its altar, each district and village its temple. They were numerous and easy to spot, for as a rule, the local temple was the most beautiful building, the pride of the area. . . . [Temples] were always built by an association or a local community. . . . In the countryside, they were erected by all the members of a village community or regional association. Management of the common property—buildings, land, furnishings, and revenue—was strictly egalitarian. . . . [W]orship in a temple is not reserved exclusively for the saint or gods to whom it is dedicated. The *miao* is a place open to all beings, divine and human. A community as well as a truly communal house, it is a place for casual and formal meetings. The elders go there daily to discuss village affairs. Grandmothers, the family delegates in religious matters, go there every day with offerings of incense and to fill the lamps with oil. Music and theater associations, along with clubs for boxing, reading, chess, charity, pilgrimages, automatic writing, medical research, kite flying, and cultural associations of all kinds create their headquarters in the temple, and find there as well a place of worship for their particular patron saint.[4]

Besides being the center of local cultural, economic, political, and social life, the local temple was traditionally the main node through which the local community was affiliated horizontally with other communities in its region.

Ties of economic and cultural exchange with other communities were established by commingling some of the ashes from the incense burner in one temple with those of another, and by the ritual interchange of visits by the people who centered themselves on different temples. As multifunctional institutions, temples were also one of the main local conduits for vertical connections with government officials intent on collecting taxes, maintaining order, and instilling proper morality.[5]

During the Maoist era, the communists shut down most local temples, took away their property, and forced their religious functionaries to give up leading religious rituals. Temples would have presented a barrier to the Party's efforts at establishing centralized political control over rural life. Meanwhile, the Party tried to establish its own forms of cultural and economic community. Of course, this project failed. In the reform era, the Party retreated from its efforts to reshape rural social and economic life at the local level. It continues to make an effort to control local politics, but the prevalence of corruption at the local level has made political control increasingly tenuous. Religion is one of the forces stepping into this vacuum, and one form it takes is the rebuilding of local temples. As they were in the past, such temples are projects of whole communities, managed by local elites who combine economic and political as well as cultural and religious roles.

Adam Yuan Chau has provided a splendid case study of the construction and management of one such temple in northern Shaanxi.[6] The temple is dedicated to the Black Dragon King. It brings in a large amount of income and has been used to build roads, irrigation systems, and a local primary school. Its annual festivals draw visitors from far and wide and become important venues for local commerce. It is not just a source of cultural pride, but an engine of local economic growth and a nexus of local political power.

The Black Dragon King Temple association is very large. "Regular employees include the caretaker, the divination poem decipherer, the accountant, the driver, the electrician, the treasurer, the custodian, the supplies procurer. . . . the gardener, and the teachers of the primary school (a dozen). There are also numerous part-time or seasonal laborers and helpers."[7] The head of the temple's governing association is "Temple Boss Wang," a former party secretary. Adam Yuan Chau suggests that leaving the party secretary's job to become temple boss was a step up in power for Boss Wang.

To play his many roles as a local political, economic, and cultural leader, Boss Wang has to establish working relationships with many different government agencies: religious affairs, public security, industry and commerce, education, cultural affairs, and even foreign affairs (because the temple attracts both foreign visitors and foreign capital). Because of the state establishment of atheism, however, all of these relationships must have a powerful informal dimension. Since its revival in 1982 until the late 1990s, the temple was, in the official classificatory system, an example of "feudal superstition," a kind of religious practice that needed to be discouraged and gradually eliminated. It would be almost impossible to shut down a thriving enterprise like the Black Dragon King Temple, however. But local officials can use the fact that the temple is formally illegal to ask for bribes to refrain from harassing it. So Boss Wang has to develop personal relationships with each of the officials responsible for overseeing aspects of the temple. These involve some exchange of favors, the nature of which varies according to the specific importance and history of each relationship.[8]

To integrate all of the various functions that the temple performs, Boss Wang also has to cultivate horizontal relationships with all the people involved. Since all of these forms of informal relationships are with Boss Wang as a person, not simply as a holder of an office, Boss Wang becomes indispensable to the successful operation of the temple.

The Black Dragon King Temple can serve to illustrate a model of "traditional" *socially embedded rural religious organization.* Order is maintained through multifunctional, particularistic bonds based upon kinship or upon exchanges of favors. The relationship networks are relatively closed: everyone knows everyone else, but they do not have many contacts outside the community, and they rely on a few community elites to mediate these contacts. The elites (like the "gentry" of old) get their power by a combination of having privileged access to higher levels of government and controlling a disproportionate amount of community property. The power is legitimated by a traditional morality that prescribes deference of clients to patrons (modeled after the deference expected of children to parents and wives to husbands) and benevolence of patrons to clients.

Many of these patterns of community organization have returned during the reform era. Often described as "local emperors," local cadres base their power on privileged access to higher levels of government, and they enrich themselves by demanding all sorts of favors from people within the communities they are supposed to govern. Temple Boss Wang operates in the same way. He is also a type of local emperor. But the difference between him and many government cadres is that he gives more back to the community. The temple is the center of an interdependent community effort that actually enhances the life of the community economically (because of the commercial enterprises it sponsors) as well as culturally (because of the meaningful religious and social activities that it makes possible).

In this socially embedded model of community organization, the boss of the local temple is as much a local political leader as he is a religious leader. But because of his ability to provide valued goods to the community, he actually has more power than the local government leaders. He would probably not want to become a government leader (by standing, for instance, in a local election), if that meant that he would have to give up his position as temple boss. Meanwhile, local government leaders may like to have some of the prestige of the temple rub off on them—to be perceived as enabling temple activities—because this might help them shed their reputation of being merely parasitical on the community.

TRANSCENDENT RELIGION: A CHRISTIAN NETWORK

In sharp contrast to traditional community-embedded religion is the Christian house church network. "House church" is the term for Protestant congregations that do not meet in officially registered venues. To be officially registered, a congregation would have to be affiliated with the Three Self Protestant Movement, which is a mass organization that cooperates closely with the government to carry out surveillance and control over Protestant groups. There are many reasons why a Christian congregation might not wish to or not be able to be officially registered. Some of these house churches may actually be very similar in theology, organization, and practice to congregations registered through the Three Self movement.[9] However, other house churches have beliefs and practices that are far removed from what would be acceptable to any group registered with the government. It is networks of this variety of house church that I am referring to in this paper.[10]

The most important networks had their origins in inland rural areas, especially in Henan Province, but they now reach much more widely throughout China. According to the journalist David Aikman, the three most important of such networks are called the Fengcheng network, the Tanghe network (both named after the towns in Henan where they originated), and the Born Again Movement.[11] Unlike the Black Dragon King Temple, which is the center of a local community consisting of families with deep roots there, these Christian networks are open networks that link many congregations of like-minded individuals over broad areas. The congregations thus linked together consist of individuals who have a born-again experience and have made a personal commitment to Jesus in adolescence or adulthood. These networks had their beginning in independent nondenominational churches founded by Chinese preachers in the early twentieth century. Influenced by the early-twentieth-century Pentecostal movement, such churches often rejected control by foreign mission organizations and emphasized faith healing and a direct, ecstatic relationship with God. Because of their resistance to any outside control, they were suppressed harshly by the Communist government after 1949.[12]

Many of their early leaders spent many years in prison, and those who survived have enormous charismatic authority in the minds of their followers. The foundations for some of the present networks were laid in the 1970s when there was enough chaos in the Chinese interior for bold evangelists, sometimes made even more determined by their sufferings in prison, to move surreptitiously from place to place to provide channels of communication between scattered congregations.[13] The networks were thus built through personal ties among itinerant preachers, but they were based on the charismatic authority of the preachers, not on the exchange of material goods that are the basis for patron-client ties with those preachers. The preachers had few material benefits to provide, and they exposed their congregations to danger instead of offering them protection. Participation in the networks separated members from local economics and politics.

It is these networks that have provided the foundation for a spectacular expansion of Christianity in rural China during the reform era—from well less than a million Christians to probably well over thirty million in the past twenty-five years. A major impetus for the expansion of the three networks mentioned here was the contact between some of their key leaders and the Pentecostal Christianity of Dennis Balcombe, an American missionary who had established a Pentecostal congregation in Hong Kong in the 1970s. Balcombe began his evangelization career in mainland China by smuggling bibles into Guangzhou, where they were taken by people from the various Christian networks and shipped into the interior. He later began showing some of the network leaders videos of spirit-filled Pentecostal meetings. In 1986, he started praying over some of the top leaders, inducing them to receive the Baptism of the Holy Spirit, manifested in the speaking of tongues. He was then invited to travel clandestinely to Fengchang in Henan (an area at the time closed to foreigners) to give the Pentecostal gifts to large assemblies of Christians in the Fengchang network. He was spectacularly successful. He was then invited to do the same for the Tanghe network. Within a short time, all of the major Christian networks, with the exception of the Born Again Fellowship whose leaders had some theological reservations about Pentecostalism, had become Pentecostal and adopted not just the speaking of tongues but styles of music, forms of worship, and patterns of belief of the late-twentieth-century worldwide Pentecostal movement.[14]

In general, these patterns of belief direct their adherents to otherworldly concerns rather than to worldly political activity. But there are beliefs that can give the government some cause for concern—especially the belief in Premillennialism, which holds that the Last Times are coming soon and that those who have accepted Jesus will be raptured up to heaven, while the world undergoes great tribulations that will end with the triumphant Second Coming of Christ.[15] The government might also worry about the public health implications of practices like faith healing.[16] But despite government attempts to stop such beliefs and practices, the networks that foster them are expanding very rapidly.

It would be difficult for the government to stop them because they are indeed networks, not dependent on a central leadership. Their members believe that each individual directly receives the gifts of the Holy Spirit. Anybody can do this; anybody can help another to do it. The networks received an enormous boost in energy from certain charismatic leaders, but they do not rely on the constant guidance of those leaders. Since the leaders' charisma is in large part connected with their willingness to undergo martyrdom for the faith, the leaders sometimes give even more respect when they are arrested than when they are actually directly engaged in their congregations. Since the experience of receiving the Holy Spirit is primarily an emotional rather than a cognitive experience, believers are not dependent on the complicated doctrinal texts that would be written by centralized theological schools. The Christian networks are even more protean than Falungong, which, after all, depended on a rather complicated body of doctrine and a centralized but flexible leadership structure.[17]

The de-centered nature of the Christian networks allows them constantly to generate new offspring with new theologies and new ways of adapting to specific environments. A few main themes remain constant—the Second Coming, speaking in tongues, faith healing—but they are given different specific interpretations. This aids in the expansion of the networks but it raises the threat of sectarian division. Local assemblies accuse each other of heresy. Out of this ferment have arisen certain new groups with beliefs bizarre even by Pentecostal standards.

The most bizarre is the "Eastern Lightning," which like the other major Christian networks began in Henan (but now is especially strong in Shaanxi), and features a belief that Christ has been reincarnated in the person of a woman. Instead of making many converts of non-Christians, the Eastern Lightning has succeeded in converting significant numbers (perhaps 400,000) of people from other Christian networks. Members of the other networks claim that the Eastern Lightning is not Christian at all, that it is indeed the "spawn of Satan" and uses lies, bribery, sexual seduction, and physical coercion to make its converts. The Eastern Lightning is only the most extreme example of breakaway offshoots of the major Christian networks.[18]

The development of such breakaway groups has stimulated attempts by the larger Christian networks to establish a better-coordinated leadership that could impose a unified orthodoxy on their networks. In 1998, leaders of the major networks issued a "Confession of Faith," in which they committed themselves to a literal interpretation of the Bible, to the classical idea of the Trinity, to the "priesthood of all believers," and to a Premillenial account of the Second Coming. These doctrines were explicitly meant to distinguish themselves from groups like Eastern Lightning. The Confession of Faith was not only directed to fellow Christians, but also to the Chinese government. The Christian networks were distancing themselves from groups that the government might find sufficiently dangerous to label "evil cults."[19]

Around the same time, the same group of leaders also issued a "United Appeal" to the government[20]:

> We call on the government to admit to God's great power and to study seriously the new trends in the development of Christianity. . . . [T]he judicial branch of the National People's Congress and the United Front system should readjust their policies and regulations on religion lest they violate God's will to their own detriment.[21]

They demanded that all "orthodox Christians" (not heretics like the Eastern Lightning) should be released from prison. Furthermore, they claimed that the house church movement had 80 million believers in China (a number that is probably greatly inflated)[22] and that they, rather than the Three Self Movement churches, represented the "mainstream of Christianity in China." They called on the Chinese Communist Party central leadership to begin a dialogue with representatives of the House Churches and warned that "attacks on Christians who fervently preach the Gospel only bring harm to China and its government."[23]

This attempt to consolidate the Christian networks did not seem to stop the growth of heretical sects like Eastern Lightning. In 1999, the government saw Eastern Lightning as enough of a threat that in some areas at least the government made it second only to Falungong as a target for suppression.[24] It is also unclear how the people who drafted the Confession of Faith and United Appeal are empowered to represent their networks. They are not elected by grassroots members. They have enormous prestige because they have been willing to act boldly for their faith, but they are not part of an organizational hierarchy that reaches down to the grassroots of their congregations and they have no ability to regularly supervise and discipline congregations composed of a "priesthood of all believers." Their willingness to suffer martyrdom by confronting the government does not make them welcome negotiating partners, even if the government might see them as better than "evil cult" leaders. The tone of their appeal—warning them not to "violate God's will to their own detriment"—seems more like a call for surrender than an appeal for dialogue.

The Christian networks can illustrate a *socially transcendent model* of rural social organization. It is disembedded from both local state and society. It is at odds with the government, though government officials might tolerate it for practical reasons in specific cases. It is also at odds with local society. Some of the most respected leaders of the Christian networks are people who accepted the faith over the objections of their families and who are now estranged from their families. For example, Ding Hui, the dynamic woman leader who was the first to receive the Holy Spirit from Dennis Balcombe, became a Christian over the fierce opposition of her parents, who were local Party leaders, and she literally ran away from home.[25]

They are linked with one another with relatively weak ties through open networks spread over wide areas. These are networks whose members do not personally know most other people in the network. Members have few of the material goods to exchange with one another that are the building blocks of tight bonds of interdependency. The ties between members are more like single-stranded channels of communication than multi-stranded bonds of economic, political, and social interdependency. They are relatively "low bandwidth" channels. They cannot convey complicated, detailed information and they cannot provide the tools to subject this information to critical scrutiny.[26] The kind of information that flows through them consists of relatively stereotyped, sketchy, yet dramatic stories of miracles and heroic witness to the faith. They are well suited to the spreading of spectacular promises of salvation, but less suited to communicating information about the prosaic business of daily life. Innovations like Dennis Balcombe's Pentecostalism that are well suited to the particular carrying capacity of these networks can cascade through them with amazing rapidity.

Because these networks are separated from reinforcing social ties of family and kinship and from political patron-client ties, they provide few points of leverage to leaders who would like to subject them to unifying discipline. They predictably produce the unpredicted. They are subject to sectarian division, but these divisions do not really weaken the network as a whole, and may actually help expand it by providing new varieties of belief for people in different circumstances.

The leadership of such networks is charismatic. One's charisma is proven by one's ability to experience and to induce unusual, ecstatic spiritual experiences, one's ability to perform miracles, and one's willingness to confront government authorities on behalf of the faith. The charisma of leaders in these rural networks is not necessarily what Max Weber could have considered pure charisma, which is unstable. Most of the charismatic leaders, in the Christian network at least, were also entrepreneurs who actually built the networks. The networks are so constructed to communicate positive stories about the exploits of those who built them. Thus they consistently spread reports of the unusual spiritual capacities—the charisma—of their creators. But the networks may be more stable than the charismatic leaders themselves. If a leader dies, or is put in jail, or otherwise disappears, he or she can quickly get replaced by another leader whose spiritual exploits become the stuff of new legends to pass through the network.

Such socially and politically disembedded networks present particular challenges to the state. They cannot easily be suppressed. If the government punishes particular leaders, the act only inspires members who revere martyrdom. If the government cuts off a part of the network, other shoots can quickly grow up elsewhere. The networks cannot easily be co-opted. Members who expect otherworldly salvation do not need anything that the government has to give them. They are relatively immune from being enmeshed in patron-client ties.

But in ordinary times, such networks might peacefully coexist with official government structures. For example, according to the descriptions of them in David Aikman's recent book, house church Christians do not seem especially interested in confronting the government on issues not directly related to religious freedom. "China's house church Christians are uniformly patriotic and cautious. They do not want to see a breakup of China by the creation, for example, of an independent Tibet. They do not want to see a Taiwan that has declared sovereign independence from China (but they also don't want to see Communist military action toward Taiwan). They want to see religious and political freedom come to China, but in an evolutionary, reformist process, not through political violence against the authorities."[27] Their leadership at least does not seem to think that China will be ready for political democracy in the near future and they do not seem interested in building grassroots democracy—by running candidates for local elections, for example—except as a means to guarantee more space for their religious activities.

HIERARCHICALLY NESTED RELIGION: THE RURAL CATHOLIC CHURCH

Rural Catholic communities occupy a middle position between socially embedded and transcendent religion. Catholic missionaries were intent on converting not just individuals but whole communities. (They were afraid that if an individual was converted without the support of his or her family and community, the individual would easily fall away from the faith, and his fate in the afterlife might be better than if he had never converted at all.) In the countryside, then, one typically finds either whole villages or at least whole lineages within villages that are Catholic. The faith is passed down from generation to generation. Marriage to non-Catholics is discouraged or allowed only if the spouse is willing to convert to Catholicism. In places like Xian County in Hebei, which is 95 percent Catholic, each sizeable village has its own church, which functions somewhat the same as temples traditionally did for non-Christian villages—as a center for the social, economic, and political life of the village.[28]

One difference between Catholic churches and village temples, however, is that they are usually not as richly appointed as temples. In his study of Daoism, Kristofer Schipper comments that "for the price of a single village temple, one can easily have built ten mission churches."[29] Before 1949, Catholic Churches were traditionally financed not by villagers themselves, but by foreign missionary organizations. Temples on the other hand represented a generations-long labor of love on the part of a village. Even today, this is still the case. A temple like the Black Dragon King temple was a product of local investment, not government subsidy. (The temple has to use its home-grown wealth to buy protection from local officials.) But many village Catholic churches are built from money provided by the government in compensation for church property confiscated or destroyed during the Maoist era. Communities that do not benefit from government subsidies often get money, sometimes surreptitiously, from Catholic organizations abroad or from former villagers now residing abroad. (Christian house churches also benefit from foreign support, but this seems to be mostly used to provide bibles and other evangelical tools rather than community church buildings.) The way of financing Catholic church buildings is indicative of the way that local Catholic communities are suspended between local social, economic, and political institutions and a larger, hierarchical ecclesiastical organization.

On the one hand, Catholic identity is profoundly identified with family and village identity. Catholic identity is less a matter of personal faith and voluntary affiliation and more a matter of community roots. Villagers distinguish between "true believer" and "lax" Catholics. But even if the latter almost never go to church and live a life at variance with church teaching, they are still considered Catholics. It is an identity that they cannot shed, so long as they remain connected to their village. (On the other hand, if they sever all roots with their village and become completely urbanized, it is easy, as one informant said, to "forget God.") When they die, they will have to be buried according to Catholic rituals, in order to become connected with their Catholic ancestors.[30] In the meantime, before 1949, they were dependent on the local church not only for spiritual solace but often for education, health care, relief money, and even investment capital.

On the other hand, Catholics saw their local church as nested within a community of communities tied together through ordered ranks of priests and bishops, regulated by canon law, and linked ultimately to the Pope.

Religious regulation and spiritual benefits descended from above. And to some degree resources not only to build churches, schools, clinics but also to support priests, teachers, and nurses came from above too.[31] Under the KMT regime, the hierarchy was also able to negotiate a degree of political protection for Catholics. Politically well-connected prelates, like Bishop Yu Bin of Nanjing, negotiated with the government to provide freedom of action for the Church.[32]

Whatever political privileges Catholics may have had under the KMT turned into major liabilities after 1949. The Church's capacity to provide education, health care, and resources for community development were also eliminated. The Catholic hierarchy itself was compromised. The government established a Catholic Patriotic Association (CPA) and demanded that only bishops and priests who belonged to the CPA could legitimately carry out their religious roles. To join the CPA one had to declare that one's allegiance to the PRC superseded allegiance to the Pope. At the direction of the Vatican, most bishops and priests refused to join or cooperate with the CPA. For their resistance, such clerics were often put into prison. Most ordinary Catholics refused to accept the legitimacy of those clergy who cooperated with the CPA, and an underground Catholic church sprang up.[33]

The CPA itself was closed down during the Cultural Revolution and all public religious practice was forbidden. During the reform era, however, churches were reopened and practice of the Catholic faith was allowed as long as it was under the general auspices of the CPA. New regulations loosened government supervision over purely theological or sacramental matters and made it possible for some bishops and priests to claim ultimate religious loyalty to the Pope even though they accepted government supervision through the CPA. At present, over two-thirds of Chinese bishops in the officially approved part of the Church have received approval of their ministry from the Vatican. However, there has also developed a parallel hierarchy of underground bishops and priests who, in the name of loyalty to the Pope, refuse to accept the hierarchy that accepts supervision by the CPA. Under some circumstances, members of official and underground hierarchies have amicable relationships, but under other circumstances they can have very hostile relationships with one another. Where relationships are hostile, sometimes whole village communities ally with one or another part of the hierarchy. Sometimes these differences are reinforced by preexisting tensions between villages over such issues as land disputes or historical grudges. The government has tried to suppress the underground Church, but so far it has been unable to do so.[34]

Despite or perhaps because of all these conflicts, practice of the Catholic faith has been vigorously revived in rural China. There were about 3,000,000

Catholics before 1949 and probably about 12,000,000 now.[35] But the numbers represent a natural population increase rather than the making of many new converts, as in the case of the house churches. Instead of bringing about a large increase in individual conversions, the flourishing of the Catholic faith involves the rebuilding of village institutions that were once associated with the faith—the rebuilding of church buildings, first of all, but also the establishment of clinics and even schools.

An example is the case of MaoVillage in Shaanxi Province, studied by Tong Zhihui on his book on elections and village government.[36] MaoVillage is a Catholic community whose roots go back to the nineteenth century. In the first half of the twentieth century, it achieved a modest prosperity, relative to other villages in its area, due in part to the organization and material aid provided by the Church. Its economy has done rather poorly during the reform era because its remote location put it at a disadvantage in a competitive market economy. The Church, however, helped to make up for some of its economic decline. In the 1980s, the village rebuilt its church and reestablished public Catholic worship. With the help of money contributed from abroad, the church helped the village address some infrastructure problems, and in the 1990s, the church helped build a new school for the village. The school was officially a public school, but the church controlled much of its organization and activities. Conflict erupted, however, when the local priest tried to get rid of the principal, a man well connected with the local Party apparatus, who resisted efforts of the church to control the curriculum. For example, the church wanted priests and nuns to teach Catholic hymns in the music class, but the principal and local department of education would not allow this. With the help of the regional bishop, the local priest forwarded to the local government an accusation of financial mismanagement and corruption against the principal. This, however, angered some villagers, who thought that the local church was getting too involved in local politics. This led to a polarization of the village, which complicated the holding of local elections. The election was a messy affair, marred by procedural irregularities that caused the first results to be invalidated. In the end, however, the principal of the school emerged as the local village head.

The story shows how Catholics, unlike house church Christians, do get involved in the messy rough and tumble of local politics—concerned not just about religious freedom but about such mundane issues as control of schools—and are willing to use the tools of pragmatic compromise, patronage, and even blackmail to get their way. In this way, the Catholic leaders (who in MaoVillage include not just the local priests, but prominent lay people) are similar to socially embedded temple leaders like Boss Wang. But unlike Boss Wang, the Catholic authorities are connected with an outside hierarchical structure, which they can call on to try to gain an edge in the political game. But this can backfire. Because of its divisions and because of its difficulties in marshalling a steady supply of resources, the hierarchy does not have the clout it may have had before the revolution. Meanwhile, non-Catholics and lax Catholics may not want Church leaders to enter too closely into political affairs.

We can abstract from such stories a model of *hierarchically nested* rural religious organization. The organization is based on multi-stranded ties that combine religion with kinship, economic interdependence, and clientalism. But the networks formed by these ties are somewhat more open than those in the socially embedded model. They are connected to a structure of authority and communication that bypasses local government officials. In the Catholic case, this hierarchy is governed by canon law, a formal legal code that might be more effective in conveying authority from top to bottom of a bureaucratic system than the corruption-ridden government bureaucracy. Conflict between official and underground factions of the Catholic hierarchy, however, hinders its effectiveness. Moreover, although the hierarchy can connect local communities with counterparts over wide regions, it is a rather rigid form of connection, compared with the Christian networks. Communications with other Catholic communities may have to go through local bishops (after questions have been resolved about the legitimacy of the local bishop). Evangelical entrepreneurship, especially by laypeople, is discouraged. The Catholic Church therefore cannot spread its influence as widely as the more nimble, flexible Christian networks. But the Catholic Church can maintain a certain unity of doctrine. It is not plagued by a multiplication of sects accusing one another of heresy. Catholic divisions are serious, but basically centered around only two poles. And these divisions, between official and underground factions, are more about lines of authority than about doctrine or forms of worship. Finally, by embedding Catholic life in the fabric of local social, economic, and political life and then nesting local Catholic communities in an outside hierarchy, this model of rural religious organization may have more potential to influence ordinary politics at the local level than the Christian networks.

CONCLUSION

During the reform era, religion has become an important social force in rural China. It is a force arising from the bottom up in the face of varying degrees of government opposition ranging from ineffectual disapproval to vigorous suppression. Religion is a multifarious force, however. The religious landscape includes revivals of older forms of religious practice and adoption of newer forms. These different practices have different social locations, different forms of organization, and different conceptions of legitimate authority. These different forms of social organization have different implications for local politics.

This paper has suggested three different models of religious social organization: a socially embedded model, a socially transcendent model, and a hierarchically nested model. The models were empirically based, respectively, on a folk religious temple, Christian house church networks, and local Catholic organizations.

These empirical examples by no means exhaust the varieties of religious belief and practice in China today. There are, for example, vigorous revivals of monastic Buddhism[37] and Daoism,[38] of Islam,[39] and of local folk religions,[40] as well as "qigong healing sects" like Falungong.[41] I would suggest, however, that the typology I have presented here might be useful to give a preliminary ordering to this variety. It reminds us, at least, that from a sociological perspective, religion is a multidimensional phenomenon. It is, as Durkheim argued, the collective representations that constitute a community's collective identity. But it is also a basis for legitimating ruling hierarchies as well as a vehicle for individual self-development. Each of these dimensions of religion has different social and political implications. All dimensions are found in all of the major world religions, but in various contexts, one dimension or another can come into prominence.

In China today, the socially embedded model can be applied not just to large folk religious temples like the Black Dragon Temple, but also to many forms of local communal solidarity based on common rituals. The hierarchically nested model can be applied to many different ways of linking local communities into a religiously justified authority structure, including Tibetan Buddhism, with its Dalai Lama and Panchen Lama. The socially transcendent model can be applied to the wide variety of cases where people seek individual salvation through syncretistic *qigong* healing sects.

The models that I have suggested are aimed at showing how different kinds of religion can be connected with different kinds of local politics. The socially embedded model is deeply implicated in informal clientalism. The nested hierarchically nested model is also implicated in local clientalism, but it can bring resources from outside into the local political struggle. The socially transcendent model is not deeply connected to local political struggle. But because its expansive open networks seem conducive for quickly spreading the visionary enthusiasms of charismatic leaders, it could under certain circumstances lead to a millenarian politics. All of these religious forms represent ways for society to organize and govern itself in at least partial autonomy from the state. In that sense they are democratic. But they are not really conducive with the ideals of modern, secular procedural democracy.

NOTES

1. Peter Tze Ming Ng, 2002, "Religious Situations in China Today: Secularization Theory Revisited," paper presented at the Association for Sociology of Religion meetings, Chicago, August 14–16, 2002.

2. See Daniel L. Overmyer, 2003, "Religion in China Today: An Introduction," in Daniel L. Overmeyer (ed.), *Religion in China Today*, Cambridge University Press, pp.1–10.

3. See Donald E. MacInnis, 1989, *Religion in China Today: Policy and Practice*, Maryknoll, NY: Orbis; and Jason Kindopp and Carol Lee Hamrin (eds.), 2004, *God and Caesar in China: Policy Implications of Church-State Tensions*, Washington, D.C.: Brookings Institution.

4. Kristofer Schipper, 1993, *The Taoist Body*, Berkeley: University of California Press, pp. 20–22.

5. Schipper, 1993, op. cit., p.23; See also, Kenneth Dean, 2003, "Local Communal Religion in Contemporary South-east China," in Daniel L. Overmeyer (ed.), *Religion in China Today*, Cambridge University Press, pp. 32–52.

6. Adam Yuet Chau, 2004, "The Channeling Zone: Between the Local State and Local Society: The Case of Popular Religion in Shaanbei, North-Central China," manuscript prepared for the Political of Religion in China Workshop, Stanford University, April 31–May 2, 2004.

7. Chau, 2004, op. cit., p. 19.

8. Chau, 2004, op. cit., pp. 15–21.

9. Daniel H. Bays, 2003, "Protestant Christianity in China Today" in Daniel L. Overmeyer (ed.), *Religion in China Today*, Cambridge University Press, pp. 182–198.

10. The following section is mostly based on David Aikman, 2003, *Jesus in Beijing*, Washington, DC: Regnery.

11. Aikman, 2003, op. cit., pp. 74–89.

12. Richard Madsen, 2003, "Chinese Christianity: Indigenization and Conflict," in Elizabeth J. Perry and Mark Selden (eds.), *Chinese Society, 2nd edition*, London: RoutledgeCurzon, p. 273, 275–277; and Daniel H. Bays, 1996, "The Growth of Independent Christianity in China," in Daniel H. Bays (ed.), *Christianity in China: From the Eighteenth Century to the Present*, Stanford: Stanford University Press, pp. 307–316.

13. Aikman, 2003, op, cit., pp. 47–71.

14. Aikman, 2003, op. cit., pp. 271–275.

15. Aikman, 2003, op. cit., pp. 93–94.

16. Daniel H. Bays, 2003, "Protestant Christianity in China Today," in Daniel L. Overmeyer (ed.), *Religion in China Today*, Cambridge University Press, p. 191;

Ryan Dunch, 2001, "Protestant Christianity in China Today: Fragile, Fragmented, Flourishing," in Stephen Uhalley, Jr. and Xiaoxin Wu (eds.), *China and Christianity: Burdened Past, Hopeful Future*, Armonk: M.E. Sharpe, p. 201.

17. See Patricia M. Thornton, 2003, "The New Cybersects: Resistance and Repression in the Reform Era," in Elizabeth J. Perry and Mark Selden (eds.), *Chinese Society, 2nd Edition*, London and New York: RoutledgeCurzon, pp. 247–270.

18. Richard Madsen, 2003, "Chinese Christianity: Indigenization and Conflict," in Elizabeth J. Perry and Mark Selden (eds.), *Chinese Society, 2nd Edition*, London: RoutledgeCurzon, p. 277. See also, Shijiazhuang Ministry of Public Security Document, 2000, in Shixiong Li and Xiqiu (Bob) Fu (eds.), *Religion and National Security in China: Secret Documents from China's Security Sector, Feb. 11, 2002*, September 14, 2000, http://www.religiousfreedomforchina.org

19. Translated in Aikman, op. cit. pp. 295–307.

20. Translated in Aikman, op. cit. pp. 293–294.

21. Translated in Aikman, op. cit. p. 293.

22. For the best scholarly discussion of the "numbers game," see Daniel H. Bays, 2003, "Protestant Christianity in China Today," in Daniel L. Overmeyer (ed.), *Religion in China Today*, Cambridge University Press, pp. 185–186.

23. Translated in Aikman, op. cit. pp. 293–294.

24. Richard Madsen, 2003, "Chinese Christianity: Indigenization and Conflict," in Elizabeth J. Perry and Mark Selden (eds.), *Chinese Society, 2nd Edition*, London: RoutledgeCurzon, p. 277.

25. David Aikman, 2003, *Jesus in Beijing*, Washington, DC: Regnery, pp. 98–108.

26. These mainly rural organizations have not developed the sophisticated Internet communication tools that were characteristic of Falungong.

27. David Aikman, 2003, *Jesus in Beijing*, Washington, DC: Regnery, p. 289.

28. Richard Madsen, 1998, *China's Catholics: Tragedy and Hope in an Emerging Civil Society*, Berkeley: University of California Press.

29. Kristofer Schipper, 1993, *The Taoist Body*, Berkeley: University of California Press, p. 21. In a footnote, Schipper continues: "This is one aspect of the problem of Christian missions in China. Not only is Western religion cheaper (it requires only a meager contribution on the part of the faithful for celebrations), but it often established owing to the gifts of foreign communities, through the intermediary of specialized organizations." Ibid. p. 220.

30. Richard Madsen, 1998, *China's Catholics: Tragedy and Hope in an Emerging Civil Society*, Berkeley: University of California Press, pp. 50–56.

31. Richard Madsen, 1998, *China's Catholics: Tragedy and Hope in an Emerging Civil Society*, Berkeley: University of California Press, pp. 25–33.

32. Eric O. Hanson, 1980, *Catholic Politics in China and Korea*, Maryknoll, NY: Orbis Books, p. 26 and passim.

33. Richard Madsen, 1998, *China's Catholics: Tragedy and Hope in an Emerging Civil Society*, Berkeley: University of California Press, pp. 34–39.

34. Richard Madsen, 1998, *China's Catholics: Tragedy and Hope in an Emerging Civil Society*, Berkeley: University of California Press, pp. 38–49.

35. Richard Madsen, 2003, "Catholic Revival during the Reform Era," in Daniel L. Overmeyer (ed.), *Religion in China Today*, Cambridge University Press, p. 163. Also, Richard Madsen, 1998, *China's Catholics: Tragedy and Hope in an Emerging Civil Society*, Berkeley: University of California Press, pp. 1–20.

36. Tong Zhihui, 2004, *Xuanju shijian yu cunzhuang zhengzhi [Elections and Village Governance]*,Beijing: Zhongguo Shehuikexuechubanshe, pp. 22–67.

37. Raoul Birnbaum, 2003, "Buddhist China at the Century's Turn," in Daniel L. Overmeyer (ed.), *Religion in China Today*, Cambridge: Cambridge University Press, pp. 122–144.

38. Lai Chi-Tim, 2003, "Daoism in China Today, 1980–2002," in Daniel L. Overmeyer (ed.), *Religion in China Today*, Cambridge: Cambridge University Press, pp. 107–121.

39. Dru C. Gladney, 2003, "Islam in China: Accommodation or Separatism?," in Daniel L. Overmeyer (ed.), *Religion in China Today*, Cambridge University Press, pp. 45–161.

40. Kenneth Dean, 2003, "Local Communal Religion in Contemporary South-east China," in Daniel L. Overmeyer (ed.), *Religion in China Today*, Cambridge University Press, pp. 32–52; Fan Lizhu, 2003, "The Cult of the Silkworm Mother as a Core of Local Community Religion in a North China Village," in Daniel L. Overmeyer (ed.), *Religion in China Today*, Cambridge: Cambridge University Press, pp. 53–66.

41. Nancy N. Chen, "Healing Sects and Anti-Cult Campaigns," in Daniel L. Overmeyer (ed.), *Religion in China Today*, Cambridge: Cambridge University Press, pp. 199–214.

Chapter Four

In Search of Positive Deviants: Social Entrepreneurs, Nongovernmental Organizations, and the Development of Civil Society in China

Anne F. Thurston

INTRODUCTION

Shortly into my first meeting with Zhu Yongzhong in the summer of 2003, our conversation was interrupted by the sound of gongs and drums and chanting. Erlang, the area's most powerful local god and the second son of the Jade Emperor, was returning home, Mr. Zhu explained. His adherents were welcoming him back. Erlang's Taoist temple was just behind the wall of the courtyard where we were sitting. We went to observe.

The local god was already in place when we arrived. The milling crowd was either very old (some of the women had bound feet) or very young—the grandchildren of the worshippers. A number of people recognized Mr. Zhu. Others came to introduce themselves. The men who greeted him took his hand and raised it to touch their foreheads—replicating the gesture lamas use to confer a blessing. At thirty-three years old, Mr. Zhu was being accorded honor well beyond his age. But he is not a lama. He is the founder and director of a small nongovernmental organization (NGO)—the Sanchuan Development Association in Guanting township, Minhe county, Qinghai.

Often since, I have seen Zhu Yongzhong receive similar displays of respect—costumed school children singing in welcome, profferings of Minhe's powerful liquor, the place of honor at a school opening, a sheep slaughtered to celebrate his visit, people stopping him on the street to solicit his advice or assistance. He is treated like a mayor, says Jessica Priselac, one of my students who spent the summer of 2004 working with him as an intern, often accompanying him to the field.[1]

Local officials in Minhe are viewed—and treated—differently. When Mr. Zhu is introduced at a public meeting, the audience claps loudly and long, sometimes cheering. Local officials receive only polite applause. Local officials are assumed to be both corrupt and uninterested in the problems of ordinary villagers. No one can quite trust the local government, people say, particularly people from the poorest villages, which are often located in mountainous areas without paved roads. Access by car is either treacherous or impossible, and local officials are not generally inclined to visit villages on foot or by bicycle. Besides, officials expect to be wined and dined, and poor villagers cannot afford the cost of such lavish entertainment.

The story is told of how one official was received when he did pay a visit to such a poor village. Several villagers were squatting in the public square, chatting, when the official arrived. No one bothered to stand up to greet him. When the official complained about their rudeness, the villagers retorted that they would have treated a Sanchuan Development Association representative differently. Not only would they have stood, but the whole village would have lined the road to applaud. Firecrackers would have been set off in welcome, and the representative would be invited to share a glass or two of water, maybe even liquor. Officials visit only to collect taxes or implement the family planning policies, the villagers pointed out. Why should they stand up in greeting?

THE BURGEONING OF CHINESE NGOS

The Sanchuan Development Association is only one of several NGOs to be established recently in Qinghai. Indeed, if numbers are any indication, China has now joined the "associational revolution" that Lester Salamon argued in 1994 "may prove to be as significant to the latter twentieth century as the rise of the nation-state was to the latter nineteenth."[2] The upsurge of nonprofit, voluntary associations formed to "deliver human services, promote grass roots economic development, prevent environmental degradation, protect civil rights and pursue a thousand other objectives formerly unattended or left to the state," says Salamon, is "permanently altering the relationship between states and citizens."[3]

Wang Shaoguang's article in this volume documents China's participation in this associational revolution. Attempting to map out the full panoply of the country's associational life, Wang concludes that China has a total of more than eight million registered and unregistered nongovernmental and quasigovernmental associations.[4] The vast majority of these, more than five million, are under the aegis of quasigovernmental mass organizations, such as the All-China Federation of Trade Unions, the Communist Youth League, and the Women's Federation. Designed as transmission belts between the party-state and the masses, Wang points out that these organizations are on the one hand "expected to carry out the directives of the party/state and pass them down to the masses." At the same time, they are also charged with collecting the "will, opinion and interests of the masses and carry[ing] them back to the policy-making of the party/state."[5]

The number of organizations more likely to be characterized as "nongovernmental," those officially registered with the Chinese Ministry of Civil Affairs, is significantly smaller. The total has fluctuated substantially with changing regulations, but by the end of 2003, according to Wang, some 142,000 organizations nationwide were officially registered with the Ministry of Civil Affairs.[6]

What are we to make of this burgeoning of Chinese associations? Is the growing number of NGOs testimony to an associational revolution heralding an important new development for early twenty-first-century China? Some hope that China's new associations might come to play a positive role, first in the development of civil society in China, and then in a long-term process of democratization. Civil society, as Omar Encarnacion describes it, is generally believed to furnish a national stock of "social capital" that serves "to protect society from the state's inherent authoritarian tendencies, grease societal collaboration on behalf of democracy and improve the performance of political institutions."[7] A diverse group of academics and policy-makers from many parts of the world, he points out, have come to see the emergence of a vibrant and robust civil society as the lynchpin of democratic development.[8] China specialists have been no exception.

Civil society became a topic of interest to China specialists following both the denouement of China's widespread popular protests in the spring of 1989 and the collapse of communism in Eastern Europe and the Soviet Union not long thereafter. Some of the early studies were long on Hegel, Habermas, and Toqueville and short on the realities of China. Some explored the possibility that economic reform was providing a new social space between the state and economic agents.[9] Some saw the emergence of a genuine civil society in the nonviolent protests in the spring of 1989.[10] Dorothy Solinger focused on China's floating population to explore fundamental questions about the nature of civil society—as either autonomous and separate from the state or inextricably joined to it.[11] Many were generally pessimistic about the development of a civil society in China.

The notion of civil society, as nearly everyone who has attempted to employ the concept with respect to China has noted, is vexingly difficult both to define and to operationalize. Not only is the concept Western in origin, but it is viewed differently even by Western philosophers. Richard Madsen notes the distinction between Anglo-American philosophers who generally distrust the power of the state and hence insist that civil society be independent of it, and Continental European thinkers who have a much more positive view of the state. European philosophers, Montesquieu and Hegel included, believe that "the state itself must organize and empower the associations of civil society and give them the moral education, the sense of community, and the security necessary for responsible participation in public affairs."[12] Viewed from the continental perspective, the five million quasigovernmental associations enumerated by Wang Shaoguang might be evidence of civil society development in China. Seen from the Anglo-American side, they probably would not.

My own interest in associational China has three dimensions.

First, China's growing number of associations—NGOs and government-organized nongovernmental organizations (GONGOs) especially—are worthy of study in their own right. Many are addressing pressing problems at the country's grassroots, focusing on ordinary Chinese who have not been greatly advantaged by the reforms. These problems include education for poor rural children, poverty alleviation, and environmental degradation. We need to understand the missions of these organizations and determine how and how well they work. Even GONGOs, which may be making little or no contributions to the development of civil society, are still making contributions to solving or ameliorating some of the country's vexing social problems.

Second, many leaders of these new associations are what David Bornstein calls "social entrepreneurs"—"people with new ideas to address major problems who are relentless in the pursuit of their visions, people who simply will not take 'no' for an answer, who will not give up until they have spread their ideas as far as they possibly can."[13] The influence of social entrepreneurs on society can be transformative, he asserts.

Moreover, as I will argue in the following pages, some of these social entrepreneurs are offering the Chinese people alternative models of leadership. As activists committed to bringing about positive social change, they stand in sharp and positive contrast to the stereotype of the local-level party official in many poor rural areas, who is commonly regarded as committed only to the perpetuation of his own power, privilege, and economic advantage. Some of the new social entrepreneurs are what some Slovakian sociologists have referred to as "positive deviants."[14]

Third, I am interested in what the nature and existence of these organizations tell us about the development of civil society in China and its potentially democratizing effects. While some do see the new organizations as evidence of a civil society beginning to take root, and some refer to them simply as civil society organizations (CSOs),[15] I am hesitant to assume that the mere existence of "associational activity" in China is evidence of civil society. I generally accept Madsen's definition of civil society as "self-governed associations through which citizens can participate in an organized way in public affairs."[16] Many see the new organizations as evidence of a civil society beginning to take root, and some refer to them simply as civil society organizations (CSOs).[17] But the vast majority of Chinese associations are not self-governed, and citizen participation is surely constrained. Whether such associations are contributing or may contribute to the development of civil society is thus an empirical question.

Omar Encarnacion, drawing largely on Robert Putnam, sets forth the logic of the relationship between civil society associations and the development of a democratic culture (though he later challenges the proposition):

> Fundamental to the development of social capital is a culture of trust, which in turn is said to emanate from the face-to-face interactions afforded to ordinary citizens by civil society associations. Every variety of civil society organization is important to the development of social capital—from trade unions and choral societies to bird-watching clubs. The fundamental requirements are simply that they are voluntary, operate outside the family, the state and the market place, and exist in order to advance mutual values and objectives. The socialization provided by civil society works in democracy's favor by spilling onto the political sphere, where civil society imparts its democratizing effect. Through participation in civil society associations, citizens learn both practical organizational and deliberative skills and become imbued with such aspects of democratic culture as "tolerance for pluralism and dissent and increasing public spiritedness."[18]

My standard for determining whether the organizations examined here are promoting the development of civil society is inspired by Richard Madsen's work on religious organizations in China[19] and relies roughly on the four criteria Robert Putnam employs to describe what he calls "civic community."

Citizens in a civic community, according to Putnam, are, first, active participants in public affairs. The ideal citizen is "virtuous," pursuing the public good while eschewing individual private ends. Less categorically altruistic, the engaged citizen is at least "alive to the interests of others."[20]

The second criterion is that of relative political equality in which the community is bound together by horizontal relationships of reciprocity and cooperation rather than vertical relations of authority and dependence. Citizens, says Putnam, interact as equals, not as patrons and clients nor as governors and petitioners. Leadership is still necessary in such a community, but leaders must be, and must conceive themselves to be, responsible to their fellow citizens.[21]

Third, citizens in a civic community are bound together by a spirit of solidarity, trust, and tolerance for diverse points of view.[22]

Finally, civic communities are rich with civil associations that serve to instill in their members habits of cooperation, solidarity, and public spiritedness. Not only do community associations contribute to effective democratic governance, but participatory local organizations are also crucial to successful rural development.[23]

Despite the importance often attributed to the emergence of what many refer to as civil society organizations, few China specialists have explored their concrete role in the development of social capital, civic community, or democratic political culture. For many years, Nick Young of *China Development Brief* provided an invaluable service by keeping track of civil society organizations, analyzing their role in Chinese society, and assessing the relationship between nongovernmental organizations and the state. But his reports generally tended to cover a broad range of NGOs rather than providing in-depth studies of a few.[24] Kang Xiaoguang, a social scientist attached to both the Chinese Academy of Sciences and Tsinghua University's Center for China Studies, has produced a valuable double-volume study categorizing, analyzing, and assessing China's nonprofit sector.[25] A growing number of U.S. and international foundations and NGOs, including the Ford Foundation, the International Republican Institute, Save the Children, the Asia Foundation, Action Aid International, Appropriate Technology Asia, The Nature Conservancy, Heifer International, and PLAN International, have cooperative projects with Chinese NGOs. Some China specialists are engaged in training and capacity-building programs to strengthen and enhance these organizations. Richard Baum and his student, Xin Zhang, have even written a piece about the aforementioned Sanchuan Development Association.[26] Richard Madsen has done an excellent, path-breaking study of the Catholic Church in China, exploring whether it is contributing to the making of a civil society.[27] But the number of detailed descriptions, intensive studies of Chinese associations that seek to understand these organizations from the inside out, is limited.

I hope this piece will both begin to fill in the gap and encourage others to undertake in-depth studies of more civil society organizations in China. I have chosen three organizations for this study: the China Youth Development Foundation's Project Hope, the Sanchuan Development Association, and the Snowland Service Group. Two of them, the Sanchuan Development Association and the Snowland Service Group, are genuine nongovernmental organizations—voluntary, self-governed, and existing to pursue shared values. Project Hope, on the other hand, more closely resembles a GONGO—a government-organized nongovernmental organization—though it has had substantial autonomy. I attempt, on the one hand, to provide a detailed description of each organization (its establishment and history, its mission, organization, and the nature of its interaction with its constituents) and, on the other, to assess its leadership, its capacity to fulfill its mission, and whether and how it is contributing to the development of civil society. I look both at the internal structure of the organizations, whether those relationships are horizontal or vertical, and at how each organization interacts with its external constituents, exploring whether constituents are treated as equals or dependent, whether leadership is consensual or directive, and whether the organization promotes solidarity, cooperation, and trust in its larger community.

I selected these three organizations simply because they are the ones I have come to know best. My acquaintance with Project Hope began in 1990 not long after its establishment. Since 1993, I have both participated in its program sponsoring the education of poor rural children and have visited a number of Project Hope schools in several areas of China—Gansu, Hubei, Jiangxi, Qinghai, Shanxi, Xinjiang, and Zhejiang. More recently, several of my students have taught English in Project Hope schools, and my contacts with the Beijing headquarters of Project Hope and its founder, Xu Yongguang, have grown deeper. In 2003, I was a member of an outside committee, funded by the Ford Foundation, investigating allegations of impropriety on the part of Project Hope leadership.[28]

My acquaintance with the Sanchuan Development Association and the Snowland Service Group is more recent, having begun in 2003, but it has been deeper and more intense. I have visited both organizations often, staying each time for several days, both conducting extensive interviews with the organizations' leaders and visiting many of their projects, as well as meeting with project directors and beneficiaries. I have met a number of local officials in the areas where these two organizations work, and, in one case, accompanied one of the directors for a negotiating meeting with a county official. My students have served as interns with these organizations. Most of the information about Sanchuan Development Association and Snowland Service Group presented in the following pages comes from my interviews conducted during these visits.

PROJECT HOPE

Set up in October 1989 under the auspices of the newly established China Youth Development Foundation (CYDF), Project Hope is one of China's earliest, and surely the most successful, "nongovernmental" (or, more appropriately, quasigovernmental) organizations. Both the foundation and its most visible project are the vision of its charismatic and indefatigable founder and longtime general secretary, Xu Yongguang.[29] Xu's determination to establish Project Hope grew out of his previous role as an official with the All-China Youth Federation (ACYF), which describes itself as a federative body of Chinese youth organizations with the Communist Youth League as its core.[30] The Communist Youth League, in turn, describes itself as a mass organization of advanced youth led by the Chinese communist party,[31] and is known as the training ground for membership in the party.

As an official of the Youth Federation, Xu traveled extensively throughout China, meeting with students and youth groups. His most lasting impressions of those visits are the persistence of poverty in many rural areas and the inability of so many poor rural children to afford schooling. Early literature from Project Hope noted that even in the early 1990s, eighty-five million people in the Chinese countryside, with average annual net incomes of less than 268 *rmb*, still did not have sufficient food and clothing. More than a million children each year were forced to drop out of school because they could not afford the 60 *rmb* then required for books.[32]

Xu Yongguang's experience with rural poverty led to his mission. He was determined both that poor rural children be given an opportunity for basic education and that primary school education take place in properly built and equipped schools. The All-China Youth Federation, in search of new purpose, agreed to support Xu's dream and thus sponsored the official establishment of the China Youth Development Foundation in March 1989. In October of the same year, the Youth Development Foundation began Project Hope, which described itself as a "public welfare undertaking . . . designed to raise funds from the people to help school dropouts in the poverty-stricken areas in China so as to enable all children to enjoy their right to education."[33]

CYDF is not entirely autonomous. It is subject to direction from the central committee of its sponsoring organization (*zhuguan danwei*), the All-China Youth Federation. At its founding, the man chosen as the China Youth Development Foundation's first president was a former president of the All-China Youth Federation, and the vice president of the CYDF was the then-president of the ACYF. Xu Yongguang, the moving force of CYDF, served as both its secretary general and its official legal representative. But Xu was still subject to directives from and the oversight of the Youth Federation. In the early years, three of the top four staff in the CYDF were drawn from the ACYF, and staff salaries were also provided by the Federation. Both ranks and salaries within CYDF corresponded to those within the Youth Federation.

The link between the China Youth Development Foundation and the party-state has always been close. From its inception, Project Hope had significant support from the highest levels of Chinese officialdom. In September 1990, less than a year after its establishment, Deng Xiaoping inscribed the characters for Project Hope—*Xiwang Gongcheng*—and became, with a contribution of 10,000 *rmb*, a major donor. Wan Li, as former head of the National People's Congress, served as its honorary president. A host of other ranking leaders, including Jiang Zemin, Li Peng, Li Xiannian, and Wang Zhen, became similarly high-profile supporters and donors, and so, later, did Hu Jintao and Wen Jiabao. Such high-level support was essential to the organization's domestic and international fund-raising efforts. Multinational corporations, determined to maintain political good will and to give back to Chinese society, would be reluctant to contribute to "nongovernmental" entities that did not have obvious government blessing.

Through the All China Youth Federation and the Communist Youth League, the China Youth Development Foundation had an instant nationwide organizational structure. The Communist Youth League has branches extending from the center, to the provinces, to the county, staffed by more than 200,000 full-time cadres.[34] The Youth Development Foundation could rely on Communist Youth League staff at the provincial and county levels to oversee the implementation of its projects.

The organization of CYDF mimicked that of government work units. Its internal structure was hierarchical, and Xu Yongguang was the unchallenged leader and decision maker. Some outsiders who have interacted with staff at Project Hope have also noted that not everyone on the staff seemed to share Xu's sense of mission and purpose. For some, work at Project Hope was a job rather than a calling.

Once established, Project Hope began soliciting contributions from both individuals and companies, domestic and foreign. Families in urban China were encouraged to provide for the education of a rural child. Many contributors were able to arrange to have their donations deducted by their work units.[35] Each sponsoring family was then matched with a child, who in turn provided a snapshot and regular reports on how his or her schoolwork was proceeding. Letters between sponsoring family and rural child often flowed back and forth, and occasionally, some rural children were able to spend parts of their summer vacations at the homes of their urban sponsors.[36]

From the beginning, Project Hope's solicitation materials were sophisticated and persuasively moving. Early brochures show pictures of children in dilapidated schools, in rooms without desks, sometimes practicing calligraphy in the sand. One snapshot shows a barefoot boy in tattered clothes, presumably too poor to attend school, looking from the outside into a classroom crowded with children. The picture of the beautiful "big-eyed girl" that appears on Project Hope's original brochure and continues to grace much of their literature has become a national icon.

Project Hope was an immediate, almost astounding, success. By early 1992, the effort had already provided support to 328,000 school dropouts in more than 648 poor counties, and had built some 68 Project Hope primary schools.[37] A decade later, at the end of 2001, Project Hope had raised more than 2 billion *rmb*, provided funding for 2,470,000 students, built 8,890 Project Hope schools, and trained nearly 16,000 village primary school teachers.[38] A substantial part of the organization's funding came from multinational companies doing business in China. Motorola, Lucent, Microsoft, Proctor and Gamble, and Coca-Cola, for instance, have been major contributors.

Both Project Hope's relationship to the All-China Youth Federation and its internal organization raise interesting questions about its nature. Is it a civil society organization, a nongovernmental organization, a government-organized nongovernmental organization, or a party-organized nongovernmental organization (PONGO)? Would it be better to avoid the issue altogether and refer to it simply as a nonprofit organization (NPO), as some Chinese scholars do?

Representatives of Project Hope might deny that the organization is a GONGO, because neither its leadership nor staff are currently government officials, and because its funding comes overwhelmingly from nongovernmental sources. But one reason for Project Hope's success is its ability to plug in to the organizational structure of the Communist Youth League for the implementation of its projects. The leadership of Xu Yongguang has been vital to the organization and his idea to involve comfortable city folk in the education of the rural poor was both innovative and compelling, but the success of Project Hope has depended on its organizational links.

Difficulties

Project Hope began to face serious difficulties early in 2002 when the Hong Kong–based newspaper *Ming Bao* began publishing a series of articles alleging financial improprieties by the Chinese Youth Development Foundation and its leadership.[39]

The major source of the allegations was a former vice-director of CYDF's finance department, a woman named Liu Yang.[40] She apparently had copies of Project Hope's account books. Among the allegations were:

- That Project Hope used some 100 million *rmb* of its donations to engage in high-risk investments, some of which lost money, in violation of a legal provision that investments by nonprofit organizations should be conducted only by authorized financial institutions.
- That the leadership of Project Hope used foundation money to purchase expensive apartments for its senior staff.
- That the leadership of Project Hope asked for and received loans from its local branches in order to make up for shortfalls.

- That many transactions took place though numerous, hard-to-trace temporary bank accounts.
- That Project Hope violated legal restrictions on the use of foreign currency.
- That Project Hope tried to raise money from the sale of gold coins in violation of a legal provision that NGOs are not permitted to engage in profit-making business.

The mainland print media never published these allegations. Indeed, 300,000 copies of the March 21, 2002, edition of the Guangzhou-based *Nanfang Zhoumo,* which carried a three-page article about the scandal, were seized by officials of the Ministry of Propaganda.[41] Nonetheless, the allegations had begun filtering into the mainland via the Internet immediately after *Ming Bao*'s original accusations, and even the confiscated *Nanfang Zhoumo* article appeared online.

Xu Yongguang's initial response was to deny any irregularities and label the allegations "sheer fabrication."[42] Later, he called the charges "a terrorist attack on the China Youth Development Foundation by vicious criminals."[43]

Hong Kong residents, who were major supporters of Project Hope and had provided some 500 million *rmb* in donations to the organization, were startled to learn of the accusations. Project Hope was the shining star of China's non-profit organizations, widely viewed as incorruptible and beyond reproof. If the best of China's NGOs could be guilty of malfeasance, what about the many others of lesser repute? Several Hong Kong members of China's National People's Congress began calling for an investigation.[44]

Several official investigations did take place. The tough and apparently universally credible National Audit Bureau sent a team of investigators to spend months sifting through CYDF's records. Another investigation was conducted by representatives of a party disciplinary committee overseeing the All-China Youth Federation. None of the investigative reports have been made public. Two conclusions are relatively certain, however. First, the allegations originally made in the series of *Ming Bao* articles are substantially true, although given the weak and fluctuating regulations governing such organizations the improprieties were not necessarily illegal. Second, the problems were a result of mismanagement and badly flawed accounting, rather than personal corruption or the pursuit of private gain on the part of CYDF leadership.[45] No one within Project Hope has been accused of having embezzled funds or of having benefited personally from financial improprieties.[46]

In the meantime, Xu Yongguang has stepped down as secretary general to become vice-chairman of the governing council (headed by Bayin Chaolu). Gu Xiaojin, who has been with Project Hope since its inception, has become secretary general. While Gu may lack Xu's charisma, she is devoted to the organization—one of the important exceptions to the perception that many staff within Project Hope see their tasks as a job rather than a calling. Under Gu's leadership, Project Hope is likely to move into a phase of greater institutionalization. The organization will survive its founder.

Project Hope's image has been tarnished as a result of this scandal, but the leadership is also rebuilding its damaged credibility, both with the public and with its major donors. CYDF has already begun to institute a series of reforms designed to prevent a repetition of previous mismanagement and accounting errors. It is making itself more transparent.[47] Donations, according to representatives of the organization, have not declined since the damaging accusations.

SOCIAL ENTREPRENEURSHIP AND CIVIL SOCIETY: THE CASE OF PROJECT HOPE

Xu Yongguang, the founder and charismatic leader of Project Hope, is surely a social entrepreneur—a man with a mission who will not take no for an answer, a person devoted to his cause. His mission of promoting the education of poor rural children, particularly at a time when so much of China seems seized with greed, sets him apart. Xu has been a leader "alive to the interests of others," an inspiration to many, an example of integrity and selflessness in the sea of greed and materialism that has infected so much of Chinese society—a positive exception in an otherwise frequently crassly materialistic society.

That the success of Project Hope has depended so heavily on its reliance on the network and structure of the Communist Youth League, and on the public support of high-ranking officials, is a tribute to the organizational effectiveness of one of China's leading "mass organizations." But the very reason that the China Youth Development Foundation has been so successful is also a reason for its limited contribution to the development of civic community. Neither its internal organization nor its relationship to its constituents is horizontal, based on principles of equality. Project Hope is not really an "association" in the sense of a self-governing organization with active, involved members. Within CYDF, Xu was the undisputed leader. Relations with the staff were hierarchical. Similarly, Project Hope's mission was implemented through the nationwide hierarchical organization of the Communist Youth League. While construction of new schools often requires a significant contribution from local governments, the relationship between CYDF and the school is still one of patron and client. While the long-term effect of education provided by Project Hope schools may prove empowering to the students as individuals, they were nonetheless relatively passive recipients of Project Hope's largesse. Nor, it seems, has Project Hope gone beyond mere provision of funds to include the promotion of the types of local-level participatory membership associations recognized by Putnam as essential to civic community.

The case of Project Hope thus suggests caution in assuming that the growth of associations, NGOs, and GONGOs is ipso facto evidence of civil society. Before drawing that conclusion, we need first to know and understand how these organizations are governed and their missions carried out.

But the limitations of Project Hope's contributions to the development of civic community ought not to detract from its astounding success. The lives of some 2.5 million students who have received an education because of Project Hope have surely changed. The consequence of education, after all, is transformative.

And in one extremely important way, Xu Yongguang, his successor Gu Xiaojin, and the Project Hope "project" have taken a first step in the development of civic community. By bringing to a vast, urban Chinese public the plight of children so poor they cannot afford to attend school, and inviting that public to take responsibility for providing those children an education, Project Hope has promoted a measure of participation in public affairs. A huge number of urban Chinese have become alive to the interests of their country's disadvantaged and are willing to contribute to better their future.

SNOWLAND SERVICE GROUP

The Snowland Service Group (SSG) describes itself, and accurately so, as a nongovernmental public welfare organization. Its realm of operation is southwest Qinghai's Yushu prefecture, an area larger than Nepal and overwhelmingly (96–98 percent) Tibetan. Indeed, Yushu prefecture is the most Tibetan place in China.[48] Of its population of 270,000, 65 percent are nomads. With an average per capita income of only 430 *rmb* ($52 U.S. dollars) a year in 2003, Yushu prefecture is also one of the poorest places in the country.

Like Project Hope, the Snowland Service Group is the brainchild of an exceptionally dynamic, energetic, and charismatic social entrepreneur, a Tibetan named Rinchen Dawa. Like Xu Yongguang, Rinchen Dawa believes in the importance of education and has taken the universalization of primary school education as one of his organization's primary goals, the first and most fundamental step in his larger mission of eradicating poverty. Rinchen Dawa himself almost missed the opportunity to go to school. He was already fourteen years old in 1981 when a primary school was finally built in his village and he was able to start his studies. Had the school been built a year later, government regulations would have prohibited him from attending, and he would never have become the person he is. He became the oldest student in the school's first class, studying for only two years before school administrators decided he was too old and sent him on to middle school. After four years in middle school, and another three at the prefectural-level normal school, Rinchen Dawa was declared a qualified teacher.

Rinchen Dawa had been teaching for only a few months when, in early 1991, he was called to work with a township-level government in a remote part of Yushu's Zaduo county. By 1998, he had been promoted to deputy chief of the county. It was that winter that Zaduo was struck with a major snow disaster that left hundreds of nomadic families devastated and thousands of their yaks dead. International organizations began offering disaster relief to help the nomads recover and rebuild their herds. Because Yushu had no locally organized NGOs, the foreign organizations had to work directly with the local governments. Rinchen Dawa was put in charge of Zaduo county's disaster relief. Within a short time, his office had received some 2 million *rmb* of international funding.

His contact with foreign NGOs introduced him to an alternative model of organization and behavior. So impressed was Rinchen Dawa with the devotion and hard work of the staff of the international organizations with whom he worked that he decided to leave government office and establish his own nongovernmental organization. He began talking to his friends—fellow teachers, monks, local businessmen, community leaders—about establishing an NGO modeled after some of the international organizations with which they had been in contact. They tried to register but were refused. NGOs were too sensitive, the officials said.

Still, the new group began drawing up plans. A primary school would be their first undertaking. They knew a village that had been petitioning local officials for more than a decade, requesting a school. The officials had always been affable. They agreed that the school should be built. But it never was. Rinchen Dawa's new NGO decided to build it.

They requested international funding. Their proposal was successful, and the new school was built. They returned to the local civil affairs office to repeat their request for official registration. What, exactly, is so sensitive about a new primary school, they wanted to know. What laws or regulations or policies would their NGO be breaking? The officials were convinced. The okay was given. Snowland Service Group was officially registered with the prefectural-level office of civil affairs in October 2001, with the department of education as its sponsoring organization.

The structure and organization of the Snowland Service Group are different from that of the China Youth Development Foundation's Project Hope. More than either of the other two organizations examined here, the Snowland Service Group is mindfully involved in building a civic community. Both its internal organization and its relationship with the community it serves are based on principles of equality, participation, and service for the public good. Snowland Service Group is a voluntary association with some 200 dues-paying members—the same teachers, monks, lamas, businessmen, and community leaders who initially came together to found it. From the outset, the association has attempted to organize itself democratically. The president, vice president, and the board of directors are elected through secret ballot by the organization as a whole, and major decisions are also discussed and decided upon as a group. Rinchen Dawa, thus, is the organization's elected leader. Members point out that the organization has to function democratically. Most of their work is voluntary and unpaid. If the organization had a bossy, undemocratic leader, no one would be willing to serve.

Nor do the paid staff function like an ordinary work unit. The dozen or so regular staff hold frequent meetings, where monthly priorities are determined, schedules are set, and work assignments are made. While Rinchen Dawa is unquestionably the leader of the organization, and everyone knows who is boss, the staff generally shares his vision and determination. If their NGO work is not yet a calling, neither is it seen as merely a job. The staff work cooperatively as a group, and there is a sense of egalitarianism among them. The staff relationships are not based on command and obedience. Moreover, the account books are transparent and audited regularly by both their international donors and the prefecture-level auditing offices.

SSG's ties with the communities it serves are similarly horizontal, based on equality, cooperation, and mutual respect. Most projects are implemented with the active participation of project beneficiaries. Projects are generally initiated through requests from villagers or village leaders. Following such a request, SSG sends a team to investigate the need for and the feasibility of the project. Staff members have all been trained in participatory rural assessment (PRA), a technique that brings villagers together to discuss their assets and strengths, to determine their needs, and to work cooperatively to organize projects designed to address those needs. The process, at its best, can take weeks, and its focus is on sustainable development.[49] In this, SSG seems to have borrowed straight from Putnam, quoting Esman and Uphoff, who say that they "cannot visualize any strategy of rural development combining growth in productivity with broad distribution of benefits in which participatory local organizations are not prominent."[50]

Half of SSG projects have focused on education—either building or repairing village primary schools or providing additions to them (student dormitories, or greenhouses, for instance). Other efforts have focused on health care. SSG has built a clinic of traditional Tibetan medicine, run by a doctor-monk, and has provided training for midwives and village doctors. They have built water delivery systems and implemented several yak loan projects. They run scholarship programs that allow a few needy students to continue studying beyond middle school, and have recently begun an English-language training program. They are setting up a yak cheese factory.

Rinchen Dawa explicitly conceives of himself as a representative of the disadvantaged of Yushu, not just a bridge between the people and the government, but an advocate, pushing and prodding on behalf of the needy. Increasingly, SSG sees its role as a teacher as well. The government, Rinchen Dawa explains, talks mostly about the obligations of the people to the government. He wants to make sure the people also know their rights.

Authorization from the local government is essential to virtually all of its projects, and Rinchen Dawa's experience as a government official is one reason for his success. As a former government official, he retains the respect of current government officials, many of whom are his friends and former colleagues. The respect he received as a government official has carried over into his nongovernmental role, together with a measure of authority. He is adept at using official government policy to justify his case before the government. Whereas some might see Jiang Zemin's "three represents" as an attempt to bring entrepreneurs and intellectuals into the party fold, Rinchen Dawa argues that the "three represents" means that poor villagers are equal to the entrepreneurs and the intellectuals, which is why they must understand their rights. While some might see the government's policy of developing the West (*xibu kaifang*) as promoting the development of infrastructure and foreign investment, Rinchen Dawa sees the policy as a means of overcoming poverty in Yushu and reducing inequalities between the Tibetans and Chinese. He promotes Hu Jintao's vision of a harmonious, peaceful society. Through his interactions with international NGOs, Rinchen Dawa has learned to regard local officials as stakeholders in SSG projects, and he has been successful in fostering official enthusiasm and cooperation for SSG's work. Many local officials, most of whom are Tibetan, are generally sympathetic to the views of Rinchen Dawa and his organization. SSG, in turn, sees the government as a resource, and knows that government support is essential to its success.

Snowland Service Group takes pride in undertaking projects more cheaply and efficiently than the government. Primary schools that ordinarily cost 400,000 *rmb* for the government to build, relying on outside materials and labor, cost only 200,000 *rmb* when undertaken by SSG. SSG endeavors to use local materials and build in the Tibetan style, relying whenever possible on local Tibetan construction workers. The result (in contrast to the ubiquitous white-tiled buildings that distinguish schools nearly everywhere in China) is schools constructed in natural stone with traditional A-style Tibetan windows painted in bright primary colors. Now, many other new buildings in Yushu are returning to the Tibetan style.

Members of SSG also cite the economic advantages of involving local communities in developmental decisions. They describe, for instance, the case of a government decision to provide a village with a new irrigation system. No one ever asked the villagers whether they wanted or needed an irrigation system, they say. Outsiders built the project without consultation with the villagers or instructions on how to use and maintain it. Not long after its completion, the irrigation ditch began to clog. When it rained, the ditch overflowed, flooding the fields and ruining the crops. Sometimes the water ran off into the street. In winter, the water would freeze, causing a series of accidents on the road that ran next to the village.

But SSG works only on projects the villagers themselves have requested. And the villagers build the projects themselves, learning in the process how they work and what to do when things go wrong. They know how to adjust and repair the water delivery systems they have constructed, for instance—and can turn to SSG when confronting problems they cannot solve.

SOCIAL ENTREPRENEURSHIP AND CIVIL SOCIETY: THE CASE OF SNOWLAND SERVICE GROUP

Of the three organizations presented here, Rinchen Dawa's Snowland Service Group is the one most clearly contributing to the development of civil community as Putnam has described it. Not only is the internal organization structured horizontally, providing the staff with experience in deliberative decision-making and respect for others' opinions, but the organization also consciously seeks to train its staff in participatory techniques—both for internal decision-making and for its community-based projects. Participatory rural assessment is, as its name implies, consciously participatory and democratic. One facet of the process even involves asking participants to provide alternative explanations for various problems faced in their daily lives—to recognize other opinions and to accord them respect.[51]

What explains Snowland Service Group's embrace of a deliberative, participatory mode of decision-making and social interaction?

Rinchen Dawa's leadership has surely been important in shaping the nature of the Snowland Service Group and in its success both within local communities and in garnering the cooperation of local governments. Not only is he an exceptional leader in Yushu, but his leadership traits would be obvious anywhere in the world. To paraphrase Putnam once more, Dawa is and conceives himself to be responsible to his fellow citizens. He is respected as a leader in Yushu but is treated by others, and in return treats them, as an equal. His staff is deferential to him—some might think too much so—but one senses little of the superior-subordinate or patron-client relationship in his personal interactions with his staff, government officials, or the local communities with which he interacts. In this, he is strikingly different from leaders elsewhere in China. Thus, Rinchen Dawa is providing an alternative model of leadership to his local community—proof that it is possible to be a local leader without being corrupt and that some leaders really do care about the people they are said to serve. He and the Snowland Service Group are yet another island of positive deviance.

Some say that Rinchen Dawa's alternative style of leadership may even be having an effect on village elections and who gets elected. A close associate of Snowland Service Group explains:

> When guys like him use a different model of leadership, people think about it. They know there are different ways to have people's needs met. We can do a lot to help ourselves.
>
> I really do believe that village elections are empowering. There was a case recently of a township telling a village that they had to elect a certain person as their village leader. The villagers didn't do it. So the township leaders came back. But the villagers encircled them. They refused to change their vote.
>
> The local NGO is tied into the local community; it understands local problems. And it changes the system. It gives people new expectations. Finally, the county governments will get this. The system changes over time.

But several other factors are also important to the character of the Snowland Service Group.

Surely, one is the nature of its funding and its interaction with international NGOs. The organization's support comes almost exclusively from international organizations, several of which both promote such methodologies as participatory rural assessment and the even more participatory "open spaces forum," and provide ongoing training in how to use these techniques. Such participatory trainings promote the notion of full, active, and equal participation by all stakeholders in grassroots development endeavors and recognize that every person has a reason for his or her opinions and that all opinions are to be respected. These are almost revolutionary concepts in China's top-down political system, and their introduction and use moves the participants further along a path of a more participatory political culture and, hence, toward the development of civil society. SSG staff are thus frequently reminded of the value and effectiveness of participatory involvement at all stages of the developmental process.

Second, the fact that SSG members and the communities the organization services are both Tibetan and Buddhist surely influences the nature of the organization. Rinchen Dawa himself is such a devout Buddhist that he claims his ideal life would be one of withdrawal from the world to a life of meditation. Other members of the organization (some of whom are lamas and monks) are also devoted Buddhists. Compassion and tolerance are fundamental tenets of Tibetan Buddhism, and people associated with Snowland Service Group note the importance of compassion in the work they do. The Buddhist tradition is also one of voluntary service, particularly to monasteries. SSG members talk about the many years of voluntary service they and their family members have given to their local monasteries. The idea of working without pay to help other people is not, therefore, new.

Finally, a shared Tibetan ethnicity and identity is also important. While the divisions within the Tibetan community are deep, and sometimes even violent, the sense of shared identity as Tibetans makes cooperation between SSG and leaders at the village and township levels where they work more cooperative than confrontational. Even at the county level, most officials are Tibetan and want to be seen as working on behalf of their own, and SSG deliberately seeks the cooperation and help of potentially sympathetic officials. Whether and how SSG would function with a stronger Chinese presence is a question. The Chinese wounds run deep, and the sense of being Tibetans also includes a perception of them, the Chinese. But in the absence of a strong Chinese presence, the combination of Buddhist values and Tibetan ethnicity allows for the relatively easy nurturing of civic communities in Yushu. The solidarity and trust necessary for civil society are already there.

If the influence of the Snowland Service Group is deep, however, its reach is extremely limited, confined as its activities are to a single, sparsely populated prefecture. Thus the anomaly: Project Hope, the organization with the least impact on the development of civil society, also has the broadest scope—and the greatest quantitative impact in terms of children educated and schools built. Snowland Service Group, the organization doing the most to promote the development of civil society, is the most limited in scope—and the most isolated from the rest of China.

SANCHUAN DEVELOPMENT ASSOCIATION

Sanchuan Development Association (SDA) is also based in Qinghai province—in Guanting township, Minhe Hui and Tu autonomous county, along the banks of the Yellow River bordering Gansu. The majority of Minhe's population are members of either the Hui or Monguor (Tu, meaning "dirt" in Chinese[52]) national minorities, and the county is officially autonomous. The current county chief is a Hui. Like many such national minority areas, the county is officially designated as poor.

SDA's founder, Zhu Yongzhong, introduced in the opening pages of this chapter, is Monguor, from a mountain village that retains the dubious honor of being the poorest in Guanting. The average per capita income was around $70 U.S. dollars a year in 2003, and Zhu Yongzhong is its proudest product.

The village had no school when Zhu was a child. He attended primary school at a neighboring village at the foot of the mountain some two kilometers away, walking up and down the zigzag path each day. His junior middle school was located in Guangting township, some twelve kilometers and a three-hour walk away. Yongzhong lived at school during the week and walked home every weekend to visit his family and stock up on his mother's homemade bread—the staple of his diet. Of the forty-eight students in his junior middle-school class, he was the only one to pass the examination to enter the Minhe county normal school.

Three years of normal school, two-and-a-half of which were spent studying English, qualified him to become an English teacher at senior middle school—one of only four qualified English teachers in the county. "By that time," Zhu says, I was seventeen years old and "what I knew and understood was only some words, expressions, a few sentences. But I could not speak English, couldn't make conversation." It was only later, when he went for further study in Xining, that he became fluent in the language.

Zhu Yongzhong cites two inspirations for the establishment of the Sanchuan Development Association. In Xining, his English teacher, the American Dr. Kevin Stuart, who has lived in Qinghai since 1987, became a major source of inspiration. Indeed, Kevin Stuart has been the inspiration for many of the internationally funded education and poverty alleviation projects throughout Qinghai and the Tibetan plateau. Since 1997, he has been the leading light in a program that brings together some sixty young Tibetans each year to study English in the Nationalities Department of Qinghai Education College in Xining. Visiting his students' families, Teacher Kevin, as he is affectionately known, often comes face-to-face with poverty. In 1998, when one of his students wondered whether international funding might be available to renovate a village school, Stuart learned that the British embassy had a small grants program for such projects. His first application to refurbish the school was funded, and over the years he and his students have cooperated on numerous endeavors. Stuart is teaching not only English, but community activism and public spiritedness as well.[53]

Zhu Yongzhong's mother was the other inspiration for his work. His childhood memories are filled with images of his mother fetching water from the well at the foot of the mountain and carrying the heavy buckets back up. His mother and younger sisters often made the trip several times a day. Water was essential not only for the human members of the family, but for the family pig, donkey, and sheep as well. And during growing season, the twenty-five *mu* of land they farmed also had to be watered. During good days, Zhu's mother might spend three or four hours walking to the well and back. On bad days, during the dry season, she could spend five or more hours, setting out in the dark of the very early morning, often having to go from well to well.

Not surprisingly, Zhu's first project was a water delivery system for his own village—a series of eight concrete boxes that collected water during the rainy season and were easily accessible to the village woman. With the water collection boxes in place, the women were freed to participate in more productive activities—and more of the young girls could go to school.

Thus, the logical choice for a second project was a school. Funds donated by the Canada Fund in Beijing were used for the renovation and reconstruction of the primary school that had been built in Zhu's village after he left home. With the improved classrooms and new teaching equipment, enrollment in the village school rose from sixteen to sixty in 1998, and to eighty in 1999. The number of students had outgrown the available space, and the Canada Fund agreed to provide funding for a new and larger classroom building and new teachers' quarters. In return, the county education bureau agreed to send and pay the salaries of properly trained teachers. The Canadian ambassador came to the opening ceremony for the new school. By 2004, Zhu's family village had become locally famous for its commitment to education. Children from surrounding villages were enrolling, and the number of students had risen to 115. The entire graduating class of 2004 was admitted to junior middle school in Guanting township.

Mr. Zhu's early projects were undertaken without an organization. He, his family, Kevin Stuart, and friends worked together on an ad hoc basis. The Sanchuan Development Association was informally established in 1999, but the organization was not officially registered. Still, the number of projects kept growing. With funding from a variety of international organizations and embassies in Beijing, the Sanchuan Development Association was building more water delivery systems, latrines, pigsties, and green houses, introducing solar cookers into villages where fuel was in short supply, and providing medical equipment to township clinics. Their sources of funding were diversifying.

Finally, in 2002, an international funder set a condition to its grant. Its donation had to be given to an NGO rather than to an individual, and the bank account had to be in the organization's name. Chinese requirements, in turn, specified that organizational bank accounts could only be established with official approval of the organization. Thus, in 2002, the Sanchuan Development Association was officially registered with the Minhe county bureau of civil affairs, and the county bureau of education agreed to serve as its sponsoring organization. Even now, Zhu Yongzhong is only seconded to the Sanchuan Development Association from the bureau of education, which continues to pay his salary.

Sanchuan Development Association's literature describes it as a nongovernmental organization "committed to empowering eastern Qinghai's most impoverished populations through projects . . . aimed at improving local education, health care, the economy and society."[54] Like Snowland Service Group, SDA is a self-governed voluntary membership organization. Some 100 SDA members, committed to improving their local communities, volunteer their time and effort to manage, implement, and evaluate SDA's growing number of projects. In 2004, only one member of the SDA staff was a paid employee. All the others were either unpaid volunteers or seconded by their work units. By the summer of 2004, SDA had implemented more than 100 projects, totaling close to US $850,000.

As with SSG, SDA projects are developed from ideas brought to the organization by a village chief, a local teacher, or the villagers themselves. While neither Mr. Zhu nor the staff are specifically trained in participatory rural assessment, implementation of most projects is a community effort, usually with international donors providing funds for materials and the local community providing labor. Every project begins with a series of forums, during which project managers "are elected, needs assessed, opinions heard, ideas debated, and group decisions made."[55] Villagers often agree that the fact of meeting, deliberating, and working together is fostering a new sense of cooperation, community, and trust.[56]

SDA's relationship with the local government is complex. Government cooperation is essential to many of its projects, especially those related to education. Because the Minhe county bureau of education is responsible for hiring primary school teachers and paying their salaries, each new school requires its approval and cooperation.

But the concept of a nongovernmental organization is new to Minhe officials, and the two sides are still feeling their way. Because Zhu Yongzhong is still only seconded to the Sanchuan Development Association by the county department of education, the department retains considerable control over his work. The relationship is, he is told, still one between leader and staff, or like father and son. Teachers are still meant to obey.

But the Sanchuan Development Association is having unintended effects beyond its goals of community-based economic and social development. Above all, like the Snowland Service Group, it is providing an alternative model of what local-level leadership can be. Village elections have recently been introduced into the area, as they have now in nearly all parts of China. Leadership changes in the initial phase of elections were minimal. The same guys who had led the villages for decades—caretaker types subordinate to the directives of township officials—were popularly elected. But the image of Zhu Yongzhong—activist, dynamic, working on behalf of the disadvantaged, holding government officials to account, pushing, prodding, trying to move communities forward—has inspired a younger generation of village leaders. In the most recent round of elections, several of these young men decided to compete, running against the old village chiefs. Many of the old guys were voted out. A new, younger, more activist group of leaders, who promise to represent the people and bring change to the village, have now assumed their positions.

SOCIAL ENTREPRENEURSHIP AND CIVIL SOCIETY: THE CASE OF THE SANCHUAN DEVELOPMENT ASSOCIATION

Zhu Yongzhong, like Xu Yongguang and Rinchen Dawa, is both a social entrepreneur with a mission to fulfill and a leader alive to the interests of others, tireless in working on the public's behalf. His leadership, both within his organization and in Minhe county, is exceptional, as the story that began this piece so tellingly illustrates. Both Zhu and his organization are promoting the development of civic community in Guanting. First, through the demonstration effect of Zhu's leadership, a new generation of activist village leaders responsible to their fellow citizens is being spawned. And second, at least some villages that have worked together on SDA-sponsored projects seem to be coming together as communities, conscious of the need to work together to pursue common, primarily economic and developmental, goals.

Still, the Sanchuan Development Association's promotion of civic community, in the sense the concept has been used here, has been limited. Conceptions of equality that would allow the development of horizontal rather than hierarchical relationships are weak in Minhe, particularly in the interactions between the government and local communities. Vis-à-vis the government,

Zhu Yongzhong, in contrast to former government official Rinchen Dawa, is the subordinate, the son, sometimes the petitioner rather than an equal. And vis-à-vis the villagers, Zhu Yongzhong is sometimes seen as the mayor and patron.

Jessica Priselac, who worked with Zhong Yongzhong in Minhe during the summer of 2004, describes a culture of dependence in the villages she visited,[57] and research by Meaghan Duthie supports that view. Duthie's study, based on numerous interviews with farmers in nine villages in Guanting township, reveals a nearly unanimous perception that government officials do not care about their plight and a continuing belief that the government is nonetheless responsible for solving their problems. As one villager said, "The government should take care of the people. It should solve problems for us, but they don't."[58] Said another, "We want [the government] to do something for us. There is nothing good about the government. All they did is for the rich. If you are poor, you don't have a chance to be helped by government."[59]

The concept of a nongovernmental organization with which they might work on their own behalf, the notion of activism in pursuit of a community goal, is still new to most villagers and sometimes difficult for them to grasp. Many villagers knew of Zhu Yongzhong and his association with foreigners before they knew of the Sanchuan Development Association. While Meaghan Duthie's investigation of the role of SDA in village empowerment suggests that working together on SDA projects did bring villages together as communities, promoting more and better cooperation in other areas as well, the perceived role of SDA in promoting that cooperation was sometimes ambiguous. Since few villagers really understood what an NGO was, not everyone could attribute the new sense of community to SDA's work. Indeed, it is quite possible that the reason Mr. Zhu is treated so often like a mayor is because people think he actually is some form of mayor. They may have no other way of conceiving his role. Villagers may be electing more activist chiefs because they want their village chief to be more like "mayor" Zhu. But Mr. Zhu and Sanchuan Development Association were universally perceived by the villagers as good. "In our opinion, SDA is a group that helps the poor people," said one representative villager.[60]

The limitations of the Sanchuan Development Association are hardly insurmountable. Rinchen Dawa's experience as a governmental official has provided him organizational experience and negotiating skills that Zhu's experience as an English teacher did not. But as Zhu becomes more experienced and the role of the Sanchuan Development Association is better understood, his success negotiating with the government is likely to improve. Further training would surely be useful to him and his staff. While SDA's funding comes almost entirely from international sources, by 2004, none of those funders had taken the same long-term interest in mentoring and oversight that was already being provided to the Snowland Service Group. International funders also need to be "alive" to the need of fledgling NGOs for mentoring and training. Increasingly, they are.

IN SEARCH OF POSITIVE DEVIANCE: SOCIAL ENTREPRENEURSHIP, LOCAL-LEVEL LEADERSHIP, AND CIVIL SOCIETY

The three organizations described in this study—Project Hope, Snowland Service Group, and Sanchuan Development Association—have three qualities in common. First, none of the organizations would have come into being without the vision of its founder. Second, the founder of each is what David Bornstein would call a "social entrepreneur." Third, each of these organizations is having a transformative effect on the communities within its sphere of influence.

Xu Yongguang, Rinchen Dawa, and Zhu Yongzhong are social entrepreneurs in every sense of Bornstein's definition presented in the introduction—"people with new ideas to address major problems who are relentless in the pursuit of their visions, people who simply will not take 'no' for an answer, who will not give up until they have spread their ideas as far as they possibly can." Each man is singularly devoted to his mission. Each has served as a transformative force within his specific sphere of influence. All have made significant personal sacrifices to pursue their goals.

Xu Yongguang, whose effect has been national in scope, has provided educational opportunities to well over two million children who would not otherwise have been able to go to school—and his work has no doubt salved the conscience of both China's new urban middle class and a host of corporations who may be troubled by the growing inequities between urban and rural, coastal and inland China that is one of the more unfortunate outcomes of China's rapid economic growth.

The transformative effects of the work of Rinchen Dawa and Zhu Yongzhong are narrower in scope but perhaps deeper in influence. The introduction of primary schools to villages where children previously had no chance for an education, of water delivery systems to women who once spent hours each day fetching water, and of basic health care to communities where poverty and ill health go hand-in-hand has surely profoundly changed the lives of the recipients.

The new social entrepreneurship represented by these three men is not a trivial phenomenon. That the Chinese government allows such social entrepreneurs to operate and thrive is a significant change, both from the Mao era and from the period of the early1980s when reform was still new. Everyone who has worked at China's grassroots in recent years has surely encountered examples of the country's new social entrepreneurs. The phenomenon is worthy of further study. In my (decidedly limited) experience, such people are generally relatively young (between thirty and fifty), usually from the countryside, and often from poor villages. Many were able to receive their education only against significant odds. Someone in their village—a teacher or relative—recognized their potential early and helped insure that their schooling continued. Many of these social entrepreneurs feel a need to repay society for the opportunities they were given—and to spread similar opportunities to wider groups of people.

Social entrepreneurship, however, does not necessarily translate into civil society. Of the three organizations examined here, the NGO with the widest scope and the greatest financial success is also the one with the least direct influence on civil society. Project Hope is a charitable organization with a top-down approach that tends to promote continual dependence rather than the empowerment of its beneficiaries. Not only does Project Hope rely on the Communist Youth League for its success (hence rendering it rather powerless to protect society from what Omar Encarnacion, quoted earlier in this piece, called "the state's inherent authoritarian tendencies"), but the hierarchical nature of its internal organization does little to promote a democratic political culture, either internally or externally. Xu Yongguang's response to criticisms of his organization, describing the charges as "a terrorist attack . . . by vicious criminals," is hardly consistent with the tolerance for diversity, transparency (and respect for a free press) that civil society is said to foster.

Nor can it be argued that Project Hope's relationship to its external constituencies, either recipients or donors, does much to foster civil society. Decisions about which students and which schools will be targeted for funds are made by Project Hope leadership in Beijing in coordination with local CYDF staff, rather than through any process of citizen-based deliberation and participation. The recipients of Project Hope's largesse remain dependent rather than participant. The one part of the Project Hope program that might have contributed in some measure to the development of civil society was the opportunity for communication between donor and recipient. Perhaps some new measure of trust and tolerance resulted from interactions between comfortable urban and impoverished rural families. But those opportunities have halted. Apparently, because of its recent commitment to provide all children with nine years of free education, the government is back at the educational helm and citizen involvement is considered unnecessary.

Rinchen Dawa and Zhu Yongzhong are not only social entrepreneurs. They are also providing alternative models of leadership in their communities—proof that it is possible to be a local leader without being corrupt and that some leaders really do care about the people they are said to serve. Their qualities of leadership are the antithesis of those that many people perceive in local party and government officials. Whereas the two NGO leaders are seen to be working on behalf of the disadvantaged, local officials are viewed overwhelmingly as corrupt, indifferent to the needs of ordinary people, and acting only for the benefit of themselves, their families, and their friends. Whereas NGO leaders, Rinchen Dawa in particular, interact with others as equals, local officials demand deference—complaining when villagers do not stand up to greet them, insisting on relationships of father-son, superior-subordinate, command-obedience. Whereas NGO leaders are trusted and admired by local people, and work to promote solidarity within the communities they serve, local-level officials are widely, profoundly, insistently mistrusted. While the NGOs are working to empower local villagers, to bring them into decisions that affect their lives, local officials continue to behave as though only they know what is right for local people—sometimes, perhaps even often, implementing projects that villagers never requested and are never taught to use, as with the failed irrigation project described in the section on Snowland Service Group. Local-level officials do not fare well in a comparison with these social entrepreneurs. Surely, no one could be guilty of accusing them of promoting civil communities. Indeed, one of the most striking observations from research at China's grassroots is how intense and widespread the disdain for local officials seems to be.

But the alternative leadership styles of Rinchen Dawa and Zhu Yongzhong are beginning to have multiplier effects, particularly in the realm of village elections. In Yushu, villagers are beginning to insist on the right to select their own leaders, without interference from the township. In Minhe, young men who have admired Mr. Zhu's activism and commitment to the community are running for office and winning. People's expectations of their leaders are changing.

All three organizations—Project Hope, Snowland Service Group, and the Sanchuan Development Association—might be considered what Slovaks used to call "islands of positive deviance"[61]—pockets of integrity and good in a sea of corruption, cynicism, and indifference. In uncivil societies, integrity comes to be regarded as deviant, as it is so often in China today. Cynics have a hard time believing, for instance, that Rinchen Dawa and Zhu Yongzhong are not reaping large financial benefits from the work they do. Who, after all, could be so naïve as to work for the public good? And when news of the allegations against Xu Yongguang began to filter out, many were quick, even relieved, to believe his guilt. Corruption is so rampant, the reasoning went, that no one can escape. Even the best are tainted.

Indeed, one of the greatest difficulties facing China's fledgling NGOs, and hence the development of civil society, is the nearly universal propensity to corruption in Chinese society today. The NGO community in western China is filled with stories of local government abuse of international funds—of officials demanding huge "management fees" in the absence of any responsibility for management, of money diverted from grassroots projects into government coffers, and of deliberate deception about how funds are spent. "All the officials lied," one community activist told me when describing the evaluation of 100 Chinese government-implemented projects that he had undertaken on behalf of a particularly generous embassy in Beijing. Every project had problems, he said. The actual per diem paid to participants in training programs was far less than that recorded in the official accounts. Fewer people participated than stated in the government books, and for less time. The officially recorded cost of food and supplies was much too high.[62]

Others tell tales of attempted subterfuge when, after an initial period of indifference, local officials awaken to the reality that local NGOs are actually able to raise funds. In one such case, township and county-level officials instructed one particularly successful NGO to continue its fund-raising efforts, but demanded that the money raised be given to them to spend. When the NGO refused, the officials issued orders and made threats. The NGO offered to consult with the donors to get their permission. "We'll do it together, then," came the official response. The NGO was ordered to cooperate. When it continued to demur, officials ordered a halt to one of the NGO's projects—construction of a new primary school. When the academic year began with the school still half built, classes had to be held outdoors. Villagers began openly to wonder about why construction had stopped. The government had no convincing answer. Villagers continued to complain. Construction resumed. The school was built.

Many NGO leaders are sympathetic to the circumstances leading local officials to corruption. They talk about how difficult it is for local government officials to do good work, how even good people who want to help their local communities are encouraged to become corrupt, often as a result of unfunded mandates. Local officials and teachers still have to be paid, even when public coffers are empty.

The pressures to succumb, as surely Xu Yongguang, Rinchen Dawa, and Zhu Yongzhong are most painfully aware, are great. They have felt the pressure, too. Perhaps an internal organization based on horizontal relationships, group decision-making, and a commitment to transparency helps some NGOs to resist. The nature of their funding might also help. The strict reporting requirements of many international funders may serve to mediate the pressure to succumb to the demands of local officials. Similarly, monitoring and oversight by international organizations may give NGO leaders an excuse to resist the pull and the means to maintain their own and the organization's integrity.

For the Slovak reformers who served as islands of positive deviants, the route to a civil society was multiplication, the transformation of islands into an archipelago, and the archipelago into a single continent. It was, said sociologist Sonia Szomoldnycova in December 1989, the police batons in Prague that served to pull "all these islands into a single continent of action."[63]

What the Chinese catalyst might be, or whether one will come, remains to be seen. Much of rural China seems to be in crisis. News from the countryside increasingly focuses on growing unrest and outbreaks of violence. The number of peasant associations, some of which are economic organizations and sanctioned by the state, others of which are rights based and sometimes confrontational, is growing. For now, both the multiplication of social entrepreneurs and the proliferation of locally based, locally governed NGOs seems not only necessary to protect the disadvantaged but also the most likely, however slow and painful, path to civil society.

NOTES

1. Presentation to the Johns Hopkins University's School of Advanced International Studies, October 18, 2004.
2. Lester M. Salamon, 1994, "The Rise of the Nonprofit Sector," *Foreign Affairs*, Vol. 73, No. 4, p. 109.
3. Ibid., p. 109.
4. Wang Shaoguang, and He Jianyu, "Associational Revolution in China: Mapping the Landscapes," in An International Conference on Grassroots Democracy and Local Government in China, Panel 4, p. 30.
5. Ibid., pp.15–16.
6. Ibid., p. 11.
7. Omar G. Encarnacion, 2003, *The Myth of Civil Society: Social Capital and Democratic Consolidation in Spain and Brazil*, New York: Palgrave Macmillan, pp. 3–4.
8. Ibid., p. 3.
9. Gordon White, 1993, "Prospects for Civil Society in China: A Case Study of Xiaoshan City," *The Australian Journal of Chinese Affairs*, Vol. 29, No. 1, pp. 63–87.
10. Lawrence R. Sullivan, 1990, "The Emergence of Civil Society in China, Spring 1989," in Tony Saich (ed.), *The Chinese People's Movement: Perspectives on Spring 1989*, Armonk, N.Y.: M.E. Sharpe, pp. 126–144.
11. Dorothy R. Solinger, 1993, "China's Transients and the State: A Form of Civil Society?" *Politics and Society*, Vol. 21, No. 1, pp. 91–122.
12. Richard Madsen, 1998, *China"s Catholics: Tragedy and Hope in an Emerging Civil Society*, Berkeley: University of California Press, p. 126.
13. David Bornstein, 2004, *How To Change the World: Social Entrepreneurs and the Power of New Ideas.* New York: Oxford University Press, p. 1.

14. See, e.g., M. Butora, 1997, "Slovakia's NGOs: A Civic Archipelago of Hope and Action." *NGOs News*, Bratislava, No. 7.

15. See, for instance, Julia Greenwood Bentley, 2003, "The Role of International Support for Civil Society Organizations in China," *Harvard Asia Quarterly*, pp. 11–21.

16. Madsen, op. cit., p. 11.

17. See, for instance, Julia Greenwood Bentley, 2003, "The Role of International Support for Civil Society Organizations in China," *Harvard Asia Quarterly*, pp. 11–21.

18. Encarnacion, op. cit., p. 4.

19. See both Madsen, op. cit., and "Religious organizations and rural self rule in rural China," in this volume.

20. Robert D. Putnam, 1993, *Making Democracy Work: Civic Traditions in Modern Italy*, Princeton, N.J.: Princeton University Press, p. 88.

21. Ibid., p. 88.

22. Ibid., pp. 88–89.

23. Ibid., pp. 89–90.

24. *China Development Brief* can be accessed online at www.chinadevelopment brief.com.

25. Hong Dayong and Kang Xiaoguang, *NGO fupin xingwei yanjiu: Diaocha baogao* (Investigation Report on Research Concerning the Behavior of Poverty Alleviation NGOs) and Kang Xiaoguang, 2001, *NGO fupin xingwei yanjiu* ,Beijing: Zhongguo Jingji Chuban She.

26. Xin Zhang and Richard Baum, 2004, "Civil Society and the Anatomy of a Rural People's NGO," *The China Journal*, No. 52, pp. 97–107.

27. Richard Madsen, *China's Catholics*, op. cit.

28. That report has not been made public. I rely here exclusively on interviews and published materials.

29. See, for instance, Fang Lilin, and Wang Rupeng (ed.), 2001, *Xu Yongguang Shuo Xiwang Gongcheng* (Xu Yongguang Talks about Project Hope). Beijing: Zhongguo Qingnian Chuban She.

30. See www.acyf.org.cn/e_about/intro.htm.

31. See www.cycnet.com/chinayouth/organs/ccyl.htm.

32. Booklet entitled *Project Hope, China Youth Development Foundation*, dated 1992, p. 1–2.

33. Undated (but probably 1991) brochure titled *Project Hope*, p. 1.

34. www.cycnet.com/chinayouth/organs/ccyl.htm.

35. Some have questioned whether such deductions were always entirely voluntary.

36. The opportunity to sponsor children directly ended around 2001, because the government had both promised to wipe out poverty by then and to guarantee universal, free education through the ninth grade. Neither goal was in fact achieved.

37. Booklet entitled *Project Hope, China Youth Development Foundation,* dated 1992, p. 1.

38. Booklet entitled *China Youth Development Foundation*, dated 2002, p. 3.

39. See "Project Hope breaks investment laws and regulations," 2002, *Ming Bao* reports, February 28, 2002; "Accounting Report Shows that China Youth Development Foundation Is Breaking Certain Rules" and "Project Hope Must Be Saved," 2002; *Ming Bao* reports, March 1, 2002; "Wherever there is charity, there must be sunshine," 2002; *Ming Bao* reports, March 21, 2002; "Project Hope Books Should Be Thoroughly Investigated to Rebuild Credibility of Charities," 2002; *Ming Bao* reports, March 22, 2002; "Fund for Chinese children accused of misusing money," 2002; *Straits Times Interactive*, March 1, 2002; "Clara Li, "Project Hope parent under investigation," 2002, *South China Morning Post*, March 1, 2002.

40. Some of Liu Yang's accusations also appeared in a four-part series on the Internet available at www.Chinesenewsnet.com.

41. See "The Mainland Prohibits Playing Up the Irregularities Case Related to the Hope Project; 300,000 Copies of the *Nanfang Zhoumo* Sealed up for Safekeeping", 2002, *Ming Bao*, March 22, 2002; and Elizabeth Rosenthal, 2002, "Under Pressure, Chinese Newspaper Pulls Expose on a Charity," *New York Times*, March 24, 2002.

42. Clara Li, 2002, "Charity accused of funds misuse," *South China Morning Post* online, March 1, 2002.

43. Elizabeth Rosenthal, op. cit. The allegation that the attack was made by vicious criminals is not quite as preposterous as it might appear. A close friend of Liu Yang, who helped her vet the allegations against Project Hope, was a convicted felon. His death sentence had been commuted, and he was released from prison in 2001 after nine years in jail.

44. *Ming Bao*, March 22, 2002, op. cit.

45. The Project Hope case may be an example of what Andrew Wedeman describes as "institutional corruption." See Andrew Wedeman, 1997, "Stealing from the Farmers: Institutional Corruption and the 1992 IOU Crisis," *The China Quarterly*, No. 152, pp. 805–832.

46. The purchase of staff apartments may seem the exception to this, but it was common practice among work units at the time.

47. See "Six Questions to Project Hope," 2003, *Beijing Youth Daily*, January 20, 2003, in which an unnamed representative of Project Hopes outlines some of the previous problems and what was being done to correct them. See also Project Hope website, www.cydf.org/cn.

48. Only Bhutan has a higher percentage of Tibetans.

49. For an examination of how participatory rural assessment is working in China, see Janelle Plummer and John C. Taylor, 2004, *Community Participation in China: Issues and Processes for Capacity Building*, Sterling, Va: Earthscan.

50. Putnam, op. cit., p. 90.

51. In one PRA report I was able to see, the different explanations for certain problems faced by villagers were quite remarkable—both for the different explanations within the village and the difference between those of the villagers and government officials.

52. Surely, this designation is one reason members of this national minority use another appellation, variously spelled Mongghul or Mangghuer. The Monguor language is Mongolic and the people are similar in many ways to the Tibetans, especially with respect to religion.

53. For a fuller description of Kevin Stuart's activities, see Anne F. Thurston, 2005, "Teacher Kevin: 17 Years in Qinghai," *The China Daily*, January 11, 2005.

54. Brochure, 2004, *Sanchuan Development Association*, June 2004.

55. Ibid.

56. An unpublished study by Meaghan Duthie offers a much more complex picture of how and whether SDA is fostering community. See Meaghan Duthie, 2003, "The Impact a Local NGO has had on Empowerment in the Communities with Which It Works: The Sanchuan development Association, Minhe Hui and Monguor Autonomous County, Qinghai Province, China," November 2003, unpublished. Duthie formerly worked with the Canada Fund in Beijing, a major funder of SDA projects.

57. Jessica Priselac, 2005, "Negotiating the State and Society: The Experiences of a Chinese Rural Development NGO," unpublished paper prepared for the Harvard East Asia Graduate Student Conference, March 4–6, 2005, pp. 16–17.

58. Meaghan Duthie, 2003, "The Impact a Local NGO has had on Empowerment in the Communities with Which It Works: The Sanchuan development Association, Minhe Hui and Monguor Autonomous County, Qinghai Province, China," November 2003, unpublished. Duthie formerly worked with the Canada Fund in Beijing, a major funder of SDA projects, p. 101.

59. Ibid., p. 101.

60. Ibid., p. 95.

61. See M. Butora, 1997, "Slovakia's NGOs: A Civic Archipelago of Hope and Action," *NGOs News*, Bratislava, No. 7, p.10.

62. In another case, people told me what happened when an international donor provided funding to replace a herd of yaks that had perished in a snow disaster. When a representative of the donor came to evaluate the fruits of the organization's funding, she was shown a healthy herd of yaks gathered near a schoolyard, but the yaks were merely on loan for the occasion by local families. When the evaluators left, the yaks were returned to their families, and the official intermediary used the yak money to buy himself a car. When another NGO provided 80,000 *rmb* for a two-month training course in veterinary medicine for nomadic Tibetan women, the local government officials spent 4,000 *rmb* for a three-day session for a handful of women and pocketed the 76,000 they had saved.

63. Quoted in Brian James, 1989, "How Peaceful Slovaks joined the Czechs' revolution," *South China Morning Post*, December 1, 1989.

Chapter Five

Socioeconomic Transformation, Grassroots Democracy, and Political Value Change in China: A Comparison with Hong Kong and Taiwan

Yun-han Chu

INTRODUCTION

China has embarked on market-oriented reform for more than twenty-five years. The implications of the resultant, rapid, socioeconomic transformation for the evolution of its political system are of great theoretical and practical importance. The prospect of further political liberalization and eventual democratization in China will not only profoundly affect the livelihood of 1.3 billion Chinese people, but it also holds the key to the future of democracy in Asia. The adaptability and resiliency of China's communist regime has so far made the region's overall environment much more hospitable for non-democratic regimes. Unless China itself embarks on a path of democratization, the prospects for a democratic breakthrough in many Asian countries within China's political and economic orbit remain extremely dim.[1]

China's economic reform has planted many seeds of democratic changes. It has gradually deprived the regime of the ability to effectively control the society. At the same time, with the growing number of private enterprises, fewer and fewer people in China depend on the state for their bread. This newly acquired economic freedom has laid the foundation for political liberalization. Economic reform has also had a significant impact on the ability of the government to control media and information. The widespread use of the Internet, e-mail, and short messages via cellular phones has made it impossible for the government to monopolize information any longer. China observers also witnessed an expanding social space between the citizens and the state. Thousands of autonomous or semi-autonomous civic organizations have mushroomed in the Chinese cities.[2] The extensive privatization of housing since 1999 has spurred the growth of home-owner self-governing organizations throughout urban China.

Most political scientists consider that China is now at the early stage of political liberalization and has not yet reached the prelude of democratization. However, certain meaningful political experiments, albeit limited in scope, have been steadily introduced by the incumbent elite to cope with the acute challenge of local governance. The first is the introduction of semi-competitive elections to select deputies at the lower levels of people's congresses. This experiment carries significance because elected deputies to various levels of people's congress are increasingly allowed to assert certain independent power. In a growing number of instances, deputies to people's congresses have not only nominated their own candidates for leadership positions but have also rejected Democratic Progressive Party (CCP) nominees. The National People's Congress (NPC) itself also has played a more important role in the political life of China.[3]

The most well-known political change in China in recent years is the introduction of semi-competitive elections, first in the rural area, and more recently in the urban area. In 1987, the NPC passed the Draft Organic Law of Village Committees, which stipulates that the chairman, deputy chairman, and members of village committees should be elected by popular vote in China. The actual implementation of the law started in 1988. Although the promotion of village autonomy was set back in the wake of 1989, the Internal Affairs Department won back approval to promote village elections in 1992. As of the end of 1997, more than 90 percent of villages on the mainland have implemented direct elections. In 1998, neighborhood committee (*juweihui*) elections were introduced to Chinese cities. Many practices of the village elections, such as the *Haixuanzhi* (elections without special restrictions on the candidates) which widened the scope of the electorate's voting rights, have since then been transplanted to the urban neighborhood committee elections. Although many China observers see a gap between this system of grassroots elections and a genuine democratic system, they also believe that such elections will eventually provide mainland China with an impetus for democratization.[4]

This article analyzes and explores to what extend the political values of the Chinese citizens have undergone some profound transformation, in particular in the direction of increasing democratic orientations, as a consequence of the far-reaching and rapid economic, social, and institutional changes occurring in China. It tries to accomplish a dynamic understanding of the sources of value changes by employing longitudinal comparative surveys conducted respectively in Mainland China, Taiwan, and Hong Kong at two time points, 1993–1994 and 2001–2002.[5] This unprecedented longitudinal trilateral data set allows us to pursue a systematic understanding of the lingering impact of their common cultural heritage, the socializing effects of their divergent political institutions, and the transformative power of their sequential, rapid, socioeconomic modernization on political culture.

Hong Kong and Taiwan are arguably the two most relevant cases of reference for exploring the trajectory of China's political future. In many ways, the CCP regime today resembles the Kuomintang (KMT) regime of yesterday. It reigns over its society as a pro-growth, market-conforming authoritarian regime and remains fused with the state in a typical Leninist fashion. The Communist leaders today are wrestling with the same kind of challenge that the KMT leadership faced two decades ago: how to retain its hegemonic presence in the society with dwindling capacity for ideological persuasion and social control, how to accommodate the rising popular demand for political representation and participation, how to co-opt the newly emerged social forces that came with a rapidly growing private sector, and how to cope with the political consequences of economic opening-up. In a similar vein, the popular conception and the orientations toward politics and authority that the citizens of the PRC held today are susceptible to a similar set of transformative forces that had prompted a shift in Taiwan's mass political culture some twenty to thirty years ago. They include the accelerating social mobility through industrialization and urbanization, expanding exposure to the potent forces of cross-border diffusion of information and ideas, the arrival of market-oriented mass media, the diffusion and penetration of modern work units and organizations, and the experiment with limited political pluralism and grassroots electoral contestation.

From the viewpoint of research design, the three societies offer a vantage point of entry for a systematic understanding of sources of culture shift as the three exhibit great diversity among themselves in terms of the level of both socioeconomic development and political democratization, while being bound together by a common cultural heritage. The three societies have traveled down different trajectories of regime transition. Taiwan has completed its democratic transition over the last two decades. Hong Kong has experienced some limited democratic experiment starting over the last fifteen years with the introduction of popular election in selecting a portion of the legislature in 1991. However, the momentum of democratization is now largely truncated as the popular demand for the popular election of the chief executive is vehemently denied. The parallel comparison of the three cases could help us decipher the relative importance of socioeconomic structural and institutional factors in driving change in political culture. In addition, our sampling design for mainland China enables us to divide the nationwide survey into two subsamples: one for urban residents (with urban household registration) and another for rural residents. The advantage of doing this lies in being able to more clearly decipher the influence of modernization while holding political system and cultural legacy constant.

The chapter will proceed in four steps. First, we briefly review the ongoing theoretical debate over the mechanism and sources of value changes. Second, we introduce our conceptualization of democratic value orientations and their measurements. Third, we report the empirical findings that emerge out of our statistical analysis of the trilateral survey. Last, we explore the implications of our empirical findings for China's democratic future.

THEORIES OF CULTURE SHIFT

There are currently three main research paradigms in comparative politics explaining cultural change: modernization (or postmodernization) theory, institutionalism, and culturalist theory. We shall examine each in some details.

Modernization and Postmodernization

Modernization theory has been developing for over a century. The central claim of Modernization theory, from Karl Marx and Max Weber to Daniel Bell, is that economic, cultural, and political changes go together in coherent patterns that change in predictable ways.[6] Modernization theory was understood by some as a variant of structural explanations[7] because many Modernization theorists emphasized social mobility and location in modern parts of the social structure as the leading cause of cultural change.[8] While there has been continuing debate over the causal linkages, many empirical findings do support the claim that socioeconomic development generates more modern attitudes and values—greater tolerance and valuing of freedom, higher levels of political efficacy, and greater capacity to participate in politics and civic life.[9] The Postmodernization theory developed by Ronald Inglehart and his colleagues agrees with the Modernization theorists on their central claim but differs from most Modernization theorists on four essential points: change is not linear, economic determinism is oversimplified, the rise of the West is not the only version of Modernization, and democracy is not inherent in the Modernization phase, but democracy does become increasingly likely as societies move beyond the Modernization phase into Postmodernization.[10] Inglehart and his colleagues have accumulated three decades of time-series data to demonstrate an intergenerational shift toward Postmaterialist values, linked with rising levels of economic development.[11] As economic development brings rising levels of tolerance, trust, political activism, and greater emphasis on freedom of speech (the components of what they defined as "self-expression values"), it leads to growing mass demands for liberalization in authoritarian societies and to rising levels of direct, mass participation in societies that are already democratic. Insofar as Postmaterialists give high priority to protecting freedom of speech and to participation in making important government decisions, this trend should bring growing mass demands for democratization and dwindling demand for authoritarian order. The three culturally Chinese societies provide the most challenging, as well as the most fertile, testing ground for the Modernization/Postmodernization perspective, because the rapid socioeconomic transformation that the three societies have experienced over the last twenty-five to forty years was unprecedented in human history. While all three societies have undergone rapid socioeconomic transformation, in terms of the level of socioeconomic modernization they are still miles apart, with Hong Kong leading the pack and China trailing far behind. Besides, during China's economic reform, the country also witnessed the glaring regional disparity between the urban and the rural, as well as between the coastal provinces and the heartland.

In short, according to Modernization theory, a decline in traditional social values and an increase in modern values (including those of civic culture, democratic orientation) will result from economic and social modernization, in particular through increasing social mobility, participation in economic activity, and cognitive mobilization brought about by mass communications. Modernization and its effect on value change can surpass differing cultural systems and the transition experiences of different political systems. It can influence both Confucian cultural areas and non-Confucian areas, and societies experiencing rapid democratic transition and those whose transitions are either slow or have not yet materialized. Other things being equal, modernization has led to a trend in global convergence of value orientations. If Modernization theory is correct, citizens of Hong Kong should register the highest level of support for democratic concepts and values, other things being equal. It should be immediately followed by that of Taiwan's citizens, then by the urban residents in mainland China, with residents in rural China trailing behind.

Institutionalism

A standard theoretical argument based on Institutionalist perspective would posit that people develop certain orientations toward democracy as well as nondemocratic regimes as a *consequence* of the organizing principles of formal and informal institutions: specifically, the incentives, disincentives, and habits created by the rules embedded in differing forms of political institutions.[12] Participation in formal procedures like voting, working for parties or candidates, attending election rallies, attending community meetings, joining with others to raise issues, or contacting elected leaders can have an educative effect increasing interest and efficacy,[13] as well as building support for democracy.[14] Also, membership in civic organizations may build up social capital and cooperative practices and organizational and communicative skills that individuals apply in other and larger political arenas.[15] The historical institutionalist perspective, in particular, emphasizes the socializing effects of institutions in shaping citizens' preferences or even identity over time.[16] Practicing democracy over time would help citizens develop a new and longer-term perspective on judging democracy, based on an appreciation of the intrinsic nature of democracy rather than its consequences.

In short, according to institutional theory, institutions guide political behavior in such a way that after a certain period of time they also help determine changes in attitude and values. If Institutionalism is correct, the socializing effect of democratic institutions should leave its clearest footprint on the soil of Taiwan where the process of democratization has run its full course. In Taiwan, democratic culture shall strengthen along with increasing experience in democratic participation, while in Hong Kong it shall stagnate as the democratization process was largely stalled. On Mainland China, the practice of grassroots democracy would also induce value change over time, but its effect shall be limited.

Culturalist

The touchstone of culturalist theory is the postulate of oriented action: actors do not respond directly to "situations" but respond to them through mediating "orientations." What divides culturalist and other theoretical perspectives involves the issue of later-in-life learning, or re-socialization. Culturalists argue from a postulate of "cumulative" socialization that privileges early learning, or what psychologists mean by "primacy." Prior learning is a basis for later learning, and therefore not only does early learning condition later learning, but also the beliefs learned early are much more resistant to change. Exceptionally great forces are needed to induce great changes in these basic orientations. Harry Eckstein, for example, describes the most likely cultural changes as pattern maintaining change.[17]

According to this perspective, East Asian political culture and liberal democracy are not compatible, since each is specific to their own respective cultures. Lucian Pye has argued that in East Asian cultures, traditional authoritarian and paternalistic relations between superiors and inferiors will remain even after modernization.[18] The pattern of dependency established in the family will interact with an individual sense of insecurity brought about by rapid socioeconomic change to create new forms of power-dependency.[19] This psychocultural analysis is consistent with how Samuel Huntington draws a sharp line between Chinese and Western civilizations—the former valuing group interests over individual interests, political authority over individual freedom, and social responsibility over individual rights.[20] The cultural relativists argue that Confucian tradition never developed a political philosophy supportive of liberal democracy like the West did. Advocacy of government by virtuous men, rather than law, is not conducive to individual rights, and modeling the state after the family leads to a paternalism that slides easily into authoritarianism. Essentially, Confucianism sees the ideal state as leading by moral suasion,[21] so as not to require coercion to fulfill its chief function of cultivating virtue and social harmony.[22] But in the absence of institutional checks against rule by men who are not virtuous, harmony and cooperation must be built on a foundation of hierarchical structures that cannot guarantee basic freedoms[23] and have the effect of hiding latent societal conflicts.[24] Furthermore, a social order based on an equivalence of societal and state interests is not conducive to the emergence of an independent civil society.

The culturalists turned our attention to the incompatibility of liberal democracy with the region's Confucian political culture and traditions to explain why so many East Asian countries have failed to complete the democratic transformation of their authoritarian or totalitarian communist states[25] Paradoxically, their view is echoed by defenders of Asian values who have claimed that Western-style liberal democracy is neither suitable for nor compatible with Confucian East Asia, where collective welfare, a sense of duty, and other principles of Confucian moral philosophy run deep in people's consciences.[26]

According to culturalist theory, value change in Confucian societies would have been rather slow and uneven, regardless of the transformative forces of modernization and globalization and/or the socializing effects of democratic practice. For ordinary citizens, values that are more compatible with traditional values, such as equality, might be relatively easy to acquire. Certain liberal values not so compatible with traditional values, such as individual freedom and rights, pluralism, and limited government, would be more difficult to make their way into the prevailing value structure. Even though the political system of a given Asian country might become formally democratized, the new democracy would still carry many illiberal characteristics due to the slow acquisition of liberal democratic values and beliefs among its elite and populace.[27] On the other hand, if the perspective of modernization is correct, then traditional Confucian values will decline in importance along with modernization, and liberal democratic values will be reinforced through improved educational standards and generational replacement.

MEASURING SYSTEM CULTURE AND TRADITIONAL VALUES

There are a plethora of philosophical studies examining the linkage between Confucian values and the universality of human rights and basic democratic norms or their absence.[28] However, with few exceptions,[29] empirical studies that systematically explore how traditional values actually affect the development of civic culture in Confucian East Asia are quite scare. Most of the political science literature is based on anecdotal or impressionistic accounts of political attitudes and behavior among the masses and political leaders.[30] A systematic exploration requires both a conceptual scheme for measuring culture-specific traditional social values that people acquired during pre-adult life and a coherent conceptual framework for a cross-system and cross-time comparison of political culture.

MEASURING DEMOCRATIC VS. AUTHORITARIAN VALUE ORIENTATIONS

Since the late 1970s, Professor Fu Hu and his colleagues pioneered the view that system culture, that is, value orientations toward the normative principles that govern the organization of political power and authority in a society, should be the pillar of the political culture approach and that the existing literature on political culture places too much emphasis on what Gabriel Almond termed *process culture*,[31] such as efficacy, compromise, trust, and tolerance. The Taiwan team has developed an original battery measuring the popular orientation toward political regime around five dimensions: *political equality, popular accountability, political liberalism, political pluralism and separation of power (or horizontal accountability)*—also known as five democratic versus authoritarian value-orientations toward power.[32]

Anchoring on these five key dimensions of democratic vs. authoritarian value orientations, Fu Hu, Yun-han Chu, Huo-yan Shyu, and their colleagues have tracked the evolution of political culture in Taiwan over more than two decades, covering the entire span of the island's regime transition, from the weakening of authoritarianism to the completion of the democratic transition.[33] They found that the acquisition of pro-democratic value orientations along the five dimensions has been uneven, suggesting the lingering influence of traditional values. Support for political equality was high from the beginning, and endorsement of popular accountability rose dramatically from 1984 to 1993 (as did belief in political pluralism, even though it remained rather low). Their data also show that by the late 1990s substantial segments of Taiwan's public still manifested the fear of disorder and preference for communal harmony over individual freedom that Lucian Pye takes to be generally characteristic of Asian attitudes toward power and authority. Yet, they also note the generally steady increase since democratization began in the mid-1980s in the proportions of the public expressing pro-democratic value orientations and rejecting the paternalistic, collectivist, illiberal norms associated with the Asian values perspective.

This approach was later applied to the comparative study of political culture among three Chinese societies: Taiwan, Hong Kong, and mainland China. The first-wave trilateral survey was conducted between summer 1993 and spring 1994.[34] The second-wave trilateral survey, which by then has become a part of a larger regionwide comparative survey known as East Asia Barometer, was conducted between summer 2001 and summer 2002.[35]

The democratic versus authoritarian value-orientation battery that has been consistently applied in all three localities consists of the following six items:[36]

Political Equality

1. People with little or no education should have as much say in politics as highly educated people.[37]

Popular Accountability

2. Government leaders are like the head of a family; we should all follow their decisions.
3. If we have public leaders who are morally upright, we can let him decide everything.

Separation of Power

4. When judges decide important cases, they should accept the view of the executive branch.

Political Liberalism

5. The government should decide whether certain ideas are allowed to be discussed in the society.

Political Pluralism

6. Stability and harmony of the community will be disrupted if people organize lots of groups.

Except for item 1, which is scaled in the democratic direction, all the remaining five items are scaled in the authoritarian direction. So, "agreement" indicates an authoritarian value orientation, while "disagreement" reveals a democratic value orientation. Each question was designed around a four-point scale, consisting of "highly disagree," "disagree," "agree," and "strongly agree." For the sake of statistical analysis, the five response categories are given numerical values: "highly disagree" for -2 points, "disagree" for -1 points, "don't know" for 0 points, "agree" for 1 point, and "highly agree" for 2 points. To construct a valid scale, essentially we combine two analytical tasks in one. Our scale enables us not only to measure the popular commitment to democratic norms, but also to identify a cluster of mass belief and attitudes that are typically nurtured under authoritarian regimes. In short, it serves as a multidimensional scale for the measurement of pro-authoritarian legitimacy orientations and conversely pro-democratic values at the same time. This conceptual formulation provides a coherent framework for a cross-system and cross-time comparison of legitimacy orientation toward political regime.

MEASURING TRADITIONAL VALUES

What are the specific components of Confucian values? How can they be defined? Values widely cited as Confucian include the importance of family, a concern for ethics and virtue, the primacy of group over individuals, an emphasis on unity or harmony, hard work, thrift, and the importance of education.[38] Our analysis largely follows Weiming Tu's elaboration of Confucian personal ethnics.[39] According to Confucian personal ethics, it is imperative to obey family elders, and the ultimate objective of one's personal behavior is to honor one's ancestors. In order to bring honor to the family, it is also imperative to take on the responsibility of bearing children and continuing the family line. Finally, in one's social relations, it is imperative to respect the opinions of nonfamily elders and the educated, so that a harmonious and well-ordered society can be preserved.

We have developed a ten-item battery for the trilateral survey to measure Confucian personal ethics. These ten items can be subdivided into ethics for three social domains, namely family-related, interpersonal-related, and work-related ethics. The following are the ten items that we employed consistently in the three localities and over time:

Traditional Family Values

Do you agree the following statement?

1. Even if parents' demands are unreasonable, children still should do what they ask.
2. The main reason to work hard and get ahead is for the glory of the ancestors and the family.

3. When a mother-in-law and a daughter-in-law come into conflict, even if the mother-in-law is in the wrong, the husband should still persuade his wife to obey his mother.
4. If one wants to have only one child, it's better to have a son than a daughter.

Traditional Interpersonal Ethnic

Do you agree the following statement?

1. When one has a conflict with a neighbor, the best way to deal with it is to accommodate the other person.
2. If there is a quarrel with others, we should ask an elder to resolve the dispute.
3. Even if you have knowledge and ability, you need not make a big show of it.

Traditional Work-Related Ethnic

Do you agree the following statement?

1. When hiring someone, even if a stranger is more qualified, the opportunity should still be given to relatives and friends.
2. It's embarrassing to accept payment for things you do for friends.
3. Wealth and poverty, success and failure are all determined by fate.

Likewise, each question was designed around a five-point scale, consisting of "highly disagree," "disagree," "don't know," "agree," and "strongly agree." The five response categories are given numerical values—"highly disagree" for -2 points, "disagree" for -1 points, "don't know" for 0 points, "agree" for 1 point, and "highly agree" for 2 points—for the sake of statistical analysis. This conversion allows us to construct three composite indexes approximating three interval variables tapping into the lingering influence of traditional Confucian personal ethics in three domains observed at the individual level. The higher the average score, the more traditionally oriented the individual is, while the lower the average score, the less traditionally oriented the individual is.

THE EMPIRICAL FINDINGS

Examining the Marco Patterns

The distribution of popular political attitudes based on our six-item battery for measuring democratic versus authoritarian value orientations in Hong

Kong, Taiwan, and mainland China over time is displayed item-by-item in figure 5.1 through figure 5.6. The most striking finding is the powerful impact of socioeconomic modernization on the growth of democratic value-orientation (indicated by the percentage of respondents who answered "agree" in figure 5.1 and the percentage of respondents who answered "disagree" in figures 5.2–5.6). For most indicators, Hong Kong's overall level of democratic value orientation is slightly higher than Taiwan's and significantly higher than that of Mainland China. This pecking order (descending with level of socioeconomic modernization) is most evident for indicators measuring the concept of popular accountability, political liberalism, and political pluralism despite the fact that Taiwan enjoys a more advanced status in terms of democratic development than Hong Kong. The only notable exception is the fact that the level of popular support for the principle of separation of power in Hong Kong is lower than that of Taiwan.

For both Taiwan and Mainland China, there is also a strikingly similar pattern of a rising level of democratic value orientation over time. For instance, on the question, "Government leaders are like the head of a family, we should all follow their decisions," 55.8 percent of our Taiwanese respondents answered "disagree" or "strongly disagree" in 1993, and it has increased to 60.3 percent in 2002. In mainland China, only 18.2 percent of our respondents expressed disagreement to this statement in 1993, but 35.7 percent of them did in 2002. This pattern holds up for the second item measuring the concept of popular accountability (see figure 5.2) and the item measuring political liberalism (see figure 5.5). However, for the paired comparison between Taiwan and Mainland China, it is difficult to tell whether this longitudinal pattern should be attributed more to the influence of socioeconomic modernization or political democratization, because during this period both societies have made progress on both scores.

The paired comparison between Taiwan and Hong Kong help us to clearly identify the socializing effects of participating in a democratic process on the growth of democratic value orientation. The political tempos in the two societies during the nine-year interval of the two surveys were quite different. Taiwan completed its democratic transition during the period, while Hong Kong's momentum for democratization suffered a setback. The divergent trajectories of regime evolution between the two societies manifest themselves in opposite patterns of value changes. In Taiwan, popular belief in political equality, popular accountability, and political liberalism have gained strength during this period (see figures 5.1, 5.2, 5.3, and 5.5). In Hong Kong, during the same period, citizens' commitment to the principles of popular accountability and political pluralism has lost ground, albeit at a modest pace. This suggests that political institutions can exert significant socializing influence independent of the forces

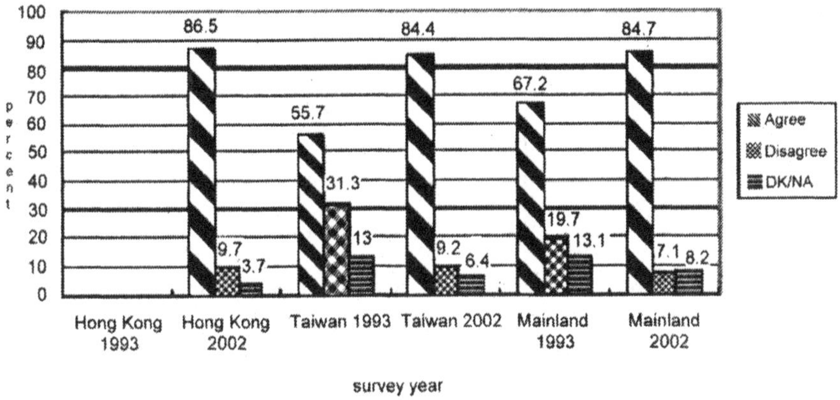

Figure 5.1

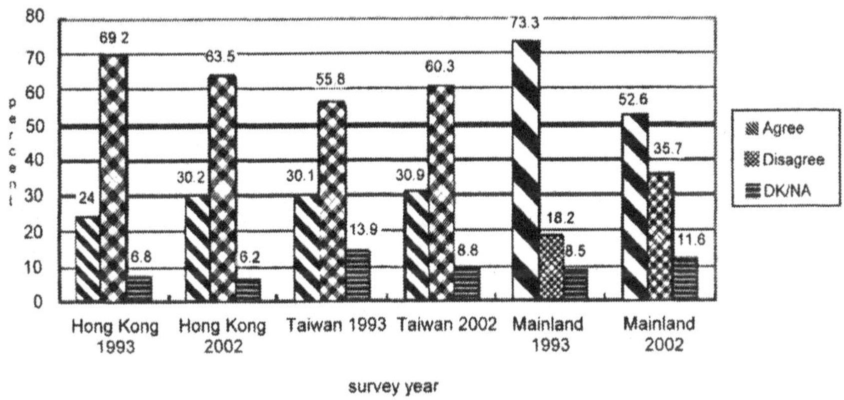

Figure 5.2

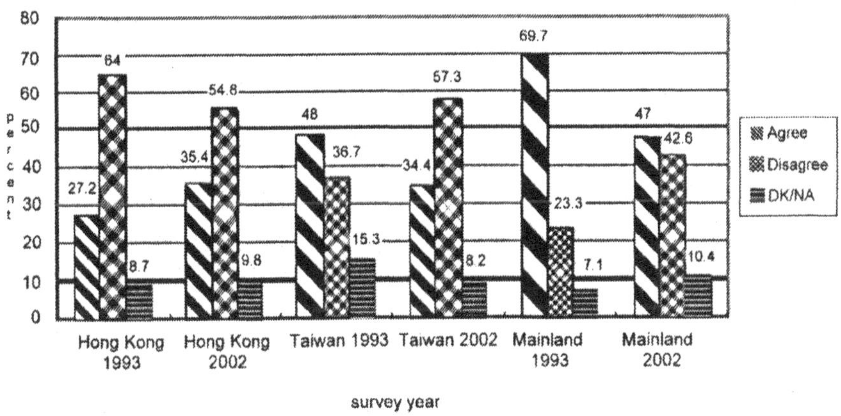

Figure 5.3

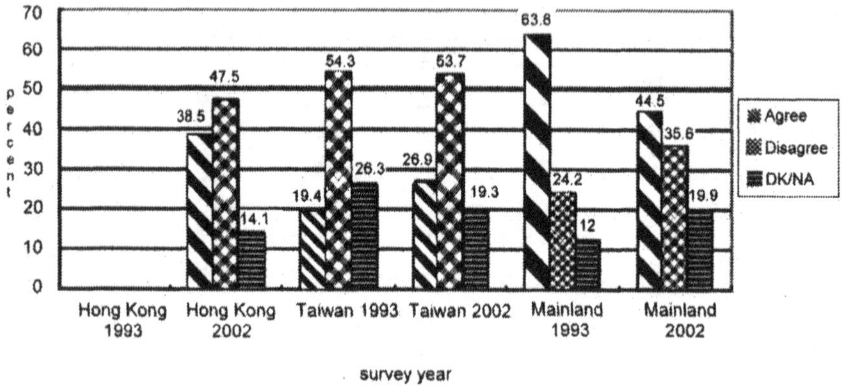

Figure 5.4

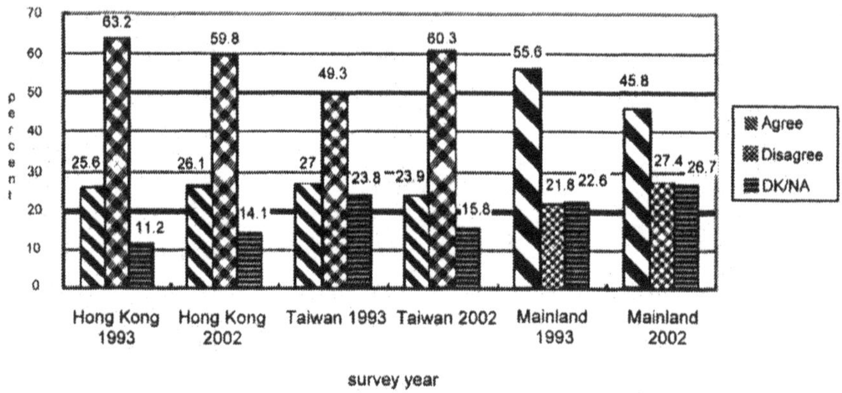

Figure 5.5

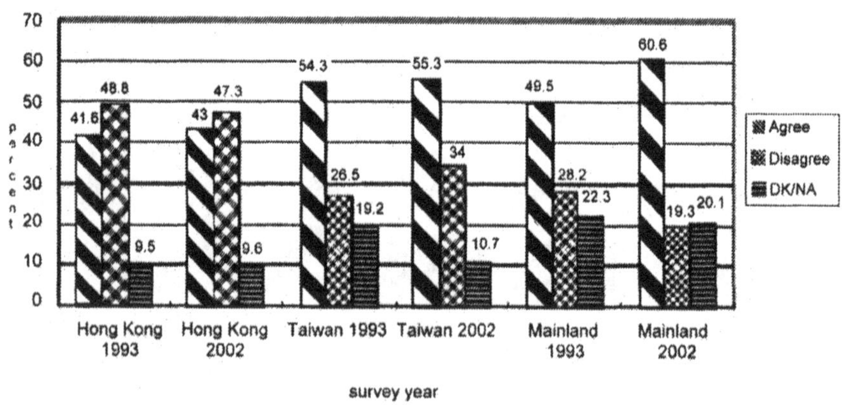

Figure 5.6

of socio-economic modernization, which are perhaps more powerful as indicated by Hong Kong's higher average level of democratic value orientation.

Across the three culturally Chinese societies, we also detect some constraining as well as enabling effects of the traditional values. Most notably, the concept of political pluralism does not bode well with the populace in all three societies (see figure 5.6). There are still a large number of citizens in all three societies who worried about the implications of competition and contestation among diverse interest groups for social stability and harmony. While Hong Kong houses the largest number of respondents who embrace of idea of political pluralism, in both surveys the level of support is still well below the 50 percent threshold. In both Taiwan and Mainland China, the number of respondents registering "disagreement" to this question has never reached 35 percent. As a matter of fact, in Taiwan, with the mushrooming of civic organizations and social movements during the 1990s, the level of support for political pluralism has actually gone down. Interestingly, in our surveys for Mainland China, we witness a similar pattern of receding support for political pluralism, just as many Chinese citizens had their first taste of associational life (see figure 5.6). The distribution of attitudes toward the principle of political equality is a mirror image of those toward political pluralism. In all three societies, the concept of political equality has reached an overwhelming consensus. In our 2001–2002 survey, there is virtually no difference among the three societies, with over 80 percent of the respondents professing a democratic orientation. This suggests that the concept of equality is more compatible with traditional Chinese ethos so that it can be more readily assimilated into the core belief (see figure 5.1). The concept of separation of power also ran into some resistance in all three localities. Despite a strong tradition of the rule of law under British rule, less than a majority of our Hong Kong respondents embraced this idea of judicial independence in our 2001 survey. It gained slightly stronger support in Taiwan, but there is virtually no change in the level of support between 1993 and 2002 (see figure 5.4).

However, the influence of traditional values has by and large steadily receded over time as the process of modernization and democratization presses on. For instance, in our 1993 Taiwan survey, more than half of our respondents embraced the idea that "If we have public leaders who are morally upright, we can let them decide everything." This traditional deference to virtuous leaders has nevertheless waned over time. This concept commands the allegiance of just a bit more than one third of respondents in Taiwan around 2002. In Mainland China, it drops from 69.7 percent to 47 percent between 1993 and 2002 (see figure 5.3).

Table 5.1 offers a summary of the characteristics of the emerging political culture in Hong Kong, Taiwan, and Mainland China. Culturally speaking,

Table 5.1. Level of Popular Support for Liberal Democratic Values

	Hong Kong 1993	*Hong Kong 2002*	*Taiwan 1993*	*Taiwan 2002*	*China 1993*	*China 2002*
Political Equality	N/A	very high	high	very high	high	very high
Popular Accountability	very high	high	modest	high	very low	low
Horizontal Accountability	N/A	modest	modest	modest	very low	low
Political Liberalism	high	high	modest	high	very low	very low
Political Pluralism	modest	modest	very low	very low	very low	very low

Above 65 percent: Very high
64 percent – 55 percent: High
54 percent – 45 percent: Modest
44 percent – 35 percent: Low
Below 34 percent: Very low

Hong Kong provides the most fertile soil for a striving liberal democracy, but that overall advantage has eclipsed slightly in the recent past. Taiwan came from behind but is catching up in a significant way. By 2002, on most of the indicators of democratic value orientation, Taiwan is on a parity with Hong Kong. The former also enjoys a more favorable trend line than the latter. By 2002, the majority of the citizens in Mainland China still embrace authoritarian orientation, despite the fact that a significant number of citizens have been shedding their attachment to authoritarian values in the recent past. China still has a long way to go before a fully fledged democratic culture emerges, albeit its trend line does offer a shining ray of hope.

Looking for Evidences at the Micro Level

The patterns that we have observed at the macro level so far provide us with only some clues to the explanatory power of different causal mechanisms. To ascertain the implied causal relationships, we have to interrogate our survey data in a more rigorous way. I will undertake this in three steps: First, I will look at the patterns of value changes at a subnational level, beginning with the urban-rural divide. Next, I will examine the impact of the level of education and the age cohort, respectively, on the level of democratic value orientation at the individual level. Third, I will run a regression analysis to examine the constraining effect of traditional Confucian values on the growth of democratic value orientation in a multivariate framework.

In table 5.2, the Mainland China sample is separated into two subsamples, one representing the urban adult population and the other the rural adult population. For each of the six indicators, an F-test is conducted to ascertain if there is a statistically significant difference in the average level of support for democratic value between the urban and rural population. As this exercise is confined to a single country, the cultural attributes and regime characteristics at the system level is in a crude sense held constant. The observed differences between the rural and urban population over time can be more conclusively attributed to the influence of socioeconomic modernization. The patterns of value changes that emerge out of table 5.2 are highly consistent with the patterns we identified earlier through trilateral comparison. Over the measures of popular accountability, separation of power, and political liberalism, residents in Chinese cities consistently exhibit a lower degree of authoritarian value orientation than do people living in the countryside. Also, for both the urban and rural populations, the level of support for authoritarian values significantly declined between 1993 and 2002. However, there are two notable exceptions. First, it is the rural people who more readily embrace the idea that "people with little or no education should have as much say in politics as

Table 5.2. Distribution of Democratic Value Orientation in China

		Mainland China			
		1993 Survey		*2002 Survey*	
Question		*Rural*	*Urban*	*Rural*	*Urban*
Political Equality					
1. People with little or no education should have as much as say in politics as highly educated people.	Mean	0.714	0.279	0.910	0.669
	Std.	0.776	0.989	0.970	0.643
	F-test	83.247 ***		3 *	
Popular Accountability					
2. Government leaders are like the head of a family; we should all follow their decisions.	Mean	−0.779	−0.396	−0.448	−0.021
	Std.	0.741	0.990	0.968	1.058
	F-test	71.454 ***		62.738 ***	
3. If we have political leaders who are morally upright, we can let them decide everything.	Mean	−0.684	−0.322	−0.327	0.140
	Std.	0.828	1.028	1.000	1.038
	F-test	55.391 ***		73.318 ***	
Separation of Power (Horizontal Accountability)					
4. When judges decide important cases, they should accept the view of the executive branch.	Mean	−0.631	−0.063	−0.473	0.141
	Std.	0.851	1.071	0.971	1.067
	F-test	118.753 ***		110.273 ***	
Political Liberalism					
5. The government should decide whether certain ideas should be allowed to be discussed in society.	Mean	−0.680	−0.198	−0.514	−0.097
	Std.	0.807	1.038	0.893	1.031
	F-test	84.372 ***		51.463 ***	
Political Pluralism					
6. Stability and harmony of the community will be disrupted if people organize lots of groups.	Mean	−0.344	−0.282	−0.504	−0.594
	Std.	1.015	1.026	0.950	0.904
	F-test	1.051		5.773 **	

Legend: *** <.001 ** <.01

highly-educated people." This suggests that the people living in the Chinese countryside, who are typically less educated than urban residents, are very conscious of their rights of political participation. This may have something to do with rural China's stronger socialist legacy as well as its longer experiences with grassroots democracy. This pattern is confirmed by both our 1993 and 2002 surveys. Our data also show that the concept of political equality continues to gain wider acceptance over time among both the rural and urban population. Next, there remains widespread aversion to political pluralism, and there is no difference between the people of the rural area and those liv-

Table 5.3. Generation and Democratic Value Orientation: An ANOVA Analysis

		Mainland China 2002 Survey		
Question		*Born before 1949*	*Born between 1949–1968*	*Born after 1968*
Political Equality				
1. People with little or no education should have as much as say in politics as highly educated people.	Mean	1.011	0.927	**0.912**
	Std.	0.607	0.673	0.660
	F-test		5.223 *	
Popular Accountability				
2. Government leaders are like the head of a family; we should all follow their decisions.	Mean	−0.366	−0.231	**0.017**
	Std.	0.990	1.030	1.081
	F-test		25.296 **	
3. If we have political leaders who are morally upright, we can let them decide everything.	Mean	−0.234	−0.102	**0.203**
	Std.	1.029	1.038	1.038
	F-test		34.494 ***	
Separation of Power (Horizontal Accountability)				
4. When judges decide important cases, they should accept the view of the executive branch.	Mean	−0.151	−0.150	**0.011**
	Std.	1.068	1.073	1.067
	F-test		5.455 *	
Political Liberalism				
5. The government should decide whether certain ideas should be allowed to be discussed in society.	Mean	−0.489	−0.308	**0.044**
	Std.	0.894	0.989	1.042
	F-test		45.273 ***	
Political Pluralism				
6. Stability and harmony of the community will be disrupted if people organize lots of groups.	Mean	−0.605	−0.494	**−0.637**
	Std.	0.917	0.949	0.873
	F-test		6.274 *	

ing in the cities. Also, this popular aversion to pluralism has gone up rather than come down in the recent past. This resembles the pattern emerging out of the trilateral comparison.

Next, we disaggregate the 2002 Mainland China sample into three age cohorts: people who were born in or before 1948 (or who were fifty-five years old by the time of the 2002 survey), between 1949 and 1968 (i.e., between the ages of fifty-four and thirty-five) and after 1968 (i.e., thirty-four years old or younger).[40] For each of the six indicators an F-test was conducted to ascertain if there is statistically significant differences in the average level of support for democratic value among the three age cohorts. The patterns of value changes that emerged out of this cross-generational analysis are highly consistent with the patterns we identified earlier through trilateral comparison. The three age cohorts vary significantly over the various measures of popular accountability and political liberalism and, to some extent, separation of power as well. More importantly, there is an easily identifiable linear pattern across these various measures: the younger the generation, the lower the support for authoritarian value orientation. Much like we found earlier, this linear pattern does not hold up for the question on political equality or political pluralism. However, the two deviate from the general pattern in the opposite way. People from all three age cohorts embrace the idea of political equality overwhelmingly, while they all harbor reservation toward political pluralism, albeit to a varying degree. Most importantly, it is among the youngest generation (aged between twenty and thirty-four) that we found that the average scores on virtually all the measures (except for political pluralism) have moved into the positive territory; that is, more people are embracing democratic value orientation than people who attach themselves to authoritarian values. By these measures, the contrast between this generation and the two older generations is truly stark. This suggests that in the midst of China's rapid socioeconomic transition, a culture shift has indeed taken place within two generations.

To dig deeper into the causal mechanisms that could account for this significant transformation, we first examine the bivariate association between level of education and democratic value orientation. We apply correlation analyses to all six indicators (plus their sum score) for both waves of Mainland China survey. We then compare the statistical results with that of the two concurrent Taiwan surveys, to ascertain whether there is one common mechanism of value changes between the two and over time despite the huge difference in their trajectories of regime evolution. The results (displayed in table 5.4) are truly impressive. For most indicators (again with the exception of measures for political equality and political pluralism), we found very significant positive correlation between levels of education and attachment to democratic value orientation. Both the strength and direction of this association are very similar over time and between the two societies. This provides very convincing evidence for confirming the potent transformative power of an improved educational standard, which is arguably a good surrogate measure of the degree of exposure to the forces of modernization at the individual level in fostering the growth of a democratic political culture. Its transformative power works

Table 5.4. Education and Democratic Orientation: Correlation Analysis of China and Taiwan

		Mainland China		*Taiwan*	
Question		*1993*	*2002*	*1993*	*2002*
Political Equality					
1. People with little or no education should have as much say in politics as highly educated people.	Correlation	−0.295	0.004	0.308	−0.016
	Sig.	0.000	0.833	0.000	0.573
	N	2849	2918	1204	1237
Popular Accountability					
2. Government leaders are like the head of a family; we should all follow their decisions.	Correlation	0.279	0.309	0.339	0.163
	Sig.	0.000	0.000	0.000	0.000
	N	2995	2807	1194	1213
3. If we have political leaders who are morally upright, we can let them decide everything.	Correlation	0.297	0.335	0.230	0.227
	Sig.	0.000	0.000	0.000	0.000
	N	3045	2851	1178	1225
Separation of Power (Horizontal Accountability)					
4. When judges decide important cases, they should accept the view of the executive branch.	Correlation	0.352	0.347	0.162	0.110
	Sig.	0.000	0.000	0.000	0.000
	N	2864	2551	1021	1121
Political Liberalism					
5. The government should decide whether certain ideas should be allowed to be discussed in society.	Correlation	0.319	0.331	0.344	0.215
	Sig.	0.000	0.000	0.000	0.000
	N	2518	2331	1058	1155
Political Pluralism					
6. Stability and harmony of the community will be disrupted if people organize lots of groups.	Correlation	0.043	−0.046	0.245	0.153
	Sig.	0.029	0.020	0.000	0.000
	N	2516	2541	1148	1198
Cumulative Index (Sum of Items 1~6)	Correlation	0.359	0.398	0.351	0.250
	Sig.	0.000	0.000	0.000	0.000
	N	2069	1878	855	1012

in all Confucian cultural contexts and works under both authoritarian and democratic regimes.

Last, we apply a regression analysis to our second-wave Mainland China survey. The dependent variable is the cumulative index of democratic value orientation (i.e., the sum score of the six indicators). On the right-hand side of the equation we include the following ten independent variables:

1. Age
2. Gender (female as the default value)
3. Education
4. Subjective social status[41]
5. Interpersonal trust[42]
6. Traditional family values
7. Traditional interpersonal ethics
8. Traditional work-related ethics
9. Perceived improvement in political rights since 1979[43]
10. Rural or urban household registration (rural as the default value)

There are three main objectives in applying the regression analysis to our China survey data. First, I would like to ascertain the explanatory power of education and urbanization, which are two good indicators of the degree of exposure to the forces of socioeconomic modernization at the individual level, while holding the influence of other control variables constant. Second, I would like to verify the cultural relativists' thesis about the inhibiting effect

Table 5.5. Regression Analysis for Index of Democratic Value Orientation (2002 China Survey)

Explanatory Variables	*Beta*	*S.E.*
Age	−0.03	(0.00)
Gender (female = 0) Male	0.05	(0.09)*
Level of Education	0.15	(0.01)***
Subjective Social Status	−0.01	(0.05)
Interpersonal Trust	−0.00	(0.05)
Traditional Family Values	−0.14	(0.02)***
Traditional Interpersonal Ethics	−0.28	(0.02)***
Traditional Work-related Ethics	−0.13	(0.03)***
Perceived Improvement in Political Rights since 1979	−0.10	(0.02)***
Household Registration (Rural = 0) Urban	0.06	(0.10)**
R-squared	0.314	
Adj R-squared	0.308	
N	1115	

Legend: * <.05, ** <.01,*** <.001

of traditional values on the growth of democratic value orientation in a multivariate framework. Third, I would like to explore the relationship between the perceived changes in the political characteristics of the political regime during the Reform era and the level of democratic value orientation.

The results of the regression analysis are reported in table 5.5.[44] There are several important findings. First, the model provides a reasonably good fit to the data, as indicated by an impressive adjusted R square. Second, there are strong evidences that certain traditional values and democratic values are incongruous belief systems. All three composite measures of traditional personal ethics exhibit a significant negative impact on the level of democratic value orientation. Their inhibiting effects are stronger than the positive impact of education, age, or urbanization. Third, among the six sociological variables, only education, urbanization, and gender (i.e., male) exert significant positive influences on the level of democratic value orientation. Age ceases to be a source of explanation once the effects of education, gender, and urbanization are taken into account. Among the three relevant sociological variables, education exerts by far the strongest positive influence on the strengthening of democratic orientation. Last, the people who perceived improvement in the areas of citizen rights and freedom since 1979 are more likely to embrace authoritarian value orientation. We suspect that the causal relationship actually works in reverse: people with a stronger attachment to democratic values tend to be more dissatisfied with the pace of changes in the areas of citizen rights and freedom during the Reform era. This implies that a further strengthening of the popular belief in democratic values will either weaken the legitimacy of the current regime (as its admissible scope of political liberalization is not fast enough) or precipitate stronger popular demand for democratic reform.

CONCLUSION

The three perspectives, institutionalism, modernization theory, and culturalist theory, are all indispensable in formulating a fully explanatory account of the steady growth of democratic orientation in the three Chinese societies.

Our empirical findings lend strong support to the modernization theory. Rapid socioeconomic changes brought about by economic reform have had significant positive influence on the growth of democratic orientation among citizens across Hong Kong, Taiwan, rural China, and urban China. I demonstrate the power of modernization theory at both the macro and micro level. Its significant contextual effect on the acquisition of democratic orientation was demonstrated through a comparison of trilateral longitudinal survey data. At the individual level, our analysis confirms the potent transformative power of improved educational standards, arguably a good surrogate measure of the degree of exposure to forces of modernization, at the individual level, in fostering the growth of a democratic political culture. Its transformative power works in all Confucian cultural contexts and under both authoritarian and democratic regimes.

The paired comparison between Taiwan and Hong Kong help us clearly identify the socializing effects of participating in the democratic process on the growth of democratic value orientation. Our regression analysis also provides supporting evidences for the culturalist perspective. It shows that in Confucian societies, traditional values do stand in the way of acquiring democratic value orientation. However, there is little ground to be pessimistic about the future of democracy in Mainland China because further socioeconomic modernization will weaken traditional values. Most encouragingly, we found that in the midst of China's rapid socioeconomic transition, a culture shift has indeed taken place within two generations. A democratic culture is emerging among China's youngest generation, the generation that has received the best education ever and grown up virtually exclusively in the Reform era. In a nutshell, our analysis offers a ray of hope for the prospect of China's further political liberalization and eventual democratization as the momentum of socioeconomic modernization continues to go strong.

APPENDIX 1

Professor Fu Hu (1998) and his colleagues conceptualize democratic versus authoritarian value orientations toward regime legitimacy, as the value orientation toward the normative principles that govern the organization of political power and authority in a society. These deeper values normative commitments lay the basis for the formation of evaluative attitudes toward regime legitimacy and support for the incumbent. A legitimacy orientation always consists of two components—desirability and feasibility. To regard some norms legitimate means they are deemed not just preferable, but also realizable or achievable.

The organizing principle of a political regime consists of three basic dimensions: (1) The legitimate power relationship among members of the political community; (2) the legitimate power relationship between the authorities and citizens; and (3) the legitimate power relationship among the government authorities themselves. The value orientation toward political equality corresponds to the first dimension. It is a set of beliefs that all members of the political community should be equal and entitled to the same citizen rights regardless of race, gender, education, religion, class, socioeconomic background, political affiliation, etc. In contrast, in some societies a majority of people might believe in a hierarchical and/or exclusionary order rather than an equalitarian/inclusionary political order, and it is widely accepted as legitimate that certain groups are privileged and that others should and can be disfranchised or discriminated against. The value orientation toward the separation of power (or horizontal accountability) corresponds to the third dimension. It is a set of beliefs that governing authority should be divided among various branches of government and that a good-order polity is achieved through a design of horizontal accountability—that is, check-and-balance. In contrast, in some societies people may believe in the necessity and the desirability of the supremacy of executive power or the fusion of legislative, executive, and judicial authority. The value orientation toward political liberty, pluralism, and popular accountability corresponds to the second dimension. The second dimension should be tapped by more than one set of beliefs because, conceptually, it can be subdivided into three subdimensions: (1) the value orientation toward political liberty is a set of beliefs that there are certain legitimate realms of individual freedom and liberty, which should be free from state intrusion and regulation; (2) the value orientation toward pluralism is a set of beliefs that there should be a legitimate realm of civil society in which the civic organizations can freely constitute themselves in an ensemble of arrangements for expressing themselves and advancing their interests without state interference; and (3) the value orientation toward popular accountability refers to a set belief that government authority should be accountable to the people and that there should be some effective means for popular control and consent. In contrast, in some societies people might believe that the realm of individual liberty should be suppressed to the minimum, civil society must be subject to state guidance and control, and the assertion of popular control over authority is unacceptable and even dangerous. Thus, we build our measures of legitimacy orientation toward a regime around five essential elements of democratic norms—in Professor Fu Hu's original formulation, the five dimensions of democratic value orientation toward power[45]:

1. Political equality
2. Popular accountability
3. Political liberalism
4. Political pluralism
5. Separation of power

What distinguishes our approach from others (Booth and Seligson 1986; Dalton 1991) is that we don't think the best measurement strategy is to state these principles in an abstract and straightforward way. Because indicators constructed this way won't be very discerning, one tends to get uniform positive answers. In this sense, legitimacy orientation is not a set of political ideals, and the belief in democratic legitimacy becomes conceptually separable from support for democratic ideals.

We recognize that most modern authoritarian regimes don't challenge (or repudiate) these democratic norms in principle; rather, the lines of defense for an authoritarian arrangement (or the lines of subtle offense against democratic norms) typically fall into one of the two camps:

1. The *Desirability Argument.* The country should develop a different form of democracy (people's democracy, Chinese democracy, socialist democracy, guided democracy) that best suits herself and that might be superior to Western democracy.
2. The *Feasibility Argument.* The country is not ready for a full democracy (due to lack of a civic culture, a low level of socioeconomic modernization, conflict with other national development priorities, and/or an imminent external threat). If the country had acquired Western democracy before its time, the society would pay a high price in terms of inefficiency, insecurity, and disorder.

To construct a valid scale, essentially we combine two analytical tasks in one. Our scale enables us not only to measure the popular commitment to democratic norms but also to identify a cluster of mass beliefs and attitudes that are typically nurtured under authoritarian or antidemocratic regimes. They are more compatible with the authoritarian arrangements and are inimical to the development of democratic values and institutions. In short, it serves as a multidimensional scale for the measurement of pro-authoritarian legitimacy orientations and, conversely, pro-democratic values at the same time. This conceptual formulation provides a coherent framework for a cross-system and cross-time comparison of legitimacy orientation toward a political regime.

NOTES

1. See Yun-han Chu, 2006, "Third-Wave Democratization in East Asia: Challenges and Prospect," *ASIEN*, Vol. 100 (July), pp. 11–17.

2. The Ministry of Civil Affairs reports 280,000 registered NGOs in China for 2005, including some 6,000 foreign NGOs, up from a total of 4,800 NGOs in 1988. The World Bank puts the present number between 300,000 and 700,000, while Wang Shaoguang and Hejian Yu (2004) estimate that China has more than eight million registered and unregistered, nongovernmental and quasi-governmental organizations.

3. See Kevin J. O'Brien, 1990, "Is China's National People's Congress a 'Conservative' Legislature?" *Asian Survey*, Vol. 30, No. 8, pp. 782–794; O'Brien, 1994, "Chinese People's Congresses and Legislative Embeddedness: Understanding Early Organizational Development," *Comparative Political Studies*, Vol. 27, No. 1, pp. 80–107; O'Brien, 1994, "Agents and Remonstrators: Role Accumulation by Chinese People's Congress Deputies," *China Quarterly*, No. 138, pp. 359–380; and Jean-Pierre Cabestan, 2006, "More Power to the People's Congresses? Parliaments and Parliamentarianism in the People's Republic of China," *Asien*, Vol. 99, pp. 42–69.

4. See Thomas Bernstein, 2006, "Village Democracy and Its Limits," *Asien*, Vol. 99, pp. 29–41.

5. This trilateral comparative survey project was co-directed by Fu Hu, Andrew Nathan, Hsin-chi Kuan, Tianjian Shi, and Yun-han Chu. It was financed by the National Science Foundation of the United States, the National Science Council of the Republic of China, the University Research Grant Council of Hong Kong, the Henry Luce Foundation, and other funding agencies and implemented under the auspices of "Political Participation and Political Culture in Mainland China, Taiwan and Hong Kong Project." After 2000, it became a sub-project of a larger region-wide survey known as the East Asia Barometer (and later on Asian Barometer, after enlargement), which is supported by the Ministry of Education, the Academia Sinica, National Taiwan University, and other national funding agencies. For more details about the project, please visit the project website at: www.asianbarometer.org.

6. See Ronald Inglehart, 1997, *Modernization and Postmodernization: Cultural, Economic and Political Change in 43 Societies*, Princeton, N.J.: Princeton University Press, p. 7.

7. See Michael Bratton, and Robert Mattes, 2003, "Learning about Democracy in Africa: Awareness, Performance and Experience," *Afrobarometer Working Paper*. www.afrobarometer.org.

8. See Alex Inkeles, and David H Smith, 1974, *Becoming Modern: Individual Change in Six Developing Countries*, Cambridge, Mass.: Harvard University Press; and Lucian W. Pye, 1990, "Political Science and the Crisis of Authoritarianism," *American Political Science Review*, Vol. 84, No. 1, pp. 3–19.

9. See Larry Diamond, 1999, *Developing Democracy: Towards Consolidation*, Baltimore: Johns Hopkins University Press.

10. See Ronald Inglehart, 1997, *Modernization and Postmodernization: Cultural, Economic and Political Change in 43 Societies*, Princeton, N.J.: Princeton University Press, pp. 10–25.

11. See Ronald Inglehart, 1977, *The Silent Revolution: Changing Values and Political Styles Among Western Publics*, Princeton, N.J.: Princeton University Press; and Ronald Inglehart, and Paul Abramson, 1999, "Measuring Postmaterialism," *American Political Science Review*, Vol. 93, No. 3, pp. 665–677.

12. See Michael Bratton, and Robert Mattes, 2003, "Learning about Democracy in Africa: Awareness, Performance and Experience," *Afrobarometer Working Paper*. www.afrobarometer.org; Peter A. Hall, and Rosemary C. R. Taylor, 1996, "Political Science and the Three New Institutionalism," *Political Studies*, Vol. 44, No. 4, pp.

936–957; Edward N. Muller, and Mitchell A. Seligson, 1994, "Civic Culture and Democracy: The Question of Causal Relationships," *American Political Science Review*, Vol. 88, No. 3, pp. 635–652; Pippa Norris, 1999, *The Growth of Critical Citizens*, Oxford: Oxford University Press; and Sven Steimo, Kathleen Thelen, and Frank Longstreth (eds.), 1992, *Structuring Politics: Historical Institutionalism in Comparative Analysis*, Cambridge: Cambridge University Press.

13. See Steven E. Finkel, 1987, "The Effects of Participation on Political Efficacy and Political Support: Evidence from a West German Panel Journal of Politics," *Journal of Politics*, Vol. 49, No. 2, pp. 441–464.

14. See Michael Bratton et al., 1999, "The Effects of Civic Education on Political Culture: Evidence from Zambia," *World Development*, Vol. 27, No. 5, pp. 807–824; and Steven E. Finkel, Christopher A. Sabatini, and Gwedolyn G Bevis, 2000, "Civic Education, Civil Society, and Political Mistrust in a Developing Democracy: The Case of the Dominican Republic World Development," *World Development*, Vol. 28, No. 11, pp. 1851–1874.

15. See Kay Lehman Schlozman, Sidney Verba, and Henry E. Brady, 1995, "Participation's not a paradox: The view from American activists," *British Journal of Political Science*, Vol. 25, No. 1, pp. 1–36; Peter McDonough, Doh C. Shin, and Jose Alvaro Moisés, 1998, "Democratization and participation: Comparing Spain, Brazil, and Korea," *Journal of Politics*, Vol. 60, No. 4, pp. 919–953; Norman H. Nie, G. Bingham Powell Jr., and Kenneth Prewitt, 1969, "Social Structure and Political Participation: Developmental Relationships, II," *American Political Science Review*, Vol. 63, No. 3, pp. 808–832; Robert D. Putnam, 1993, *Making Democracy Work*, Princeton, N.J.: Princeton University Press; and Doh Chull Shin, 1999, *Mass Politics and Culture in Democratizing Korea*, Cambridge: Cambridge University Press.

16. See Sven Steimo, Kathleen Thelen, and Frank Longstreth (eds.), 1992, *Structuring Politics: Historical Institutionalism in Comparative Analysis*, Cambridge: Cambridge University Press.

17. See Harry Eckstein, 1988, "A Culturalist Theory of Political Change," *American Political Science Review*, Vol. 82, No. 3, pp. 789–804.

18. Lucian W. Pye, 2001, "Civility, Social Capital, and Civil Society in Asia," in Robert I. Rothberg (ed.), *Patterns of Social Capital: Stability and Change in Historical Perspective*, Cambridge: Cambridge University Press, p. 381.

19. Lucian W. Pye, 1985, *Asian Power and Politics*, Cambridge, Mass: Harvard Belknap, p. 325.

20. Samuel P. Huntington, 1996, *The Clash of Civilizations*, New York: Simon and Schuster, p. 108.

21. Frederick W. Mote, 1989, *Intellectual Foundations of China*, New York: McGraw-Hill, p. 41.

22. Leonard Hsu, 2005, *The Political Philosophy of Confucianism*, London: Rutledge, p. 102.

23. Wm Theodore de Bary, 1996, *The Trouble with Confucianism*, Cambridge, Mass.: Harvard University Press, p. 49.

24. Lucian W. Pye, 1985, *Asian Power and Politics*, Cambridge, Mass.: Harvard Belknap, p. 186.

25. See Shaohua Hu, 1997, "Confucianism and Western Democracy," *Journal of Contemporary China*, Vol. 6, No. 15, pp. 347–363; Shipping Hua (ed.), 2001, *Chinese Political Culture, 1989–2000*, Armonk: M.E.Sharpe; Samuel P. Huntington, 1991, *The Third Wave: Democratization in the Late Twentieth Century*, Norman, Okla.: University of Oklahoma Press; Fareed Zakaria, 2003, *The Future of Freedom: Illiberal Democracy at Home and Abroad*, New York: W. W. Norton; Donald K. Emerson, 1995, "Singapore and the 'Asian Values' Debate," *Journal of Democracy*, Vol. 6, No. 4, pp. 95–105; Joseph B. Tamney, 1995, *The Struggle over Singapore's Soul: Western Modernization and Asian Culture*, Berlin: Walter de Gruyter.

26. See Michael D. Barr, 2002, *Cultural Politics and Asian Values: The Tepid War*, London; Routledge.

27. See Fareed Zakaria, 2003, *The Future of Freedom: Illiberal Democracy at Home and Abroad*, New York: W. W. Norton.

28. See, for instance, Daniel A. Bell, 2000, *East Meets West*, Princeton, N.J.: Princeton University Press; Jack Donnelly, 1999, "Human Rights and Asian Values: A Defense of 'Western' Universalism," in Joanne R. Bauer and Daniel A. Bell, *The East Asian Challenge for Human Rights*. Cambridge: Cambridge University Press; Joseph B. Tamney and Linda Hsueh-Ling Chiang, 2002, *Modernization, Globalization and Confucianism in Chinese Societies*, Conn.: Praeger Publishers; Christopher Tremewan, 1993, "Human Rights in Asia," *Pacific Review*, Vol. 6, pp.17–30; Tu Weiming, Milan Hejtmanek, and Alan Wachman (eds.), 1992, *The Confucian World Observed: A Contemporary Discussion of Confucian Humanism in East Asia*, Honolulu: East-West Center Press.

29. See Chong-Min Park and Doh Chull Shin, 2004, "Do Asian Values Deter Popular Support for Democracy? The Case of South Korea," paper presented at the 2004 Annual Meeting of the Association for Asian Studies, San Diego, March 4–7; and Yu-Tzung Chang, Yun-han Chu, and Frank Tsai, 2005, "Confucianism and Democratic Values in Three Chinese Societies," *Issues and Studies*, Vol. 41, No. 4, pp. 1–33.

30. See Samuel P. Huntington, 1996, *The Clash of Civilizations*. New York: Simon and Schuster; Lucian W. Pye, 1985, *Asian Power and Politics*, Cambridge, Mass.: Harvard Belknap; Robert A. Scalapino, 1989, *The Politics of Development: Perspectives on Twentieth Century Asia*, Cambridge, Mass.: Harvard University Press.

31. Gabriel A. Almond and G. Bingham Powell (eds.), 1980, *Comparative Politics Today: A World View*, Boston: Little, Brown.

32. See Fu Hu, 1998, *Zhengzhi wenhua yu zhengzhi shenghuo*, Political culture and political life), Taipei: Sanmin; Yun-han Chu and Fu Hu, 1996, "Neo-authoritarianism, Polarized Conflict and Populism in a Newly Democratizing Regime: Taiwan's Emerging Mass Politics," *Journal of Contemporary China*, 5, 11 (Spring). For an elaboration on the conceptual underpinning of the five-dimensional measure, please refer to Appendix 1.

33. See Fu Hu, 1998, *Zhengzhi wenhua yu zhengzhi shenghuo*, Political culture and political life), Taipei: Sanmin; Yun-han Chu, and Fu Hu, 1996, "Neo-authoritarianism, Polarized Conflict and Populism in a Newly Democratizing Regime: Taiwan's Emerging Mass Politics," *Journal of Contemporary China*, Vol. 5, No. 11, pp. 23–41; Doh Chull Shin and Huoyan Shyu, 1997, "Political Ambivalence in South Korea and

Taiwan," *Journal of Democracy*, Vol. 8, No. 3, pp. 91–124; Yun-han Chu, and Yu-Tzung Chang, 2002, "Confucianism and Democracy: Empirical Study of Mainland China, Taiwan and Hong Kong," see www.asianbarometer.com.

34. For the first-wave trilateral survey, in all three localities territorywide stratified samples based on the PPS (probability proportional to size) criterion were drawn. Each sample represents all the adult population above voting age in a given territory. Our Hong Kong survey yields 892 valid cases, the Taiwan survey 1,402 cases, and the mainland survey 3,296 cases. All three samples are sufficiently large, relative to their respective degree of demographic heterogeneity.

35. For the second-wave trilateral survey, the same stratified sampling strategy was applied. Our Hong Kong survey yields yields 811 valid cases, the Taiwan survey 1,415 cases, and the mainland survey 3,183 cases.

36. However, Items 1 and 4 were not asked in the 1993–1994 Hong Kong survey.

37. The wording of this item for the 1993–1994 survey is slightly different.

38. See Joanne R Bauer, and Daniel A. Bell (eds.), 1999, *The East Asian Challenge for Human Rights*, Cambridge: Cambridge University Press.

39. See Weiming Tu, (ed.), 1996, *Confucian Traditions in East Asian Modernity*. Cambridge, Mass.: Harvard University Press. Tu classifies Confucian values into two categories: political Confucianism and Confucian personal ethics.

40. The Chinese people born after 1968 were little affected by the Cultural Revolution and they are the best-educated generation that China has ever known. They have grown up almost exclusively under the Reform since their adolescent years.

41. The wording of the question for measuring Subjective Social Status is as follows: "People sometimes think of the social status of their families in terms of upper class, middle class, or lower class. Where would you place your family on the scale? Upper class, upper-middle class, middle class, lower-middle class, or lower class." It yields a five-point scale ranging from 5 to 1.

42. The question measuring interpersonal trust is worded as follows: "Generally speaking, would you say that 'Most people can be trusted' or 'you can't be too careful in dealing with them'?"

43. The index of "Perceived Improvement in Political Rights since 1979" is the sum score of the five questions asking the respondents to evaluate the changes between now and the era before 1979 (the beginning of the Reform) in five areas: a. freedom to express one's view; b. government treats everyone equally; c. people like me can have a say in government policy; d. judges and courts are free from political interference; and e. join any organization you like. The five questions are preceded with the following lead statement: "We would like you now to compare the present system of government with the one our country had before the Reform. In each of the following areas, would you say that today things are MUCH BETTER THAN BEFORE, SOMEWHAT BETTER, MUCH THE SAME, SOMEWHAT WORSE, or MUCH WORSE?" Each question yields a five-point scale, ranging from –2 to +2.

44. We adopted list-wise deletion of cases with missing values. As a result, we had to throw out almost two-thirds of the cases. So, this scaled-down sample is no longer

a true representative sample of the population. People with better political knowledge and higher education are overrepresented in this scaled-down sample.

45. The principle of majority rule is not explicitly included in our conceptual formulation. If Arend Lijphart (1984) is correct, then the majoritarian rule is not a first-order principle of Western democracy, or at least it is always qualified by the respect for minority and requirement of consensus.

Chapter Six

Elite Mobility in Post-Reform Rural China

Chih-Jou Jay Chen

INTRODUCTION

China has the world's fastest-growing economy but one of its most unequal societies. Economic reforms since the late 1970s have allowed China to grow at a staggering pace—close to 10 percent a year—but the new wealth has spread unevenly. In June 2005, China's government announced that the income gap had further widened in the first three months of the year, with the most affluent 10 percent of the population controlling 45 percent of the country's wealth, while the poorest 10 percent of the population held little more than 1 percent of the wealth.[1] In particular, the urban-rural cleavage further exacerbates the income gap. In addition to the widening income gap, other measurements of inequality—like concentration of political power and social status—appear to have remained the same, or even increased. In the countryside, the Communist Party–centered power structure, characterized by the dominance of village cadres, has not changed much in the post-reform era. Meanwhile, private entrepreneurs have emerged to form a notable rural elite-group representing a lucrative new occupation that enjoys very large income advantages. The Maoist era of egalitarian collectivism has decidedly come to an end. The trends that show growing disparities in income and power distribution in rural China highlight the significance of studying social change and social differentiation brought about by China's post-1978 economic reforms and consequent transformation.

There are several key questions to ask concerning socioeconomic disparities. The fundamental one is: what are the mechanisms of social mobility—the means by which some in society move ahead? Other questions are, who wields political power and who champions entrepreneurial spirit, and where did they come from?

This study examines the mechanisms and factors that affect rural stratification in post-reform China. It investigates whether the status attainment processes in the Chinese rural reforms have varied over time due to the country's rapid economic development and substantial structural changes. It also explores whether elite mobility varies across regions due to their diverse socioeconomic conditions and institutional environment. Empirically, two questions are posed. First, to what extent do individual and village-level factors affect one's career opportunities (i.e., being a village cadre, private entrepreneur, or a farmer or peasant worker) and do clearly separated career advancement paths exist? Second, what is the relationship between individual characteristics and status attainment across villages? Thus, the contextual sources of the variation are identified and the effects of institutional changes (i.e., privatization and democratization) and structural changes (i.e., industrialization and urbanization) on the mechanisms of status attainment in Chinese villages are examined.

RESEARCH ON THE DYNAMICS OF CHINA'S SOCIAL STRATIFICATION

Over the past decade, rigorous empirical research has been conducted on socioeconomic inequalities and social mobility in China. This research shows both continuity and change in what was once a politicized social mobility regime. However, we still lack convincing answers to long-standing questions and some preliminary answers to more recent ones.

First, despite the fact that the countryside has experienced greater and more profound transformations than urban areas, relatively little research has been conducted on rural China.[2] Of those studies that do deal with rural China, Victor Nee's "market transition theory" has pioneered mainstream sociological research on China's social stratification dynamics. It conceptualizes economic transformation as a shift of resource allocation from state redistribution to market institutions, leading to the decline of political power and the rise of human capital and entrepreneurial abilities.[3] Over the past two decades, the once homogeneous "peasant class" has become socially differentiated, and new rural classes have emerged.[4] Market expansion, the transformation of property rights, and the recently introduced grassroots democracy have deeply transformed the social structure of rural China and thus prompted a closer examination of the stratification of Chinese villages.

Second, much less attention has been paid to elite stratification than to income distribution in contemporary China studies. Income is only one of several scarce resources in a society and only one indirect indicator, rather than the proxy, of power and political position. Occupations in rural China today are more diversified and thus serve as better indicators for the Weberian concept of authority and neo-Marxist concept of control. In a recent survey, Chinese researchers identified and defined eight emerging rural status groups, among which cadres, private entrepreneurs, managers, and petty bourgeois comprise the new elites.[5] In the transformation of postcommunist countries, the liberalization of political markets is no less important than the liberalization of economic markets.[6] Indeed, there are studies that examine the economic returns of political power.[7] Nevertheless, with the exception of recent works by Andrew Walder and his colleagues, little has been done to determine how such elite occupations as cadre posts and entrepreneurial positions are achieved in rural China.[8] Some scholars look forward to seeing market reforms change the political mechanisms of the Chinese Communist regime from a virtuocracy to a meritocracy.[9] Market competition changes the stratification order by rewarding skill and ability rather than rank and authority, and creates a new class of entrepreneurs whose incomes rise relative to administrators and former Party cadres.[10] Meanwhile, the literature also reveals that power and influence persist and generate disproportionate benefits in China's emerging market economy.[11] Walder's study of urban Chinese elites demonstrates that urban China has two distinct career paths that lead to a divided elite. The political path requires both educational and political credentials; the professional path requires educational but not political credentials.[12] As rural China moves away from a planned to a market economy, one question to be addressed is whether dual career paths have emerged, like those existing in urban China.

Third, the ways that contextual factors and regional variations in the extent of institutional change affect stratification mechanisms need to be scrupulously examined. Much existing research on income stratification in China focuses on the individual characteristics that have allowed people to reap more rewards during the reform era.[13] The effects of institutional arrangements on the relationship between individual factors and the stratification order need to be further addressed. Recent studies employ multilevel analysis to examine regional variations in income distribution resulting from economic growth and industrialization.[14] This paper will address these studies by examining elite stratification and emphasizing the contextual effects of key institutional arrangements in Chinese villages.

Institutional analysis is crucial for a better understanding of the dynamics and mechanisms of status attainment in Chinese villages. In addition to addressing how individuals are rewarded according to their individual characteristics, a study of institutional sources of inequality would further explain inequality structures. The same situation prevails if one considers regional heterogeneity in rural China and the new rural electoral institutions. Treating rural China as a homogeneous entity is both methodologically unsound and theoretically wasteful. It is unsound because regional variations in social stratification are obvious and substantial, and it is wasteful because we can take advantage of the regional variation in career determination to test theories that relate stratification order to the progress of institutional changes and industrialization. Regional heterogeneity in rural China is significant and considerable, not only because of the dissimilar pace and degree of economic growth in different parts of the Chinese countryside, but also, and more importantly, because there have been different models of rural reform, all of which lead to industrialization and development.[15] Privatization and local state-led growth characterize the most recent rural transformation in the post-reform era, and these have had significant effects on the stratification mechanism.[16] In addition to variations in economic institutions, regional disparities of grassroots democratization in both degree and kind are partly due to economic development and to a deliberate trial scheme imposed at the outset by the central state.[17] Therefore, contextual variations in industrialization, property rights arrangements, and grassroots political institutions may have clear impacts on stratification mechanisms.

Finally, the impacts of social networks on status attainment in rural China are noteworthy. They have not been tested with survey data, although useful conceptual frameworks and findings have been generated from sophisticated case studies. Based on the Blau-Duncan paradigm, which emphasizes the effects of achieved status (education and prior occupational status) on the ultimate attained status, studies of social stratification attribute individual opportunities for upward mobility to personal resources, namely personal qualifications and their positional power.[18] The research tradition of social networks, in contrast, emphasizes the effects of social capital on attained status. According to Nan Lin's theory, social capital exerts an important influence on attained status because it contains four elements of one's instrumental and expressive actions: information, influence, social credentials, and reinforcement.[19] Applying this proposition to Chinese societies directly relates to the Chinese culture of *guanxi* or interpersonal connections of sentiment and obligation that dictate social interaction, mutual anticipation, and behavioral patterns. While this application of social relations in instrumental actions is not unique to China, it appears that the pervasiveness of *guanxi* as a social fact gives credence to the claim that social relationship occupies a core position in the Chinese way of life far beyond its status elsewhere.[20] More important, the practice of *guanxi* involves not only symmetric economic exchange of transactional rationality, but also asymmetric social exchange of relational rationality. *Guanxi* may serve as the instrumental means to obtain economic or social rewards, but on other occasions, *guanxi* itself becomes the end while instrumental action becomes the means.[21] In postrevolutionary China, the use of *guanxi* in the form of patron-client relations in the workplace has been the chief way in which workers secure resources and opportunities under Party clientelism.[22] *Guanxi* networks, predominantly strong-tie relations, were also found to promote occupational and career opportunities in urban China.[23]

In rural China, kinship networks, one particular type of social network, have been a distinctive and prominent feature in economic institutions and grassroots politics. Martin King Whyte argues that Chinese family patterns and lineage ties may have facilitated economic growth since the 1980s. Chinese familism provided resources under changed and uncertain conditions.[24] In Chinese villages, the bonds and obligations involved in lineage ties become a distinctive kind of social capital available for use by members of the lineage. Yusheng Peng argues that kinship networks facilitate the founding and growth of private enterprises by conferring three types of social capital benefits on private entrepreneurs: the protection of private property rights, the reduction of uncertainty and transaction costs, and the building of better bridges to market information and entrepreneurial opportunities.[25] In grassroots politics, the revived strength of lineage is clearly demonstrated in the village elections that have been institutionalized throughout rural China. A number of case studies reveal that village elections are dominated by sublineage alliances or by prominent lineage groups.[26]

The above overview indicates that scholars have still to address certain outstanding issues of rural status attainment (particularly elite status attainment, as far as social capital and kinship capital are concerned). The institutional arrangements that may affect stratification order in Chinese villages vary because of different degrees and kinds of marketization, property rights transformation, and local state behaviors. Also, Chinese villages are small communities in which local social networks, including kinship networks, have continued to play a key role in both political governance and business activities. As a result, elite stratification defining the occupation of cadre posts and positions as private entrepreneurs would be better explained by considering the effects of social networks in general and kinship networks in particular.

DATA, MEASUREMENT, AND METHOD

The present analysis employs data from a 2002 China Survey, conducted under the auspices of the Comparative Study of Democratization and Value Changes in East Asia (also known as the East Asia Barometer Survey).

The project was launched in the summer of 2000 under the Program for Promoting Academic Excellence of the Universities in Taiwan,[27] under the co-directorship of Professors Fu Hu and Yun-han Chu at National Taiwan University.

The survey used a nationally representative multistage stratified random sample of 3,183 urban and rural individuals (drawing from sixty-seven cities or districts and sixty-two counties), representing China's adult population over eighteen years old residing in family households at the time of the survey. In addition, a village survey was conducted in conjunction with the larger countrywide survey, in which between five and eight villagers were selected and interviewed in each randomly selected village. The village administrations were also approached for assistance in filling out a village survey questionnaire. Among the 3,183 national cases, village-level data are available for 1,202 cases from 214 villages, accounting for 83 percent of the sampled villages across the country. This subsample is a fair representation of the rural population in China. The present analysis employs the individual-level data of this rural subsample and its village-level data.

Villages are important social and economic units in the Chinese countryside. In 2003, there were 678,589 villages across rural China, each with an average of 365 households and an average population of 1,381.[28] Often a village comprises very few lineages and lineage branches, giving rise to extensive social networks and social cohesion. Almost all revenue for investment and welfare must come from the village itself—in the form of levies on villagers and production, rent from factory premises, and the profits of village collective enterprises or real estate. In rich coastal provinces from Jiangsu to Guangdong, many villages now draw their main income from selling or renting out village farmlands for industrial manufacturing. Villagers—in contrast to resident outsiders (such as managers and migrant peasant workers in village enterprises)—are effectively "shareholders" in the resources of the village, although village elites retain the lion's share of benefits. Over the past twenty-five years, the rapid development of rural industry has enabled some villages to get richer than others and has thus produced a new source of stratification among villages. There is significant variation even within the same township, with some villages engaging in nonagricultural activities or selling off village farmland, which is the result of their having enterprising cadres, a good location, infrastructure and transport facilities, or access to funds. Therefore, some villages have been launched into virtuous circles of development while others are trapped in vicious circles. As villagers' well-being and opportunities are strongly linked to the village they belong to, the effect of the village on one's socioeconomic status should be very significant and deserves closer examination.

This study implies multilevel relationships between village context and individual determinants of career opportunities, and the data includes measures at both the individual and contextual level. That is, it implies a relationship not only between a respondent's individual characteristics and his/her career opportunities, but also between the village's sociopolitical characteristics and the impact of individual characteristics on one's career opportunities. The estimation methods must therefore take account of the multilevel hypotheses and data. Multilevel or hierarchical models, which nest one level of data (in this case, individuals) within another level (in this case, villages), are appropriate for testing such hypotheses. Dealing with multilevel data by simply assigning macro-level values to each individual in a village creates statistical problems: it ignores nonindependent errors for individuals within the same village, and heteroscedasticity across villages, and exaggerates the degrees of freedom for village-level variables.[29] These problems bias downward the estimates of standard errors. Multilevel or hierarchical models correct these problems by including a separate error term for the macro-level units, and allow for appropriate tests of significance for macro-level variables.[30]

Dependent Variables

Status attainment is the central theme of this study. *Village cadre* and *private entrepreneur,* the political and economic elites in rural China, are dummy variables for individuals who serve as some kind of village cadre (*cunganbu*), or are involved in business, including being self-employed and owning private firms. Considering the fact that Chinese village cadres are not on state salaries but only on local subsidies, it is quite common for villagers to simultaneously hold more than one job. In this survey, respondents were asked about their "primary occupation." The omitted reference category is farmer and wage employee, including farmers working in local enterprises and outside the village. The survey sample reports that roughly 4 percent of the rural population were serving as village cadres at the time of the survey in 2002, 10 percent were involved in business (*zuo shengyi*) or had established a private business, and the other 86 percent were farmers or peasant workers.

In Chinese villages, village cadres play a key role in villagers' day-to-day life and the village's economic development and social solidarity. No matter whether they are appointed from above or elected from below, cadres continue to wield power in village affairs. The question is, to what extent are village cadres and private entrepreneurs an economic elite; that is, do they make significantly money than the average farmer? The answer can be found in this study's national survey data: the income gaps between village cadres, private entrepreneurs, and farmers are significant. Specifically, the average household income for a private entrepreneur was 10,019 *yuan*, slightly higher than that of village cadres who earned an average household income of 6,967 *yuan*, with farmers lagging far behind with a household income of 6,381 *yuan*.

Individual-Level Measures

Human capital is the most important individual-level independent variable. In previous research, measures of human capital are intended to capture changes introduced by markets in China's transitional economy.[31] For this purpose, the conventional measures of human capital used are education and experience. The literature highlights the particular importance of education for the development of rural industries in China.[32] In this study human capital is measured by the levels of formal schooling and experience. *Primary*, *junior*, and *advanced* are dummy variables for individuals who graduated from primary schools; junior middle schools; and senior middle schools, technical schools, colleges, or universities. Because there were so few cases with education above the senior middle school level, those who had attended technical schools, colleges, or universities were polled together with those who had received senior middle school education. The omitted reference category is the individual who never attended school or failed to graduate from primary school. The *age* of the individual is employed to approximate work experience. *Gender* (1 if male; 0 if female) serves as a control in the analysis. *Father's years of education* of the individual indicates the respondent's family background. *Party membership* is a dummy variable indicating whether an individual is a Party member (1 if yes; 0 if no).

Social capital is conceptualized as "resources embedded in a social structure that are accessed and/or mobilized in purposive actions."[33] These resources are not possessed by individuals but tied to social relations. Social capital theory predicts that having greater access to social capital may enable one to realize status attainment.[34] More specifically, the quantity and quality of social capital are expected to contribute to its value as a means of social mobility. Nan Lin pioneered the usage of the position generator approach to measure social capital.[35] The position generator approach samples a number of hierarchically ranked positions and asks respondents to indicate whether they have contacts in each of the positions. In this study the respondent is asked about eight occupations: primary school teacher, deputy of people's congress, section chief or township mayor, division chief or county magistrate, bureau chief, entrepreneur, lawyer, and bank official. The occupations in this survey questionnaire swing to more prestigious occupations in government and highlight the upper reachability in the position generator approach. Excluding the primary school teacher, which is more commonly reachable, only 18 percent of respondents had contacts with any of the abovementioned occupations. This study employs a dummy variable measured by whether an individual has contact with any of the abovementioned seven prestigious occupations (1 if yes; 0 if no) as indicators of social capital. Since the analysis aims to test the influence of social capital on status attainment, it is important to rule out the possibility of reverse causal link in which social capital is gained by one's occupational position. To ensure that the respondents' access to social capital was available before they acquired any resources, only ties that had been established for more than *five* years were counted.

Kinship capital is a dummy variable measured by whether an individual belongs to the largest lineage branch in the whole village (1 if yes; 0 if no). Empirical studies in rural China document that it is primarily the lineage branch in a village, not the surname group or grand lineage, that serves to provide its members with common vested interests, networks, capital, and assistance. Members of the same lineage branch often establish loyalty networks and, through branch rites and activities, consolidate their identity and have assistance networks.[36]

VILLAGE-LEVEL MEASURES OF INSTITUTIONAL ENVIRONMENT

In addition to the above set of individual-level variables, there are contextual variables indicating economic development and the institutional environment. The core question that motivates the analysis is whether the relative net returns from education, Party membership, social capital, and kinship capital vary by the level of economic development or in qualitatively different types of local institutional arrangements.

The following village-level measures are drawn from the village survey to indicate the extent of a village's economic development and industrialization. *Industrialization and commercialization* is a dummy variable, gauging the structural change that defines economic development in a village by reference to the most important sector (agriculture, industry, and tertiary industry) in the village economy (1 if industry or tertiary industry; 0 if agriculture). The survey shows that 14 percent of villages report that their most important sector is industry or tertiary industry. *Requisitioning of farmland* is also a dummy variable that specifies whether the village's farmland was ever requisitioned by the state over the past ten years. This is an index to show the intervening role of the local state in the structural change of local development. The village survey shows that farmland had been requisitioned in 30 percent of villages.

To assess the property rights arrangements in a village, *private enterprise output* gauges the relative importance of the private sector in the village. It is defined as the proportion of output contributed by individual and private enterprises. The lowest value is 0; the highest is 1. The average village derives 29 percent of its village output from individual or private production.

In addition to measures of village economic context, this study also examines the contextual effects brought about by political and social institutions. *Democratization* measures the institutionalization of grassroots democracy. It is a count variable (ranging from 0 to 7) defined as how many times the village committee members, including the village chief, have been directly elected by villagers. A village's experience in handling its village committee election is presumed to serve as a good indicator of village-level political reform. The average number of elections per village in this study is just under four.

Urban proximity is the variable that purports to measure the extent of the market in the area. It is defined as the distance from the village to the neighboring county town. The average distance between a village and its nearest county town is forty-three kilometers.

Farmland per capita indicates the amount of arable land usable by peasants. This may affect one's choice of staying in agriculture or seeking outside employment.

STATISTICAL MODELS AND RESULTS

After excluding observations whose information is missing on any of the variables used in the analysis, the working sample consists of 870 individuals in 196 villages. The deleted cases are mostly missing data on the respondent's individual occupation, or his/her village-level variables. A further analysis with missing data was employed: from EM (expectation-maximization) estimated statistics, the null hypothesis of MCAR (missing completely at random) cannot be rejected, indicating that the data were missing completely at random.

Statistical Models

Hierarchical multinomial regression analyses are employed to test hypotheses, drawing from hierarchical generalized linear models (HGLMs).[37] The models use "farmers" (including farmers and peasant workers) as the reference category for the dependent variable in the multinomial logistic regressions, thus contrasting those who are village cadres with those who are farmers, and those who are private entrepreneurs with those who are farmers. This study hypothesizes that individual- and village-level variables that predict being a village cadre are somewhat different from those that predict entering private entrepreneurship.

HGLMs use the logit link function when the level-1 sampling model is multinomial. Define η_{mij} as the log-odds of falling into category m relative to that of falling into category M. Specifically,

$$\eta_{mij} = \log\,[\psi_{mij}/\psi_{Mij}]$$

Where

$$\phi_{Mij} = 1 - \sum_{m=1}^{M-1} \phi_{mij}$$

In words, η_{mij} is the log odds of being in m-th category to M-th category, which is known as the "reference category." In the present study, η_{1ij} is the log odds of being in the "village cadres" category relative to the third category, "farmers or peasant workers." Similarly, η_{2ij} is the log odds of the "private entrepreneurs" category relative to the third category, "farmers or peasant workers."

At the individual level, father's years of education, male, age, primary school, junior middle school, advanced schooling, Party membership, social capital, and kinship capital are used as predictors, so that η_{mij} can be written as

$$\begin{aligned}\eta_{mij} = {} & \beta_{0j(m)} + \beta_{1j(m)*}\,(\text{Father's years of education})_{ij} + \beta_{2j(m)*}\,(\text{Male})_{ij} + \beta_{3j(m)*}\,(\text{Age})_{ij} \\ & + \beta_{4j(m)*}\,(\text{Primary school})_{ij} + \beta_{5j(m)*}\,(\text{Junior middle school})_{ij} \\ & + \beta_{6j(m)*}\,(\text{Advanced schooling})_{ij} + \beta_{7j(m)*}\,(\text{Party membership})_{ij} \\ & + \beta_{8j(m)*}\,(\text{Social capital})_{ij} + \beta_{9j(m)*}\,(\text{Kinship capital})_{ij}\end{aligned}$$

for m = 1,2. For this example, with M = 3, there would be two level-1 equations, for η_{1ij} and η_{2ij}.

At the village level, industrialization and commercialization, democratization, private output, farmland per capita, urban proximity, and requisitioning of farmland are used as predictors. The level-2 model has a parallel form like the individual-level models.

Furthermore, this study allows these intercepts to vary randomly, even after controlling for other variables. It constrains all other level-1 coefficients to be fixed for the sake of parsimony and computational stability. These level-1 predictors, such as "father's education" and "age," have been centered on their group means. The level-2 predictors, such as "democratization," "private output," "farmland per capita," and "urban proximity," have been centered on their grand means.

Results

Table 6.1 shows the individual- and village-level characteristics of the general sample. Table 6.2 further shows the characteristics of three occupation groups: village cadre, private entrepreneur, and farmer or peasant worker. ANOVA tests, Kruskal-Wallis tests, or Chi-square tests are employed for different variables to see if there is any significant difference in the characteristics among the three status groups. For individual-level characteristics, there is no statistically significant difference in family background (indicated

Table 6.1. Mean and Standard Deviation of Sample Villagers and Villages, 2002

	Mean	*S.D.*
Individual-level variables (N = 870)		
Father's years of education	2.35	3.21
Male	0.51	0.50
Age	43.72	12.52
Education		
Under primary school	0.43	0.49
Primary school	0.27	0.45
Junior middle school	0.24	0.43
Advanced schooling	0.06	0.24
Party membership	0.11	0.31
Occupation		
Village cadre	0.04	0.19
Private entrepreneur	0.10	0.29
Farmer/peasant worker	0.86	0.34
Social capital	0.18	0.39
Kinship capital	0.21	0.41
Village-level variables (N = 196)		
Industrialization and commercialization	0.14	0.35
Democratization	3.85	1.92
Private enterprise output	0.29	0.42
Farmland per capita	1.28	1.09
Urban proximity	42.90	32.24
Requisitioning of farmland	0.30	0.46

Table 6.2. Descriptive Statistics of Chinese Rural Elites, 2002 (Percentage/Mean)

	Village Cadre (n = 33)	*Private Entrepreneur (n = 83)*	*Farmers/Peasant Workers (n = 754)*	*Total (n = 870)*	*Test*
Individual-level variables					
Father's education	2.73	2.36	2.33	2.35	ANOVA = 0.241
Male	73	70	48	51	Chi-squarc = 21.5***
Age	45	39	44	44	K-W test = 15.5***
Education					Chi-square = 52.2***
Under primary school	30	27	45	43	
Primary school	12	18	29	27	
Junior middle school	36	47	21	24	
Advanced schooling	21	8	5	6	
Party membership	49	12	9	11	Chi-square = 50.4***
Social capital	42	28	16	18	Chi-square = 19.7***
Kinship capital	33	17	22	22	Chi-square = 3.8
Village-level variables					
Industrialization & commercialization	9	34	10	12	Chi-square = 39.1***
Democratization	4.94	3.31	3.89	3.88	ANOVA = 8.56***
Private output	.20	.46	.26	.28	K-W test = 19.2***
Farmland per capita	1.29	1.01	1.33	1.30	ANOVA = 3.4*
Distance to nearest county town	37	32	46	44	ANOVA = 6.7***
Requisitioning of farmland	27	64	25	29	Chi-square = 53.9***

by father's education) and kinship capital among three occupation groups. Statistically significant relations appear in such characteristics as gender, education, Party membership, and social capital. Compared with ordinary peasants (i.e., farmers and peasant workers), more village cadres are male (73 versus 48 percent), better educated (57 percent attending junior middle school or higher versus 26 percent attending junior middle school or higher), Party members (49 versus 9 percent), and possess more social capital (42 percent having contacts with prestigious occupations versus 16 percent for peasants). Similarly, differences in the abovementioned characteristics between private entrepreneurs and ordinary peasants (i.e., farmers and peasant workers) also exist. For village-level characteristics, in comparison with ordinary peasants, private entrepreneurs come from villages that are more industry- and commerce-based (34 versus 10 percent), democratized (3.31 versus 3.89 times), private-sector dominated (46 versus 26 percent), closer to a county town (32 versus 46 kilometers), and that have had farmland requisitioned (64 versus 25 percent).

In table 6.3, the intercept of the village cadre is the expected log odds of a villager being a village cadre relative to being a "farmer or peasant worker," holding all other variables constant and a random effect of zero. It is adjusted for the between-village heterogeneity in the likelihood of being a village cadre relative to being a "farmer or peasant worker." The estimated conditional expected log-odds is −4.86.

The predicted probability that the same villager responds as being a village cadre is exp{-5.27}/(1 + exp{-5.27} + exp{-4.15}) = 0.005. The predicted probability that the same villager gives a private entrepreneur response is exp{-4.15}/(1 + exp{-5.27} + exp{-4.15}) = 0.015. Thus, the predicted probability of a farmer or peasant worker response for the same villager is 1 − 0.005 − 0.015 = 0.98.

The individual-level effects associated with heightened odds of becoming a village cadre (relative to a farmer or peasant worker) include being male, having advanced schooling (relative to under primary school), being a Party member, possessing social capital, and holding kinship capital (all $p < 0.05$).

To be specific, the odds of a male becoming a village cadre rather than a farmer or peasant worker are {0.96} = 2.61 times greater (increase about 161 percent) than for a female, controlling for other variables. The odds of a villager who attended senior high school or above becoming a village cadre rather than a farmer or peasant worker are exp{1.43} = 4.18 times greater (increase about 318 percent) than those of one who did not finish primary school, controlling for other variables. The odds of a Party member becoming a village cadre rather than a farmer or peasant worker are exp{1.81} = 6.11 times greater (increase about 511 percent) than those of a non-Party member, controlling for other variables. The odds of a villager with social capital becoming a village cadre rather than a farmer or peasant worker are $\exp\{1.01\} = 2.75$ times greater (increase about 175 percent) than those of one who lacks social capital, controlling for other variables. The odds of a villager with kinship capital becoming a village cadre rather than a farmer or peasant worker are $\exp\{0.98\} = 2.66$ times greater (increase about 166 percent) than the odds of one who lacks kinship capital, controlling for other variables.

In predicting the odds of becoming a private entrepreneur (relative to a farmer or peasant worker), each of the corresponding coefficients is smaller and only gender, age, and junior middle schooling have coefficients that are significantly different from zero. The individual-level effects are found to be associated with negative heightened odds in age ($p < 0.01$). Those who are male or attended junior middle school (relative to having no primary schooling) may have heightened odds of becoming a private entrepreneur (both $p < 0.01$) rather than a farmer or peasant worker.

The odds of a male becoming a private entrepreneur rather than a farmer or peasant worker are $\exp\{0.91\} = 2.48$ times greater (increase about 148 percent) than those of a female, controlling for other variables. The odds of a villager who attended junior middle school becoming a private entrepreneur rather than a farmer or peasant worker are $\exp\{1.01\} = 2.75$ times greater (increase about 175 percent) than one who did not finish primary school, controlling for other variables. The odds of becoming a private entrepreneur rather than a farmer or peasant worker are multiplied by $\exp\{-0.04\} = 0.96$ (decrease about 4 percent) with each one-year increase in age, controlling for other variables.

Switching to the village level, controlling for individual-level variables, despite a slight and small effect of urban proximity, the only village characteristic associated with being a village cadre (versus being a farmer or peasant worker) is the village's level of democratization. An average villager who lives in a village with more institutionalized village committee elections is more likely to become a village cadre than a counterpart who lives in a village with less experience of village committee elections. In these latter villages, becoming a village cadre is only associated with particular individual characteristics such as Party membership, social capital, and kinship capital.

As for predicting the odds of becoming a private entrepreneur (relative to a farmer or peasant worker), village-level effects associated with heightened odds include "industrialization and commercialization" and "requisitioning of farmland" (both $p < 0.01$). The odds of someone living in an industry-based or commerce-based village becoming a private entrepreneur rather than a farmer or peasant worker are $\exp\{1.11\} = 3.03$ times greater (increase about 203 percent) than those of someone living in an agriculture-based village,

Table 6.3. Multinomial Multilevel Model

	Village Cadres		*Private Entrepreneurs*	
	Coefficient	*P-value*	*Coefficient*	*P-value*
Village-level variables				
Industrialization and commercialization	−0.46	0.56	1.11**	0.01
Democratization	0.33**	0.01	−0.05	0.52
Private enterprise output	−0.48	0.42	0.51	0.16
Farmland per capita	−0.11	0.64	0.12	0.48
Urban proximity	−0.01	0.33	−0.01	0.11
Requisitioning of farmland	−0.12	0.81	1.35***	0.00
Individual-level variables				
Father's education	−0.08	0.32	−0.07	0.17
Male	0.96*	0.03	0.91**	0.01
Age	0.01	0.69	−0.04**	0.01
Education (under primary school as reference group)				
Primary school	−0.55	0.40	−0.11	0.79
Junior middle school	0.85	0.12	1.01**	0.01
Advanced schooling	1.43*	0.03	0.57	0.30
Party membership	1.81***	0.00	−0.11	0.81
Social capital	1.01*	0.02	0.35	0.30
Kinship capital	0.98*	0.04	−0.19	0.60
Intercept	−5.27***	0.00	−4.15***	0.00

Note: The outcome variable is: (1) village cadres; (2) private entrepreneurs; and (3) farmers or peasant workers (the reference group).
* $p < 0.05$ ** $p < 0.01$ *** $p < 0.001$.

controlling for other variables. The odds of someone living in a village that has had its farmland requisitioned by the government becoming a private entrepreneur rather than a farmer or peasant worker are $\exp\{1.35\} = 3.86$ times greater (increase about 286 percent) than those of one who lives in a village whose farmland has never been requisitioned, controlling for other variables.

DISCUSSIONS AND CONCLUSIONS

This study provides new and convincing evidence on the status attainment of political and economic elites in post-reform rural China. Using intervillage variations in economic structure and institutional arrangements and measurements of social capital and kinship capital, it has achieved significant findings that have important theoretical implications. This study shows that dual career paths exist for rural elite positions, and that political and educational credentials are screened differently for entry into cadre posts and into entrepreneurial positions. Party membership, which is a prerequisite for holding administrative posts in the urban state apparatus, also remains a fundamental determinant for cadre posts in villages. Political screening is still the key filter in recruiting village leaders. Educational credentials are paramount for achieving both cadre posts and entrepreneurial positions. In this respect, the results correlate with Walder's research in urban China, which finds two paths to urban elite status: one emphasizing educational credentials leading to high prestige professional positions, and the other emphasizing a combination of Party and educational credentials leading to administrative posts within the government.[38] In a later study, Walder and his colleagues add that a college education did not become a criterion for administrative positions until the post-Mao period.[39] The present analysis of rural China also finds that there are two distinct paths into political and economic elite groups: Party loyalty and meritocratic principles.

In addition, this study examines the effects of social networks and kinship support, linking these factors to the fundamental institutions governing status attainment in Chinese society. The enduring, essential impact of political credentials on administrative career may reflect the fact that state socialist practices are still alive, and have not been eroded by the expanding market economy as some theorists have predicted. At the same time, the political payoff of social capital and kinship networks further shows the forces of local institutions in driving stratification in rural China. For a Chinese villager pursuing a cadre post today, the effects of political capital increase notably when it is combined with social capital and kinship capital in addition to human capital. Being equipped with contacts in politics and business outside the village, and having been born into a dominant lineage branch inside the village, boost one's chance of achieving a cadre post. This study demonstrates that the attainment of rural cadre positions is closely related to five aspects: gender, human capital, political capital, kinship capital, and social capital.

The significant effects of social capital and kinship networks on achieving cadre posts may be an unintended consequence of the introduction of village elections in the 1990s. In contrast to the previous practice of village cadres being appointed from above within the Party, village cadres, including the Party branch secretary, are now selected through popular elections. As a result, the ability to mobilize majority support among ordinary villagers is more crucial now in order to become a village cadre. This explains why social capital and kinship networks play a major role in today's village politics. This trend actually reflects a return to generic familism and clanism practices in rural China that were rejected during the Mao years.

In contrast to the path to a village cadre post, the path to private entrepreneurship is quite different. Political, social, and kinship capital lose ground to human capital, which plays a determining role when it comes to entry into entrepreneurship. Formal schooling facilitates the development of management skills and widens the horizons of entrepreneurs. The present study finds that the typical private entrepreneur tends to be male, younger, and with a better than average education.

The insignificant effect of social capital and kinship capital on a villager's likelihood of becoming an entrepreneur deserves further discussion and exploration in later research. Anecdotal evidence indicates the importance of *guanxi* in doing business in China. The findings here do not necessarily contradict the thesis that business performance is closely related to the entrepreneur's social capital. The message here is that a villager's initial action of becoming a private entrepreneur (rather than his/her subsequent performance) may not be affected by his/her deposit of social capital at the time of entering the business. What matters for becoming a private entrepreneur is one's human capital, sex, age, and, more important, the macro-market environment in which he/she is situated.

Two village-level factors—the degree of industrialization and commercialization and the existence of a developmental local state—are found to have significant effects on one's likelihood of becoming an entrepreneur. Other things being equal, the more industrialized or commercialized a village is, the more likely its villagers are to become private entrepreneurs. Again, a history of the village's farmlands being requisitioned by the local state significantly increases the likelihood of its villagers becoming private entrepreneurs. This finding is in line with Nee's market transition theory, which argues that the shift from plan to market changes the stratification order of society.[40]

From a nationwide survey in rural China in 1989–1990, Nee finds that only in the inland provinces does political capital (measured by holding former cadre positions) increase the odds of entering into entrepreneurship; political capital has no significant effect in the coastal provinces which are presumed to be more industrialized and commercialized. Rather than relying on indirect and proxy indicators of market institutions, the present study employs a much more direct measurement to tackle the "market transition" issue. It measures the village's degree of industrialization and commercialization to gauge the extent to which individuals are influenced by the market mechanism. It finds that the main factors contributing to an individual becoming an entrepreneur are the individual's human capital and the market institutions of his/her village. Political capital, social capital, and kinship capital are hard to convert into significant and helpful forces in the entrepreneurial career path, in contrast to their significant advantages in advancing one's career in village administration.

In conclusion, in terms of stratification order, post-reform rural China cannot be simply characterized as moving along a one-dimensional road from a redistributive institution to a market or capitalist institution. The distinct paths of status attainment for political and economic elites in Chinese villages are products of the workings of distinctive political, social, and economic institutions. This highlights the fact that post-reform rural China has qualitatively unique features that merit study more from the point of view of institutional specificity. In addition to market institutions, some particular institutional arrangements—such as property rights, urbanization, grassroots democratization, social networks, and clanism—have played a role in the dynamic stratification mechanism in rural China. It remains to be seen whether these institutional arrangements will decline, persist, or transform and significantly impact on Chinese society.

NOTES

1. "Income Gap in China Widens in First Quarter," 2005, *Xinhua*, June 20, 2005, http://news.xinhuanet.com/english/2005-06/20/content_3107515.htm.

2. For a comprehensive review of the literature on Chinese social stratification and social mobility, see Yanjie Bian, 2002, "Chinese Social Stratification and Social Mobility," *Annual Review of Sociology*, Vol. 28, pp. 91–116; and Yanjie Bian, 2003, "Sociological Research on Reform-Era China," *Issues & Studies*, Vol. 38, No. 4/ Vol. 39, No. 1, pp. 139–174.

3. Victor Nee, 1989, "A Theory of Market Transition: From Redistribution to Markets in State Socialism," *American Sociological Review*, Vol. 54, No. 5, pp. 663–681; Victor Nee, 1996, "The Emergence of a Market Society: Changing Mechanisms of Stratification in China," *American Journal of Sociology*, Vol. 101, No. 4, pp. 908–949; and Yang Cao and Victor Nee, 2000, "Comment: Controversies and Evidence in the Market Transition Debate," *American Journal of Sociology*, Vol. 105, No. 4, pp. 1175–1189.

4. For the once homogeneous "peasant class," see William L. Parish, 1975, "Socialism and the Chinese Peasant Family," *Journal of Asian Studies*, Vol. 34, No. 3, pp. 613–630.

5. The eight rural status groups are: (1) village administrators (i.e., village cadres), (2) private entrepreneurs, (3) managers of township and village enterprises, (4) self-employed laborers and individual merchants, (5) rural intellectuals and professionals, (6) peasant workers, (7) wage laborers, and (8) farmers. See Lu Xueyi, 2002, *Dangdai Zhongguo shehui jieceng yanjiu baogao* (a research report on social stratification of contemporary China), Beijing: Shehui kexue wenxian chubanshe, p. 178.

6. William L. Parish and Ethan Michelson, 1996, "Politics and Markets: Dual Transformations," *American Journal of Sociology*, Vol. 101, No. 4, pp. 1042–1059.

7. See, for example, Yang Cao and Victor Nee, 2000, "Comment: Controversies and Evidence in the Market Transition Debate," *American Journal of Sociology*, Vol. 105, No. 4, pp. 1175–1189; and Andrew G. Walder, 2002, "Income Determination and Market Opportunity in Rural China, 1978–1996," *Journal of Comparative Economics*, Vol. 30, No. 2, pp. 354–375.

8. For studies of career mobility in urban China, see Andrew G. Walder, 1995, "Career Mobility and the Communist Political Order," *American Sociological Review*, Vol. 60, No. 3, pp. 309–328; and Andrew G. Walder, Bobai Li, and Donald J. Treiman, 2000, "Politics and Life Chances in a State Socialist Regime: Dual Career Paths into the Urban Chinese Elite, 1949 to 1996," *American Sociological Review*, Vol. 65, No. 2, pp. 191–209. One of the few works on elite mobility in rural China is Andrew G. Walder, 2002, "Privatization and Elite Mobility: Rural China, 1979–1996" (Working Paper, Asia/Pacific Research Center, Stanford University, July 2002).

9. Susan L. Shirk, 1984, "The Evolution of Chinese Education: Stratification and Meritocracy in the 1980s," in Norton Ginsburg and Bernard A. Lalor (eds.), *China: The 80s Era*, Boulder, Colo.: Westview Press, pp. 245–272; and Hong Yung Lee, 1991, *From Revolutionary Cadres to Party Technocrats in Socialist China*, Berkeley: University of California Press.

10. Victor Nee, 1989, "A Theory of Market Transition: From Redistribution to Markets in State Socialism," *American Sociological Review*, Vol. 54, No. 5, pp. 663–681; Victor Nee, 1996, "The Emergence of a Market Society: Changing Mechanisms of Stratification in China," *American Journal of Sociology*, Vol. 101, No. 4, pp. 908–949.

11. Yanjie Bian and John R. Logan, 1996, "Market Transition and the Persistence of Power: The Changing Stratification System in Urban China," *American Sociological Review*, Vol. 61, No. 5, pp. 739–758; and Xueguang Zhou, 2000, "Economic Transformation and Income Inequality in Urban China: Evidence from Panel Data," *American Journal of Sociology*, Vol. 105, No. 4, pp. 1135–1174.

12. Andrew G. Walder, 1995, "Career Mobility and the Communist Political Order,",*American Sociological Review*, Vol. 60, No. 3, p. 309; and Andrew G. Walder, Bobai Li, and Donald J. Treiman, 2000, "Politics and Life Chances in a State Socialist Regime: Dual Career Paths into the Urban Chinese Elite, 1949 to 1996," *American Sociological Review*, Vol. 65, No. 2, p. 191.

13. For example, see Victor Nee, 1989, "A Theory of Market Transition: From Redistribution to Markets in State Socialism," *American Sociological Review*, Vol. 54, No. 5, pp. 663–681; Victor Nee, 1991, "Social Inequalities in Reforming State Socialism: Between Redistribution and Markets in China," *American Sociological Review*, Vol. 56, No. 3, pp. 267–282; Yusheng Peng, 1992, "Wage Determination in Rural and Urban China: A Comparison of Public and Private Industrial Sectors," *American Sociological Review*, Vol. 57, No. 2, pp. 198–213; Yanjie Bian and John R. Logan, 1996, "Market Transition and the Persistence of Power: The Changing Stratification System in Urban China," *American Sociological Review*, Vol. 61, No. 5,

pp. 739–758; and Nan Lin and Yanjie Bian, 1991, "Getting Ahead in Urban China," *American Journal of Sociology*, Vol. 97, No. 3, pp. 657–688.

14. Yu Xie and Emily Hannum, 1996, "Regional Variation in Earnings Inequality in Reform-Era Urban China (in Symposium on Market Transition)," *American Journal of Sociology*, Vol. 101, No. 4, pp. 950–992; Victor Nee, 1996, "The Emergence of a Market Society: Changing Mechanisms of Stratification in China," *American Journal of Sociology*, Vol. 101, No. 4, pp. 908–949; Andrew G. Walder, 2002, "Income Determination and Market Opportunity in Rural China, 1978–1996," *Journal of Comparative Economics*, Vol. 30, No. 2, pp. 354–375; and Yanjie Bian and Zhanxin Zhang, 2002, "Marketization and Income Distribution in Urban China, 1988 and 1995," in Kevin T. Leicht (ed.), *The Future of Market Transition*, Stamford, Conn.: JAI Press, pp.377–415.

15. William A. Byrd and Qingsong Lin (ed.), 1990, *China's Rural Industry: Structure, Development, and Reform*, Oxford: Oxford University Press; Chih-jou Jay Chen, 2004, *Transforming Rural China: How Local Institutions Shape Property Rights in China*, London: Routledge/Curzon; Kellee S. Tsai, 2002, *Back-Alley Banking: Private Entrepreneurs in China*, Ithaca, N.Y.: Cornell University Press, pp. 254–265; and Jean C. Oi and Andrew G. Walder (eds.), 1999, *Property Rights and Economic Reform in China*, Stanford, Calif.: Stanford University Press.

16. Jean C. Oi, 1999, "Two Decades of Rural Reform in China: An Overview and Assessment," Special Issue: The People's Republic of China after 50 Years, *The China Quarterly*, No. 159, pp. 616–628.

17. Kevin J. O'Brien, 2001, "Villagers, Elections, and Citizenship in Contemporary China," *Modern China*, Vol. 27, No. 4, pp. 407–435; and Tianjian Shi, 1999, "Economic Development and Election in Rural China," *Journal of Contemporary China*, Vol. 8, No. 22, pp. 425–442.

18. Peter M. Blau and Otis D. Duncan, 1967, *The American Occupational Structure*, New York: Free Press.

19. Nan Lin, 2001, *Social Capital: A Theory of Social Structure and Action*, New York: Cambridge University Press, p. 20.

20. Fei Xiaotong, 1992, "Guanyu xiangzhen fazhan de sikao" (Pondering the development of villages and townships), *Beijing daxue xuebao* (Beijing University Journal), No.1, pp. 89–97; and Yanjie Bian, 1994, "*Guanxi* and the Allocation of Urban Jobs in China," *The China Quarterly*, No. 140, pp. 971–999; and Thomas B. Gold, Doug Guthrie, and David Wank, 2002, "An Introduction to the Study of *Guanxi*," in Thomas B. Gold, Doug Guthrie, and David Wank (ed.), *Social Connections in China: Institutions, Culture, and the Changing Nature of Guanxi*, Cambridge: Cambridge University Press, pp. 3–20.

21. Nan Lin, 2001, "*Guanxi*: A Conceptual Analysis," in Alvin Y. So, Nan Lin, and Dudley Poston (ed.), *The Chinese Triangle of Mainland China, Taiwan, and Hong Kong: Comparative and Institutional Analysis*, Westport, Conn.: Greenwood, pp. 153–66.

22. Andrew G. Walder, 1986, *Communist Neo-Traditionalism: Work and Authority in Chinese Industry*, Berkeley: University of California Press; and David Wank, 2002, "Business-State Clientelism in China," in Thomas B. Gold, Doug Guthrie,

and David Wank (ed.), *Social Connections in China: Institutions, Culture, and the Changing Nature of Guanxi*, Cambridge: Cambridge University Press, pp. 97–115.

23. Yanjie Bian, 1997, "Bringing Strong Ties Back in: Indirect Ties, Network Bridges, and Job Searches in China," *American Sociological Review*, Vol. 62, No. 3, pp. 366–385.

24. Martin King Whyte, 1995, "The Social Roots of China's Economic Development," Special Issue: China's Transitional Economy, *The China Quarterly*, No. 144, pp. 999–1019.

25. Yusheng Peng, 2004, "Kinship Networks and Entrepreneurs in China's Transitional Economy," *American Journal of Sociology*, Vol. 109, No. 5, pp. 1045–1074. For an in-depth case study on kinship networks and private entrepreneurs in southern Fujian, see Chih-jou Jay Chen, 1999, "Local Institutions and the Transformation of Property Rights in Southern Fujian," in Jean C. Oi and Andrew G. Walder (ed.), *Property Rights and Economic Reform in China*, Stanford, Calif.: Stanford University Press, pp. 49–70.

26. Xiao Tangbiao, *Cun zhi zhong de zongzu: dui jiuge cun de diaocha yu yanjiu* (Lineage in the village administration: a survey and research in nine villages) (Shanghai: Shanghai shudian chubanshe, 2001); Xiao Tangbiao, *Zongzu, xiangcun quanli yu xuanju: dui Jiangxisheng shierge cunweihui xuanju de guancha yanjiu* (Clans, village power, and elections: a study of twelve villager committee elections in Jiangxi Province) (Xi'an: Xibei daxue chubanshe, 2002); Gregory A. Ruf, *Cadres and Kin: Making a Socialist Village in West China, 1921–1991* (Stanford, Calif.: Stanford University Press, 1998); and Chen, *Transforming Rural China*, 173–177.

27. This program was jointly sponsored by the ROC Ministry of Education and the National Science Council.

28. Calculated from *Zhongguo tongji nianjian 2004* (China statistical yearbook 2004), Beijing: Zhongguo tongji chubanshe.

29. Guang Guo and Hongxin Zhao, 2000, "Multilevel Modeling for Binary Data," *Annual Review of Sociology*, Vol. 26, pp. 441–462.

30. Ita Kreft and Jan de Leeuw, 1998, "Introducing Multilevel Modeling," in Michèle Lamont and Marcel Fournier Lamont (ed.), London: Sage; and Stephen W. Raudenbush and Anthony S. Bryk, 2002, "*Hierarchical Linear Models: Applications and Data Analysis Methods,*" Thousand Oaks, Calif.: Sage.

31. Victor Nee, 1989, "A Theory of Market Transition: From Redistribution to Markets in State Socialism," *American Sociological Review*, Vol. 54, No. 5, pp. 663–681; Victor Nee, 1996, "The Emergence of a Market Society: Changing Mechanisms of Stratification in China," *American Journal of Sociology*, Vol. 101, No. 4, pp. 908–949; and Yu Xie and Emily Hannum, 1996, "Regional Variation in Earnings Inequality in Reform-Era Urban China (in Symposium on Market Transition)," *American Journal of Sociology*, Vol. 101, No. 4, pp. 950–992.

32. See, for example, Samuel P. S. Ho, 1994, *Rural China in Transition: Non-Agricultural Development in Rural Jiangsu, 1978–1990*, New York: Oxford University Press, pp. 195, 206; and Jati K. Sengupta and Bo Q. Lin, 1993, "Recent Rural Growth in China: The Performance of the Rural Small-Scale Enterprises, 1980-86," *International Review of Applied Economics*, Vol. 7, No. 2, pp. 177–196.

33. Nan Lin, 2001, *Social Capital: A Theory of Social Structure and Action*, New York: Cambridge University Press, p. 29.

34. Ibid.; Chih-Jou Jay Chen, 2009, "The Distribution and Return of Social Capital in Taiwan," in Ray-May Hsung, Nan Lin, and Ronald L. Breiger (ed.), *Contexts of Social Capital: Social Networks in Communities, Markets and Organizations*, London: Routledge/Curzon, pp.193–215.

35. Nan Lin and Mary Dumin, 1986, "Access to Occupations through Social Ties," *Social Networks*, Vol. 8, pp. 365–385.

36. Anita Chan, Richard Madsen, and Jonathan Unger, 1992, *Chen Village under Mao and Deng*, (expanded and updated edition), Berkeley: University of California Press; Chih-jou Jay Chen, 1999, "Local Institutions and the Transformation of Property Rights in Southern Fujian," in Jean C. Oi and Andrew G. Walder (ed.), *Property Rights and Economic Reform in China*, Stanford, Calif.: Stanford University Press, pp. 61–67; and Chih-jou Jay Chen, 2004, *Transforming Rural China: How Local Institutions Shape Property Rights in China*, London: Routledge/Curzon, pp. 172–177.

37. Stephen W. Raudenbush and Anthony S. Bryk, 2002, "*Hierarchical Linear Models: Applications and Data Analysis Methods*," Thousand Oaks, Calif.: Sage, p. 291.

38. Andrew G. Walder, 1995, "Career Mobility and the Communist Political Order," *American Sociological Review*, Vol. 60, No. 3, p. 309.

39. Andrew G. Walder, Bobai Li, and Donald J. Treiman, 2000, "Politics and Life Chances in a State Socialist Regime: Dual Career Paths into the Urban Chinese Elite, 1949 to 1996," *American Sociological Review*, Vol. 65, No. 2, p. 191.

40. Victor Nee, 1989, "A Theory of Market Transition: From Redistribution to Markets in State Socialism," *American Sociological Review*, Vol. 54, No. 5, p. 663; and Victor Nee, 1996, "The Emergence of a Market Society: Changing Mechanisms of Stratification in China," *American Journal of Sociology*, Vol. 101, No. 4, p. 908.

Chapter Seven

Contracting and Dispute Resolution among Chinese Firms: Law and Its Substitutes

Susan H. Whiting

INTRODUCTION

Litigation of contract disputes in China has increased markedly since the initiation of economic reform three decades ago. Yet, the decision of firms to enter the court system is surprising, given the widely accepted views of Chinese courts as handmaidens of party-state officials and of Chinese citizens and firms as nonlitigious. This chapter analyzes the contracting practices and choice of dispute-resolution mechanisms on the part of Chinese firms in the domestic political economy. It explores the hypothesis that, in the rapidly changing context of China's transition from socialism, both the informal networks in which firms are embedded and the bureaucratic structures by which firms are governed fail to provide adequate information and sanctions for the resolution of disputes, making the courts an increasingly important element in the process of dispute resolution. Indeed, despite the emphasis of the party state on mediation and arbitration and the establishment of an array of new institutions for these purposes, litigation increased at an average annual rate of 24 percent per year during the 1980s and 1990s, before leveling off in the 2000s.[1]

In theory, courts, as neutral third-party arbiters of disputes, become increasingly important as the volume of arms-length market transactions in the economy increases. This research explores the changing role of the courts in the Chinese political economy in order to evaluate this claim. In 1996, Chinese Communist Party (CCP) General Secretary Jiang Zemin called for China to build a "socialist rule of law state," and in 1999, the constitution was amended to assert that "The People's Republic of China exercises the rule of law, building a socialist country governed according to law." Thus, litigation increased simultaneously with an ambitious political initiative to promote legal development.

Table 7.1. Cases Accepted by Courts of First Instance

	Economic	*Civil*	*Administrative*	*Criminal*
1983	44,080	756,436		
1984	85,796	838,307		
1985	226,695	846,391		
1986	322,153	989,409		299,720
1987	366,456	1,213,219	5,240	289,614
1988	508,965	1,455,130	8,573	313,306
1989	690,765	1,815,385	9,934	392,564
1990	588,143	1,851,897	13,006	459,656
1991	563,260	1,880,635	25,667	427,840
1992	652,150	1,948,786	27,125	422,991
1993	894,410	2,089,257	27,911	403,267
1994	1,053,701	2,383,764	35,083	482,927
1995	1,278,806	2,718,533	52,596	495,741
1996	1,519,793	3,093,995	79,966	618,826
1997	1,483,356	3,277,572	90,557	436,894
1998	1,455,215	3,375,069	98,463	482,164
1999	1,535,613	3,519,244	97,569	540,008
2000	1,297,843	3,412,259	85,760	560,432
2001	1,155,992	3,459,025	100,921	628,996
Avg growth	18.8	8.3	21.8	4.7

Sources: *Quanguo renming fayuan sifa tongji lishi ziliao huibian 1949-1998 (Mingshi bufen)*, 2000 (Beijing: renming fayuan chubanshe; Zhongguo falu nianjian), various years.

Note: while 2002 data is available, the revision of the Contract Law in 1999 led to changes in the handling and reporting of economic disputes in the courts. Those changes were implemented at the district court level by 2002, resulting in incomparable reporting categories. At present, adequate data to correct for those changes is not available.

This study addresses major theoretical debates in the fields of comparative politics, political economy, law and development, and China studies. Dramatic increases in litigation raise anew questions about the necessity of effective courts for sustainable economic growth.[2] The work of Max Weber establishes the claim that a rational legal system, which lends the predictability of universally applied rules to market activity, is essential for economic growth.[3] Douglass North's work further establishes the importance of legally constraining potentially predatory state actors from undermining property rights and thereby economic growth.[4] North also emphasizes the importance of providing a neutral third party to underpin arms-length contracting. "How effectively agreements are enforced is the single most important determinant of economic performance. The ability to enforce agreements across time and space is the central underpinning of efficient markets."[5] These claims have been accepted and propagated in recent years not only by scholars but also by multilateral institutions like the World Bank and the United Nations Development Program.[6]

However, these theoretical claims have also been challenged in both Western and Asian contexts. Stewart Macaulay's seminal work on noncontractual relations in U.S. business highlights the high frequency of dispute resolution without resorting to formal, legal processes or legal sanctions.[7] Similarly, Robert Ellickson finds that community norms rather than the law govern the resolution of everyday disputes in rural communities in the United States.[8] In the context of contemporary Chinese society, the works of Jane Winn and Carol Jones both emphasize the importance of the cultural practice of *guanxi* (social connections) in enforcing contracts and resolving disputes.[9] Traditional cultural norms against litigation are vividly captured in phrases, such as "to enter a court of justice is to enter a tiger's mouth."[10]

Indeed, in the contemporary context, not only cultural norms and practices but also the flawed nature of the legal system itself may mitigate against using the courts.[11] Courts in the PRC are subordinate to the party, lack competent judges, and have weak enforcement powers.[12] In light of these cultural and institutional features of the Chinese system, the dramatic increase in the litigation of economic disputes appears surprising.

Others, following the law and development literature, argue that an increase in arms-length market transactions and a growing role for the courts must inevitably go hand-in-hand in China.[13] While the economic growth of the Chinese economy over the past quarter century hardly needs substantiation, a debate exists around the theoretical centrality of nonlitigious, relational versus formal, institutionalized dispute resolution mechanisms in underpinning this growth. The debate has larger implications for the study of comparative politics; in particular, it contributes to arguments about the relationship between institutions and culture that arise with respect to both legal development and democratization.[14]

Finally, this study seeks to contribute to the growing literature on the empirical study of law by focusing on the arena of disputes over contracts for exchange of goods and services.[15] In doing so, it builds on recent research in the economics of transition, which offers empirically based and theoretically nuanced assessments of the relationship between relational contracting and formal legal institutions in transition economies, including the former Soviet Union, Eastern Europe, and Vietnam.[16] Scholars of China have also begun to redress the relative lack of empirical evidence on dispute resolution—and on the legal system more generally.[17] This chapter is based upon results of analysis of a representative sample of seventy-six purchase and sales contract disputes from 1999 to 2001 from one district court in Nanjing, and a convenience sample survey implemented through face-to-face interviews with seventy-six enterprise managers conducted in Nanjing and Shanghai between 2002 and 2004.[18] The questionnaire focuses on firms' experiences with contracting and dispute resolution. In particular, it explores the full range of mechanisms for resolving contract disputes, ranging from informal and formal mediation, arbitration, and litigation, to nonlegal, coercive mechanisms. The paper also draws on original data provided by the World Bank Study of Competitiveness, Technology, and Firm Linkages.[19] On this basis, the chapter seeks to evaluate the extent to which a well-functioning legal system—as opposed to political and/or cultural substitutes—provides the basis for securing intertemporal transactions and, therefore, economic growth. Both the Nanjing and Shanghai data and the World Bank data are drawn from large cities, where economic exchange is concentrated, where judges are likely to be better educated, and where lawyers are available; thus, these data are more likely to reflect the most advanced segments of the economy and the legal system.

The paper proceeds as follows: it first examines the evolution of contract law governing exchange of goods and services in order to explicate the legal/regulatory basis for contracting and to provide a starting point for assessing the relevance of these rules for contracting behavior. The second section looks at the nature of contracting behavior, evaluating the extent to which firms engage in arms-length vs. relational contracting. The next section analyzes the range of dispute resolution mechanisms in order to evaluate the role of law and its substitutes. The fourth section presents a discussion of attitudes of business owners and managers toward the legal system and its role in the economy. The conclusion addresses the relevance of this research to larger arguments about China's "rule-of-law" initiative and the relationship between institutions and culture.

EVOLUTION OF CONTRACT LAW

The first reform-era laws governing contracts—the 1981 Economic Contract Law (ECL), the 1985 Foreign Economic Contract Law (FECL), and the 1987 Technology Contract Law (TCL)—evince significant flaws when evaluated on the basis of the following criteria of a well-regulated market economy: (1) Does the legislation create a level playing field for all firms? (2) Does it enable parties injured by breaches to enforce the rules and receive compensation? and (3) Does it allow nonstate actors to put the coercive machinery of the state in motion in service of their legitimate interests? As subsequent paragraphs demonstrate, these weaknesses were ameliorated in part by the amendment of the ECL in 1993 and the promulgation in 1999 of a new, unified Contract Law (CL), which was much better suited to a market economy characterized by a diversity of ownership forms. In addition, the new law addressed the "inconsistent norms and competing institutions" created or codified by the three initial contract laws and the 1986 General Principles of Civil Law.[20]

The first Economic Contract Law of the PRC, promulgated in 1981, embodied many of the concepts developed through regulations put in place in the 1950s and 1960s.[21] The Soviet concept of "economic contract" was adopted with the socialist transformation of the economy in 1956 and perpetuated by the ECL into the early reform era.[22] Under planning, economic contracts were nothing more than a means of implementing the plan, and contracts violating the plan were void.[23] At the same time, administrative changes to the plan were common reasons for nonperformance.[24] Other aspects of the law were also restrictive, including the requirement that contracts be in writing.[25] As Bing Ling notes, this requirement was "one of the major problems of the pre-1999 law, whereby a contract [could] easily become void."[26] Moreover, according to the ECL, only legal persons[27] (*fa ren*) could sign economic contracts; the intent of the law was that only enterprises "subject to state control could enter into meaningful economic activity."[28] However, the growing participation of individuals, who by definition were not legal persons, and private enterprises, which were often unable to obtain legal person status but which were increasingly parties to contracts, presented a challenge to the ECL.[29]

While political and social substitutes for law created openings for individuals and private enterprises that were not legal persons to enter into contracts, the absence of a basis in law still hindered the development of the nonstate economy prior to the early 1990s.[30] Although the literature provides only anecdotal and case study evidence here, one can surmise that the growth of the private sector might have advanced more quickly under a more encompassing contract regime. Legal obstacles in the ECL were evident even in places like Wenzhou, where the private economy enjoyed strong local political support and extensive social networks. According to an official in Yueqing County, Wenzhou, before the amendment to the ECL in 1993, many firms outside of Wenzhou refused to enter into contracts with private enterprises there.[31] Furthermore, private enterprise owners felt they had no recourse when they encountered contract disputes, since courts were unwilling to recognize their claims.[32] Moreover, informal solutions to these contracting problems were vulnerable during the 1980s and early 1990s to official crackdowns, like the closure of Wenzhou's informal commodities markets (supplying steel, lumber, and cement to private firms) by the State Administration of Industry and Commerce—the state agency responsible for administering economic contracts.[33] Thus, under the ECL regime, private enterprises functioned only within the quasi-legal or illegal interstices of the planned economy.[34]

Amendment of the ECL in 1993, along with authoritative interpretations of civil law by the Supreme People's Court (SPC) in the early 1990s, addressed many of these problems. The amended ECL did away with many provisions that perpetuated the dominant role of the state plan and greatly "expanded the scope of the 'economic contract' concept."[35] These changes included allowing "other economic organizations" to qualify as parties to economic contracts. Authoritative interpretations by the SPC had already defined "other organizations" to include properly registered and licensed solely owned private enterprises, partnerships, foreign-invested enterprises, and branches of legal persons.[36] Essentially, any properly registered and licensed business entity could now enter into legal contracts. With the changes in the contract regime beginning in the early 1990s, firms that were properly registered and licensed, like those in Yueqing, Wenzhou, alluded to above, could enter into legally enforceable contracts.

The unified Contract Law, passed by the National People's Congress in 1999, reflects the principles of good faith, fostering transactions, and freedom of contract.[37] For example, natural individuals—not just legal persons—can now enter into legally enforceable contracts, and oral contracts are recognized as valid for the first time, significantly expanding the scope of contract. The principle of freedom of contract signals a definitive move away from the planned economy.[38] The law limits the scope of contracts to be monitored by administrative organs; for example, it limits administrative supervision of contracts by the SAIC to illegal acts.[39]

These changes are clearly reflected in court records. This paragraph draws on the analysis of a representative sample (n = 76) of purchase and sales contract disputes from 1999 to 2001, from one district court in Nanjing, the capital of Jiangsu Province. It is possible to identify the ownership form of the plaintiff in 70 percent of the court records in the sample. Private enterprises are the plaintiffs in 34 percent of the cases; firms with mixed public/private investment are the plaintiffs in another 15 percent of the cases. While it is possible to identify the ownership form of the defendant in only 37 percent of the cases, private enterprises are the defendants in 36 percent of those cases and mixed public/private firms are the defendants in another 14 percent of the cases. Thus, the records show that the principle of freedom of contract enables private enterprises to enter into legally enforceable contracts and enjoy recourse to the courts—features of the contract regime that were absent through the early 1990s. The records also show how the law served to foster transactions by recognizing oral contracts. In 89 percent of the cases, it is possible to identify the form of the contract—oral versus written—and oral contracts are in dispute in 46 percent (n = 31/68) of those cases. Moreover, reliance on oral contracts does not, in and of itself, appear to unduly prejudice the hearing a plaintiff can receive. In the Nanjing court sample, the court found for the plaintiff, resulting in payment of compensation by the defendant, in 55 percent (n=17/31) of the cases involving oral contracts.

Having examined the evolution of contract law and its growing ability to serve a more marketized economy featuring a range of ownership forms, the chapter proceeds in the next section to focus on the actual contracting behavior of firms.

ARMS-LENGTH VS. RELATIONAL CONTRACTING

Stewart Macaulay opens his seminal 1963 article on noncontractual relations in business with the question, "What good is contract law?" While changes in the legal contract regime that level the playing field and improve access to legal recourse are central to the work of both Weber and North, scholars working in contexts as diverse as American and Chinese business communities emphasize the extent to which contractual relations are grounded in informal social ties and not in legal rules and sanctions.

The treatment of relational contracting in Chinese societies focuses on the concept of *guanxi*. As Wai-Keung Chung and Gary Hamilton indicate, "Chinese relational rules personalize transactions, making them part of the interpersonal social matrix of daily life . . . thereby increasing the calculability of economic outcomes."[40] In the context of the People's Republic of China in particular, the discussion of *guanxi* links not only relations among entrepreneurs, but also relations between entrepreneurs and government officials.[41] One explanation of the expansion of economic exchange, then—even preceding significant legal change—centers on dense, interpersonal networks that extend into the government apparatus. Victor Nee and Sijin Su focus on "long-standing social ties based on frequent face-to-face interactions" as an important basis for trust and cooperation between entrepreneurs and the government in the Chinese political economy.[42] They emphasize that "transaction costs are lower in institutional settings where trust and cooperation flow from informal norms and established social relationships." Dense interpersonal networks provide information as well as opportunities to impose sanctions that are important to the establishment of trust. In a similar vein, Nan Lin and Chih-jou Chen emphasize thick relationships based on familial ties.[43] Ambrose King finds that "network building is used (consciously or unconsciously) by Chinese adults as a cultural strategy in mobilizing social resources for goal attainment in various spheres of social life.[44] To a significant degree the cultural dynamic of *guanxi* building is a source of vitality in Chinese society." As this statement suggests, the social network explanation of trust in contractual relations is related to accounts of Chinese culture that emphasize the importance of networks of relations (*guanxi*) as a widespread sociocultural phenomenon.

However, recent studies raise questions about the extent of reliance on *guanxi* as markets for factors and products become more complete.[45] Identifying contracting partners through social ties is important, particularly in the absence of well functioning legal institutions. In theory, social ties provide an alternative set of opportunities for monitoring and enforcing contractual performance, since social ties facilitate the flow of information within a defined network.[46] What does available data tell us about the social basis of contractual relations? Zhou Xueguang et al. find that, while social networks are important, firms rely on a range of search channels to identify contractual partners.[47] Social networks (47.1 percent) and open information sources including advertisements, media, and trade information (47.0 percent) predominate, followed by self-initiative. The survey data in my study of Nanjing and Shanghai firms show that professional ties predominate over social ones; in identifying suppliers, firms rely on business associates (41.4 percent), trade conferences (12.9 percent), advertising (11.4 percent), and self-initiative (10 percent) as the major sources of contacts. Friends account for only 8.6 percent[48] (figure 7.1). In identifying customers, firms report relying upon business associates (42.9 percent), competitors (21.4 percent), trade conferences (18.6 percent), and advertising (14.3 percent), as well as self-initiative (i.e., approaching the potential client directly; 10 percent), and friends' companies (10 percent) (figure 7.2). Thus, social networks are only one of many search channels for contractual partners. This finding is consistent with the extremely rapid expansion of economic exchange, particularly in major cities.

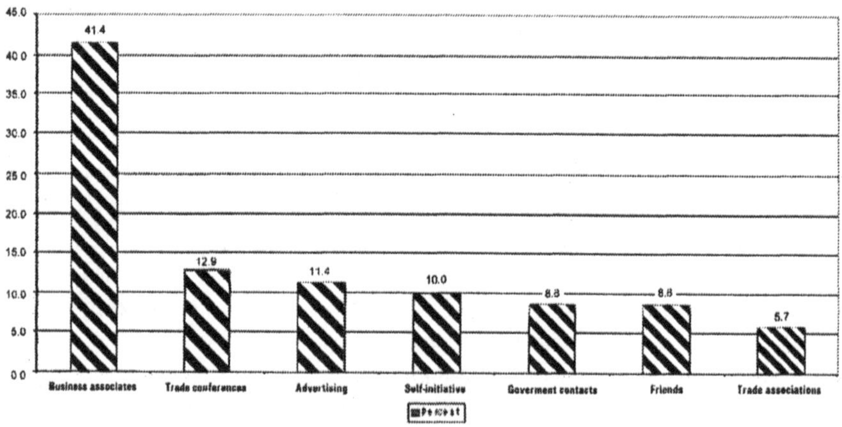

Figure 7.1

Moreover, despite the role of social networks, formal, written contract provisions have become the norm; more than 75 percent of the firms in the study by Zhou et al. used such provisions to specify volume, quality, price, deadlines, and contractual safeguards.[49] Written contracts appear even more pervasive in other studies. The data from Nanjing and Shanghai demonstrate that firms use written contracts with suppliers in 90.5 percent of cases, while they use written contracts with customers in 98.6 percent of the cases. Similarly, the World Bank data also show that the use of written contracts is the norm, found in 90.1 percent of contracts with clients and 82.2 percent of contracts with suppliers. Zhou et al. find that "contracts initiated through social networks have a higher probability of having informal provisions," but, crucially, the effect is small: "Network ties play a statistically significant but substantively minor role in the choice of contract forms and provisions."[50] In other words, business people in these studies rely overwhelmingly on formal contracts in economic exchange. The reliance on formal contracts has important implications for the nature of dispute resolution. As one manager interviewed said, if we have delivery or product problems with a supplier, we first go to the contract.[51]

Trade associations perform an important function in promoting the use of formal contracts and are often involved in popularizing the use of state-approved, industry-specific form contracts.[52] For example, according to the Shanghai Municipality Regulations on the Management of Form Contracts (*Shanghaishi geshihetong guanlitiaoli*), trade associations in Shanghai draft form contracts, which are reviewed and approved by the municipal level of the State Administration for Industry and Commerce and by the relevant

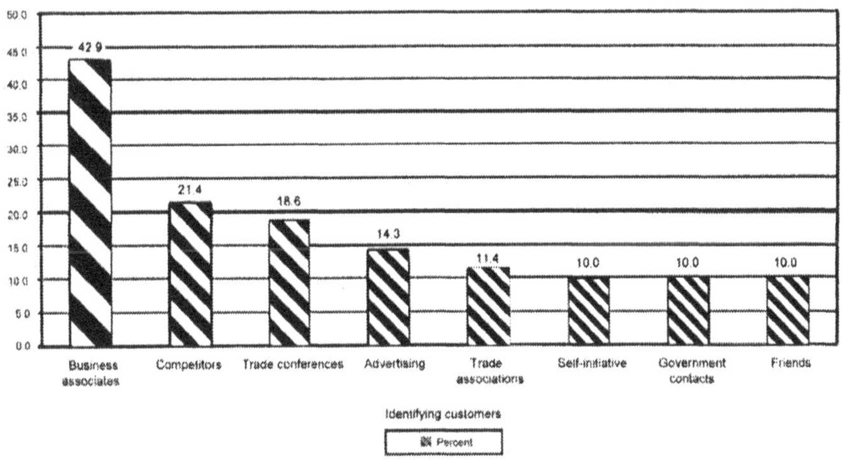

Figure 7.2

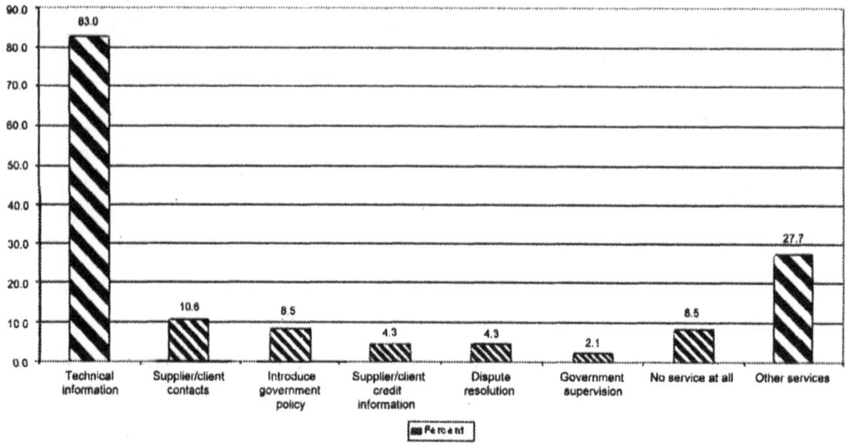

Figure 7.3

ministerial bureau. Trade associations then provide these form contracts for use by their members.[53]

However, trade associations are limited in their ability to provide information about contractual partners that would underpin relational contracting without recourse to the formal legal system. In the Shanghai and Nanjing survey, 67.1 percent of respondents were members of trade associations, yet managers dismissed their role in contract formation or enforcement. Most managers reported relying on trade associations for technical information (83 percent), while only some reported that trade associations provide a forum for making supplier or client contacts (10.6 percent; figure 7.3). Revisiting figure 7.1, we can see that 5.7 percent of managers reported actually identifying suppliers through trade associations, and 11.4 percent reported actually identifying customers through this means (figure 7.2). Indeed, trade associations appear limited as a basis for evaluating potential trade partners. Very few respondents said that associations provided information on credit worthiness (4.3 percent; figure 7.3). A smaller percentage of firms (54.5 percent) were members of trade associations in the World Bank dataset, and the survey taps a somewhat different array of functions: With respect to evaluating the creditworthiness of potential business partners, less than one third of the managers reported that these associations could "accredit members to suppliers or customers"[54] (figure 7.4). Rather than providing contacts and information that would underpin relational contracting, trade associations appear to link firms to the formal, legal system.

Other institutions that could provide information to facilitate the evaluation of potential contractual partners were largely absent or faced significant

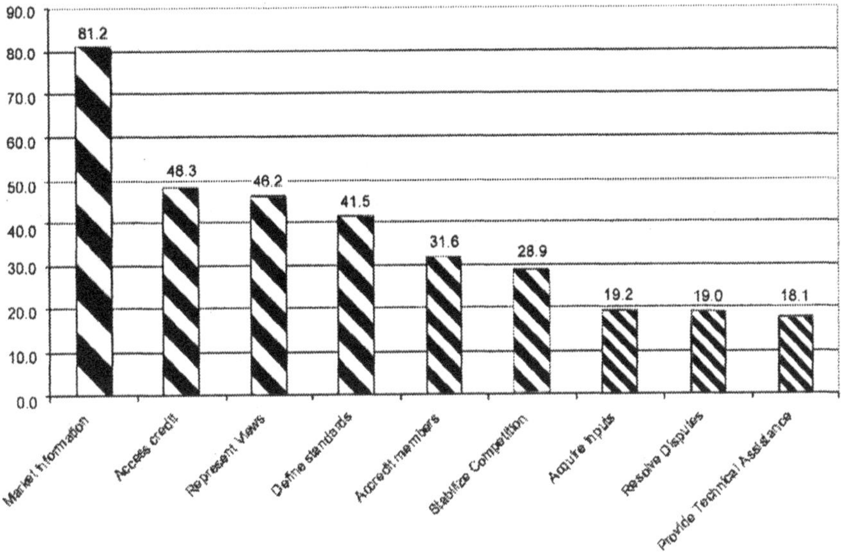

Figure 7.4

regulatory hurdles at the time of the enterprise survey. Credit bureaus are a noteworthy example. Only a few specially approved credit bureaus were in existence. A lawyer in Nanjing commented, "China's credit system is underdeveloped. There is no unified system for [evaluating] enterprise credit; there's no way to investigate an individual manager's creditworthiness (*zhongguode xinyongzhidu bufada, meiyou yige tongyide qiyexinyongtixi, wufakaocha mougejingyingzhede xinyu*)."[55] In 2001, the State Council set up a "Group for Enterprise and Personal Credit Investigation" to propose legislation governing business and consumer credit bureaus.[56] As of July 2005, Wan Enxiang, Vice President of the Supreme People's Court, described the credit reporting system as "lacking (*queshi*)," with the result that enterprises and individuals who don't pay their debts are never sanctioned.[57] In 2007, the State Council Office issued "Several Opinions Regarding Building a Social Credit System."[58] These guidelines highlighted the importance of information for contract performance and product quality as well as for loan repayment. To date, the People's Bank of China has been the central player, and regulations for credit-reporting agencies are likely to require a "very high level of minimum capitalization, as if they were financial institutions."[59] This requirement is, in essence, a barrier to entry. As Su Ning, Deputy Governor of the People's Bank of China, has commented, "In the preliminary stage of the credit reporting industry, supervision by the government might be quite strong."[60] In the Shanghai and Nanjing survey, when asked explicitly how they evaluated the creditworthiness of customers, managers indicated using credit bureaus in only 9 percent of the cases and banks in only 15 percent of the cases. Managers reported seeking information from other suppliers of a client in 26 percent of the cases. The most common response was "other"—39 percent.

In open-ended responses, managers indicated that they invested a large amount of time and energy in trying to assess the credit-worthiness of new customers on their own. Managers described visiting new customers—including customers in different provinces with attendant travel expenses—at least three times on average.[61] One manager initially took the fancy apartment and famous-make car of one contract partner to be signs of credit-worthiness—until he failed to pay (Enterprise #1).

Managers also rely on the two parties' narrow self-interest in the shadow of the future to reduce risk. They intentionally keep the size of the first few deals small before expanding the size of contracts. One manager commented, "We mainly look at a series of deals and ability to pay. Before, we didn't pay much attention to this and got burned. Now we pay attention. The key is not to have unpaid accounts payable" (Enterprise #61).

At the same time, however, managers face significant competition, generating pressure for them to contract at arm's length in order to offer the best terms on price and quality to customers. Fully 80 percent (81.8 percent) of respondents in the Shanghai and Nanjing survey characterized competition in their core product markets as "intense" or "very intense." Managers interviewed suggested that foregoing the most efficient contracting opportunities could result in a loss of market competitiveness for their firms.

The picture of contracting presented here is one of transactions divorced in most cases from pre-existing social ties, and yet not well supported by other state or nonstate institutions like trade associations or credit agencies.[62] The findings from major cities suggest less reliance on relational contracting and greater use of formal, written contracts than expected, based on the existing literature. These findings have implications for dispute resolution. We can contrast such contract-based approaches to economic exchange with more trust-based approaches:

> When two enterprises trade with one another over an extended period, their officials might develop bonds of personal trust that override any fears of contractual non-performance. Then, the relationship no longer depends upon a detailed calculus of the other party's motives. In such cases, the written contract is largely superfluous. Any specific element of agreement between the two parties can only be understood in the context of the whole relationship. If problems arise, they are resolved through negotiations, without involving outsiders. Adjustments occur without recontracting. Resorting to the courts or even bringing in lawyers can be corrosive, since such actions signal a decline of personal trust.[63]

The results presented in this section suggest that when firms do encounter disputes, there are few effective substitutes for an institution like the courts in dispute resolution. The following section investigates this hypothesis in detail.

DISPUTES AND DISPUTE RESOLUTION

In the survey of firms in Shanghai and Nanjing, 55 percent reported experiencing one or more self-defined "disputes" in the preceding year. According to data drawn from the World Bank survey of 1,500 Chinese firms, in the year 2000, 31.1 percent of firms had one or more "major disputes" with clients, while 21.9 percent of firms had one or more major disputes with suppliers. Once enterprises encounter disputes, what mechanisms do they rely upon to resolve these disputes? Theorists from Weber to North emphasize the importance of formal, state-sponsored legal recourse. As Weber asserts, "In a capitalist society, economic exchange is quite overwhelmingly guaranteed by the threat of legal coercion . . . a stable private economic system of the modern type [would be] unthinkable without legal guarantees."[64] Yet, as noted above, there is a large literature on contractual relations, spanning cases from the United States to Asia, which indicates that contract disputes are often resolved outside the courts. This section examines the dispute resolution mechanisms employed by Chinese firms and finds that the courts play a moderately important role in the strategies firms employ. The importance of the courts likely reflects a number of factors, particularly the relative absence of effective alternatives in the context of cut-throat competition. The following paragraphs address self-enforcing contracts, direct negotiation, mediation, arbitration, litigation, and the ability to enforce judgments.

Self-enforcing Contracts

Self-enforcement, in which two parties bargain to attain a long-term cooperative solution based on the anticipated value of future contracts, is an important mechanism in contractual relations with Chinese firms; enforcement is based in part on the threat to stop trading. As one manager in Nanjing noted, "If a client is very late with payment, we stop doing business with them."[65] Moreover, in the study of businesses in Shanghai and Nanjing, 90.6 percent of firms reported that in the event of a serious dispute, their long-term reciprocal relations with a supplier or contractor would be broken.

It is possible for reputation to function within the dyadic contractual relationship. In the Shanghai and Nanjing data, the average length of contractual

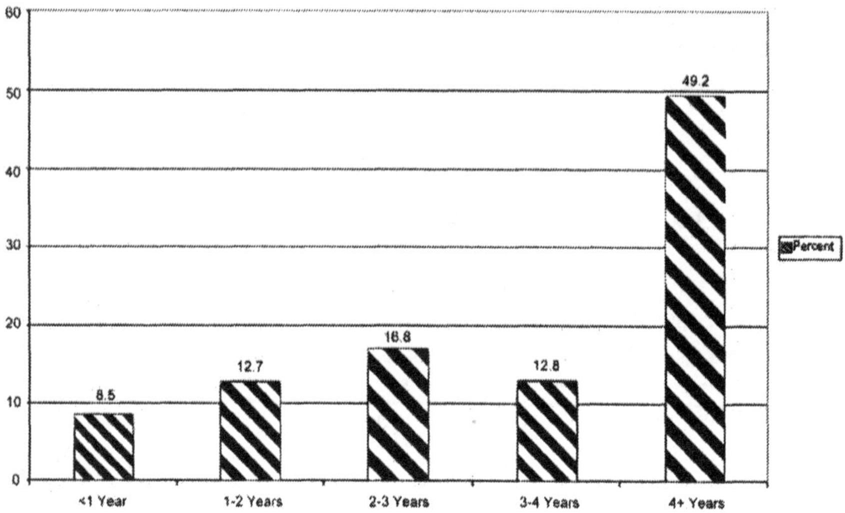

Figure 7.5

relations with major clients was about 7.5 years, while the median length of the relationship was 5.5 years. In nearly 50 percent of firms in the World Bank dataset, the average length of the business relationship with major suppliers and clients was four years or longer (figure 7.5). Furthermore, reputation also functions within business circles to help police contractual relations. Contract partners are concerned with the future value of contracts not only with one firm but with a group of firms. In Shanghai and Nanjing, 74.2 percent of firms said that other businesses would know about it if a dispute arose between the firm and one of its suppliers. Here, economic (as opposed to strictly social) networks are important sources of information, not only in the search for contractual partners, but also in the attempt to enforce contracts—particularly in the absence of credit evaluation services as noted above.

Partial prepayment is another common strategy to minimize risk in an information-poor environment without reliance on the formal legal system; this practice builds in conditions that encourage enforcement.[66] In 28 percent of cases, managers described relying on partial prepayment, particularly for new customers. In these cases, typical payment terms were: 30 percent in advance, 40–60 percent upon delivery, and 10–30 percent within thirty days of delivery.[67]

Direct Negotiation and Mediation

Negotiation directly between the contracting parties is the norm for resolving contract disputes. "No matter what firm or what dispute, enterprises' first [step]

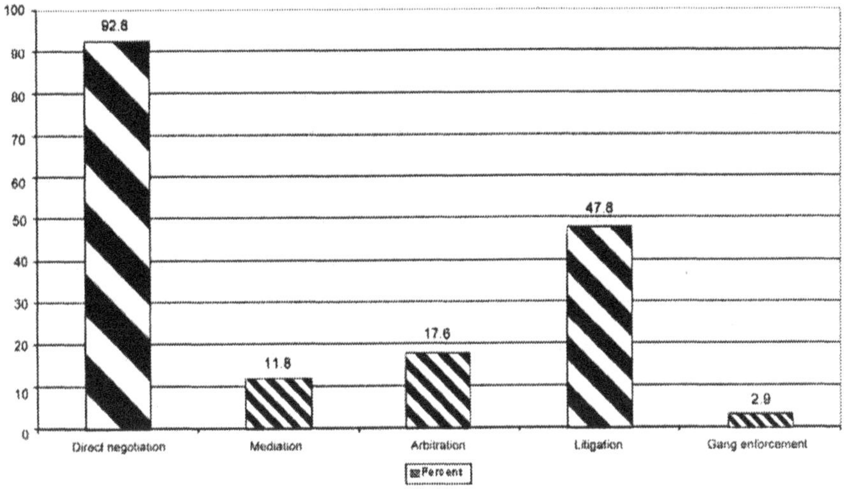

Figure 7.6

is direct negotiation. On the one hand, [this approach] minimizes costs, and, on the other hand, it maintains good relations (*buguanshishemeqiye, shemejioufen, qiyeshouxiande kengdingshi xieshang, yifangmian keyijieyuechengben, lingyifangmian haikeyibaochi haodeguanxi*)."[68] In Shanghai and Nanjing, 92.8 percent of firms attempted direct negotiation (*xieshang*) to resolve disputes. (figure 7.6.) In the World Bank survey, 87.1 percent of firms used negotiation in the final resolution of disputes with at least one client, while 93.2 percent used negotiation in the final resolution of disputes with at least one supplier. (figures 7.7 and 7.8.)

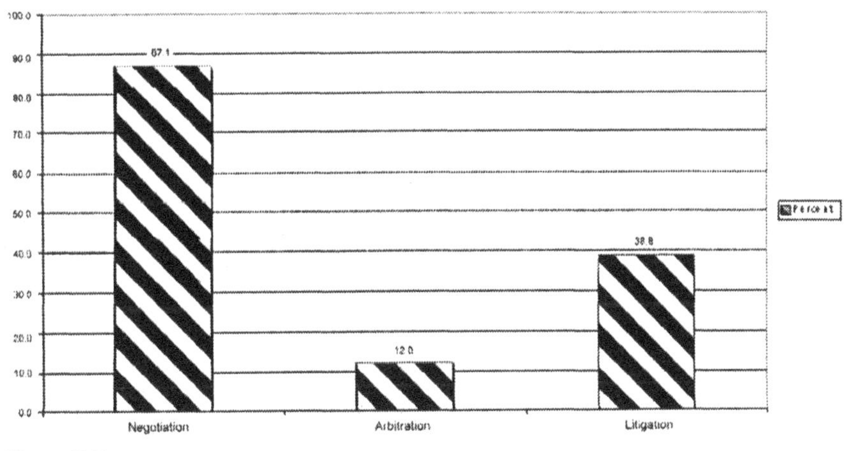

Figure 7.7

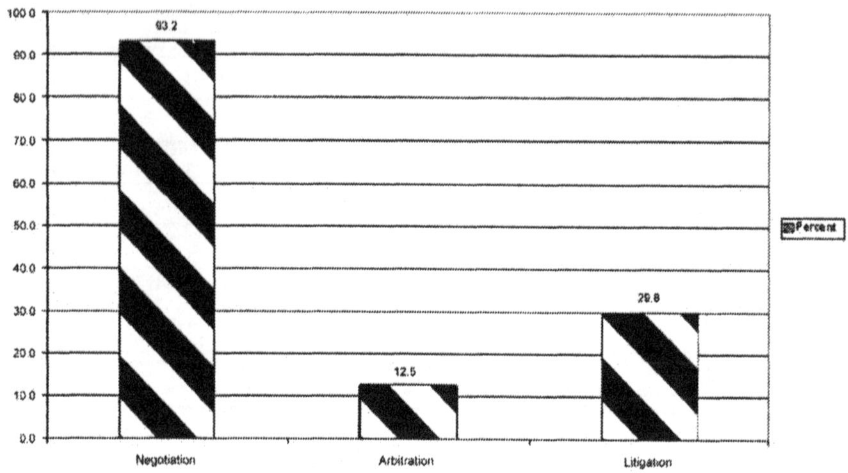

Figure 7.8

In direct negotiation, business leverage is likely to be an important factor in determining the outcome.[69] One Nanjing manager who sourced steel from Baoshan Steel (*Bao Gang*) described them as "tough (*niou*)," and said that when disputes arose with that company, he had to "take it or leave it."[70] An unrelated lawyer also from Nanjing commented on Baoshan Steel's business leverage: "In some disputes, the cause and the solution are determined by the enterprise's leverage, for example, Baoshan Steel. Baoshan Steel is a large enterprise—a supplier with a lot of leverage and with a lot of long-term business partners. But, if a Baoshan product has a problem, the buyer won't look to Baoshan [to make good]. Because Baoshan has tremendous market leverage, you can't afford to offend them. Of course, after such a problem [has occurred], it [i.e., Baoshan] may [choose to] give some other form of compensation (*haiyoude jioufende chanshenghejiejue qujueyu qiyezhijiande shili, biru Baogang delizi. Baogang shidaqiye, henyoushilide guenghuoshang, youhenduo changqihezuohuoban. danruguo Baogang dechanpin youlewenti, dueifang yebuhuei laizhaota. yinwei Baogang juyou henqiangde jingzhengshili, nidezueibuqi. dangranle, shihou tayehuei geiyu mouzhuengxingshide buchang*)."[71]

The Shanghai and Nanjing data further differentiate direct negotiation and negotiation employing a third party—informal mediation (*tiaojie*). In the latter case, only 11.8 percent of firms typically turned to a third-party. This raises the question of what entities can serve as third parties in the mediation of a dispute. In questions regarding the functions of associations, 19 percent of firms in the World Bank dataset agreed that the business association performed the function of "helping resolve disputes" for any member (not

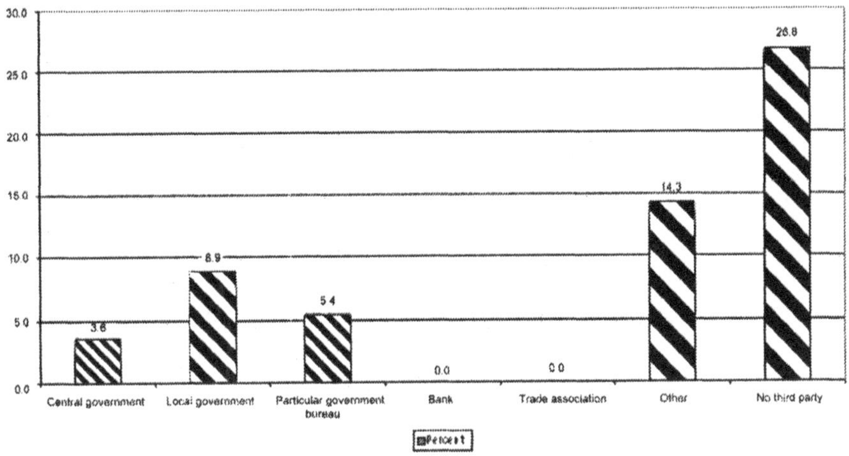

Figure 7.9

necessarily themselves). As a Nanjing lawyer commented, "China also has trade associations, but they have little influence; they're of no use in resolving disputes (*zhongguo yeyou hangyexiehuei, danshi tamende lilianghenxiao, zaijiejue jioufenfangmian fahueibuliao shemezuoyong*).[72] Only 4.3 percent of respondents in the Shanghai-Nanjing data indicated that trade associations contributed to dispute resolution. In the context of their direct experience with dispute resolution, moreover, no managers reported having the assistance of their trade associations. Strikingly, the most common response (26.8 percent) was that there was no suitable third party available to mediate (figure 7.9.) "Other" alternatives (14.3 percent) commonly referred to a respected individual known to both parties. In only a small percentage of cases were government bureaus at any level deemed useful as third-party mediators.[73] This represents a major change from the role of government under the planned economy, in which government bureaus often undertook the mediation of disputes between subordinate firms, and challenges Lubman's claim of the "persistence of devotion to mediation."[74] Overall, what is most striking is the apparent lack of appropriate third parties—formal or informal—available to business people to mediate disputes. This finding is consistent with the rapidly changing market environment in which there is significant new entry by firms.

Arbitration

While arbitration is the "preferred method" of dispute resolution by foreign investors in China,[75] leading some scholars to characterize it as "a key part of the official legal system" more broadly,[76] arbitration plays a surprisingly small role in the resolution of disputes over sales and purchase contracts among domestic firms.[77] As one lawyer remarked, "Domestic enterprises mainly sue; very few choose arbitration as a method to resolve disputes (*guoneiqiye yisusongweizhu, xuanzezhongcai zuowei zhengyi jiejuefangshidehenshao*)."[78] The Arbitration Law went into effect only in 1995. Prior to 1995, similar functions for local firms were handled by Economic Contract Arbitration Commissions administered by the State Administration for Industry and Commerce and were pursued in a highly bureaucratic and often arbitrary manner.[79] The 1995 law called for the abolition of all old arbitration commissions and the establishment of new arbitration commissions, independent in principle, yet licensed and recognized by the state, to arbitrate economic disputes.[80]

The Shanghai Arbitration Commission was established in 1995. However, the arbitration commission in Nanjing, the capital of one of the wealthiest coastal provinces, was not established until 1998. In the first five years (combined) following passage of the law, all domestic arbitration commissions nationwide accepted only 17,000 cases, involving 25.7 billion rmb.[81] This compares to 1,329,020 strictly economic contract disputes involving 413.4 billion rmb accepted by courts in one year alone (1998). Table 7.2 shows the small number of cases handled by the Shanghai Arbitration Commission during its first five years; the commission handled only 189 cases in 1998, increasing to 649 cases in 2003. In the Nanjing and Shanghai survey, some respondents had arbitration clauses in their contracts, but many fewer used them.

Arbitration requires the agreement of both parties. Moreover, many standard form contracts contained imprecise clauses like the following: "All disputes arising from this contract should be resolved through direct negotia-

Table 7.2. Shanghai Arbitration Commission

	Number of Cases	*Total Value of Contracts in Dispute (10,000 rmb)*	*Average Value of Contracts in Dispute (rmb)*
1998	189	27,180	1,438,109
1999	253	58,570	2,315,024
2000	341	36,400	1,067,449
2001	431	72,030	1,671,230
2002	479	57,879	1,208,330
2003	649	128,833	1,985,100
Avg Growth	22.8	29.6	5.5

Source: Shanghai Arbitration Commission, August 2004

tion. If direct negotiation is unsuccessful, the parties can apply for arbitration through the arbitration commission or sue in the court (*youbenhetong yinqide yiqiezhengyi youshuangfang xieshangjiejue. xieshangbucheng, buchengbili shuangfangjunkexiang zhongcaijigou shengqingzhongcai huoxiangfayuan tichususong*)" (contract provided by Enterprise #1). When a specific arbitration commission is named by one party to a contract, the other party is often suspicious of personal ties between the first party and the arbitrator. In the World Bank survey of 1,500 firms, only 12 percent used arbitration even once in the final resolution of disputes with suppliers or customers, and only 2 percent used arbitration at least half of the time (figures 7.7 and 7.8). In the Nanjing and Shanghai sample, most respondents had little awareness or understanding of the potential role for arbitration. Only 17.6 percent of respondents mentioned it as a viable dispute resolution mechanism (figure 7.6). Comments like "Where is there an arbitration commission? (*na er you zhongcaiweiyuanhuei*)?" (Enterprise #16) were common. Furthermore, many respondents perceived it as less authoritative than the courts—despite the fact that, in principle, they could apply for enforcement of arbitral decisions by the courts in the same way that they could for court decisions.

What is noteworthy, however, is the relatively large value of contracts in dispute brought to the Shanghai Arbitration Commission—roughly 1.5 million rmb on average in 1998 (table 7.2), compared to an average value of only about 300,000 rmb for economic contract disputes in the courts (nationwide) in that year.

In the Shanghai and Nanjing sample, managers of large state-owned enterprises (SOEs) accounted for fully two-thirds of the small share of responses identifying arbitration as a viable dispute resolution mechanism.[82] Given the prominence of arbitration among foreign firms, I would have expected the Sino-foreign joint ventures in the sample to choose arbitration disproportionately. However, the prominence of large SOEs among those indicating arbitration commissions as a viable option may be due to their earlier experience with arbitration by the Economic Contract Arbitration Commission under the State Administration for Industry and Commerce.[83]

Litigation

Between 1983 and 2001, economic disputes, broadly defined, accepted by the court of first instance increased at an average annual rate of 18.8 percent, peaking in 1999[84] (table 7.1). Put in wider domestic context, civil disputes increased at less than half that rate on average—8.3 percent per year over the same period—while criminal cases grew at only 4.7 percent per year on average. Data for administrative cases is available only for the period 1987–2001,

Table 7.3. Economic Contract Disputes Handled in the Courts of First Instance

	Number of Cases Accepted	*Total Value of Contracts in Dispute (10,000 rmb)*	*Average Value of Contracts in Dispute (rmb)*	*Change in Average Value*	*Change in Number of Cases Accepted*
1983	36,274	171,055	51,541		
1984	69,204	149,659	24,443	−52.6	90.8
1985	206,582	897,804	48,611	98.9	198.5
1986	292,599	788,339	28,144	−42.1	41.6
1987	332,496	814,621	24,552	−12.8	13.6
1988	467,872	1,110,392	25,033	2.0	40.7
1989	634,941	1,935,130	31,426	25.5	35.7
1990	543,613	1,731,293	31,277	−0.5	−14.4
1991	516,507	1,987,858	37,101	18.6	−5.0
1992	598,610	2,970,257	49,878	34.4	15.9
1993	824,448	6,342,211	77,834	56.0	37.7
1994	971,432	9,727,423	100,875	29.6	17.8
1995	1,184,377	14,830,833	125,865	24.8	21.9
1996	1,404,921	21,406,425	153,641	22.1	18.6
1997	1,373,355	26,303,090	192,336	25.2	−2.2
1998	1,329,020	41,343,216	310,167	61.3	−3.2
1999	1,410,107	n/a	n/a	n/a	6.1
2000	1,184,613	n/a	n/a	n/a	−16.0
2001	1,062,302	n/a	n/a	n/a	−10.3

Notes:
As of 1998, statistics on economic contract disputes accepted by the courts include cases involving foreign entities.
As of 1988, statistics on cases involving transport of goods were removed from the larger category of economic contract disputes.
Sources: *Quanguo renming fayuan sifa tongji lishi ziliao huibian 1949-1998 (Mingshi bufen)*, 2000 (Beijing: renming fayuan chubanshe); Zhongguo falu nianjian, various years.

and only administrative cases outpaced the growth of economic dispute cases, increasing at an average annual rate of 21.8 percent from a small base. While it is difficult to specify a meaningful metric for evaluating the pace of growth, the courts appear to play an increasingly important role in economic disputes during the reform period.

Contract dispute litigation in particular, which accounts for the lion's share (more than 90 percent) of all economic dispute cases accepted by the courts, increased at an average annual rate of 20.1 percent between 1983 and 2001. A definitional change means that data for the years 2002 to 2006 is not strictly comparable with earlier years. Moreover, data on the average value of disputes is available only through 1998: from 1983 to 1998, the total value of disputes grew 40.9 percent per year on average, while the average value of disputes grew at 11.9 percent per year on average. In 1998, the average value of a contract dispute heard in the courts nationwide was 310,167 rmb (table 7.3). As noted above, the average value of arbitrated cases was much larger, but the number of disputes heard by arbitration commissions was miniscule in comparison.[85] In China, as elsewhere, litigation of contract disputes is rarely the first resort.[86] Nevertheless, in the World Bank survey of 1,500 firms in the year 2000, 38.8 percent of firms used litigation in the final resolution of disputes with at least one client, while 29.8 percent used litigation in the final resolution of disputes with at least one supplier (figures 7.7 and 7.8). In the study of seventy-six firms in Shanghai and Nanjing, 36.8 percent of respondents had used the courts in their *most recent* dispute.

As with litigation of economic disputes more broadly, litigation of contract disputes peaked in 1999, declined slightly and leveled off since. In interpreting the reasons for the peak (1996–1999) and subsequent decline in litigation of contract disputes, judges in district and intermediate courts in Shanghai identified several factors with a lagged effect (Interview sh040721p; sh040817p). They include the prevalence of oral contracts, which are more likely to end up in court; the tightness of macroeconomic policy, which contributes to the incidence of nonpayment disputes; the pace of transition from plan to market; and the pace of transformation of state-owned enterprises.

Oral contracts are more likely to end up in litigation and may have been more prevalent in the mid-1990s. In the World Bank survey of 1,500 firms in the year 2000, less than 10 percent of contracts with clients were oral, and less than 20 percent of contracts with suppliers were oral. Yet, in the Nanjing court sample, more than 40 percent of the court cases between 1999 and 2001 involved oral contracts. This finding suggests a greater propensity to litigate oral contracts.

The transition from plan to market, most notably in terms of the transformation of small- and medium-sized state-owned enterprises, may have generated a transitory wave of disputes. Indeed, anecdotal evidence suggests that nonpayment disputes may move from multiple renegotiations of payment terms to litigation when new owners repudiate debt (interview Enterprise #77). Another practice that occurs during enterprise restructuring is the concentration of valuable assets in one spin-off, leaving the debts; it is then difficult to recover any amount owed by the original firm (interview with lawyer nj020925p). Litigation is also a strategy for verifying outstanding accounts payable. One case record in the Nanjing court sample indicates that despite "a long-term cooperative relationship," the dispute was propelled into litigation by the fact that the plaintiff was facing restructuring (Nanjing Case #5). Similarly, according to Zhou et al., "One manager in a state-owned firm said: 'We use formal contracts and sometimes take our contractual partners to court. Most of the time we do not expect to get any tangible outcome from court decisions. But court decisions will put it on record that the contract failures are not the result of our irresponsibility or acceptance of bribes.'"[87] A practicing lawyer in Shanghai confirmed the propensity of SOEs to use the courts to verify the status of accounts (interview with lawyer sh040818p).

Lawyers and managers alike pointed to the substantial number of disputes arising from chains of unpaid "triangular debts (*sanjiaozhai*)," which increase when the state-run banking system tightens the credit supply (interview with lawyer nj020935p). Although tight macroeconomic policies also contribute overall to the high incidence of nonpayment disputes, private enterprises are much more strategic with respect to the likely outcome of the case; in other words, they are motivated by the expected value of suing. They are more likely to sue in case of nonpayment if they believe that the plaintiff has resources that can be captured or, in case of nonperformance, if they believe that the plaintiff can perform (interview with lawyer sh040818p). Indeed, the manager of a real estate development company in Shanghai commented, "One shouldn't sue like Qiu Ju did. . . . One shouldn't pursue matters in which one can obtain only justice/winning and not material gains (*buyaoxiang Qiu Ju nayang daguansi; zhengqi buzhengcaideshibuzuo*)" (Enterprise #11).[88] This view was confirmed by a partner in a Nanjing law firm; in fact, he evaluated not only the likelihood of winning but also the likelihood of the defendant's paying up before accepting new cases (interview with lawyer nj020925p).[89]

Supply of Legal and Judicial Services

Recourse to the courts is supported by the increasing supply of legal services. Indeed, in Nanjing and Shanghai, 91.6 percent of managers surveyed indicated that they had legal representation. Such representation took a range of forms, from legal departments internal to the firm, to retained counsel, to

Table 7.4. Supply of Legal Services

Year	Law Firms (Units)	Lawyers (Individuals)	Law Firms (% increase)	Lawyers (% increase)
1997	8441	98902		
1998	8946	101220	6.0	2.3
1999	9144	111433	2.2	10.1
2000	9541	117260	4.3	5.2
2001	10225	122585	7.2	4.5
2002	10873	136684	6.3	11.5
2003	11593	142534	6.6	4.3
2004	11823	145196	2.0	1.9
2005	12988	153846	9.9	6.0
Avg Growth	4.9	5.0		

Source: *Zhongguo falu nianjian*, various years.

lawyers hired on an as-needed basis. Judges similarly report that most parties to contract disputes come to court with legal representation (interview with judges).[90] Underpinning this representation is the expansion of the legal profession. The number of both lawyers and law firms has increased at an average annual rate of 4–5 percent since the mid-1990s, when such data became available (table 7.4). More strikingly, law is among the fastest growing undergraduate majors, increasing at an average annual rate of 20 percent between 1994 and 2006; at the graduate level, it is the fastest growing field, increasing at an average annual rate of 23 percent per year (table 7.5.) Information available for the year 2000 indicates that 185,169 people sat for the bar, while 21,700 attained the passing score of 231 points, yielding a pass rate of 10.05 percent.[91]

Trends in the number of judges show different characteristics, however. As of October 2004, there were 3,133 basic-level people's courts with 148,555 judges (*faguan*), of which 91,099 were front-line judges (*yixian faguan*; i.e., those hearing cases), a reduction of 13.07 percent from 2000.[92] Published reports suggest that the reduction may reflect a new emphasis on training and appropriate educational attainment. Those judges deemed unqualified may be removed from the courtroom.[93]

Judgments and Their Enforcement

Three major trends in the national data (1983–2001) on the disposition of economic contract disputes by the court bear on the issue of enforcement of court judgments[94] (table 7.6). First, withdrawals of cases by the plaintiffs have increased from approximately 8 percent in the mid-1980s to more than

Table 7.5. Expansion of Legal Education

	Philosophy	*Economics*	**Law**	*Education*	*Literature*	*History*	*Sciences*	*Engineering*	*Agriculture*	*Medicine*	*Admin.*	*Total*	*Law Share*
Graduates at the Bachelor's Level													
1994	2117	80,981	**17650**	35,234	92,928	16794	87,845	228,922	27,856	47,090	n/a	637,417	2.77
1995	2110	119,042	**23170**	41,898	115,969	18117	100,566	295,839	32,975	55,711	n/a	805,397	2.88
1996	1960	127,018	**25852**	40,620	120,051	16423	97,260	315,005	33,032	61,417	n/a	838,638	3.08
1997	1183	132,988	**28270**	39,595	116,115	14559	90,513	314,418	30,190	61,239	n/a	829,070	3.41
1998	1183	132,900	**29649**	40,716	119,583	14179	92,729	308,574	28,941	61,379	n/a	829,833	3.57
1999	1067	134,258	**31500**	40,271	120,957	13374	90,395	326,180	28,070	61,545	n/a	847,617	3.72
2000	916	159,299	**44124**	42,052	146,997	13661	98,200	354,291	30,370	59,857	n/a	949,767	4.65
2001	925	57,254	**61474**	52,563	157,837	10220	115,829	349,097	28,543	62,638	139,943	1,036,323	5.93
2002	1012	65,942	**79966**	79,812	198,535	11683	131,494	459,842	36,284	79,500	193,239	1,337,309	5.98
2003	1196	88,181	**110416**	117,072	286,889	13905	173,031	644,106	50,057	111,356	281,283	1,877,492	5.88
2004	1331	113,687	**133364**	146,685	367,133	14502	207,490	812,148	59,564	154,187	381,061	2,391,152	5.58
2005	1275	162,977	**163529**	280,134	415,206	10694	164,867	1,090,986	69,531	202,577	506,180	3,067,956	5.33
2006	1417	203,957	**186164**	322,317	524,806	10605	197,231	1,341,724	77,177	253,252	656,058	3,774,708	4.93
Avg Growth	−3.0	7.4	**19.9**	18.6	14.2	−3.5	6.4	14.6	8.2	13.8	29.4	14.7	
Graduates at the Master's and Doctorate Levels													
1994	454	1,967	**1,296**	540	1,575	506	5,521	12,463	945	2,780	n/a	28,047	4.62
1995	460	2,165	**1,370**	577	1,607	593	6,039	14,675	1,111	3,280	n/a	31,877	4.30
1996	581	3,666	**1,864**	736	2,228	745	6,646	17,621	1,418	4,144	n/a	39,649	4.70
1997	664	4,988	**2,258**	902	2,584	926	7,625	19,918	1,788	4,886	n/a	46,539	4.85
1998	659	4,740	**2,385**	893	2,795	859	7,473	20,681	1,715	4,877	n/a	47,077	5.07
1999	649	6,302	**3,257**	1,008	3,310	970	8,251	23,369	1,949	5,605	n/a	54,670	5.96
2000	775	7,308	**3,820**	1,221	3,714	1,026	8,077	24,378	2,282	6,166	n/a	58,767	6.50
2001	904	3,981	**4,504**	1,550	4,193	1,179	8,637	24,873	2,136	6,992	8,860	67,809	6.64
2002	n/a	n/a	**5,139**	n/a	n/a	n/a	n/a	n/a	n/a	n/a	n/a	80,841	6.36
2003	1,562	6,578	**7,484**	2,764	7,426	1,926	13,220	41,337	3,849	12,207	12,738	111,091	6.74
2004	1,854	8,098	**11,097**	4,276	10,483	2,407	17,540	56,074	5,165	16,128	17,655	150,777	7.36
2005	2,249	10,930	**14,103**	5,101	13,314	2,657	22,028	72,941	6,038	19,405	20,962	189,728	7.43
2006	3,117	14,784	**19,413**	767	20,107	3,497	29,137	94,516	8,853	26,415	28296	255,902	7.59
Avg Growth	16.0	16.8	**23.1**	22.8	21.6	16.0	13.7	16.9	18.8	18.9	21.4	18.5	

Sources: China Statistical Yearbook on Science and Technology (Beijing: China Statistics Press, 2000), p. 9; Educational Statistics Yearbook of China (Beijing: People's Education Press, various years).

Table 7.6. Disposition of Economic Contract Disputes by the Courts of First Instance (Share of Total)

	Accepted	Mediated by Court	Decided by Court	Transferred to Relevant Bureau	Rejected	Withdrawn	Resolved	Other	Total
1983		79.3	5.5	4.2		8.5	2.4		100.0
1984		80.6	5.6	3.2		8.7	1.9		100.0
1985		81.8	5.7	3.1		8.5	0.9		100.0
1986		79.6	7.5	3.9		8.2	0.8		100.0
1987		77.3	9.5	2.8		9.6	0.8		100.0
1988		80.2	8.6	1.9	0.0	8.8	0.5		100.0
1989		76.8	10.5	2.0	0.0	10.2	0.5		100.0
1990		69.5	14.7	2.1	0.0	13.0	0.7		100.0
1991		61.6	20.0	2.2	0.0	14.7	1.5		100.0
1992		61.7	20.8	1.6	0.5	14.8	0.7		100.0
1993		63.1	19.5	1.5	0.3	14.9	0.6		100.0
1994		60.0	20.8	1.5	0.3	16.8	0.6		100.0
1995		57.7	22.1	1.3	0.3	17.9	0.6		100.0
1996		53.7	25.5	1.3	0.3	18.4	0.8		100.0
1997		49.9	29.1	1.5	0.4	18.3	0.8		100.0
1998		43.2	34.6	1.4	0.6	18.8	0.4	1.0	100.0
1999		41.3	35.5	0.0	0.8	19.3	0.0	3.1	100.0
2000		34.6	40.3	0.0	1.3	20.7	0.0	3.2	100.0
2001		30.8	43.8	0.0	1.4	21.3	0.0	2.7	100.0
2002		27.4	45.3	0.8	1.5	23.4	0.3	1.4	100.0
2003		26.5	44.8	0.8	1.6	24.4	0.2	1.6	100.0
2004		28.0	42.4	0.8	1.8	25.5	0.3	1.3	100.0
2005		28.7	41.3	0.9	1.6	26.3	0.3	1.1	100.0
2006		28.4	41.4	0.8	1.4	26.9	0.2	0.8	100.0

Source: *Quanguo renming fayuan sifa tongji lishi ziliao huibian 194—1998 (Mingshi bufen)*, 2000 (Beijing: renming fayuan chubanshe).

27 percent in 2006. Interviews with lawyers and enterprise managers suggest that the threat of litigation is just another step in the bargaining process; initiating litigation is one strategy to elicit performance from the contractual partner. Firms thereby make a credible threat to use the courts and then bargain within the "shadow of the law."[95] Settlement is often cheaper than litigation. In the Nanjing court sample, 29 percent of the cases (n = 22/76) were withdrawn; in general, these cases receive no further notation. However, in a few instances, court records include notations such as "defendant already paid" (Case #36) and "performed contract" (Case #27), indicating that bargaining in the shadow of the law can be effective.

In a second major trend, a higher percentage of cases nationwide go all the way to judgment than in the past, increasing from roughly 5 percent in the 1980s to more than 40 percent in 2006. Third, and relatedly, the data show declines in the occurrence of court-mediated settlements from roughly 80 percent of the total in the mid-1980s to 28 percent as of 2006. The decline is significant, since official interference has been reported to occur often during court-sponsored mediation. According to Pittman Potter, "The dominance of consensual methods of resolution [including court-sponsored mediation] permitted the personal and organizational relationships of the parties to affect the outcome, thus undermining contract autonomy."[96] However, interviews with lawyers, judges, and enterprise owners and managers in Shanghai and Nanjing confirm the decline in court-sponsored mediation.

Based on the Shanghai and Nanjing survey, it appears that court-sponsored mediation involving government officials occurs most commonly when fulfillment of unpaid contractual obligations may result in lay-offs or nonpayment of wages by an enterprise in difficulty. Such government intervention may reflect the priority of the Wen Jiabao administration on more timely payment of migrant labor wages. In this situation, judges may proactively invite government officials to participate in court-sponsored mediation, pressuring the plaintiff to accept smaller or delayed settlement in order to maintain the work force of the defendant (interview with district and intermediate court judges sh040817p).[97] In this regard, judges are like other government officials and bear political responsibility for any incidents affecting social stability. When the enterprise in difficulty is a state enterprise, the State Assets Commission (*guoziwei*) and the labor bureau are typically the state agencies brought in to the court-sponsored mediation process (ibid.). As a Nanjing lawyer commented, "Enterprise workers may resist implementation [of a judgment]; moreover, the enterprise and the workers may combine to hinder implementation even with covert support from the local government. If a large enterprise collapses, there is an impact on the local economy, the firm, and the workers" (interview nj020925p). Overall, however, the decline in court-sponsored mediation reduces one source of opportunity for official interference in court actions, and government interference was not a major complaint of managers who had taken contract disputes to court.[98]

Enforcement of judgments is an on-going problem. In March 2004, Xiao Yang, President of the China's Supreme People's Court, stated in his work report to the NPC, "The difficulty of executing civil and commercial judgments has become a major 'chronic ailment,' often leading to chaos in the enforcement process; there are few solutions to the problem."[99] According to Ge Xingjun, head of the SPC's Judgment Enforcement Division, approximately 60 percent of civil and economic judgments were enforced at the basic-level court, 50 percent at the intermediate-level court, and 40 percent at the provincial high-level court.[100] In general, inadequate data are available to assess the nature of implementation, but the Nanjing court sample sheds some light on this issue.[101] Of the seventy-six cases in the sample, 29 percent (n = 22/76) were withdrawn by the plaintiff; court-sponsored mediation occurred in 21 percent (n = 16/76) of the cases; and cases went to judgment in 47 percent of the cases (n = 36/76).

The latter two types of cases (68 percent of the total, n = 52/76) are subject to enforcement by the courts. Of the cases subject to enforcement, in only 3.8 percent (n = 2/52) were judgments "automatically" implemented. In 52 percent of the cases (n = 27/52), winners applied for compulsory enforcement (*qiangzhi zhixing*), and the vast majority of these applications came from cases that went all the way to judgment.[102] Only five of the cases resolved by court-sponsored mediation applied for compulsory enforcement, and one might presume that implementation was smoother in mediated outcomes in which creditor plaintiffs did not apply for compulsory enforcement. Of the twenty-seven cases that sought compulsory enforcement, the records indicate results for twenty of them, showing that 55.5 percent (n = 15/27) were implemented successfully and 18.5 percent (n = 5/27) failed to be implemented. Notations accompanying "successfully" implemented cases include, "Defendant paid debt by handing over factory land and equipment" (Case #52); "No assets to be implemented, except 5500 rmb attachment and auction" (Case #57); and "Defendant paid 3,350 rmb and a case of cigarettes; case closed" (Case #61). In most of the failed cases, records indicate that either there were no assets to be implemented (Cases #116, 23, 39) or the defendant was already in bankruptcy proceedings (Case #1). In the remaining case, the records indicate that a Shandong Province court rejected implementation of a Nanjing, Jiangsu Province judgment (Case #10).

Local protectionism—the failure of local courts to enforce judgments by outside courts on local firms—is a common explanation for failed implementation.[103] Locally, implementation branches of the courts can be more proactive; in Shanghai, the economic courts even engage in public shaming, periodically publishing the names of those who have unenforced judgments against them in a popular evening newspaper.[104] Shanghai court representatives also report organizing "enforcement delegations," which travel as a group to other provinces to seek—often unsuccessfully—enforcement of their judgments. Donald Clarke notes that the Chinese legal system may have a lower tolerance for nonimplementation of judgments than other societies, notably the United States.[105] Indeed Martin Shapiro writes,

> In most societies courts have had only the most rudimentary enforcement mechanisms. . . . Courts typically do not monitor compliance, and they reintervene to exact compliance only at the request of one of the parties. The reintervention often takes the form of a simple repetition of the previous order. The successful suitor even in a modern industrial society frequently finds that the decree is only the first in a long series of painful, expensive, and often inconclusive steps aimed at getting his remedy. Courts, we are repeatedly and rightly told, have neither the purse nor the sword.[106]

Private Coercion

In light of the lack of success of formal enforcement efforts, and in light of the attention received by mafia enforcement in other transition economies—most notably Russia—one might expect a greater role for private enforcement in China.[107] In the Nanjing and Shanghai sample, only 2.6 percent of firms reported resorting to private coercion to enforce contracts. In one case, a Shanghai manager described "resolving" a nonpayment dispute by "splitting the amount owed 50-50 with a gang (literally, "black society") ("*heishehuei yaoshoujioufen jin e de baifenzhiwushi zuowei shouduanfei*"), which then forcibly collected the money owed (Enterprise #1).[108] In another case, a manager in the food service industry used the biggest men in the warehouse to intimidate a recalcitrant business partner, who, in the manager's view, had supplied a defective refrigerator. The warehouse workers exacted money from the supplier to recover the original price of the refrigerator (Enterprise #12). Some managers alluded to privately engaging local police and splitting the payments recovered. As one lawyer noted, "There are many different illegal methods. For example, in Zhejiang [Province], some private bosses will put their lives on the line to get their money (*feifalushouduan jiouhenduole. biruzai Zhejiang, yixiesiyinglaoban, tamenpinleming yeyaobaqian zhueihueilai*)" (interview with lawyer nj020925p). However, private enforcement appears to be employed in a small number of disputes.[109]

Attitudes toward the Legal System

Courts appear to play a role in contract disputes because they are seen as authoritative (despite problems with enforcement), but not necessarily fair or just. According to one private business owner interviewed in Nanjing, "Going to court is not because it's fair but rather because it's authoritative (*zhaofayuan bushiyinwei tagkongzheng ershiyinwei tadequanwei*)" (interview nj021127p). Strikingly, an intermediate court judge echoed this sentiment, "*xuyaoyige youquanderen laichuli; zueiyouquanweixing zueirongyijieshou; buyidingzueikongzheng; buyaobakongzheng zuoweibiaozhuen; guanjiandeshi jiejuewenti* (You need an authoritative person to handle [the dispute], and the resolution of the most authoritative person is the easiest to accept)" (interview sh040817p).[110] Somewhat surprisingly, attitudes toward the legal system as a whole are solid: 56.3 percent of respondents in Shanghai and Nanjing rated the legal system as average, while 25.3 percent found it to be low or very low, and 18.3 percent found it to be high or very high. Paraphrasing Shapiro, Hendley et al. wrote, "Submitting a dispute to the courts implies an acceptance of the legitimacy of the institution and a willingness to abide by its decision."[111] Thus, the courts play a key role as a third-party arbiter, while this role is undersupplied by other institutions in China and mutual trust among businesses appears low. The contrast with attitudes toward other business people's trustworthiness in contracting is noteworthy, since it is more negative: 42.9 percent of respondents found it to be average, while 53 percent found it to be low or very low, and only 4.1 percent found it to be high or very high. As one manager put it, "There's no trust to speak of. The Cultural Revolution destroyed the normal relations between people; there's no more mutual trust. Under the planned economy, one wouldn't even call it trust; just irresponsibility. The situation of trust is pretty bad (*meiyouxinyongkeyan. wengedapole renyurenzhijian zhengchangdeguanxi, buzaixianghuxinren. jihuajingjishiqi nabujiaoxinyong, shibufuzeren. xinyongzhuangkuanghencha*)" (Enterprise interview #39).

These findings do not imply that courts are free of corruption. Business owners and managers interviewed suggest that they held their lawyers responsible for entertaining judges and cultivating positive relationships with judges. At the same time, owners and managers recognized that both parties to a dispute would engage in this behavior, and they regarded the expenses involved as part of the "cost of doing business." As one manager noted, "It's better than it was before, and in the future it will definitely be good; we've entered the WTO. The effectiveness of the courts is okay; in Nanjing, we're set with respect to justice. When the company does business it considers legal factors relatively often (*biyiqianhao, yihouyekendinghao, womenjiaru shijiemaoyizuzhi. fayuandexiaolu haikeyi, zai Nanjing me, kongzhengxingfangmian womendougaodingle. kongsi zaizuoyewudeshihou kaolu falu yinsu bijiaoduo*)" (Enterprise interview #39). The reference to being "set" with respect to justice suggests an important investment in a good relationship with the court.

CONCLUSION

Weber and North may be incorrect to the extent that they claim that well-functioning legal institutions are a *prerequisite* for economic growth, but they are correct in identifying limits to the expansion of contracting in the absence of such institutions. Business people in urban China clearly seek recourse to the courts to underpin economic transactions. With respect to contract disputes—the most common type of economic dispute—courts are not as completely flawed as they have been portrayed, nor are disputants as nonlitigious as they have been portrayed. In the context of China's transition from socialism to a fast-growing market economy, contracts are often not grounded in social networks, but rather occur more at arm's length. Institutional alternatives to courts for underpinning contracts—mediation and arbitration—appear to be unavailable or are underdeveloped for local firms. At the same time, the role of the government bureaucracy in directly supervising contracts has declined markedly. In this context, the courts are an increasingly important element in the process of dispute resolution. But this role for the courts is by no means inevitable, as scholars like Pan Wei suggest.[112] The implementation of major policy changes, ranging from successive revisions of the body of law governing contracts to the training of legal professionals, are necessary in order for courts to play this role.

These findings have implications for broader arguments about the nature of the relationship between culture and institutions.[113] Many observers, drawing on the "normative tradition articulated by the Confucian elite,"[114] have concluded that litigation plays a minor role in East Asian societies.[115] Randall Peerenboom describes the Confucian tradition as follows:

> Confucius' politics of harmony requires the voluntary participation of the individuals who collectively comprise society. If conflicts arise, as they inevitably will, each person must evidence a willingness to look for a mutually acceptable

> solution. Of course a willingness to cooperate is not enough to overcome all conflicts. There must also be sufficient common ground to provide a basis for discussion, understanding, and potential mutually agreeable solutions. The li (rites) provide this essential communally owned repository of shared meaning and value on which to draw in times of conflict. One is inextricably a part of one's tradition. However different one may be from one's neighbor, there are still deep chords of affinity that bind one to other members of one's community. . . . The li are better understood as customary norms that . . . constitute . . . culturally valued, though negotiable, guidelines for achieving harmony in a particular context.[116]

However, Haley and Winn, among others, challenge the "myth of the reluctant litigant" by highlighting the *limited institutional capacity* of the courts and the legal professional in Japan, Taiwan, and Korea at levels of economic development comparable (or even more advanced) than China's today.[117] Peng describes these countries from the 1950s through the 1990s as "lawyerless wonderlands."[118] Haley, for example, focuses on the high barriers to entry to the bar—with a pass rate of 1.7 percent in 1975—and the lack of meaningful access to the courts: "The simplest trial can take over a year at the district court level, and the average is two years."[119] But, in contrast, he also highlights the ready supply of alternatives to the courts, such as private mediation companies. Haley concludes, "What distinguishes Japan [from most societies] is the successful implementation of this interdiction [to litigate] through institutional arrangements."[120]

In contrast to the experience of other Northeast Asian countries, China is rapidly expanding the supply of legal services at a much earlier stage of economic development. China—at a per capita income of about US $960.00 in 2002 compared to Korea's US $11,280.00—had one lawyer for every 9,510 people in that year, while Korea had one lawyer for every 9,383 people.[121] In 2004, Shanghai alone had more than 6,000 lawyers in 592 law firms, while Korea had 6,273 lawyers in 258 law firms nationwide.[122]

This contrast in the supply of legal services at a relatively early stage of economic development in China is most likely explained by the Chinese Communist Party's attempt to develop "rule of law" as a new means to both legitimate itself and promote continued rapid economic growth. In 1996, Jiang Zemin articulated the official policy of ruling the country in accordance with law and establishing a socialist rule of law state (*yifazhikuo jianshe shehueizhuyizhikuo*). These principles were enshrined in a constitutional amendment in 1999; the relevant article now reads, "The People's Republic of China exercises the rule of law, building a socialist country governed according to law." It is important to note that contract disputes not only are among the most common type of dispute, but are also among the least politically sensitive in the legal system;

thus, the present study is not directly generalizable to other, more directly political, types of disputes. Indeed, the state in urban China has removed itself to a large extent from day-to-day economic exchange, and an important part of the CCP's motivation for pursuing the "rule of law" is precisely to gain the economic benefits of a more market-oriented economy and deeper links to the international economy that are supported by reformed legal institutions.[123] Moreover, when contract disputes do become politically sensitive—as in the enforcement of judgments in nonpayment disputes that might result in large lay-offs affecting political stability, for example—the "rule of law" does not always hold sway, as demonstrated above. While the prominence of "rule of law" rhetoric in contemporary PRC politics may be instrumental to the goals of regime maintenance, it nevertheless has measurable implications for the development of legal institutions in the realm of economic exchange.

NOTES

1. The average annual rate of increase for 1983–1999 (the years for which strictly comparable data is available) is 24 percent. *Quanguo renming fayuan sifa tongji lishi ziliao huibian 1949–1998 (Mingshi bufen)*, 2000, Beijing: renming fayuan chubanshe; Zhongguo falu nianjian, various years. Donald C. Clarke, 1991, "Dispute Resolution in China," *Journal of Chinese Law*, Vol. 5, No. 2, pp. 245–296; Stanley Lubman, 1997, "Dispute Resolution in China after Deng Xiaoping: 'Mao and Mediation' Revisited," *Columbia Journal of Asian Law*, Vol. 11, No. 2, pp. 229–391; Stanley Lubman, 1999, *Bird in a Cage: Legal Reform in China after Mao*, Stanford, Calif.: Stanford University Press.

2. Katharina Pistor, and Philip A. Wellons (eds.), 1999, *The Role of Law and Legal Institutions in Asian Economic Development*, New York: Oxford University Press.

3. Max Weber, Guenther Roth, and Claus Wittich (trans.), 1978, *Economy and Society: An Outline of Interpretive Sociology*, Berkeley: University of California Press.

4. Douglass C. North, 1990, *Institutional Change and Economic Performance*, New York: Cambridge University Press.

5. Douglas C. North, 1992, "Institutions, Ideology and Economic Performance," *The Cato Journal*, Vol. 11, No. 3, p. 481.

6. Frank Upham, 1995, "Speculations on Legal Informality: On Winn's 'Relational Practices and the Marginalization of Law," *Law and Society Review*, Vol. 28, No. 2; John Gillepsie, 1999, "Law and Development in 'The Market Place': An East Asian Perspective," in Kanishka Jayasuriya (ed.), *Law, Capitalism, and Power in Asia: The Rule of Law and Legal Institutions*, London Routledge, pp. 118–150.

7. Stewart Macaulay, 1963, "Non-Contractual Relations in Business: A Preliminary Study," *American Sociological Review*, Vol. 28, No. 1, pp. 55–67.

8. Robert C. Ellickson, 1991, *Order Without Law: How Neighbors Settle Disputes*, Cambridge: Harvard University Press.

9. Jane Kaufman Winn, 1994, "Relational Practices and the Marginalization of Law: Informal Financial Practices of Small Businesses in Taiwan," *Law and Society Review*, Vol. 28, No. 2, pp. 193–232; Carol Jones, 1994, "Capitalism, Globalization and Rule of Law: An Alternative Trajectory of Legal Change in China," *Social and Legal Studies*, Vol. 3, pp. 195–221. While Winn and Jones address contracting and dispute resolution specifically, there is a much broader literature on social connections (*guanxi*) in Chinese societies. Among recent contributions, see, for example: Thomas Gold, Doug Guthrie, and David Wank, 2002, *Social Connections in China*, New York: Cambridge University Press; Gary H. Hamilton, 1996, *Asian Business Networks*, Berlin: Walter de Gruyter; Nan Lin, and Chih-jou Chen, 1994, "Local Initiatives in Institutional Transformation: The Nature and Emergence of Local Market Socialism in Jiangsu," Paper presented to the Annual Meeting of the Association of Asian Studies, Boston, March 24–27; Victor Nee, and Sijin Su, 1996, "Local Corporatism and Informal Privatization in China's Market Transition," in John McMillan and Barry Naughton (eds.), *Reforming Asian Socialism: The Growth of Market Institutions*, Ann Arbor, Mich.: University of Michigan Press, pp. 111–134; Yunxiang Yan, 1996, *The Flow of Gifts: Reciprocity and Social Networks in a Chinese Village*, Stanford, Calif.: Stanford University Press; and Mayfair Mei-hui Yang, 1994, *Gifts, Favors, Banquets: The Art of Social Relationships in China*, Ithaca, N.Y.: Cornell University Press.

10. Kathryn Bernhardt, and Philip C. C. Huang, 1994, *Civil Law in Qing and Republican China*, Stanford, Calif.: Stanford University Press. The work of Kathryn Bernhardt and Philip Huang (1994) has sparked debate regarding the role of law and the courts in the traditional Chinese legal system. They challenge the extent to which traditional China had a "non-litigious" culture that privileged harmonious relations over overt conflict and mediation over litigation. See also Diamant (2000), which draws on the work of Bernhardt and Huang. Neil J. Diamant, 2000, "Conflict and Conflict Resolution in China: Beyond Mediation-Centered Approaches," *Journal of Conflict Resolution*, Vol. 44, No. 4, pp. 523–596.

11. See Stanley Lubman, 1999, *Bird in a Cage: Legal Reform in China after Mao*, Stanford, Calif.: Stanford University Press; Lester Ross, 1990, "The Changing Profile of Dispute Resolution in Rural China: The Case of Zouping County, Shandong," *Stanford Journal of International Law*, Vol. 26, No. 1, pp. 15–66.

12. Donald C. Clarke, 1995, "The Execution of Civil Judgments in China," *China Quarterly*, No. 141, pp. 65–81; Donald C. Clarke, 1991, "Dispute Resolution n China," *Journal of Chinese Law*, Vol. 5, No. 2, pp. 245–296; Anthony Dicks, 1995, "Compartmentalized Law and Judicial Restraint: An Inductive View of Some Jurisdictional Barriers to Reform," *China Quarterly*, No. 141, pp. 82–109; Pitman B. Potter, 1992, *The Economic Contract Law of China*, Seattle: University of Washington Press; David Zweig, Kathy Hartford, James Feinerman, and Deng Jianxu, 1987, "Law, Contracts, and Economic Modernization: Lessons from the Recent Chinese Rural Reform," *Stanford Journal of International Law*, Vol. 23, No. 2, pp. 319–364.

13. Pan Wei, Beijing University, commentary presented at the International Conference on "Grassroots Democracy and Local Governance in China During the Reform Era," Chinese Association of Political Science and National Chengchi University,

Taiwan, November 2–3, 2004. This view was also evident in the early law and development literature, which was strongly influenced by modernization theory. "'Law' was seen as both a necessary element in 'development' and a useful instrument to achieve it" (David M. Trubek and Marc Galanter, 1974, "Scholars in Self-Estrangement: Some Reflections on the Crisis of Law and Development Studies in the United States," *Wisconsin Law Review*, No. 4, p. 1073). See also Tom Ginsburg, 2000, "Does Law Matter for Economic Development? Evidence From East Asia," *Law & Society Review*, Vol. 34, No. 3, p. 832. This paper adopts the view that there is nothing inevitable about the development of legal institutions.

14. John Haley, 1978, "The Myth of the Reluctant Litigant," *Journal of Japanese Studies*, Vol. 4, No. 2, pp. 359–390; Edward N. Muller, and Mitchell A. Seligson, 1994, "Civic Culture and Democracy: The Question of Causal Relationships," *American Political Science Review*, Vol. 88, No. 3, pp. 635–652; Sidney Tarrow, 1996, "Making Social Science Work Across Space and Time: A Critical Reflection on Robert Putnam's *Making Democracy* Work," *American Political Science Review*, Vol. 90, No. 2, pp. 389–397. *Institutions* here are defined as formal organizations (state or non-state) that set or embody rules shaping the behavior of their constituents; *culture* is defined as a relatively stable pattern of attitudes and values regarding, e.g., the political or legal system.

15. It is important to note that disputes over labor contracts are handled through a distinct set of laws and institutions. On labor disputes see Mary Gallagher, 2005, *Contagious capitalism: globalization and the politics of labor in China*, Princeton, N.J.: Princeton University Press; and Ching Kwan Lee, 2007, *Against the law: Labor protests in China's rustbelt and sunbelt*, Berkeley: University of California Press.

16. Kathryn Hendley, Peter Murrell, and Randi Ryterman, 2000, "Law, Relationships, and Private Enforcement: Transactional Strategies of Russian Enterprises," *Europe-Asia Studies*, Vol. 52, No. 4, pp. 627–656; Simon Johnson, John McMillan, and Christopher Woodruff, 2002, "Courts and Relational Contracts," *Journal of Law, Economics, and Organization*, Vol. 18, No. 1, pp. 221–277.

17. Neil J. Diamant, 2000, "Conflict and Conflict Resolution in China: Beyond Mediation-Centered Approaches," *Journal of Conflict Resolution*, Vol. 44, No. 4, pp. 523–546. On Japan, see T. Ginsburg, and G. Hoetker, 2006, "The Unreluctant Litigant? An Empirical Analysis of Japan's Turn to Litigation," *Journal of Legal Studies*, Vol. 35, pp. 31–59; and Veronica Taylor. Only a few years earlier, scholars bemoaned the lack of empirical research. Stanley Lubman lamented, "Most Western study has necessarily focused on the texts of the rules, which tell nothing about their impact on practice" (Stanley Lubman, 1999, *Bird in a Cage: Legal Reform in China after Mao*, Stanford, Calif.: Stanford University Press; p. 35). Minxin Pei describes the "paucity of empirically based scholarship on the actual operation of the emerging legal system," which he attributes to the poor access to relevant materials and to the small number of social scientists as opposed to lawyers engaged in such research. Minxin Pei, 2001, "Does Legal Reform Protect Economic Transactions? Commercial Disputes in China," in Peter Murrell (ed.), *Assessing the Value of Law in Transition Economies*, Ann Arbor: University of Michigan Press, pp. 180–210. See also William P. Alford, 2000, "Law, Law, What Law? Why Western Scholars of

China Have Not Had More to Say about Its Law," in Karen G. Turner, et al. (eds.), *The Limits of the Rule of Law in China*, Seattle: University of Washington Press, pp. 45–64. There were always exceptions to the general lack of empirical studies, of course, including Stanley Lubman's (1999) study of dispute resolution based not only on textual and institutional analysis, but also on formal and informal interviews and secondary literature in Chinese; Lester Ross' (1990) study of dispute resolution based on interviews conducted in a single county; Isabelle Thireau and Hua Linshan's (1997) analysis of 130 court cases from a basic-level civil court in single city; Phyllis Chang's (1989) case-study analysis of rural responsibility contract disputes; Thomas Lyons' (1994) analysis of rural disputes based on newspaper accounts; and Pei Minxin's (2001) analysis of cases reported in *Zhongguo shenpan anli yaolan* (*Anthology of Adjudicated Cases in China*). In other cases, path-breaking research, such as Randall Peerenboom's study of enforcement of arbitral awards based on the author's own snowball sample, focuses exclusively on cases involving foreigners, thus neglecting the domestic legal arena. Randall Peerenboom, 2001, "Seek Truth From Facts: An Empirical Study of Enforcement of Arbitral Awards in the PRC," *American Journal of Comparative Law*, Vol. 49, pp. 249–327. Moreover, work like that of Pei (1997; 2001), which is based on the *Zhongguo shenpan anli yaolan*, suffers from certain methodological problems. First, as Lubman (1999, 288) indicates, the source "is not representative of ordinary judicial decisions because it is a compilation of decisions submitted from courts all over China that have been chosen, edited, and often extensively rewritten by law professors before publication." Moreover, as Pei acknowledges, the cases in no way constitute a representative sample; there is no indication of any attempt by the editors to select cases that reflect the characteristics of the population of cases. Therefore, one cannot make descriptive inferences to the population based on the sample. For example, he states, "The data on the background of the litigants in the sample show that the majority of litigants are state-owned enterprises and government-affiliated nonprofit institutions" (2001, 201). Based on the available data, it cannot be shown that this statement accurately describes the population of cases. Melanie Manion's (1994) statistical study of unrepresentative samples suggests that, at best, one may use an unrepresentative sample to examine *relationships among variables*, so long as one can measure or estimate the bias in the sample and so long as that bias is not systematically related to either of the variables of interest in the relationship (Melanie Manion, 1994, "Survey Research in the Study of Contemporary China: Learning from Local Samples," *China Quarterly*, No. 139, pp. 741–765). Moreover, Manion looks specifically at unrepresentative *local* samples, which render estimation of the bias somewhat easier. Interviews conducted during the summer of 2001 with the editors and publishers of several case anthologies highlight the difficulty—if not impossibility—in assessing the bias in the sample of published cases.

18. Eighty percent of the firms are located in Nanjing; 20 percent in Shanghai. Twenty-one percent of firms are foreign (including foreign joint ventures), 21 percent private, 7 percent collective, and 48 percent state (including domestic joint ventures). Firms represent a wide range of manufacturing and service sectors, and firm size ranged from 8 to more than 10,000 employees.

19. World Bank, "Competitiveness, Technology and Firm Linkages in Manufacturing Sector, 1998-2000" (WDI ID 0359). "The dataset is created from a firm-level survey conducted by the World Bank in 2001. The survey covers 1,500 Chinese firms, which are evenly distributed across five big cities: Beijing, Chengdu, Guangzhou, Shanghai and Tianjin. The sample firms are drawn within ten sectors, of which five are manufacturing . . . and the other five are service sectors." The data cited here are for the year 2000.

20. Bing Ling, 2002, *Contract Law in China*, Hong Kong: Sweet & Maxwell Asia, p.14.

21. Regulations governing the use of contracts were first set forth in 1950 following the founding of the PRC state and the abolition of the ROC Civil Code and Nationalist law, then elaborated with the establishment of economic planning in the mid-1950s, and subsequently revived in the early 1960s during the retrenchment following the Great Leap Forward. They fell into disuse during the Cultural Revolution and were reintroduced in industry and agriculture in 1978 and 1979, respectively (Bing Ling, 2002, *Contract Law in China*, Hong Kong: Sweet & Maxwell Asia, p.11; Pitman B. Potter, 1992, *The Economic Contract Law of China*, Seattle: University of Washington Press, pp. 19–20). In 1979, the State Administration for Industry and Commerce was established and tasked with overseeing economic contracts, and in the same year economic divisions were put in place in the court system to hear economic disputes (Ling 2002: 11-12).

22. Liming Wang, and Xu Chuanxi, 1999, "Fundamental Principles of China's Contract Law," *Columbia Journal of Asian Law*, Vol. 13, No. 1, p. 3.

23. Bing Ling, 2002, *Contract Law in China*, Hong Kong: Sweet & Maxwell Asia, p. 43.

24. Pitman B. Potter, 1992, *The Economic Contract Law of China*, Seattle: University of Washington Press, p. 79.

25. Liming Wang, and Xu Chuanxi, 1999, "Fundamental Principles of China's Contract Law," *Columbia Journal of Asian Law*, Vol. 13, No. 1, p. 31.

26. Bing Ling, 2002, *Contract Law in China*, Hong Kong: Sweet & Maxwell Asia, p. 22.

27. A legal person is an entity other than a human being (e.g., a corporation) that is recognized by the legal system as having various capacities such as the ability to own property, bear liability, and undertake contractual commitments.

28. Pitman B. Potter, 1992, *The Economic Contract Law of China*, Seattle: University of Washington Press, p.32.

29. Bing Ling, 2002, *Contract Law in China*, Hong Kong: Sweet & Maxwell Asia, p.139; Pitman B. Potter, 1992, *The Economic Contract Law of China*, Seattle: University of Washington Press, p.87; Liming Wang, and Xu Chuanxi, 1999, "Fundamental Principles of China's Contract Law," *Columbia Journal of Asian Law*, Vol. 13, No. 1, p. 4.

30. Donald C. Clark, 1992, "Regulation and Its Discontents: Understanding Economic Law in China," *Stanford Journal of International Law*, Vol. 28, No. 2, pp. 282–322; He Rongfei, 1987, *Wenzhou jingji geju: women de zuofa he tansuoxing yijean (The Economic Structure of Wenzkou)*, Zhejiang: Zhejiang renmin chubanshe;

Susan H. Whiting, 2001, *Power and Wealth in Rural China: The Political Economy of Institutional Change*, New York: Cambridge University Press.

31. Susan H. Whiting, 2001, *Power and Wealth in Rural China: The Political Economy of Institutional Change*, New York: Cambridge University Press, p.150.

32. Susan H. Whiting, 2001, *Power and Wealth in Rural China: The Political Economy of Institutional Change*, New York: Cambridge University Press, p.150.

33. Susan H. Whiting, 2001, *Power and Wealth in Rural China: The Political Economy of Institutional Change*, New York: Cambridge University Press, p. 141.

34. Zhang, Houyi, and Qin Shaoxing, 1989, "pinyin title" ("The Current Situation of Development of Private Enterprises with One Million Yuan in Assets and Policy Responses"), *Journal title in pinyin* (Economic Research Reference Materials), No. 39, reprinted in "pinyin title" (*Reprinted Periodical Materials – Economic System Reform)*, 1989, No. 6, pp. 59–67.

35. Bing Ling, 2002, *Contract Law in China*, Hong Kong: Sweet & Maxwell Asia, p. 14.

36. Bing Ling, 2002, *Contract Law in China*, Hong Kong: Sweet & Maxwell Asia, p. 140.

37. Liming Wang, and Xu Chuanxi, 1999, "Fundamental Principles of China's Contract Law," *Columbia Journal of Asian Law*, Vol. 13, No. 1, p. 10.

38. As Ling (2002:43) indicates, the principle put forward in the CL is "voluntariness," but the "substantive rights recognized under the principle of voluntariness are almost identical to those under the conventional notion of freedom of contract."

39. Bing Ling, 2002, *Contract Law in China*, Hong Kong: Sweet & Maxwell Asia, p. 49.

40. Wai-keung Chung, and Gary H. Hamilton, 2001, "Social Logic as Business Logic: Guanxi, Trustworthiness, and the Embeddedness of Chinese Business Practices," in Richard Appelbauj, et al. (ed.), *The Legal Culture of Global Business Transactions*, Oxford: Hart Publishing, p. 325.

41. Thomas Gold, Doug Guthrie, and David Wank, 2002, *Social Connections in China*, New York: Cambridge University Press; and Chung and Hamilton (2001) provide good reviews of the massive literature on this topic.

42. Victor Nee, and Sijin Su, 1996, "Local Corporatism and Informal Privatization in China's Market Transition," in John McMillan and Barry Naughton (eds.), *Reforming Asian Socialism: The Growth of Market Institutions*, Ann Arbor: University of Michigan Press, pp. 111–134.

43. Nan Lin, and Chih-jou Chen, 1994, "Local Initiatives in Institutional Transformation: The Nature and Emergence of Local Market Socialism in Jiangsu," Paper presented to the Annual Meeting of the Association of Asian Studies, Boston, March 24–27.

44. Abromse King, 1991, "Kuan-his and Network Building: A Sociological Interpretation," *Daedalus*, Vol. 120, No. 2, p. 79.

45. Doug Guthrie, 1999, *Dragon in a Three-Piece Suit: The Emergence of Capitalism in China* , Princeton, N.J.: Princeton University Press; Lisa A. Keister, 2002, "Guanxi in Business Groups: Social Ties and Formation of Economic Relations," in Thomas Gold, et al., (eds.), *Social Connections in China*, New York: Cambridge

University Press, pp. 77–96 ; Susan H. Whiting, 1998, "The Mobilization of Private Investment as a Problem of Trust in Local Governance Structures," in Valerie Braithwaite and Margaret Levi (eds.), *Trust and Governance*, New York: Russell Sage Foundation, pp. 167–193; and Susan H. Whiting, 2001, *Power and Wealth in Rural China: The Political Economy of Institutional Change*, New York: Cambridge University Press.

46. Avner Greif, 1989, "Reputation and Coalitions in Medieval Trade: Evidence on the Maghribi Trader," *Journal of Economic History*, Vol. 49, No. 4, pp. 857–882; Janet Landa, 1981, "A Theory of the Ethnically Homogenous Middleman Group: An Institutional Alternative to Contract Law," *Journal of Legal Studies*, Vol. 10, No. 2, pp. 349–362.

47. Zhou Xueguang et al., 2003, "Embeddedness and Contractual Relationships in China's Transitional Economy," *American Sociological Review*, Vol. 68, No. 1, pp. 75–102. This study of contracting behavior is based on a convenience (non-random) sampling method and includes 620 firms in Beijing and Guangzhou.

48. Xueguang et al. indicate the difficulty of separating networks that arise from social ties as opposed to business contacts. The present study attempts to distinguish relationships that originate in business contacts from those that have their origins among family and friends. Ibid.

49. Xueguang et al., 2003, "Embeddedness and Contractual Relationships in China's Transitional Economy," *American Sociological Review*, Vol. 68, No. 1, p. 91.

50. Xueguang et al., 2003, "Embeddedness and Contractual Relationships in China's Transitional Economy," *American Sociological Review*, Vol. 68, No. 1, p. 96.

51. Enterprise #35.

52. Interview with lawyer sh040818p.

53. Interview with trade association representative sh040827.

54. This apparently more positive assessment of the role of trade associations in underpinning contractual relations may be a function of wording. The World Bank survey asked managers to respond to queries about the functions of associations "in regards to general members, not only to your firm in particular."

55. Interview with lawyer nj020925p.

56. Alex Xu, 2002, "First Personal Credit Law Expected Early Next Year," China Internet Information Center December 20, 2002, http://www.china.org.cn.

57. "*duobanminshangshipanjue xuqiangzhizhixing mingezhongyangjianyi sifagaige* (More than half of judgments in civil commercial matters need compulsory enforcement)," http://news.tom.com/1002/20050707-2285205.html.

58. "*kuowuyuan bankongting guanyu shehueixinyongtixi jianshederuokanyijian* (Several Opinions Regarding Building a Social Credit System) *kuobanfa* [2007]#17," http://www.gov.cn/zwgk/2007-04/02/content_569314.htm.

59. Personal communication, Donald Clarke, Faculty of Law, George Washington University, October 2004.

60. Su Ning, 2004, "Fostering Modern Credit Culture in China," speech delivered to the International Conference on "Public Policy for Credit Reporting Systems," September 28, 2004, http://www.pbc.gov.cn. Subsequent speeches document the developments to date: Su Ning, 2006, "Major Progress in the Building of a

Credit Registry System in China," *BIS Review* (October 2006); and Su Ning, 2007, "The Evolution of a Credit Information System for China," *BIS Review* (December 2007).

61. This is a preliminary finding based on coding of eighteen out of seventy-six transcripts of open-ended interview questions.

62. Despite China's gradual approach to market transition, which, beginning in 1984, allowed the coexistence of plan-administered contracts and market transactions, most exchanges were taking place in the market by 1992. More than a decade later in the early twenty-first century, government is no longer directly underpinning contracts through the economic plan, and even informal contacts introduced through government bureaus are increasingly rare. Indeed, figure 7.1 shows that, in Shanghai and Nanjing, only 8.6 percent of firms reported finding suppliers through government contacts, and only 10 percent reported finding customers this way (figure 7.2). Zhou et al. (2003) also find that government sources play a minor role in the search for contracting partners, accounting for only 6.6 percent.

63. Kathryn Hendley, Peter Murrell, and Randi Ryterman, 2000, "Law, Relationships, and Private Enforcement: Transactional Strategies of Russian Enterprises," *Europe-Asia Studies,* Vol. 52, No. 4, p. 629.

64. Max Rheinstein (ed.), 1954, *Max Weber on Law in Economy and Society,* Cambridge, Mass.: Harvard University Press, pp. 29–30.

65. (Enterprise #39).

66. Kathryn Hendley, Peter Murrell, and Randi Ryterman, 2000, "Law, Relationships, and Private Enforcement: Transactional Strategies of Russian Enterprises," *Europe-Asia Studies,* Vol. 52, No. 4, pp. 627–656; Oliver Williamson, 1985, *The Economic Institutions of Capitalism,* New York: Free Press.

67. Enterprises #61, 66, 69, 75, 1.

68. Interview with lawyer nj020935p.

69. This is often the case in the United States as well. Daniel Keating, 1997, "Measuring Sales Law against Sales Practice: A Reality Check," *Journal of Law and Commerce,* Vol. 17, No. 1, p. 125.

70. Enterprise #29.

71. Interview with lawyer nj020925p.

72. Interview with lawyer nj020925p.

73. Stanley Lubman refers to economic dispute mediation centers (*jingji jioufen tiaojie zhongxin*) during the early 1990s, but it is not clear how widespread they were, and they do not appear in accounts of mediation offered by managers in Shanghai and Nanjing (Stanley Lubman, 1999, *Bird in a Cage: Legal Reform in China after Mao,* Stanford, Calif.: Stanford University Press, pp. 276–277).

74. Stanley Lubman, 1999, *Bird in a Cage: Legal Reform in China after Mao,* Stanford: Stanford University Press, p. 276.

75. Andrew Jeffries, and James Kwan, International Arbitration Group, Allen & Overy, Hong Kong, July 27, 2004.

76. Donald C. Clarke, 2003, "Empirical Research in Chinese Law," in Erik Jensen and Thomas Heller (eds.), *Beyond Common Knowledge: Empirical Approaches to the Rule of Law,* Stanford, Calif.: Stanford University Press, p. 171.

77. Note that arbitration for foreign firms has typically taken place within a distinct set of institutions, including international arbitration enforceable under the Convention on the Recognition and Enforcement of Foreign Arbitral Awards adopted in New York on June 10, 1958 and arbitration enforeceable under the China International Economic and Trade Arbitration Commissions' rules. Randall Peerenboom, 2001, "Seek Truth From Facts: An Empirical Study of Enforcement of Arbitral Awards in the PRC," *American Journal of Comparative Law*, Vol. 49, p. 251.

78. Interview with lawyer nj020925p.

79. Stanley Lubman, 1999, *Bird in a Cage: Legal Reform in China after Mao*, Stanford, Calif.: Stanford University Press, pp. 242–244. As Stanley Lubman notes, other state agencies handled special types of arbitration, for example, Science and Technology Commissions established special arbitration commissions to handle disputes within their bailiwick.

80. Arbitration Law of the People's Republic of China (*zhonghuarenmingongheguo zhongcaifa*), 2001, Beijing: zhongguo fazhi chubanshe.

81. Bing He, 2002, "Reconstructing the Mechanism of Dispute Resolution," *Peking University Law Journal*, Vol. 14, No. 1, p. 28.

82. *State enterprises* here refers to state-run firms or shareholding enterprises in which the state is the majority shareholder. *Large* is indicated by employment levels above the median in the sample.

83. In reviewing the history of arbitration, staff members at the Shanghai Arbitration Commission highlighted the larger role for the earlier state-administered arbitration commission in the 1980s, when state enterprises dominated the economy (interview with Shanghai Arbitration Commission sh040817a).

84. *Quanguo renming fayuan sifa tongji lishi ziliao huibian 1949–1998 (Mingshi bufen)*, 2000, Beijing: renming fayuan chubanshe; Zhongguo falu nianjian, various years.

85. Bing He, 2002, "Reconstructing the Mechanism of Dispute Resolution," *Peking University Law Journal*, Vol. 14, No. 1, p. 28.

86. Litigation of contract disputes in the United States typically involves uncommon circumstances, including failed businesses, abandoned product lines, very high stakes, or extreme miscalculations (Daniel Keating, 1997, "Measuring Sales Law against Sales Practice: A Reality Check," *Journal of Law and Commerce*, Vol. 17, No. 1, pp. 99–130).

87. Zhou Xueguang et al., 2003, "Embeddedness and Contractual Relationships in China's Transitional Economy," *American Sociological Review*, Vol. 68, No. 1, p. 91.

88. Qiu Ju is the protagonist in Zhang Yimou's 1992 film adaptation ("The Story of Qiu Ju") of Chen Yuanbin's novella "The Wan Family's Lawsuit."

89. This is consistent with the findings in Ethan Michelson, 2006, "The Practice of Law as an Obstacle to Justice: Chinese Lawyers at Work," *Law & Society Review*, Vol. 40, No. 1, pp. 1–38.

90. Stanley Lubman, 1999, *Bird in a Cage: Legal Reform in China after Mao*, Stanford, Calif.: Stanford University Press.

91. New China News Agency (xinhuashe), 2000, "*quanguo lushi zigekaoshi gongbufenshuxian,*" December 8, 2000, accessed at www.people.com.cn/GB/channel1/12/20001208/342830.html.

92. "*woguojicengfaguan renshujiejinshiwuwanrenfayuan cuenzaisidawenti* (The Number of Basic-Level Judges in Our Courts nears 150,000; Four Major Problems Exist in the Courts)" October 26, 2004, www.xinhuanet.com/newscenter/2004-10/26/content_2141302.htm.

93. "*zhongguojiangjingjian faguanrenshu, tueixingfaguanzhiyehua* (China Reduces the Number of Judges, Implements Professionalization of Judges)," July 7, 2002. www.news.xinhuanet.com/zhengfu/2002-07/08/content_472993.htm.

94. Note that both court-sponsored mediation and court decisions are enforceable decisions.

95. Kathryn Hendley, Peter Murrell, and Randi Ryterman, 2000, "Law, Relationships, and Private Enforcement: Transactional Strategies of Russian Enterprises," *Europe-Asia Studies,* Vol. 52, No. 4, pp. 627–656.

96. Pitman B. Potter, 1992, *The Economic Contract Law of China,* Seattle: University of Washington Press, p. 99.

97. Here it is important to distinguish interference due to the institutional interests of the state from interference due to the personal interests of powerful state officials (i.e., outright corruption).

98. This experience is in contrast with the experiences of parties to other kinds of disputes. With respect to administrative litigation, for example, see Veron Hung, 2004, "China's WTO Commitment on Independent Judicial Review: Impact on Legal and Political Reform," *The American Journal of Comparative Law,* Vol. 52, No. 1, pp. 77–132.

99. www.court.gov.cn as cited in *China Law and Governance Review* (June 2004) www.chinareview.info. See also Donald C. Clarke, 1996, "Power and Politics in the Chinese Court System: The Enforcement of Civil Judgments," *Columbia Journal of Asian Law,* Vol. 10, No. 1, pp. 1–125.

100. Donald C. Clarke, 1996, "Power and Politics in the Chinese Court System: The Enforcement of Civil Judgments," *Columbia Journal of Asian Law,* Vol. 10, No. 1, pp. 1–125.

101. Donald C. Clarke, 1996, "Power and Politics in the Chinese Court System: The Enforcement of Civil Judgments," *Columbia Journal of Asian Law,* Vol. 10, No. 1, p. 28.

102. The court records suggest that the minimum fee for court-sponsored implementation was 150 rmb, but for larger awards, more typically approximately 1.25–1.5 percent of the award amount (a fee incurred by the winning side).

103. Donald C. Clarke, 1996, "Power and Politics in the Chinese Court System: The Enforcement of Civil Judgments," *Columbia Journal of Asian Law,* Vol. 10, No. 1, pp. 1–125; Stanley Lubman, 1999, *Bird in a Cage: Legal Reform in China after Mao,* Stanford, Calif.: Stanford University Press, p. 268.

104. In interviews, lawyers, judges, and managers alike commented on the publication of unenforced judgments in the Xinmin Evening News (Xinmin wanbao). See

also the national publicity this practice received in the People's Daily: "Shanghai guaqi'zhixing baofeng'" *Renmin ribao*, 2001.09.21, accessed at www.people.com .cn/GB/paper40/4279/492229.html.

105. Donald C. Clarke, 1996, "Power and Politics in the Chinese Court System: The Enforcement of Civil Judgments," *Columbia Journal of Asian Law*, Vol. 10, No. 1, p. 34.

106. Martin Shapiro, 1981, *Courts: A Comparative and Political Analysis*, Chicago: University of Chicago Press, p. 13.

107. Jonathan R. Hay, and Andrei Schleifer, 1998, "Private Enforcement of Public Laws: A Theory of Legal Reform," *American Economic Review*, Vol. 88, No. 2, pp. 398–403.

108. The manager further described the gang as composed of members of the local public security bureau.

109. Of course, the small role reported for such practices may reflect an unsurprising reticence about discussing these methods.

110. The perception of authority combined with unfairness may stem from the excessive formalism of judgments in many Chinese courts (Potter 2002).

111. Martin Shapiro, 1981, *Courts: A Comparative and Political Analysis*, Chicago: University of Chicago Press; Kathryn Hendley, Peter Murrell, and Randi Ryterman, 2000, "Law, Relationships, and Private Enforcement: Transactional Strategies of Russian Enterprises," *Europe-Asia Studies*, Vol. 52, No. 4, p.6 32.

112. See note 4, above.

113. Related debates occur, for example, with respect to the relationship between political culture and democracy/democratization (Edward N. Muller, and Mitchell A. Seligson, 1994, "Civic Culture and Democracy: The Question of Causal Relationships," *American Political Science Review*, Vol. 88, No. 3, pp. 635–652; Sidney Tarrow, 1996, "Making Social Science Work Across Space and Time: A Critical Reflection on Robert Putnam's *Making Democracy* Work," *American Political Science Review*, Vol. 90, No. 2, pp. 389–397).

114. Hugh T. Scogin Jr., 1994, "Civil 'Law' in traditional China: History and theory," in Kathryn Bernhardt and Philip C. C. Huang (eds.), *Civil law in Qing and Republican China*, Stanford, Calif.: Stanford University Press, p. 15.

115. For the debate with respect to Japan, see John Haley, 1978, "The Myth of the Reluctant Litigant," *Journal of Japanese Studies*, Vol. 4, No. 2, pp. 359–390; on Taiwan, see Jane Kaufman Winn, 1994, "Relational Practices and the Marginalization of Law: Informal Financial Practices of Small Businesses in Taiwan," *Law and Society Review*, Vol. 28, No. 2, pp. 193–232; on Korea, see Tae-kyu Park, 1997, "Confucian Values and Contemporary Economic Development in Korea," in Timothy Brook and Hy V. Luong (eds.), *Culture and Economy: The Shaping of Capitalism in Eastern Asia*, Ann Arbor, MI: University of Michigan Press, pp. 125–136.

116. Randall Peerenboom, 2001, "Seek Truth from Facts: An Empirical Study of Enforcement of Arbitral Awards in the PRC," *American Journal of Comparative Law*, Vol. 49, pp. 249–327.

117. John Haley, 1978, "The Myth of the Reluctant Litigant," *Journal of Japanese Studies*, Vol. 4, No. 2, pp. 359–390; Jane Kaufman Winn, 1994, "Relational Practices

and the Marginalization of Law: Informal Financial Practices of Small Businesses in Taiwan," *Law and Society Review*, Vol. 28, No. 2, pp. 193–232.

118. Shin-yi Peng, 2000, "The WTO Legalistic Approach and East Asia: From the Legal Culture Perspective," *Asian-Pacific Law and Policy Journal*, Vol. 13, p. 32.

119 John Haley, 1978, "The Myth of the Reluctant Litigant," *Journal of Japanese Studies*, Vol. 4, No. 2, p. 381.

120. John Haley, 1978, "The Myth of the Reluctant Litigant," *Journal of Japanese Studies*, Vol. 4, No. 2, p. 389. This situation began to change in Japan, Korea, and Taiwan during the 1990s.

121. Korean data from the Korean Bar Association (accessed at www.koreanbar.or.kr/eng/03.asp) and the World Bank (accessed at www.worldbank.org).

122. Ibid. and "Database Keeps Tabs on Lawyers," China Economic Net, August 5, 2004 (en.ce.cn/National/Law/200408/05/t20040805_1419061.shmtl).

123. Rosemary Foot, 2000, *Rights Beyond Borders: The Global Community and the Struggle over Human Rights in China*, Oxford: Oxford University Press, p. 258.

Chapter Eight

Developing into a Developmental State: Explaining the Changing Government-Business Relationships behind the Kunshan Miracle

Shu Keng

"Today's Kunshan will be tomorrow's China."—Junru Li[1]

"Every student of China study should go to Kunshan and observe the county carefully, finding out where the Kunshan miracle comes from and in which direction it is heading."—Fei Xiaotong[2]

INTRODUCTION: MAKING SENSE OF THE KUNSHAN MIRACLE

Back in the early 1980s, Kunshan was an inconspicuous agriculture-based area of the countryside, notorious for an endemic parasitic disease.[3] Some twenty-five years later, however, Kunshan has achieved phenomenal economic success (table 8.1). Today's Kunshan is at the top of the list among China's "most prosperous counties" (*baiqiangxian*, table 8.2). In particular, in terms of what has been eagerly encouraged, "export-oriented development"(*waixiangxin fazhan*), Kunshan is leading all the way in the country, even comparing with other rapidly growing county-level economies in coastal China (table 8.3). Nowadays, Kunshan is the world's largest production base for laptop computers—one out of every three laptops is manufactured there. In addition, every year, the county also fabricates ten million computer monitors, ten million digital cameras, and ten million cellular phones, mostly for export. Kunshan is thus a microcosm of the "world's workshop"[4] and China's "export-oriented economy."[5] It is no wonder that the question as to where the Kunshan miracle comes from has aroused the interests of many students of Chinese political economy.

Table 8.1. Selected Indicators for Kunshan's Socioeconomic Development

	1978	*1988*	*1998*	*2007*
GDP (in billion RMB)	0.24	1.63	15.05	115.18
GDP per capita (in 1000 RMB)	0.466	2.96	25.7	102.1
Total Industrial Outputs (in billion RMB)	0.28	4.59	29.37	403.07
Fixed Asset Investments (in billion RMB)	0.01	0.76	5.80	32.10
Sales of Consumer Goods (in billion RMB)	0.07	0.59	3.85	16.10
Total Fiscal Income (in billion RMB)	0.04	0.12	0.74	20.18
Contracted FDI (in billion USD)	0.0015(84)	n.a.	1.10	2.99
Actual Flow of FDI (in billion USD)	0.0003(84)	n.a.	0.60	1.44
Total Trade (in billion USD)	0.0405(90)	n.a.	2.12	53.44
Total Exports (in billion USD)	0.03807(90)	n.a.	1.19	32.32
Total Savings (in billions RMB)	0.06	0.67	10.97	106.95
Disposal Income of Urban Residents (in RMB)	479(83)	1,692	8,039	21,927
Disposal Income of Rural Residents (in RMB)	201	1,276	5,351	12,168

Source: Shucheng Zhang, 2008, *Erliji: Kunshan Gaige Kaifang Sanshinian Jubian* (Hong Kong: Zhongguo Wenhua), p. 303. Double checked with *Kunshan Statistical Yearbook.*

Apart from being adjacent to Shanghai, Kunshan enjoys almost no advantages over other county-level economies (refer to Appendix: Map of Kunshan). However, among cities in the lower Yangtze Delta region, it needs to be asked why Kunshan has been able to have the most stellar performance in terms of socioeconomic development. There are two mainstream explanations for the conundrum. The first one highlights Kunshan's institutional innovations, and argues that Kunshan has always been "one step ahead" in making adjustments to the broader politicoeconomic environment.[6] Such innovations are presumably contingent, are located in different layers, and involve the mutual adjustments of various players.[7] This account, though unquestionably valid, is a little vague in failing to point out the exact direction in which innovations have been introduced into Kunshan's institutional arrangements. As I will show in this paper, these innovations in fact reveal different patterns at different stages of Kunshan's development. More importantly, this explanation ignores the fact that almost every institutional innovation in Kunshan is initiated by the local government. The local government plays a central role

Table 8.2. Changes in the Top Ten among China's One Hundred Most Prosperous Counties/County-Level Cities (*baiqiangxian*), 2000–2006

	2000	2001	2002	2003	2004	2005	2006
1	Sunde	Sunde	Sunde	Sunde	**Kunshan**	**Kunshan**	Jiangyin
2	Nanhai	Nanhai	Nanhai	**Kunshan**	Sunde	Sunde	**Kunshan**
3	**Kunshan**	Zhangjia-gang	**Kunshan**	Jiangyin	Jiangyin	Zhangjia-gang	Zhangjia-gang
4	Jiangyin	Jiangyin	Zhangjia-gang	Zhangjia-gang	Zhangjia-gang	Jiangyin	Changshu
5	Zhangjia-gang	**Kunshan**	Jiangyin	Changshu	Changshu	Nanhai	Jinjiang
6	Changshu	Changshu	Changshu	Nanhai	Nanhai	Changshu	Wujiang
7	Taichang	Xiaoshan	Xiaoshan	Xiaoshan	Xiaoshan	Xiaoshan	Cixi
8	Nanhui	Taichang	Shaoxing	Wujin	Wujin	Wujin	Shaoxing
9	Xiaoshan	Nanhui	Taichang	Wujiang	Wujiang	Taichang*	Yixing
10	Jinjiang	Shaoxing	Wujiang	Shaoxing	Shaoxing	Wujiang	Rongcheng

Source: *Kunshan Statistical Yearbook 2007*, pp. 286–97, updated with data from http://www.chinagate.com.cn/chinese/MATERIAL/41723.htm, available by July, 31, 2008.
Note: Taichang and Wujiang both ranked number 9 in 2005.

in adopting creative approaches to secure property rights, improve service efficiency, and save businesses from administrative harassments. When all is put together, it gives rise to the Kunshan miracle.

Therefore, the other even more widely accepted explanation for the Kunshan miracle stresses the role of the local state.[8] According to this perspective, the government of Kunshan is the "primary actor" (*diyi xingdong jituan*) in relation to various institutional innovations,[9] and the close ties and collaboration

Table 8.3. Kunshan's Achievements on "Export-Oriented Development" in Comparison with Other County-Level Economies in Costal China, 2006 (in million USD)

Ranking	Counties	Actual FDI*	Growth 05-06(%)	Counties	Total Export	Growth 05-06(%)
1	**Kunshan**	1,171.90	15.9	**Kunshan**	24,366.43	35.8
2	Wujiang	678.00	13.0	Shunde	9,680.17	13.2
3	Changshu	642.68	9.9	Wujiang	7,173.00	12.9
4	Jiangyin	520.53	24.6	Zhangjia-Gang	5,487.33	33.7
5	Jiading	497.86	10.2	Jiading	5,244.60	19.5
6	Haimen	487.07	91.8	Nanhai	4,635.54	32.6
7	Xiaoshan	469.62	47.6	Jiangyin	4,570.69	43.3
8	Yinzhou	450.40	12.0	Yinzhou	4,298.02	26.7
9	Tongzhou	449.87	102.9	Changshu	4,202.00	30.1
10	Zhangjia-Gang	449.12	59.7	Xiaoshan	4,095.57	24.8

Source: Kunshan Statistical Yearbook, 2007, pp. 281–82.
Note: Actual FDI refers to the actual flow of the foreign direct investment of the year.

between local officials and foreign investors is the key that generates those innovations.[10] Not just these studies, but various surveys and reports also suggest that Kunshan's "business-friendly style" (*qinshang zuofeng*) and the performance of local government is the single most critical factor that attracts all of the foreign enterprises to Kunshan.[11]

If the local state is central to the Kunshan miracle, then what exactly is its role? As I will show in this chapter, the Kunshan government has played different roles at different stages of Kunshan's development. The purpose of the chapter is thus to illustrate how and why the local state has shifted its role. Such a shift, as I will argue later, reflects the relative bargaining power of the local state and foreign enterprises, which is in the end determined by the relative scarceness of the resources controlled by the local state and foreign enterprises, that is, land and capital, respectively. As the economic development modifies the demand for and supply of land and capital, the state-business relationships have to adapt themselves accordingly. As a result, unlike other cases, Kunshan has gradually developed into a strong state.

The remainder of the chapter is divided into four sections. What follows is a brief summary of the recent literature, which gives the background to the recent debates over the role of the state in China's market transition. With that as the basis, section three distinguishes several ideal-typical roles of the local state in terms of their relationships vis-à-vis business classes, namely, the entrepreneurial state, the service state, and the developmental state. The two sections that follow after that are devoted to characterizing the transformation of the government-business relationships in the past two decades, with section four dealing with the rise of a service state in Kunshan as the response of a late-developer to China's marketization, and section five with the shift of Kunshan toward a developmental state as a reflection of its economic achievements. In the conclusion with which the paper ends, I draw broader implications from the case study of Kunshan by providing an explanation based on the demand and supply of land and capital for the dynamics of government-business relationships in Kunshan.

BEHIND THE KUNSHAN MIRACLE: LOCAL STATE AND FOREIGN ENTERPRISES

There are two recurrent themes in the study of post-Mao China. One is how to explain China's spectacular economic success in the past three decades.[12] The other is how to pinpoint China's dynamic state-society relations during its market transition.[13] Both issues, I would argue, could be best elucidated by being studied together, especially in light of the government-business relations at the local level. In this study, I will take Kunshan as an example to show how local-level government-business relationships may facilitate economic achievements and how such achievements may in return modify the government-business relationships. In this section, I will set the stage for the discussions that follow.

Explaining the Success of China's Reforms and State-Society Dynamics

In terms of economic performance, China is undoubtedly among the world's fastest-growing economies. When compared with the records of other transitional economies, her achievements are even stunning. The question thus arises: How did China make it? A quick answer might be: China made it by following almost none of the formulas in economics textbooks.[14] It is no wonder that making sense of the "China miracle" has generated a great deal of academic interest and debate.[15]

Those who try to figure out China's success story often focus their attention on government-business relations at the local level.[16] The reason is quite obvious: although the nonstate sector is the real source of the "China miracle," it could never have possibly created the miracle by itself. In most cases, local governments either actually own (e.g., *xiangzhen qiye*, the TVE sector) or effectively control enterprises (e.g., the private sector) under their respective administrative jurisdictions and thus usually play a crucial role in making the transactions happen.[17] The interactions between local governments and nonstate enterprises thus always hold the key to our understanding of China's economic dynamism. To make sense of the China miracle or individual success stories, we had better draw attention to the government-business relations at the local level.

On the other hand, China's post-Mao reforms have been initiated with a view to maintaining the existing political institutions.[18] However, it is almost impossible to create an energetic market economy without giving people substantial freedom of exchange. China's party-state has thus had to loosen its grip over economic transactions and certain social activities. These liberalization policies, however, have set in motion the process of sea changes in China's society and politics. The social forces unleashed by the economic reforms have then affected the state-society relationships inherited from Mao's China.[19] Likewise, the dynamic state-society relationships can be most clearly observed through government-business relations at the local level and especially when they finally get involved in market activities and economic dynamism.

The paper thus seeks to characterize changes in government-business relations in Kunshan to illustrate how such a transformation may facilitate rapid development. Before proceeding with our case study, let me first briefly review the current debates over the topic.

Debates over the Success of China's Reforms: State or Market?

Recent studies on China's local government-business relations in the market transition, however, have resulted in more controversy than agreement. Broadly speaking, there are two competing analytical perspectives: the "institutional convergence" thesis and the "institutional path-dependence" perspective.[20] The former underscores the institutional transformation and thereby explains China's reform success in terms of emerging market institutions—that is, the withdrawal of pre-existing sociopolitical institutions. By contrast, the latter highlights the institutional legacies and underscores China's economic achievements in light of either the adaptation of pre-established institutions or the mix of markets and pre-established institutions.

Institutional Convergence vs. Institutional Path-Dependence

The "institutional convergence" thesis begins with an assumption that the market and the state are organized on the basis of two fundamentally different institutional principles, that is, "free exchange" versus "redistribution."[21] Therefore, the emergence of market institutions would naturally lead to the decline of the state, with the process appearing to be a "displacement."[22] The transition thus ends up with a convergence of market societies (i.e., Western-style "market societies"). For example, Victor Nee claims that "[w]here market reform has resulted in bypassing hierarchies, the extent of the vertical segmentation characteristic of socialist economies is reduced to *horizontal market relationships between private buyers and sellers.*"[23]

The contrasting conceptualization is the "institutional path-dependency" perspective. Unlike the market convergence thesis, this view begins with a different assumption: the co-existence and/or co-evolution of different institutions.[24] In the transition, newly emerging institutions do not simply replace pre-established institutions. Instead, they can always co-exist with each other, gradually adapt to each other, and reciprocally support each other.[25] This perspective is best illustrated by Wank's study of private entrepreneurs in Xiamen.[26] In this study, he skillfully shows that private enterprises have been actually expanding through the state-centered clientelistic networks: they both count on the symbiotic ties between them.

According to this perspective, after constant adjustments, the institutional legacies of the *ancient regime* can be turned into the institutions underpinning the new socioeconomic system. For example, Oi's work on the development of the rural industrial sector has effectively illustrated such adjustments.[27] In that study, she demonstrates that once the incentives have been redirected, the local state will then provide the support/protection that is essential for the growth of these rural industries. In this sense, the market transition does not necessarily lead to the decline of the state. Instead, it may give the state an opportunity to adjust itself to be able to play a new and active role in the economy following the transition.

In contrasting the two competing institutional accounts of China's transition, the "institutional convergence" thesis is founded on a strong neo-classical theoretical base. However, it is still a uni-institutional theory for too much emphasis has been given to the one institution. In addition, it is also too deterministic because it underestimates the adaptability of the state. On the other hand, the "institutional path-dependency perspective" is firmly grounded on the Chinese realities.[28] While it does offer a more balanced multi-institutional theory, it is still uncertain how the state might interact with the market as well as its agents in a dynamic way. To overcome this limitation, we need more detailed case studies to broaden our understanding of the interactions between institutional legacies and the market.

The Great Consensus: Hybrid Institutions and the Stage Metaphor

With respect to China's market transition, different scholars also take different positions: some favor the "institutional convergence" thesis,[29] while others prefer the "institutional path-dependency" perspective.[30] No matter what their positions are, these scholars have found similar institutional arrangements in their empirical research, especially in studies on TVEs in the late 1980s and early 1990s: it is the "hybrid form of institutions" that coordinated this fast growing sector.[31] Although both camps found evidence regarding the "symbiotic relations" between local government and business entrepreneurs, they held divergent interpretations. For example, the scholars assuming the "institutional path-dependency" perspective often regard the symbiosis as "the institutional process of marketization"[32] and are thus most likely to treat it as "the equilibrium in market societies."[33] On the other hand, the advocates of the "institutional convergence" thesis interpret the symbiosis as a "*pro tem* arrangement," existing only in the transitional period and under "partial reforms," that will gradually give way to market mechanisms.[34]

The debate does not seem to end yet. However, from the mid-1980s to the mid-1990s, it was probably the "institutional path-dependency" perspective that dominated the China field with its rich empirical evidence. After the corporate restructuring that took place in 1996–1997 (*chanquan gaizhi*, especially in the TVE sector), in the end, following China's accession to the WTO; however, the "institutional convergence" thesis seems to have prevailed. In other words, both camps that used to be debating have now reached a compromise on a "stage metaphor" inspired by economic rationale—that is, a market transition has to go through two separate phases: market transition and market maturity.[35] In the earlier transition stage, the state still reigns supreme and pre-established institutions remain largely intact, while in the later maturity stage, as markets gradually deepen, the state finally gives way to the market. More and more scholars seem to accept that China's transition is simply part of the process of "growing out of the plan" as the country moves toward a Western-style market society.

This paper seeks to challenge this simplified interpretation of China's transition in particular and the nature of the market transition in general. To be specific, I would like to use the case of Kunshan to demonstrate that there is more than one common path to capitalist development. As will be shown later, with its institutional innovations and socioeconomic development, the local state of Kunshan has been gradually becoming stronger rather than weaker, in contrast to what the above-mentioned stage metaphor would predict. However, it still needs to be asked why Kunshan has followed such a unique pattern of market transition. There must be other factors that contribute to the Kunshan model than those we already know, such as property rights for incentives and market mechanisms as forms of discipline. This paper thus hopes to make sense of these factors and thereby offer a broader explanation of the state-society dynamics in the market transition.

AN ANALYTICAL FRAMEWORK FOR THE STATE IN MARKET TRANSITION

Once it has been acknowledged that the Kunshan state does make a difference and that economic achievements have to be understood in light of the collaborations between the local state and foreign capital, our analysis should shift to the local-level government-business relationships. Under such circumstances, as Peter Evans suggests, the question that should be asked is not "whether" or "how much" the state matters, but "what kind" of state matters.[36] Before characterizing and explaining the dynamics of Kunshan's government-business relationships, however, we need to develop a framework to distinguish the different roles that the local state plays at different stages of Kunshan's development, similar to those developed by Linda Weiss and John Hobson,[37] Peter Evans,[38] and Richard Baum and Alexei Shevchenko.[39]

However, in accordance with this paper's argument, this section offers several ideal-typical categories for the roles of the state vis-à-vis those of the business class, primarily on the basis of two criteria, namely, "property rights" and "policy making." The former criterion involves how to split profits and the latter how to make the decisions when the state and businesses cooperate with each other in promoting local development. Based on those two criteria, we can then identify three types of roles of the local state: the entrepreneurial state, the service state, and the developmental state.

The Role of the State in the Economy: A Typology for China Study

Market transition involves constant adaptations of both state and society/business.[40] The role of the state and government-business relationships in the market transition should thus be very dynamic. To distinguish the changing state roles in the market transition, as mentioned, we need a typology for the roles of the local state. The typology proposed in this section is grounded in the relations between the state and businesses, highlighting how they might collaborate with each other—to venture across the "public-private divide"[41] and to survive and thrive in a market transition. Before establishing such collaboration, however, two questions stand out: (1) How do they share the profits they make? (2) How do they negotiate the rules they have to follow? The former has more to do with behavioral incentives and the latter with power relationships.

The first criterion involves the arrangements of property rights. The key issue here is concerned with what the state can get from the income flows, or, how it can provide state officials with the incentives to support businesses and promote growth. As we already know, their support is very critical in a transitional period. With respect to this "income flow," we have two ideal typical arrangements, namely, "sharing" or "monopolizing." The former refers to splitting the profits between the state and businesses in a direct fashion (i.e., at the local level). By contrast, the latter indicates that the businesses can enjoy all of the profits, while the state can only benefit from bureaucratic redistribution—usually through taxation. As Jean C. Oi and Andrea G. Walder maintain, the key to the economic transition is the "reassignment of property rights."[42] The arrangement of profit-sharing constitutes an essential institutional criterion that characterizes the role of the state in the transitional economy.

The second characteristic of the local-level institutional arrangement has more to do with the distribution of policy-making power. The key issue here is whether the business reserves the power to set rules in its own way, or what kind of policy-making process would attract foreign enterprises to move in and work closely with the local state to cross the "public-private divide." With respect to the policy process, we can also distinguish two ideal typical categories, namely, the "joint" or "unilateral." The former thus refers to a policy process with coordination, consultation, and mutual adjustments between the state and businesses, while the latter refers to the policy process without those interactions. As we know, the concept of "autonomy" is commonly employed to observe the role of the state in making policy.[43] If state autonomy refers to whether or not the policy goals are shaped by the social forces/business class, then the process through which those policy goals are shaped and reshaped should be our focus in observing the role of the state in the economy.

Based on the two criteria mentioned above, we can then distinguish three types of state roles in the economy: the entrepreneurial state, the service state, and the developmental state, all of which are ideal types of the state role (table 8.4).[44] First of all, in the case of the entrepreneurial state, the state and its subordinate agencies directly "undertake entrepreneurial activity"[45] and it is thus difficult to separate the state from business. Because it is the state that makes the decisions and bears the risks, it, of course, shares the profits earned.[46] In addition, as a consequence of the "state-business synergy," the state will always take into account the interests of the businesses: they are in fact their own interests.[47]

Secondly, in the case of the service state, the property rights of businesses are usually well-specified and the state-business boundary is clear cut, so that states cannot easily encroach upon businessmen's profits. As a result, the state "suppl[ies] a number of overhead facilities in partial return for taxes."[48] However, through the repeated interactions between states and businesses, ties of trust and norms of reciprocity have gradually been generated between them.[49] On the basis of these ties and norms, when making decisions, the businesses will be consulted and their interests accommodated. In this way, the ideal type of service state is constructed.[50]

Finally, in the case of the developmental state, the property rights of the businesses are similarly well-specified and the state generally cannot reap any profits directly. However, unlike the other two cases, the state leads the

Table 8.4. Contrasting Three Roles of Local Government in Terms of Their Relationships vis-à-vis Local Business Class

	Entrepreneurial State	*Service State*	*Developmental State*
Profit-Splitting Mechanisms	Sharing	Monopolizing	Monopolizing
Rule-Making Processes	Jointly	Jointly	Unilateral

Source: Marc Blecher, 1991, "Developmental State, Entrepreneurial state: The Political Economy of Socialist Reform in Xinju Municipality and Guanghan County," in Gordon White, ed., *The Chinese State in the Era of Economic Reform: The Road to Crisis* (Armonk, NY: M. E. Sharpe), pp. 265–91; Linda Weiss and John M. Hobson, 1995, *States and Economic Development: A Comparative Historical Analysis* (Cambridge, Mass.: Polity), pp. 238–53; Peter B. Evans, 1995, *Embedded Autonomy: States and Industrial Transformation* (Princeton, N.J.: Princeton University Press), pp. 43–73.

economy with its unilateral etatist planning, which should benefit society/enterprises in the long run.[51] In other words, the policy process under a developmental state does not involve any prior consultation with the businesses and does not allow sequential adaptation once opposition from businesses is faced.[52]

In addition to the three ideal-typical roles of the state, we, of course, still have two other genres, namely, "the predatory state"[53] and "the minimal state."[54] Following our previous criteria, however, for the former case, the property rights are generally poorly specified and the policy process is definitely unilateral.[55] For the latter case, because the state plays no significant role in the economy, no profit-splitting mechanisms nor policy-making processes will make much of a difference.[56] In other words, these two models of government-business relations are irrelevant in our understanding of the Kunshan case. The paper thus directs all of the attention to these three types of state roles. In the next section, we will rely on this typology to outline the economic development of Kunshan. And, please note that such typology is designed mainly for the study of China's local-level government-business relationships; thus, some of the definitions might be different from those drawing from state literature, which is rich but a bit discordant.[57]

The Empirical Research: Government and Businesses in Kunshan

Our field site, Kunshan, is located between Shanghai and Suzhou. Historically, it was often referred to as the "city of the deer" (*lucheng*) and was transformed into a county-level city within the larger Suzhou district-level city (*dijishi*) in 1989. Kunshan City occupies an area of 921 square kilometers and consists of one state-level development zone (the Kunshan Economic and Technical Development Zone/*Kunshan Jingji Jishu Kaifaqu,* KETD) and ten towns (*zhen*), with 620,000 inhabitants and about 470,000 registered migrant employees.

In 2007,[58] the GDP of Kunshan was 115.18 billion RMB in total and 102,000 RMB per capita; that is, about US $16.82 billion in total and US $14,890 per capita. Its total imports and exports amounted to US $53.44 billion for the year and attracted US $1.44 billion in actual flows of FDI in that year, for an accumulated FDI of US $10.96 billion, invovling 4,848 cases from fifty-four countries and twenty-seven cases from Fortune 500 companies. As for the foreign investment, about 2,500 Taiwanese enterprises were established in Kunshan, bringing in roughly "50% of its fiscal revenue, 60% of its tax revenue, 70% of gross sales, 80% of foreign capital, and 90% of total trade."[59] Kunshan's Taiwanese investments account for more than half of those of Suzhou, one fourth of those of Jiangsu, and one-ninth of those of China. Accompanying the Taiwanese investments, there are more than 20,000 Taiwanese businesspeople, managers, and their families settled there—which has also resulted in one Taiwanese school ("Huadong Taiwan Businessmen's School") and the one and only Taiwanese bank branch (CHB Bank in Kunshan) in China.

As mentioned earlier, Kunshan has followed a different track of market transition since the very beginning (i.e., "the Kunshan way"). Unlike most neighboring districts in southern Jiangsu (*Sunan*), due to its lagging-behind, Kunshan did not follow the common pattern of TVE-led development—that is, rural industrialization organized by an entrepreneurial state. Without an industrial base to compete with neighboring districts, the poor county then devoted its efforts to attracting outside investments (first from Shanghai, and then inland, and finally from foreign regions) and building up its "Self-Supported Economic Development Zone" (*zifei kaifaqu,* SSEDZ, later becoming the KETD). Through self-reinforcing virtuous circles between attracting foreign investments and adjusting institutional arrangements, Kunshan gradually established its well-known business-friendly "service state." Under the guidance of the local state, Kunshan witnessed a rush of FDI, and then joined the ranks of the most prosperous counties in China. That is how "the Kunshan miracle" was created. However, the story of Kunshan does not stop there. After a transitional period between 1998 and 2000, to the surprise of many observers, the Kunshan government abandoned its earlier service state and adjusted itself toward a developmental state, in which the local government not only became more capable, but also more autonomous. Nowadays, Kunshan is famous among Taiwanese businessmen for its "attracting investments with discretion" (*zhaoshang xuanzi,* in contrast with "attracting investments with efforts," *zhaoshang yinzi*) and "industrial upgrading by replacing old enterprises" (or *tenglong huanniao,* or literally translated, "emptying the cage to let in new birds").

Kunshan is picked as our case study because it follows a different path of market transition and thus is ideal to contrast with what has been widely acknowledged as *the* pattern of China's transition. In the earlier stage, Kunshan did not rely on "vague property rights," TVE-led industrialization, or moving toward an entrepreneurial state, as found in other studies on southern Jiangsu.[60] In the later period with a full opening up, the Kunshan government has become stronger and stronger, and has increasingly assumed the characteristics of a developmental state. The experiences of Kunshan thus suggest that the paths of economic transition might probably be more diverse than what we have recognized. This paper then seeks to make sense of the logic shaping Kunshan's unique path of market transition and then to hopefully shed light on the general pattern of the dynamics of government-business relationships.

The primary focus of this paper is on the interactions between Kunshan's local state and foreign enterprises in Kunshan, especially investors from Taiwan (*Taishang*). The essential part of this empirical research consisted of multiple field trips to Kunshan. Staring in the summer of 2002, I first visited Kunshan on an IIR-funded field project. After that, under the support of Taiwan's National Science Council, I visited Kunshan, collecting data and conducting interviews there once in July 2003, once in July 2004, once in August 2005, twice in 2006 (March and August), twice in 2007 (March and August), and twice in 2008 (April and August). In total, I have interviewed about eighty foreign investors, local officials, and relevant scholars at least twice and stayed for more than three and a half months there. With these contacts there, four graduate students under my supervision, Jiahuang Lin (2004), Chen-Wei Chen (2004), Weifeng Zeng (2006), and Jincan Lin (2007), also chose Kunshan as their field site for their master's thesis research. They all helped to collect background information, thereby updating my knowledge. Given the nature of my research—small N, sensitive issues, and categorical variables—this was essentially a qualitative project. Yet, to gain more diverse sources of information, the study combined three types of data-collecting strategies: (1) in-depth interviews, (2) standardized interviewing (based on semi-structured questionnaires), and (3) an intensive study of case history. All of these methods have been proven effective by one or several successful studies on similar subject matter in the Chinese context.[61]

THE RISE OF THE SERVICE STATE IN KUNSHAN, 1985–1998

Section four and section five are devoted to the characterization of the role of the local state in Kunshan and how that may affect Kunshan's economic transformation over the past quarter century. Section four stresses the rise of the service state in the earlier stage (1985–1998) and section five the shift to the developmental state in the later one (since 2002).[62] In this section, therefore, the emphasis of my analysis will be placed on the question as to why the politicoeconomic context in the mid- and late 1980s contributed to the rise of the service state instead of the entrepreneurial state in Kunshan. In the next section, I will seek to show why this service state had to adapt itself and gradually move toward a developmental state.

The Service State vs. the Entrepreneurial State in Kunshan

Among different models of economic success in post-Mao China, the "Sunan/southern Jiangsu model" is probably the most well-known.[63] As we know, the industrial transformation in Sunan was led by their township and village enterprises (TVEs), which are largely collective-owned and government-controlled. Since most TVEs grew out of collective funds and collective-owned land (*jiti tudi*) and are strongly supported by local governments, their property rights are as a rule unspecified. Through such unspecified property relationships, local governments often intervene directly in making managerial decisions, bearing all the risks, and, in the end, claiming the profits earned by the TVEs. On the other hand, in the name of the collective, local governments also hold the TVEs under strict controls, treating these enterprises just like their administrative subordinates. Local officials can give orders at any time and make rules unilaterally. These two characteristics—sharing profits and unilateral decision-making—together make the government-business relationships under the Sunan model a typical case of an entrepreneurial state.[64]

The Kunshan way, however, is very different from the experiences of other districts in southern Jiangsu. At the very beginning, Kunshan relied on outside investments rather than their own, such as TVEs, as the primary source of outputs and income. In addition, in order to compete with other neighboring cities for those outside investments, Kunshan has developed the property right arrangement in a way that is even further away from the Sunan model. On the one hand, most of Kunshan's foreign investments do not take the form of "joint ventures" (*hezi qiye*), and the county is *the* first in Jiangsu and one of the first in China to allow foreign capital to take the form of "single-ownership" (*duzi qiye*). On the other hand, unlike many other districts in the country, especially the investments in the Zhu River Delta, the lion's share of Kunshan's foreign enterprises do not pay rent for their land, but instead make "transfers with monetary compensation" (*youchang churang*). With respect to "transferring" the land to foreign capital, again, Kunshan leads the province and is among the first in the country as a whole.

For Kunshan, these innovations in property right arrangements are designed with a view to attracting more outside investment. Without such property links, unlike governments in neighboring Suzhou or Wuxi, the local state of Kunshan cannot share the profits from most of the enterprises located in their administrative jurisdiction. At the same time, in order to compete with other districts for limited foreign investments, the Kunshan government must work very hard to serve the foreign enterprises—this is where the "business-friendly style" comes from—and cannot make any rules or policies without prior consultation or repeated follow-up adjustments. These two characteristics—no profit sharing and joint decision-making—together then make the government-business relationships in Kunshan quite different from those elsewhere in Sunan, and the role of the local state becomes very close to that of a service state.

Origins of Kunshan's Service State: Incentives and Constraints

Why did Kunshan deviate from the common development model of Sunan and create the service state? The answer is found in the politicoeconomic context of the mid- and late 1980s, when Kunshan's economy was ready to take off. We can make sense of the background and the course of Kunshan's transformation by focusing on the leadership's incentives, the constraints of an agriculture-based economy, and the processes accompanied by some unexpected opportunities. All these have contributed to Kunshan's different path toward economic success.

Incentives

The broader context of Kunshan's development is still the post-Mao reforms: the Kunshan miracle would not have happened without the reforms, especially the fiscal reforms combining the "devolution of decision power" (*fangquan*) and "reserving shares of revenues" (*rangli*).[65] The local state of Kunshan thus obtained strong incentives and the ability to play a role in promoting economic growth. However, the story of the Kunshan miracle did not start until 1984, when Wu Kequan was formally appointed the magistrate of Kunshan. Wu, having served at the State Planning Commission (*Guojia Jiwei*) and having worked in Gansu and Wuhan, was an experienced economic technocrat and a true believer of "once serving a term, being obliged to bring profits" (*weiguan yiren, zaofu yifang*). Once appointed, Wu and his colleagues felt that they must lead the county out of poverty. At that time, Kunshan was still the most backward county in Suzhou, often being referred to as the "always number six" (*xiaoliuzi*). With the inducement granted from fiscal reforms and the leadership's devotion to economic development, the incentives for Kunshan to take off were largely in position.

Constraints

Since the leaders' motivation alone could not bring about an economic takeoff, they had to find ways to remove the tight constraints on a latecomer. Kunshan in the early 1980s was still an agricultural economy—until 1984, more than 80 percent of its inhabitants were engaged in agriculture.[66] In addition, when neighboring areas seized the chances to develop their TVEs in the early 1980s, Kunshan was still content with its stable production of rice and nonstaple food. Furthermore, as we know through "increasing returns" and "economic agglomeration," if it fell behind, it would be very difficult for it to catch up. Therefore, when urged to build up Kunshan's industrial development, the leadership faced the quandary of the "five shorts" (*wuque*): Kunshan had no funds, no technology, no markets, no facilities, and no managerial skills/experiences.[67] Even worse, being merely a county, Kunshan enjoyed no advantages to bargain with superiors for scarce resources and preferential policies (*youhui zhengce*). Kunshan was trapped in the vicious circle of underdevelopment. According to many historical overviews, the efforts of Wu and his colleagues had been repeatedly frustrated due to Kunshan's disadvantageous conditions. Wu had to find an innovative way to make the dream come true. The key to the success of the new strategy was to introduce what Kunshan did not have from the outside. This strategy led Kunshan along a new path of development, that is, outward-oriented development and a service state to manage such development.

Processes

To find a way out of the "latecomers' trap," Kunshan's highly motivated leaders introduced a series of institutional innovations. However, these innovations did not come all of a sudden; they were found and adopted through a process that was mixed with chances and learning. The window of opportunity first opened to Kunshan in the early 1980s when Wu and his colleagues found that some of the natives of Kunshan held critical positions in the Shanghai government. Through their mediation, Kunshan successfully built "cross-regional cooperation" (*hengxiang lianhe*) with Shanghai, selling agricultural products to Shanghai and introducing some of the factories to Kunshan. The experiences of setting up "joint-ventures" with Shanghai companies taught the leadership of Kunshan that they had to offer "incentives" to attract "outside" investments and technology, and that they should not ask for too much so as not to "kill the hen to get the eggs" (*shaji qunuan*). With the experience of dealing with "outside" investors, the second opportunity knocked on the door: many Third Front (*sanxian*) enterprises looked for the possibility to move back to Shanghai—this was where they were previously located as hometown employees. Since Shanghai had really no incentive to accept these firms, Kunshan again seized the opportunity to build up its industrial bases. In addition, in the meantime, purely out of chance, a Japanese company making leather gloves, named Swany, settled in Kunshan, making Kunshan the county with the first joint-venture in Jiangsu.

Through dealing with Shanghai and Third Front enterprises, the leadership of Kunshan learned how to deal with outside investors, with what they wanted, and how they could solve their problems. They strongly felt that Kunshan needed more "privileged conditions" to attract more outside investments. So, under Wu's guidance, Kunshan finally launched its "Self-supported Economic Development Zone" (SSEDZ) in 1985. Once it became a "development zone," the Kunshan leadership then reassessed their strengths and weaknesses in promoting growth. They found that investments had become the primary source of economic growth, and that most of the regions were competing for limited capital. As a result, it would be more and more difficult for Kunshan to attract investment from neighboring regions. They also found that their adjoining Shanghai was one of the advantages Kunshan possessed and that they should target the foreign investment that Shanghai had left over. Therefore, after the SSEDZ was completed in late 1980, Kunshan increasingly relied on foreign investments and made more successful attempts to attract foreign capital. This direction then led to Kunshan's unique path of market transition.

Consolidation of Kunshan's Service State: Institutional and Noninstitutional Arrangements

Given the leadership incentives and the structural constraints, plus the process of continuous learning and adjustments through virtuous cycles of adaptation and success, Kunshan assumed more and more characteristics of a service state, which was based on certain institutional and noninstitutional arrangements that are specified in this section.

Institutional Foundations of the Service State

The Kunshan miracle was established on both institutional and noninstitutional practices. Among them, some involved arrangements for property rights, some frameworks for reaching decisions, and some customs or traditions that sustained these institutional features. Put together as a package, Kunshan then looked most attractive and the economic miracle was finally generated. Among these characteristics, arrangements regarding property rights were the most fundamental: they made the most effort, made the most political effort, and contributed most to Kunshan's early advantages in attracting foreign capital. While maintaining these arrangements, the government of Kunshan later became famous for its "business friendliness," which can be considered to be value added to these fundamental arrangements.

In terms of the government and business relationships, the role of the Kunshan government as a service state was derived from these institutional and noninstitutional practices. On the one hand, the arrangements regarding property rights—single-ownership and land possession—saved businesses' profits from being shared by the local state. After all, joint ventures and land tenure are the primary sources of state encroachment. On the other hand, certain institutional and noninstitutional practices helped safeguard the businesses' right to be consulted and their interests accommodated prior to policy-making. These practices together give rise to the service state.

Property Right Arrangements

Kunshan was among the first counties in Jiangsu and even in China to allow or even encourage "single ownership" and "land ownership" while introducing foreign capital.[68] In the late 1980s, it was common to introduce foreign investment in the form of joint-ventures, and it was much safer politically. Although its approach was questioned and criticized, Kunshan still decided to take the initiative in allowing foreign investments to take the form of single ownership. This was because of the following three reasons, according to the founder, Wu Kequan. First of all, it was easier to introduce foreign capital: those foreign enterprises preferred single ownership to save potential disputes. Kunshan adjusted its approach to fit the demands of foreign capital so that it could attract foreign capital faster—it was very eager to catch up—and to beat opponents—as the neighboring regions also rose to compete for foreign investments. Second, single ownership enabled foreign capital to be introduced more rapidly: Kunshan did not need to prepare to match funds to set up "joint ventures." Third, the leadership of Kunshan knew that only when foreign enterprises were allowed single ownership and to enjoy all the profits, would they be willing to introduce up-to-date technology, hand over foreign markets, and bear all the risks of making investments in Kunshan. From its previous experiences, Kunshan learned what foreign investors really wanted and the leadership was willing to adjust its approach to serve the demands of foreign capital. In this way, we then have the first pillar of the Kunshan miracle.

As in most developing counties, being a latecomer, Kunshan was also caught in a "vicious cycle" of capital shortage: the county needed foreign capital but, before inviting foreign investment and, in particular, making itself competitive, Kunshan had to invest in land acquisition (*zhengdi*) and infrastructural set-up (*santong yipin* in the 1990s and *qitong yipin* in the 2000s). Kunshan had to find the source of money for the start-up fund, and probably the only source at that time was to sell foreign investors something they genuinely wanted: land for industrial use. So the "land transfer with monetary compensation" was initiated in order to collect the start-up fund and also as a strategy to attract foreign capital. Furthermore, at the same time, the principle guiding land transfer, that is, the "cycle development" (*gundong kaifa*), was also practiced in Kunshan: the state first took over a small piece of land and improved its infrastructure, then sold the land to foreign enterprises to set up factories, and finally made use of the money to acquire and improve another small piece of land. That was the other pillar of the Kunshan miracle.

Decision-Making Coordination Mechanisms: Formal Institutions

In addition to the property right arrangements, which established the basis of Kunshan's competitiveness, Kunshan was particularly famous for being a "business friendly" environment for foreign enterprises, which significantly added to Kunshan's competitiveness among neighboring regions. As claimed earlier, such a reputation was grounded on institutionalized mechanisms and noninstitutionalized traditions or practices. The former consisted of the following three categories of arrangements.

The first had to do with channels to facilitate government-business coordination and consultation. First of all, the government of Kunshan encouraged foreign investors to establish their associations, such as the Taiwanese Business Association (*taizi qiye xiehui,* TBA), and Associations of Foreign Investors (*waizi qiye xiehui*) to facilitate the government-business interactions. Once these platforms were ready, local officials, usually the vice mayor in charge and the heads of the branches responsible for economic affairs, would participate in these associations' activities, both formal or informal. On the other hand, the Kunshan government also called for a bi-monthly "Salon for Foreign Investors" (*waishang touzi qiy salong*), to announce policy proposals and collect responses from the foreign investor community. The government also invited representatives from these associations to the Kunshan City People's Congress, both to regular meetings and occasional public hearings, such as the Assembly of Urban Planning (*chengshi guihua huiyi*). Even though they did not have the right to cast votes, these representatives would be kept informed of policy proposals and debates and encouraged to express their concerns or support, especially when they were stakeholders.

The second was the design of a mediation system among different branches inside the Kunshan government (e.g., the Industry and Commerce Administration Bureau, the Tax Bureau, and the Office of Taiwan Affairs), among different levels under the Kunshan government (say, town governments and village governments), and between foreign enterprises and local enterprises. The center of the system was the "Service Center for Foreign Investors" (*waizi qiye fuwu zhongxin*), which was a private enterprise controlled by the Management Committee of the KETD. The Center provided a "packaged service"(*yitiaolong fuwu*), taking care of everything related to setting up a business—starting from the investment advice, contract negotiations, formal registration, land acquisition, electricity, and water supply, to applications for tax reductions and environmental impact assessments, as well as all the regular services afterwards, such as recruiting workers, the provision of meals, finding transportation, locating markets, the supply of materials and parts, establishing local subcontracting networks, and providing all the living necessities for the employees.[69] To make the system work smoothly, the

Kunshan government established an office referred to as the "Joint Center for Application Reviewing" (*shenpi duwu zhongxin*), that was put together with staff from all related bureaus and headed by the vice mayor to back up the service center.

Finally, institutions were designed to make quick responses and solve unexpected problems, including the "Immediate Problem-Tackling Center" (*mashangban zhongxin*) and the "Complaint Processing Center" (*waishang tousu zhongxin*). The former was open twenty-four hours a day and carefully handled every case, as their rule said, "The first one who takes the case should take care of it, and the second visit for the same case will receive the final decision" (*shouwen fuzezhi, liangwen zhongjiezhi*).[70]

Decision-Making Coordination Mechanisms: Informal Institutions

Informal connections between cadres and entrepreneurs have always been a key to local-level government-business relationships.[71] In addition to the institutional foundation specified above, there were other, not-yet-institutionalized, customs and practices that also significantly contributed to the collaboration and partnership between the local state foreign enterprises. These practices took two different forms: some as principles and norms and others as practices and customs.

For the former, Kunshan officials dealing with foreign enterprises had to observe the "old three" rules (*laosantiao*). First, "never say no or I can't to foreign investors"; the only thing Kunshan officials can say is "let's work on that." Second, they needed to be friendly to and helpful toward (foreign) businesses (*qingshang*). Third, they needed to always treat foreign investors as tax-payers; you must serve them just as you serve those who feed you. After the mid-1990s, those rules were replaced by the "new three" rules (*xinantiao*) in order to avoid common mistakes while attracting foreign investments. According to these rules, all the local cadres of Kunshan needed, first, to keep every promise they made: "no misleading and no cheating." Second, they needed to observe the principle of the "rule of law," and could not promise anything illegal. Third, they had to make every effort to reduce the foreign investors' costs—production as well as transactions costs, such as tariffs and red tape while passing through the customs.

In addition to these principles and norms, there were some other common practices inherited from the leaders in the 1980s. For example, cadres who worked in KETD, or were in any way related to foreign enterprises, had to keep their mobile phones on twenty-four hours a day so that they could be reached twenty-four hours a day. If a foreign investor wanted to meet the vice mayor of Kunshan in charge of economic affairs, an appointment was to be arranged in two hours, and if it was for the mayor, four hours at the most, and for the party secretary, a day at the most.[72] In the mid-1990s, the then–party secretary even moved his office to the Kunshan Hotel to live next door to most of the foreign entrepreneurs interested in Kunshan. In addition to these, there were many legends making their rounds in the Taiwanese investors' community about how local cadres helped out foreign investors, ranging from helping establish one of the two Taiwan Businessmen's Schools, and negotiating the level of personal income tax with higher levels of government, to helping out a Taiwan businessman involved in a traffic accident or urgently looking for a dentist to pull a bad tooth.

In a relationship-oriented society like China, formal institutional arrangements must be sustained and lubricated by informal *guanxi*. This is exactly the case with Kunshan. Let us take the most critical interactions between the Kunshan government and TBA as an example. To act as an institutional channel for Taiwanese investors and local governments, the TBA formally arranged positions for all the relevant local cadres, for example, the Kunshan mayor as their honorary chair, the director of KETD as the vice-honorary chair, the heads of relevant bureaus of the Kunshan government—in charge of economic affairs, industries and business, taxation, land management, and the police office—on their advisory board. All would be invited to participate in the regular meetings of the TBA. However, more importantly, Taiwanese entrepreneurs also met with these officials in various ceremonies—such as Donations for Establishing Primary Schools in Inland China or for someone's wedding ceremony. Sometimes, they just had a toast, but on other occasions they might have also grabbed the chance to discuss the problems that needed to be solved. Local officials really cared about the opinions of Taiwanese entrepreneurs and were willing to help them solve any problems they had. As a result, the TBA was referred to as the fifth government branch in Kunshan (next only to the Party, the Government, the People's Assembly, and the Political Consultative Conference).[73] Furthermore, based on the advice of the TBA, the Kunshan government later decided to launch the country's first export processing zone (i.e., the "*Kunshan Chukou Jiagong Qu*," or KEPZ, in 2002).

As a conclusion, and partly due to structural constraints and partly to historical path-dependence, Kunshan gradually assumed the defining characteristics of the Kunshan way, unlike most other success stories in southern Jiangsu (e.g., Oi's "local state corporatism" and Ding Lu and Xiaobo Lu's rent-seeking networks).[74] It is these institutional and noninstitutional arrangements together—constituting what I call the service state—that made the Kunshan miracle a reality.

KUNSHAN'S SHIFT TO A DEVELOPMENTAL STATE, 2002–NOW

The Kunshan miracle is grounded on the ability of the state to meet the needs of foreign capital. However, unlike the expectations of the liberalist version of global transformation, Kunshan has not maintained its service state, while increasingly integrating itself into the global economy. On the contrary, as our field research suggests, due to the demand for further development, the government of Kunshan gradually gave up its role as a service state and gradually assumed the characteristics of a developmental state after the year 2002. How and why does this unexpected trend happen? In this section, I briefly characterize the process and explain the reasons.

Minimalist State vs. Developmental State in Kunshan

As we can see from the earlier discussions, the service state of Kunshan was created as a response to the problem the Kunshan leadership faced in the mid- and late 1980s. In addition, the service state helped Kunshan attract a great deal of foreign capital so that it became the most successful example in China's "outward oriented development," and dominated coastal China in the early or mid-1990s. However, with certain advantages brought about by "one step ahead," Kunshan met another problem in the late 1990s and early 2000. Partly because of a shortage of land that was partly due to the competition from neighboring regions, Kunshan had to make adjustments to maintain its growth rate. In order to deal with these challenges, the role of the Kunshan government has assumed more and more characteristics of being a developmental state.

The adaptation of Kunshan can also be viewed as the result of both China's and Kunshan's response to globalization. For the country, accession to the WTO has led to more and more FDI and, after being rewarded by the model, the central government has gradually leaned toward the rule of evaluating the performance (*zhengji*) of local officials by not just the GDP growth but also the amount of FDI. Being motivated by such a criterion, the leaders of Kunshan then tried their best to maintain the level of economic growth and FDI flow.[75] However, it is not easy to maintain the level of FDI flow, and Kunshan faces the new challenges while trying to catch new opportunities. Among these challenges, the shortage of land and the competition from neighboring regions are the most serious. To be able to solve the problem of the shortage of land and to upgrade its industrial structure to attract more technological- and capital-intensive industries, the government of Kunshan has had to insulate itself from the community of foreign entrepreneurs.

The path along which Kunshan has traveled is quite different from what most scholars would expect. In order to grab the opportunities brought about by embracing the global market, the local government of Kunshan has been forced to adjust itself to better the expectation of the foreign capital and the maintenance of its leading role in the "outward development." In other words, to fight for its survival in the new politicoeconomic context, the state of Kunshan has gradually built up its autonomy and has thus adjusted itself from a service state to a developmental state.

The Road to the Developmental State

Why has Kunshan deviated from the common path of "state shrinking" or "state retrenching" and instead moved in the opposite direction toward a developmental state? The answer again can only be found in the politicoeconomic context of the late 1990s and early 2000s, when the previous success formula faced a dead end and serious challenges. We can make sense of the background and the course of such transformation by looking at its incentives, constraints, and processes. These factors altogether bring Kunshan to a different path of economic success.

Incentives

Again, Kunshan's transformation is driven by the motivation of the local leadership, although it was somewhat due to the leadership's incentives that Kunshan took off. The new generation of Kunshan leaders was eager to bring about economic development, because this was the key to demonstrating their performance. As we know, after the mid-1990s, the central government of China tended to evaluate the performance of local government based on criteria that were mainly composed of indicators of economic development.[76] Under the new system of performance, the record of Kunshan is of course the most dazzling one. Therefore, those who are appointed to positions in charge of Kunshan are definitely among the most promising and ambitious leaders in Suzhou or Jiangsu. Furthermore, anyone in charge of Kunshan also expects to follow the example of his or her predecessors to climb up on the ladder in order to create a promising career. Among the former leaders of Kunshan, two have been promoted to vice-governor of Jiangsu and almost everyone has been elevated to the mayor or party secretary of a district-level city (say, Changzhou, Zhenjiang, Yangzhou, and Xuzhou). Therefore, the new leaders of Kunshan are competing with their predecessors for performance: they cannot just continue to attract FDI and maintain the GDP growth rate, but they must also seize remarkable investment cases such as major projects,

projects with Fortune 500 companies, or projects introducing unique technology. Therefore, the leadership of Kunshan has tried its best to boost its performance.

Constraints

For the new leaders of Kunshan, it is not easy to keep the existing record, let alone constantly set new ones. Serious challenges to the previous developmental model come in both ways, the first being due to the shortage of land and the second the harsh competition from other neighboring latecomers. After several major efforts to break through the limits and get rid of followers, Kunshan has gradually assumed the characteristics of being a developmental state.

The most serious challenge facing Kunshan in maintaining its continued growth is the shortage of land. As mentioned in a previous discussion, the earlier success of Kunshan in attracting foreign capital was at least partly based on the transfer of land ownership. As a result, the rapid development of Kunshan has been accompanied by the rapid consumption of land. According to recently released statistics, in Suzhou,

> According to a previous estimate, every percent in the growth of industrial output would cost Suzhou about 4000 mu (one-sixth of an acre) of arable land. Therefore, with an average 22% annual growth rate of industrial output, Suzhou would lose 100,000 mu of arable land in each year. However, in reality, the situation is worse: just in the year 2002, the cultivated area of Suzhou has shrunk by 225,000 mu, leading to a decrease of 8.2% in grain production, a 22% decrease in vegetable oil production and a 42% decrease in cotton production.[77]

Kunshan's shortage of land stems from not just heavy consumption but also from its limited supply, the latter being mainly due to the following three reasons. First of all, the supply of land is by nature limited: the boundary of the administrative jurisdiction is fixed and the land can neither be subjected to double use nor be recycled. For the Kunshan leadership, once it is occupied, the land is gone. They must therefore make use of the land wisely. Second, in 2002 and 2003, the Central Government set a strict limit on the "land-use quota" (*yongdi zhibiao*) with a view to guarding against the overuse of arable land (*guodu kaifa*) and also to slow down the "development fever" (*kaifare*) or "economic overheating" (i.e., the policy package referred to as "macro-economic stabilizing policies" *hongguan tiaokong*).[78] Third, unlike in the old days, local governments could no longer collect the land from the tillers/villages so easily without much resistance and handsome compensation.[79] This was partly due to the policy of the central government: the Sixteenth Party Congress of the CCP (2002) marked a shift in its development strategy from chasing only for GDP growth to pursuing a "Well-Off Society" (*jianshe xiaokang shehui*, 2002) and then also "a Harmonious Society" (*hexie shehui*, 2003). These policies stressed the protection of the disadvantaged, especially the peasants losing their farming land. On the other hand, following the national trend, Jiangsu also announced the policy of "Two Pioneerings" (*liangge shuaixian*, reaching the well-off society and simultaneously realizing a modern society, 2004) and set Kunshan as the model for the province. This policy then led to Kunshan's movement "To Learn to Be the Pioneer of the Two Pioneerings" (*xuexi zuo liangge shuaixian de paitoubin*, 2004), the "Making the People Rich" Project (*fumin gongcheng*, 2004), and a later announced standard to compensate the peasants who sacrificed their farm land. The compensation included immediate monetary transfers, housing replacement, or relocation (one square-foot built-up for one square-foot torn-down, *chaiyi huanyi*), social security (medical and unemployment insurance), and an annually paid pension (first the "3-6-9 Project" and then the "4-8-12 Project").[80] All these policies and people's expectations entailed enormous costs of land transfer.

As a result, it has become more and more costly for Kunshan to offer cheap land to foreign investors. If Kunshan chooses to keep offering land ownership, its land will soon all be gone and the consequences will be frightening, regardless of whether it is for food security or in order to attract FDI. However, if Kunshan stops offering land ownership, the investors looking for a "location" will also turn to other places and Kunshan's FDI will soon slow down, if not grind to a halt. The shortage of land is thus an absolute and pressing constraint on Kunshan's sustainable development. The leadership of Kunshan has had to make the best of this extremely limited resource.

Processes

Kunshan's earlier success is grounded on several premises, namely, institutional arrangements for land ownership and single ownership and a state always ready to offer help. However, the limited supply of land and the harsh competition from neighboring regions suggests that the existing formula for success is running out of advantages. Without significant adjustments, the Kunshan road is leading toward a dead end. The role of the Kunshan government has thus gradually shifted toward a developmental state.

The pressures pushing for a modification of Kunshan's growth strategy have included the shortage of land. However, while Kunshan is strictly in need of land, its neighboring regions are trying their best to offer free or almost free land to foreign investors. These regions include neighboring counties in Suzhou such as Wujiang and Suzhou New District and other places in Jiangsu (such as Wuxi New District), Zhejiang (such as Xiaoshan and Jiaxing), and even the suburban counties of Shanghai (mainly, Songjiang). These late-late-comers have all tried to copy the earlier Kunshan model to attract foreign investors. They have all been ready with land ownership, single-ownership, and a service-oriented government. In addition, each of them offers something more to attract the foreign capital that should have come to Kunshan, such as even cheaper land, cheaper labor, tax deductions compensated from local fiscal revenue, and a government that works even harder. Without the land and all its effective innovations soon being copied, Kunshan is thus in a difficult situation to compete with these followers.

In the meantime, several developments led to Kunshan's decision to give up its earlier strategy to attract foreign capital and save itself from the "race to the bottom." First of all, some commentaries on the economic slow-down/stagnation of the Zhu River Delta in the late 1990s and the so-called "northbound migration of foreign capital" (*waizi beiyi,* foreign investments moving to the Yangtze River Delta) showed up in about 2002 and caused a panic in Kunshan, since the problem of Shenzhen and Dongguan was also reportedly caused by the shortage of land. In learning from these experiences, Kunshan had to take measures before it was too late. Second, the competition from neighboring regions became even harsher and some of the foreign investments even set up new factories with Kunshan's competitors because they offered cheaper land and labor and a lighter tax and social security burden. Kunshan was losing the war on cutting the costs of foreign investments.

It was thus time for Kunshan to redefine its competitiveness. The reason for this is quite obvious: without inexhaustible land and the prohibition of the copying of innovations, there was no chance of Kunshan winning the race by lowering its production and transaction costs, that is, the "race to the bottom." Kunshan could only give up those foreign enterprises concerned primarily with cost cutting—largely small or medium-sized labor-intensive enterprises—and focus on those that cared for a broader range of business goals or even the living environment—mostly high-tech, large capital-intensive enterprises. It was unclear whether this strategy might work, but two additional trends helped consolidate the transition. One was the above-mentioned "performance factor," where every region was looking for FDI and had made certain progress. In this regard, some local governments needed remarkable cases to impress their superiors: a major investment case was usually worth more than a dozen smaller projects. In addition, and more importantly, the further opening-up of China also led to huge numbers of multinational conglomerates being highly interested in making investments in Kunshan—partly because of the "agglomeration effects" and partly because of its transparent business-running environment and capable and efficient bureaucracy. The continued and increasing flow of FDI proved that such a transition was a successful move.

In order to attract the high-tech, large-scale, capital-intensive enterprises, Kunshan had to eliminate many kinds of pollution, significantly improve the living environment, relocate labor-intensive enterprises, and empty the land for targeted foreign enterprises. In other words, to make this transition possible, Kunshan needed more urban planning and vision and the capacity to fulfill the plan. The government-business relationships in Kunshan thus gradually assumed the characteristics of a developmental state when Kunshan gradually embraced the new growth strategy.

The Developmental State Takes Shape: Institutional and Noninstitutional Arrangements

As claimed earlier, the government-business relationships in the Kunshan government were gradually transformed from those of a service state to those of a developmental state. During the transition, some institutional arrangements were maintained while others were modified. As in the previous section, my discussion that follows can be divided into institutional and noninstitutional aspects of the new coping strategy of Kunshan toward the shortage of land and the competition from neighboring regions.

Institutional Foundations of the Developmental State

As shown above, the institutional arrangements for property rights and facilitating decision-making play a key role in the operation of government-business relationships at the local level. While the government of Kunshan adjusted its role to act more like a developmental state, it maintained most of the features with regard to the property right arrangements. As before, when making deals with foreign enterprises, "single ownership" was still encouraged and "land ownership" was normally granted. However, in order to meet Kunshan's development goals, land ownership ceased to be the absolute right that it had been in the past. Sometimes, factories would be torn down and moved away (i.e., the "emptying the cage to let in new birds" policy) because of infrastructure construction, industrial upgrading, or just in order to appropriate the land. Of course, these enterprises would be given a monetary compensation that was much higher than in other neighboring regions. This is why such deals were considered to be fair in the eyes of Kunshan officials. Furthermore, all of these were "necessary" for the future development of Kunshan.

At the same time, the Kunshan government placed an emphasis on industrial upgrading as the criterion for inviting investments. According to the government, the criterion for accommodating foreign enterprises shifted from "everybody is welcome" (*laizhe buju*) to "picking the best" (*zeyou jiena*). This was because the guiding principle for Kunshan's development had been transformed from targeting "the plainer, the easier, and the faster" (*duan, ping, kuai*) to pursuing "the higher, the bigger, and the more modern" (*gao, da, xin*), an objective that was formally announced in 1999.[81] Given the principle of industrial upgrading and the shortage of land, the Kunshan government also proposed the "5-4-3-2 Rule": to appropriate one *mu* of land in the export processing zone (KEPZ), a foreign enterprise had to invest at least US $500,000 in the state-level development zone (KETD), it had to invest at least US $400,000, in the provincial-level development zone, US $300,000, and in the town-founded industrial zone, also US $200,000.[82]

By the same token, in addition to emphasizing some general rules based on the "high-tech, large-scale, low-pollution" principle, in order to establish its nationwide leadership via the mechanism of agglomeration, Kunshan targeted three industrial sectors for investment: information technology, precision machinery, and bio-technology. For example, the government devoted much effort to establishing industrial networks or supply chains for the IT industry in Kunshan. Everywhere in Kunshan one can hear about how the local official in charge of foreign investments served as the boss of a Taiwanese dragon-head enterprise for foot-washing to win over investment deals and how a vice mayor had taken apart a notebook computer and asked his subordinates to find out which parts were not yet manufactured in Kunshan.

To sum up, while Kunshan has embraced a new development strategy, it has maintained most of the institutional arrangements in the earlier years, but has also made considerable adjustments in regard to the institutional rules. These new rules have been firmly implemented, which constitutes the topic of the next section.

Decision-Making Coordination Mechanisms: Formal and Informal Institutions

Similar to the above-mentioned institutional features, the institutional mechanisms facilitating coordinated decision-making seem to be the same as they used to be. The channels between business associations such as the TBA and local government are maintained, and congressional meetings/hearings are held periodically. Casual and informal contacts and exchanges of concerns and ideas are similarly as frequent as before. However, in reality, the mode of the interactions between local officials and foreign enterprises has changed dramatically. As two Taiwanese businesspeople comment:

> Things have been changing a lot. When we express concerns or give advice, they [local officials] look like they are listening. However, in the end, they al-

> ways have their own way. They think they know and are thus quite willful now. Sometimes, I suspect that they have a development plan that we don't know and, in the plan, we [normal Taiwanese enterprises] are all gone. (Personal interview, August 3, 2004)

> When we go complaining about things, taking last time as an example, about the rule only allowing factories with over 1000 employees to build a dorm, it is quite clear they [local officials] no longer care about you anymore. You are not coming from Europe or America, and neither are you huge enterprises like Foxconn. They won't think about your survival while making policies. But what can you do? Leave Kunshan? This is probably just what they want. (Personal interview, July 30, 2004)

In other words, in terms of the decision-making process, the local state of Kunshan has become more autonomous and insulated from most of the demands or pressures of the business community, with the exception of a few VIP enterprises. On the other hand, while implementing the policies, the local government has also been getting stronger:

> Let's take my neighbor, a Taiwanese investor, as example. That was early this year. The Yushan Town wanted to extend the road from 40 meters to 80 meters wide and thus tear down his factory buildings. This was very difficult for him, for there was no place to relocate the buildings and assembly lines. So he went to talk to the director of the town's industrial zone, the town mayor, and the party secretary, claiming that the traffic did not need a road 80 meters wide and suggesting that the town could make this a two-step plan and this time just extend the road to 60 meters wide. All the local officials were willing to listen. However, in the end, they still decided to extend the road just like their original plan, with a counter offer of reserving a piece of land in the new development zone for my neighbor so he could move all of the factory away. (Personal interview, July 26, 2004)

> Unlike in the old days, rules usually have exceptions. Many things can be bargained for. If you told them [local officials] frankly what's the problem, you would normally get some special considerations. Nowadays, the policy-implementing generally cannot be discounted. Their [local official] "special services" [tebie zhaogu] are really selective, only very few "earlier pioneers" (laobin) like us can get some. (Personal interview, August 10, 2006)

In conclusion, as Kunshan adopts a new development strategy, the local state also has to play a new role, assuming more of the characteristics of a developmental state. To keep its arms open to foreign capital, the state remains unconnected to foreign entrepreneurs' profits. However, to carry out the development plan that promises sustainable prosperity, the state has to insulate itself from vested interests and is determined to crack down on resistance. The state has thus become increasingly autonomous and capable, becoming close to the archetype of the developmental state in East Asia. In this sense, the transformation of the local-level government-business relationships can be understood to be a function of the shift in development strategy.

Responses from the Business Community: The Transitional Confrontation

Of course, the mode of government-business interaction cannot be decided by the government side only: the government can play a stronger role only when the business community accepts it. However, as we can imagine, the business community would be inclined to resist the state's transition from a service state to a developmental state. According to our interviews, the sudden drop in Kunshan's ranking on TEEMA's list of the "Highly Recommended Chinese Cities for Taiwanese Investors" in 2003 can be considered to result from the protests of the Taiwanese business community against the Kunshan government's new policies.[83]

However, we can also find on the same list that Kunshan's ranking has soon returned, from No. 16 in 2003 to No. 9 in 2004 and then No. 4 in 2005. This trend indicates that the Taiwanese community, the largest in Kunshan, has gradually accepted the new role of the Kunshan government. According to our field research, their reasons and processes are as follows. First of all,

Table 8.5. TEEMA's Ranking of the Highly Recommended Chinese Cities for Taiwanese Investors, 2001–2007

Ranking	*2001*	*2002*	*2003*	*2004*	*2005*	*2006*	*2007*
1	Wujiang	Suzhou	Xiaoshan	Xiaoshan	Minhang	Suzhou	**Kunshan**
2	Ningbo	**Kunshan**	Qingdao	Yangzhou	Xiaoshan	Ningbo	Lanfang
3	Hangzhou	Yangzhou	Zhangzhou	Jiangyin	Chengdu	**Kunshan**	Suzhou
4	**Kunshan**	Wuxi	Ningbo	Chengdu	**Kunshan**	Yangzhou	Jianning
5	Ningbo	Xiaoshan	Zhongshan	Shanghai	Jiangyin	Hanzhou	Nanchang
6	Shanghai	Ningbo	Yangzhou	Xuzhou	Xuzhou	Jiangyin	Xiaoshan
7	Wuxi	Ningbo	Wuxi	Jiaxing	Yangzhou	Suzhou	Ningbo
8	Suzhou	Shanghai	Suzhou	Shantou	Nanchang	Jinan	Qingdao
9	Zhenjiang	Hangzhou	Shantou	**Kunshan**	Pudong	Tianjing	Tianjing
10	Wenzhou	Pudong	Shanghai	Nanchang	Tianjing	Nanchang	Weihai
:			:				
:			:				
:			:				
16			**Kunshan**				

Source: Taiwan Electrical and Electronic Manufacturers' Association, 2007, "Zichuang Pinpai: The 2007 Investigation of Investing Environment and Risks in China," Taipei: *Business Weekly*, 2007: 59; and Taiwan Electrical and Electronic Manufacturers' Association, 2004, "Liangli Liangdu: The 2004 Investigation of Investing Environment and Risks in China," Taipei: *Business Weekly*, 2004: 82.

after the result had been publicized, there was a series of efforts to facilitate the dialogue between the Kunshan government and the Taiwanese business community. Nevertheless, these were just explanations and communications, without any concessions and deal-cutting. After those efforts, some entrepreneurs, mostly hi-tech factory owners, found that they would actually have benefited if the new development plan could have been successfully carried out. Some others recognized that this trend was irreversible, and the only thing they could do was to accept it and make adjustments themselves. The rest, largely labor-intensive industries that would lose the most, still continued to resist such change. However, under the new policy regime, some moved away and others got ready to move out in the coming years. The former could no longer protest, and the latter had no time to protest.[84]

In conclusion, the transition of the role of the Kunshan state from a service state to a developmental state was motivated by the problems associated with the earlier development strategy. Without an unlimited supply of land, Kunshan could not defeat its competitors and, in the end, the earlier "business-friendly" strategy could not be sustained. After a determined shift to the new development strategy, the local state had to bring in a new development plan and had to adjust its relations with the business community in order to carry out that plan. The local state became more development-oriented, autonomous from the demands of the business community, and capable of cracking down on both direct or indirect resistance and implementing the plan. In this way, the Kunshan government gradually moved toward a developmental state.

CONCLUSION: TOWARD AN EXPLANATORY FRAMEWORK FOR THE CHANGING GOVERNMENT-BUSINESS RELATIONSHIPS IN KUNSHAN

About twenty years ago, after reviewing the literature up to that time, Peter Evans wrote: "Third-world states have clearly not shrunk as a result of the penetration of their economies by transnational capital, regardless of the specific form of that penetration."[85] According to him, the state may get stronger to survive in a context of global competition and capital mobility: the state sometimes acts as a capable partner of foreign capital, sometimes as a countervailing power of foreign capital, and, at other times, as a functional intermediary between foreign capital and the local economy. In other words, once it is merged into the world economy, the role of the state in developing countries will be shaped by foreign capital and its strength vis-à-vis foreign capital.[86]

In this sense, the traditional wisdom that assumes that developing countries will "race to the bottom" and that their state will be truncated as a result of globalization is questionable.[87] However, how should we observe and explain the dynamics of government-business relationships with an emphasis on the role and strength of the state in developing countries that are integrated into the global economy? In this paper, on the basis of the Kunshan study, I propose a framework that may help to make sense of the continuities and changes at the local level of government-business relationships. Of course, this framework must be further tested against different cases undergoing rapid economic transition in this age of globalization.

The Case of Kunshan: The Road Less Traveled?

As described in the previous sections, throughout these years of rapid development, the local state in Kunshan has shifted from a service state to a developmental state. It seems that the Kunshan case is quite different from the overall trend of China's economic take-off: the model of Sunan, characterized by a strong TVE sector and an entrepreneurial state, usually represents China's success story. Quite different from that, Kunshan was among the first counties in the country to target foreign investments; to do so, Kunshan transformed its government into a business-friendly "service state." The Kunshan-way later achieved enormous success and Kunshan became one of the most prosperous counties in the country. However, after a time of rapid FDI and explosive development, Kunshan seemed to come to a dead end, due to a shortage of land and harsh competition for FDI. The Kunshan government refused to "race to the bottom" and thus abandoned its earlier strategy and drew up a development plan and established itself as a developmental state accordingly. Once again, Kunshan seemed to take "the road less traveled," as compared with most other regions in China and even in the developing world.

In this paper, I propose a framework for the understanding of the dynamics of local-level government-business relationships. However, many exemplary studies tend to address state-society relations in the comparative context of a couple of counties.[88] These studies, however, might further exacerbate the classical problem in comparative politics, "too many variables, too few cases," for when applying control over cross-country variations, the approach would easily run out of cases.[89] In this sense, methodologically speaking, a single case with multiple observations in different periods of time—as in Jean Oi[90] and David Wank[91]—might probably be a better choice, for such a design involves less "potentially confounding variables."[92]

This research adopts the same approach to make sense of Kunshan's unique transition by asking the following questions: What factors led to such a transition? Why is the local state forced to, and also able to, shift its role? Why are foreign enterprises willing to let the local state assume such a stronger position? In the following section, I propose an explanatory framework to explain the experiences of Kunshan. I show how structural changes reshape the resources of the local state vis-à-vis foreign capital and thus modify the relative bargaining power between them and, in the end, rewrite the government-business relationships in Kunshan. The explanatory framework in this chapter is on the basis of the resources of the local state and foreign enterprises. It is the relative scarceness of these critical resources that defines their respective "relative bargaining power," which then shapes the seemingly unique development path of Kunshan.

An Explanation: Relative Bargaining Power Based on Land and Labor

The explanation provided in this chapter draws from the existing literature of government-business relationships.[93] The most popular perspective employed to analyze the dynamics of government-business relationships might be to look at the relative bargaining power of the state vis-à-vis society.[94] This approach has been embraced by the study on the students in China and thus generates many exemplary studies.[95] This perspective is thus also borrowed to make sense of the transformation of government-business relationships in Kunshan. However, to provide a specific explanation for the Kunshan case, we need to go further to discover the resources more.

As shown in our earlier discussion, the rapid "outward development" of Kunshan can be considered to result from the collaboration of the local state and foreign enterprises. As we know, to make such industry-led development possible, all the "factors of production," such as land, labor, and capital, must be available. Given China's policies to allow migrant workers to move to the cities, the supply of labor for the coastal regions of China is normally inexhaustible.[96] Therefore, the most scarce and critical resources for the collaboration are land and capital: almost every success story of "industrial transformation" can be characterized by the alliance of land and capital—which is also the partnership of local government and foreign enterprises, for the former usually controlled the land and the latter the capital. Since land and capital are critical, they can be easily employed as bargaining chips for the local state vis-à-vis the foreign enterprises, or vice versa. In addition, since none of the land and capital can be done without, the relative scarcity of land and capital will affect the relative bargaining power of the local state and foreign capital, regardless of whether it is a buyer's market or seller's market.

We can apply this explanatory framework to the experiences of Kunshan. Let us start with the earlier years of Kunshan's development. After granting enough incentives and discretionary power to promote local development,[97] every region was in urgent need of capital which almost always meant there were opportunities for industrial transformation and then getting rich. The resource in short supply at that time was the capital, especially foreign capital, with the latter usually being accompanied by advanced technology and export opportunities. For the same reason, attracting foreign capital also deserved the most credit and visibility for evaluating the performance of local officials. As a result, after the decline of TVE-led development, almost every region in the coastal China regions was competing for foreign capital. Some offered free land, tax-cuts, and other preferential policies to attract foreign investment. This was because Kunshan, which started with a feeble industrial base and administratively was only a county-level city, enjoyed few advantages and could offer no special deals to attract foreign capital. This is the reason why Kunshan had to accept the supremacy of foreign capital and, based on that

Table 8.6. The Growth of China's Foreign Direct Investments (in billion USD)

Year	*Case No.*	*Contracted FDI*	*Actual Flow of FDI*
1979–1984	3,724	97.50	41.04
1985	3,073	63.33	19.56
1986	1,498	33.30	22.44
1987	2,233	37.09	23.14
1988	5,945	52.97	31.94
1989	5,779	56.00	33.93
1990	7,273	65.96	34.87
1991	12,978	119.77	43.66
1992	48,764	581.24	110.08
1993	83,437	1,114.36	275.15
1994	47,549	826.80	337.67
1995	37,011	912.82	375.21
1996	24,556	732.76	417.26
1997	21,001	510.03	452.57
1998	19,799	521.02	454.63
1999	16,918	412.23	403.19
2000	22,347	623.80	407.15
2001	26,140	691.95	468.78
2002	34,171	827.68	527.43
2003	41,081	1,150.69	535.05
2004	43,664	1,534.79	606.30
2005	44,001	1,890.65	603.25
2006	41,485	2,001.74	694.68

Source: *China Statistical Yearbook*, 2007, available at http://www.stats.gov.cn/tjsj/ndsj/2007/indexch.htm, available by July, 31, 2008.

assumption, develop its unique property arrangements and excellent value-added service, or when put together, the service state. In other words, when foreign capital is relatively scarce while land is rather abundant, the owner of capital definitely has the upper hand in terms of its bargaining with whoever owns the land. The service state is in this sense a refection or a response of Kunshan's weakness in its bargaining power vis-à-vis foreign enterprises.

However, later on, as more and more foreign capital kept flowing into China, Kunshan also became well-known for its attractiveness for foreign capital—partly because of Kunshan's brilliant services and partly due to its "conglomeration effects." Both conditions caused foreign capital to come in rather large amounts for Kunshan (for the trend of China, refer to table 8.6, and for the case of Kunshan, table 8.7). At the same time, however, these foreign enterprises used up huge tracts of land to set up or expand their factories. After the central government started to worry about the unlimited use of land, leaving arable land in danger and peasants in peril, the shortage of land became increasingly serious. In comparison with the land, however, the capital appeared to become less and less scarce. As a result, Kunshan proposed a series of rules to set a lower limit to the land-FDI ratio. In addition, other policies were also proposed, such as "attracting investments with discretion" (*zhaoshang xuanzi*), "holding the industrial sector and promoting the service sector" (*tui'er jinsan*), "industrial upgrading by replacing old enterprises" (*tenglong huanniao*), and "development and industrialization without using land" (*wudi kaifa*).[98] As a result of these efforts, the usage of land and the imbalance in the land-FDI ratio started to improve after the year 2002 (see also

Table 8.7. Growth in FDI and Land Consumption in Kunshan, 1996–2004

Year	*Total FDI (in 1000 USD)*	*Land Use by FDI Firm (in mu*)*
1996	45.5	2,103
1997	56.0	3,889
1998	60.0	8,918
1999	60.0	3,011
2000	70.4	4,170
2001	75.1	8,795
2002	101.8	17,735
2003	120.1	12,279
2004	122.0	8,614

Note: One mu equals 0.165 acre and one acre equals to 6.07 mu.
Source: Policy Research Institute of Ministry of Commerce, MNC Research Center of Nankai University, and Bureau of Foreign Trade and Economic Cooperation of Kunshan City, 2006, Liyong Waizi yu Kunshan Jingji Fazhan, Shanghai, Shanghai Sanlian, pp. 162–163.

table 8.7). However, to maintain Kunshan's growth level with a minimal consumption of land, the local state conceived a sustainable development plan and struggled with the business community to implement it. In the meantime, the state became more and more autonomous and increasingly strong; that is, it assumed the characteristics of a developmental state.

In conclusion, as Kunshan keeps on developing, the relative scarcity of land and capital has gradually shifted. The local state controlling the land has gained higher bargaining power over the foreign enterprises directing the capital. It is thus the reason why Kunshan has adopted a unique path of economic transition. Kunshan has been developing into a developmental state.

APPENDIX: MAP OF KUNSHAN

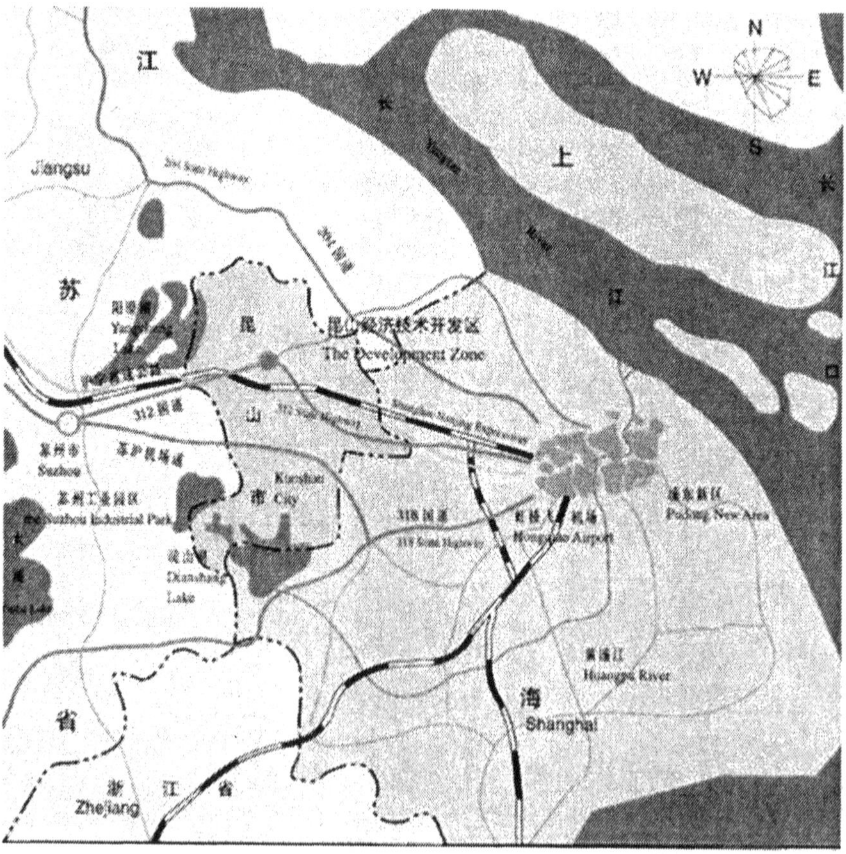

NOTES

1. Shucheng Zhang, 2008, *Erliji: Kunshan Gaige Kaifang Sanshinian Jubian* (Transformation in the Thirty Years of Reform), Hong Kong: Zhongguo Wenhua, p. 203.

2. Xiaotong Fei, 2004, "Preface," in Kunshan Association of Talents (*Kunshan Rencai Xuehui*) (ed.), *Jinri Kunshan: Tozi, Chuangye, Lvyou, Jiuye Daodu* (Today's Kunshan: A Guide for Investment, Tourism and Job-hunting), Beijing: Jinghua, pp. 1–3.

3. Kequan Wu, 2005, *Weishi, Yangchang, Fendou: Kunshan Jingji Fazhan de Tansuo yu Shijian* (Practical, Vision, and Struggles: An Inquiry into the Practices and Experiences of Kunshan's Economic Development), Suzhou: Guwuxuan, p. 19.

4. Yehua Dennis Wei, 2000, *Regional Development in China: States, Globalization, and Inequality*, London: Routledge, pp. 191–196; and 2002, "Beyond the Sunan Model: Trajectory and Underlying Factors of Development in Kunshan, China," *Environment and Planning A*, Vol. 34, pp. 1725–1747.

5. David Zweig, 2002, *Internationalizing China: Domestic Interests and Global Linkages*, Ithaca, N.Y.: Cornell University Press, pp. 83–85.

6. Shiuh-Shen Chien, 2008, "Isomorphism of Regional Development Policy in China- Case Study of National-Level Development Zones in Jiangsu," *Urban Studies*, Vol. 45, No. 2, pp. 273–294.

7. Jenn-Hwan Wang, and Chuan-Kai Lee, 2007, "Global Production Networks and Local Institution Building: The Development of the Information-Technology Industry in Suzhou, China," *Environment and Planning A*, Vol. 39, No. 8, pp. 1873–1888.

8. Yehua Dennis Wei, 2002, "Beyond the Sunan Model: Trajectory and Underlying Factors of Development in Kunshan, China," *Environment and Planning A*, Vol. 34, pp. 1725–1747.

9. Ruilong Yang, 1999, "*Zhongjian Kuoshan de Zhidu Bianqian Fangshi yu Difang Zhengfu de Chuangxin Xingwei: Jiangsu Kunshan Zifei Jingji Jishu Kaifaqu Anli Fengxi*" (Expanding from the Middle: The Source of Institutional Changes and the Innovations of Local Government, The Case Analysis of KETD), in *Zhongguo Zhidu Bianqian de Anli Yanjiu II* (Case Study of Institutional Change in China Vol. II), Beijing: Zhongguo Caizheng Jingji, pp. 353–381.

10. Lanchih Po, and Ngai Pun, 2003, "*Kuajia Zhili: Taizhi Canyu Kunshan Zhidu Chuangxin de Ge'an Yanjiu*" (Making Trans-border Governance: A Case Study of the Role of Taiwanese Capital in Kunshan's Institutional Change), *Chengshi yu Sheji Xuebao* (Journal of Urban Design), Vol. 15/16, pp. 69–70.

11. Zhentao Liu, and Baoming Li, 2003, "*Kunshan Jiaqiang Touzhi Huanjing Jianshe de Jingyan*" (Lessons of Kunshan's Efforts to Improve Investing Environment), *Haixia Keji yu Chanye* (Cross-Strait Technology and Industry), No. 6, p. 4; Taiwan Study Institute, Qinghua University, 2004, *Congtouyue: Dui Kun-Tai Jingji Guanxi de Guoqu, Xianzai he Weilai de Sikao* (Crossing in the Sky: Reflections on the Economic Ties between Kunshan and Taiwan: The Past, the Nowadays, and the

Future), Beijing: Taiwan Study Institute, Qinghua University; and Joint Research Group of Institute of Policy Research, Ministry of Commerce, MNC Research Center, Nankai University, Bureau of Foreign Trade and Economic Cooperation, City of Kunshan, 2006, *Liyong Waizhi yu Kunshan Jingji Fazh* (FDI and Kunshan's Economic Development), Shanghai: Sanlian, pp. 294–295.

12. Andrew G. Walder. (ed.), 1996, *China's Transitional Economy*, Oxford & New York: Oxford University Press; Thomas G. Rawski, 1999, "Reforming China's Economy: What Have We Learned?" *China Journal*, No. 41, pp. 139–156; Wing Thye Woo, 1999, "The Real Reasons for China's Growth," *China Journal*, No. 41, pp. 115–137; Wing Thye Woo, 2003, "A United Front for the Common Objective to Understand China's Economic Growth: A Case of Non-antagonistic Contradiction," *Issues & Studies*, Vol. 39, No. 2, pp. 1–23; Yu-Shan Wu, 2002/2003, "Chinese Economic Reform in a Comparative Perspective: Asia vs. Europe," *Issues & Studies*, Vol. 38, No. 4/Vol. 39, No. 1, pp. 93–138; and Yu-Shan Wu, 2003, "Institutions and Policies Must Bear the Responsibility: Another Case of Non-antagonistic Contradiction," *Issues & Studies*, Vol. 39, No. 2, pp. 24–40.

13. Gordon White (ed.), 1991, *The Chinese State in the Era of Economic Reform: The Road to Crisis*, Armonk, N.Y.: M. E. Sharpe; Andrew G. Walder (ed.), 1995, *The Waning of the Communist State: Economic Origins of Political Decline in China and Hungary*, Berkeley: University of California Press; Paul Bowles, Barrett L. McCormick, and Jonathan Unger (eds.), 1996, *China after Socialism: In the Footsteps of Eastern Europe or East Asia?* Armonk, N.Y.: M. E. Sharpe; Merle Goldman, and Roderick MacFarquhar (eds.), 1999, *The Paradox of China's Post-Mao Reforms*, Cambridge, Mass.: Harvard University Press.

14. Thomas G. Rawski, 1999, "Reforming China's Economy: What Have We Learned?" *China Journal*, No. 41, pp. 139–156; Andrew G. Walder (ed.), 1995, *The Waning of the Communist State: Economic Origins of Political Decline in China and Hungary*, Berkeley: University of California Press.

15. John McMillan, and Barry Naughton (eds.), 1996, *Reforming Asian Socialism: The Growth of Market Institutions*, Ann Arbor, Mich.: University of Michigan Press; Andrew G. Walder. (ed.), 1996, *China's Transitional Economy*, Oxford: Oxford University Press; Wing Thye Woo, Stephen Parker, and Jeffrey D. Sachs (eds.), 1997, *Economies in Transition: Comparing Asia and Europe*, Cambridge, Mass.: MIT Press; Thomas G. Rawski, 1999, "Reforming China's Economy: What Have We Learned?" *China Journal*, No. 41, pp. 139–156; Wing Thye Woo, 1999, "The Real Reasons for China's Growth," *China Journal*, No. 41, pp. 115–137; Yu-Shan Wu, 2002/2003, "Chinese Economic Reform in a Comparative Perspective: Asia vs. Europe," *Issues & Studies*, Vol. 38, No. 4/Vol. 39, No. 1, pp. 93–138; Wing Thye Woo, 2003, "A United Front for the Common Objective to Understand China's Economic Growth: A Case of Non-antagonistic Contradiction," *Issues & Studies*, Vol. 39, No. 2, pp. 1–23; and Yu-Shan Wu, 2003, "Institutions and Policies Must Bear the Responsibility: Another Case of Non-antagonistic Contradiction," *Issues & Studies*, Vol. 39, No. 2, pp. 24–40.

16. Andrew G. Walder (ed.), 1995, *The Waning of the Communist State: Economic Origins of Political Decline in China and Hungary*, Berkeley: University of Califor-

nia Press; Lynn T. White, 1998, *Unstately Power, Vol. I. Local Causes of China's Economic Reforms*, Armonk, N.Y.: M. E. Sharpe; Jean C. Oi, 1999, *Rural China Takes Off: Institutional Foundations of Economic Reforms*, Berkeley: University of California Press; Susan H. Whiting, 2001, *Power and Wealth in Rural China: The Political Economy of Institutional Change*, Cambridge: Cambridge University Press.

17. William A. Byrd, and Qingsong Lin (eds.), 1990, *China's Rural Industry: Structure, Development, and Reform*, Oxford: World Bank/Oxford University Press; Marc Blecher, 1991, "Developmental State, Entrepreneurial State: The Political Economy of Socialist Reform in Xinju Municipality and Guanghan County," in Gordon White (ed.), *The Chinese State in the Era of Economic Reform: The Road to Crisis*, Armonk, N.Y.: M. E. Sharpe, pp. 265–291; Jean C. Oi, 1999, *Rural China Takes Off: Institutional Foundations of Economic Reforms*, Berkeley: University of California Press; Susan H. Whiting, 2001, *Power and Wealth in Rural China: The Political Economy of Institutional Change*, Cambridge: Cambridge University Press; Chih-Jou Jay Chen, 2004, *Transforming Rural China: How Local Institutions Shape Property Rights in China*, London: Routledge.

18. Harry Harding, 1987, *China's Second Revolution: Reform after Mao*, Washington, D.C.: Brookings Institution; Dorothy J. Solinger, 1993, *China's Transition from Socialism: Statist Legacies and Market Reforms 1980–1990*, Armonk, N.Y.: M. E. Sharpe.

19. Gordon White (ed.), 1991, *The Chinese State in the Era of Economic Reform: The Road to Crisis*, Armonk, N.Y.: M. E. Sharpe; Richard Baum, and Alexei Shevchenko, 1999, "The State of the State," in Merle Goldman and Roderick MacFarquhar (eds.), *The Paradox of China's Post-Mao Reforms*, Cambridge, Mass.: Harvard University Press, pp. 333–360; Paul Bowles, Barrett L. McCormick, and Jonathan Unger (eds.), 1996, *China after Socialism: In the Footsteps of Eastern Europe or East Asia?* Armonk, N.Y.: M. E. Sharpe; Elizabeth J. Perry, and Mark Selden (eds.), 2003, *Chinese Society: Change, Conflict and Resistance*, London: Routledge/Curzon.

20. Eyal Gil, Iván Szelényi, and Eleanor R. Townsley, 1998, *Making Capitalism without Capitalists: Class Formation and Elite Struggles in Post-communist Central Europe*, London: Verso, pp. 36–45; Xueguang Zhou, 2000, "Economic Transformation and Income Inequality in Urban China: Evidence from Panel Data," *American Journal of Sociology*, Vol. 105, No. 4, pp. 1135–1174; Shu Keng, 2002, "The Changing Government-Business Relations in Rural China, 1979–1999," *Chinese Political Science Review*, No. 23, pp. 116–119.

21. Victor Nee, 1989, "A Theory of Market Transition: From Redistribution to Markets in State Socialism," *American Sociological Review*, Vol. 5 4, No. pp. 663–81; Victor Nee, 1991, "Social Inequality in Reforming State Socialism: Between Redistribution and Markets in China," *American Sociological Review*, Vol. 56, No. 3, pp. 267–282.

22. Victor Nee, 1989, "A Theory of Market Transition: From Redistribution to Markets in State Socialism," *American Sociological Review*, Vol. 54, No. 4, pp. 663–681; Victor Nee, 1991, "Social Inequality in Reforming State Socialism: Between Redistribution and Markets in China," *American Sociological Review*, Vol. 56, No. 3, pp. 267–282; Douglas Guthrie, 1998, "The Declining Significance of Guanxi

in China's Economic Transition," *China Quarterly*, No. 154, pp. 31–62; Douglas Guthrie, 1999, *Dragon in a Three-Piece Suit: The Emergence of Capitalism in China*, Princeton, N.J.: Princeton University Press.

23. Victor Nee, 1989, "A Theory of Market Transition: From Redistribution to Markets in State Socialism," *American Sociological Review*, Vol. 54, No. 4, p. 668. It's my emphasis.

24. Andrew G. Walder, 1994, "The Decline of Communist Power: Elements of a Theory of Institutional Change," *Theory and Society*, No 23, pp. 297–323; Xueguang Zhoû, 2000, "Economic Transformation and Income Inequality in Urban China: Evidence from Panel Data," *American Journal of Sociology*, Vol. 105, No. 4, pp. 1135–1174.

25. Jean C. Oi, 1995, "The Role of the Local State in China's Transition Economy," *China Quarterly*, No. 144, pp. 1132–1149; Jean C. Oi, 1998, "The Collective Foundation for Rapid Rural Industrialization," in Eduard B. Vermeer, Frank N. Pieke, and Woei Lien Chong (eds.), *Cooperative and Collective in China's Rural Development: Between State and Private Interests*, Armonk, N.Y.: M. E. Sharpe, pp. 93–109; Peter B. Evans, 1997, "Government Action, Social Capital, and Development: Reviewing the Evidence of Synergy," in *State-Society Synergy: Government and Social Capital in Development*, Berkeley: University of California–Berkeley, International and Area Studies, pp. 178–209.

26. See David L. Wank, 1995, "Bureaucratic Patronage and Private Business: Changing Networks of Power in Urban China," in Andrew G. Walder (ed.), *The Waning of the Communist State: Economic Origins of Political Decline in China and Hungary*, Berkeley: University of California Press, pp. 153–183; 1995, "Private Business, Bureaucracy, and Political Alliance in a Chinese City," *Australian Journal of Chinese Affairs*, No. 33, pp. 55–71; 1996, "The Institutional Process of Market Clientelism: Guanxi and Private Business in a South China City," *China Quarterly*, No. 147, pp. 820–838; and 1999, *Commodifying Communism: Business, Trust, and Politics in a Chinese City*, Cambridge: Cambridge University Press.

27. See Jean C. Oi, 1999, *Rural China Takes Off: Institutional Foundations of Economic Reforms*, Berkeley: University of California Press, Chapters 3 and 4.

28. Thomas G. Rawski, 1999, "Reforming China's Economy: What Have We Learned?" *China Journal*, No. 41, pp. 139–156.

29. Victor Nee, 1989, "A Theory of Market Transition: From Redistribution to Markets in State Socialism," *American Sociological Review*, Vol. 54, No. 4, pp. 663–681; Victor Nee, 1991, "Social Inequality in Reforming State Socialism: Between Redistribution and Markets in China," *American Sociological Review*, Vol. 56, pp. 267–282; Wing Thye Woo, Stephen Parker, and Jeffrey D. Sachs (eds.), 1997, *Economies in Transition: Comparing Asia and Europe*, Cambridge, Mass.: MIT Press; Douglas Guthrie, 1998, "The Declining Significance of Guanxi in China's Economic Transition," *China Quarterly*, No. 154, pp. 31–62; Douglas Guthrie, 1999, *Dragon in a Three-Piece Suit: The Emergence of Capitalism in China*, Princeton, N.J.: Princeton University Press; Wing Thye Woo, 1999, "The Real Reasons for China's Growth," *China Journal*, No. 41, pp. 115–137; Wing Thye Woo,

2003, "A United Front for the Common Objective to Understand China's Economic Growth: A Case of Non-antagonistic Contradiction," *Issues & Studies*, Vol. 39, No. 2, pp. 1–23.

30. Andrew G. Walder, 1994, "The Decline of Communist Power: Elements of a Theory of Institutional Change," *Theory and Society*, No. 23, pp. 297–323; Jean C. Oi, 1995, "The Role of the Local State in China's Transition Economy," *China Quarterly*, No. 144, pp. 1132–1149; Andrew G. Walder. (ed.), 1996, *China's Transitional Economy*, Oxford: Oxford University Press; Jean C. Oi, 1999, *Rural China Takes Off: Institutional Foundations of Economic Reforms*, Berkeley: University of California Press; Thomas G. Rawski, 1999, "Reforming China's Economy: What Have We Learned?" *China Journal*, No. 41, pp. 139–156; David L. Wank, 1999, *Commodifying Communism: Business, Trust, and Politics in a Chinese City*, Cambridge: Cambridge University Press; Xueguang Zhou, 2000, "Economic Transformation and Income Inequality in Urban China: Evidence from Panel Data," *American Journal of Sociology*, Vol. 105, No. 4, pp. 1135–1174; Yu-Shan Wu, 2002/2003, "Chinese Economic Reform in a Comparative Perspective: Asia vs. Europe," *Issues & Studies*, Vol. 38, No. 4/ Vol. 39, No. 1, pp. 93–138; Yu-Shan Wu, 2003, "Institutions and Policies Must Bear the Responsibility: Another Case of Non-antagonistic Contradiction," *Issues & Studies*, Vol. 39, No .2, pp. 24–40. The distinction draws from Shu Keng, 2002, "The Changing Government-Business Relations in Rural China, 1979-1999," *Chinese Political Science Review*, No. 23, pp. 116–119.

31. Victor Nee, 1992, "Organizational Dynamics of Market Transition: Hybrid Forms, Property Rights, and Mixed Economy in China," *Administrative Science Quarterly*, Vol. 37, No. 1, pp. 1–27; Nan Lin, 1995, "Local Market Socialism: Local Corporatism in Action in Rural China," *Theory and Society*, Vol. 24, No. 3, pp. 301–354; Victor Nee, and Sijin Su, 1996, "Institutions, Social Ties, and Commitment in China's Corporatist Transformation," in John McMillan and Barry Naughton (eds.), *Reforming Asian Socialism: The Growth of Market Institutions*, Ann Arbor, Mich.: University of Michigan Press, pp. 111–134; David L. Wank, 1995, "Bureaucratic Patronage and Private Business: Changing Networks of Power in Urban China," in Andrew G. Walder (ed.), *The Waning of the Communist State: Economic Origins of Political Decline in China and Hungary*, Berkeley: University of California Press, pp. 153–183; Jean C. Oi, 1999, *Rural China Takes Off: Institutional Foundations of Economic Reforms*, Berkeley: University of California Press.

32. David L. Wank, 1996, "The Institutional Process of Market Clientelism: Guanxi and Private Business in a South China City," *China Quarterly*, No. 147, p. 838.

33. David L. Wank, 1999, *Commodifying Communism: Business, Trust, and Politics in a Chinese City*, Cambridge: Cambridge University Press, p. 228.

34. Douglas Guthrie, 1998, "The Declining Significance of Guanxi in China's Economic Transition," *China Quarterly*, No. 154, pp. 31–62; Douglas Guthrie, 1999, *Dragon in a Three-Piece Suit: The Emergence of Capitalism in China*, Princeton, N.J.: Princeton University Press; Wing Thye Woo, 1999, "The Real Reasons for China's Growth," *China Journal*, No. 41, pp. 115–137.

35. Akos Rona-Tas, 1994, "The First Shall Be Last? Entrepreneurship and Communist Cadres in the Transition from Socialism," *American Journal of Sociology*, Vol. 100, No. 1, pp. 40–60.

36. Peter B. Evans, 1995, *Embedded Autonomy: States and Industrial Transformation*, Princeton, N.J.: Princeton University Press, p. 13.

37. Linda Weiss, and John M. Hobson, 1995, *States and Economic Development: A Comparative Historical Analysis*, Cambridge, Mass.: Polity, pp. 238–253.

38. Peter B. Evans, 1997, "Government Action, Social Capital, and Development: Reviewing the Evidence of Synergy," in *State-Society Synergy: Government and Social Capital in Development*, Berkeley: University of California–Berkeley, International and Area Studies, pp. 178–189.

39. Richard Baum, and Alexei Shevchenko, 1999, "The State of the State," in Merle Goldman and Roderick MacFarquhar (eds.), *The Paradox of China's Post-Mao Reforms*, Cambridge, Mass.: Harvard University Press, pp. 334–360.

40. What Xueguang Zhou called, the "co-evolution," see Xueguang Zhou, 2000, "Economic Transformation and Income Inequality in Urban China: Evidence from Panel Data," *American Journal of Sociology*, Vol. 105, No. 4, pp. 1135–1174.

41. Peter B. Evans, 1997, "Government Action, Social Capital, and Development: Reviewing the Evidence of Synergy," in *State-Society Synergy: Government and Social Capital in Development*, Berkeley: University of California–Berkeley, International and Area Studies, pp. 178–179.

42. Jean C. Oi, and Andrew G. Walder (eds.), 1999, *Property Rights and Economic Reform in China*, Stanford, Calif.: Stanford University Press, pp. 6–8.

43. Theda Skocpol, 1985, "Bringing the State Back In: Strategies of Analysis in Current Research," in Peter B. Evans, Dietrich Rueschemeye, and Theda Skocpol (eds.), *Bringing the State Back In*, Cambridge: Cambridge University Press, pp. 9–20.

44. See, also, Peter B. Evans, 1995, *Embedded Autonomy: States and Industrial Transformation*. Princeton, N.J.: Princeton University Press, pp. 43–73.

45. Marc Blecher, 1991, "Developmental State, Entrepreneurial State: The Political Economy of Socialist Reform in Xinju Municipality and Guanghan County," in Gordon White (ed.), *The Chinese State in the Era of Economic Reform: The Road to Crisis*, Armonk, N.Y.: M. E. Sharpe, p. 267.

46. Peter K. Eisinger, 1988, *The Rise of the Entrepreneurial State: State and Local Economic Development Policy in the United States*, Madison, Wis.: University of Wisconsin Press, p. 8; Yves Tiberghien, 2007, *Entrepreneurial States: Reforming Corporate Governance in France, Japan, and Korea*, Ithaca, N.Y.: Cornell University Press, pp. 13–23.

47. Jane Duckett, 1998, *The Entrepreneurial State in China: Real Estate and Commerce Departments in Reform Era Tianjin*, London: Routledge, pp. 14–15.

48. Linda Weiss, and John M. Hobson, 1995, *States and Economic Development: A Comparative Historical Analysis*, Cambridge, Mass.: Polity, pp. 245–246.

49. Ben Ross Schneider, and Sylvia Maxfield, 1997, "Business, the State, and Economic Performance in Developing Countries," in Sylvia Maxfield and Ben Ross Schneider (eds.), *Business and the State in Developing Countries*, Ithaca, N.Y.: Cornell University Press, pp. 6–15; Peter B. Evans, 1997, "Government Action, Social

Capital, and Development: Reviewing the Evidence of Synergy," in *State-Society Synergy: Government and Social Capital in Development*, Berkeley: University of California–Berkeley, International and Area Studies, pp. 178–189.

50. Linda Weiss, and John M. Hobson, 1995, *States and Economic Development: A Comparative Historical Analysis*, Cambridge, Mass.: Polity, pp. 245–246.

51. Juhana Vartiainen, 1992, *Capital Accumulation in a Corporatist Economy*, Berlin: Springer-Verlag; Cheng-Tian Kuo, 1995, *Global Competitiveness and Industrial Growth in Taiwan and the Philippines*, Pittsburgh: University of Pittsburgh Press; Robert Wade, 2004, *Governing the Market: Economic Theory and the Role of Government in East Asian Industrialization*, Princeton, N.J.: Princeton University Press (2nd. ed.).

52. Gordon White, and Robert Wade, 1988, "Developmental States and Markets in East Asia: An Introduction," in Gordon White (ed.), *Developmental States in East Asia*, New York: St. Martin's Press, pp. 1–2; Peter B. Evans, 1995, *Embedded Autonomy: States and Industrial Transformation*. Princeton, N.J.: Princeton University Press, pp. 47–50; Steve Chan, Cal Clark, and Danny Lam (eds.), 1998, *Beyond the Developmental State: East Asia's Political Economies Reconsidered*, Basingstoke, Hampshire, UK: Macmillan and New York: St. Martin's.

53. Peter B. Evans, 1995, *Embedded Autonomy: States and Industrial Transformation*. Princeton, N.J.: Princeton University Press, pp. 45–47.

54. Paul P. Streeten, 1992, "Against Minimalism," in Louis Putteman and Dietrich Rueschemeyer (eds.), *State and Market in Development-Synergy or Rivalry*, Boulder, Colo.: Lynne Rienner, pp. 16–20.

55. Peter B. Evans, 1995, *Embedded Autonomy: States and Industrial Transformation*. Princeton, N.J.: Princeton University Press, pp. 12; 45–46.

56. Paul P. Streeten, 1992, "Against Minimalism," in Louis Putteman and Dietrich Rueschemeyer (eds.), *State and Market in Development-Synergy or Rivalry*, Boulder, Colo.: Lynne Rienner, pp. 16–17.

57. Gordon White, and Robert Wade, 1988, "Developmental States and Markets in East Asia: An Introduction," in Gordon White (ed.), *Developmental States in East Asia*, New York: St. Martin's Press, pp. 1–29; Peter B. Evans, 1995, *Embedded Autonomy: States and Industrial Transformation*, Princeton, N.J.: Princeton University Press; Meredith Woo-Cummings (ed.), 1999, *The Developmental State*, Ithaca, N.Y.: Cornell University Press.

58. Kunshan Bureau of Statistics, 2007, *Kunshan Statistical Yearbook*, Kunshan: Kunshan Bureau of Statistics, Various Years.

59. This calculation, as quoted from Lanchih Po and Ngai Pun, 2003, "*Kuajia Zhili: Taizhi Canyu Kunshan Zhidu Chuangxin de Ge'an Yanjiu*" (Making Transborder Governance: A Case Study of the Role of Taiwanese Capital in Kunshan's Institutional Change), *Chengshi yu Sheji Xuebao* (Journal of Urban Design), Vol. 15/ Vol. 16, pp. 59–91, was performed in the early 2000s and thus is a little out of date. Since the investments of the Taiwanese are not listed as a separate category, we do not have any more up-to-date data.

60. Jean C. Oi, 1999, *Rural China Takes Off: Institutional Foundations of Economic Reforms*, Berkeley: University of California Press, 1999, pp. 134–138.

61. Jean C. Oi, 1999, *Rural China Takes Off: Institutional Foundations of Economic Reforms*, Berkeley: University of California Press, 1999; David L. Wank, 1999, *Commodifying Communism: Business, Trust, and Politics in a Chinese City*, Cambridge: Cambridge University Press.

62. As will be explained later, my classification is based on the government-business relationships in Kunshan. Different researchers tend to divide the development of Kunshan into different stages: among these classifications, the one proposed by Binglong Xuan might be the most popular, see Xuan Binglong, 2004, *Tansuo, Chuangxin: Kunshan Jingji Jishu Kaifaqu de Shijian* (Explorations and Innovations: The Experiences of KETDs), Beijing: Zhongguo Caizheng Jingji, pp. 1–2. He divides the history into three periods, 1985 to 1991, 1992 to 1999, and 2000 until today). However, this classification has little to do with Kunshan's government-business relationships.

63. Erliu Zhou, and Yuling Zhang (eds.), 1994, *Zhongguo Chengxiang Xietiao Fazhan Yanjiu* (The Study of Coordinated Development of Urban and Rural China), Hong Kong: Oxford/Chinese; Susan H. Whiting, 1996, "Contract Incentives and Market Discipline in China's Rural Industrial Sector," in John McMillan and Barry Naughton (eds.), *Reforming Asian Socialism: The Growth of Market Institutions*, Ann Arbor, Mich.: University of Michigan Press, pp. 63–110; Jean C. Oi, 1999, *Rural China Takes Off: Institutional Foundations of Economic Reforms*, Berkeley: University of California Press; Chih-Jou Jay Chen, 2004, *Transforming Rural China: How Local Institutions Shape Property Rights in China*, London: Routledge.

64. Jean C. Oi, 1999, *Rural China Takes Off: Institutional Foundations of Economic Reforms*, Berkeley: University of California Press, 1999; Susan H. Whiting, 2001, *Power and Wealth in Rural China: The Political Economy of Institutional Change*, Cambridge: Cambridge University Press; Chen, Chih-Jou Jay, 2004, *Transforming Rural China: How Local Institutions Shape Property Rights in China*, London: Routledge, pp. 31–124.

65. Jean C. Oi, 1992, "Fiscal Reform and the Economic Foundation of Local State Corporatism," *World Politics*, Vol. 45, No. 1, pp. 99–126.

66. Shousong Yang, 1991(1992/1995/2002), *Yang Shoushou Wenji Juan 10: Kunshan Zhilu I, Suzhou Laoxiang, Kunshan Zhilu II* (Collective Works of Yang Shousong Vol. 10: *The Kunshan's Way I, The Kunshan's Way II, Comrade from Suzhou*), Nanjing: Jiangsu Wenyi, pp. 2–3.

67. Kequan Wu, 2005, *Weishi, Yangchang, Fendou: Kunshan Jingji Fazhan de Tansuo yu Shijian* (Practical, Vision, and Struggles: An Inquiry into the Practices and Experiences of Kunshan's Economic Development), Suzhou: Guwuxuan.

68. Among our interviewees, many of them, especially those who came to Kunshan in the early 1990s, were attracted by the land ownership and single ownership. However, some of our interviewees in Dongguan and Zhongshan told us that they were also attracted to and thus considered moving to Kunshan. Nevertheless, Dongguan and Zhongshan soon learned from "the experiences of the Yangtze River Delta" (in actual fact the case of Kunshan) and adjusted their property right arrangements. In other words, the experience of Kunshan triggered a wave of "property right transformation," first in regions targeting foreign investors, and then later all over the country.

69. Xuan Binglong, 2004, *Tansuo, Chuangxin: Kunshan Jingji Jishu Kaifaqu de Shijian* (Explorations and Innovations: The Experiences of KETDs), Beijing: Zhongguo Caizheng Jingji, pp. 152–153.

70. Xuan Binglong, 2004, *Tansuo, Chuangxin: Kunshan Jingji Jishu Kaifaqu de Shijian* (Explorations and Innovations: The Experiences of KETDs), Beijing: Zhongguo Caizheng Jingji, pp. 5–6.

71. Yasheng Huang, 1990, "Web of Interests and Patterns of Behavior of Chinese Local Economic Bureaucracies and Enterprises during Reforms," *China Quarterly*, No. 123, pp. 430–458; Youtien Hsing, 1996, "Blood, Thicker than Water: Interpersonal Relations and Taiwanese Investment in Southern China," *Environment and Planning A*, Vol. 28, pp. 2241–2261; David L. Wank, 1999, *Commodifying Communism: Business, Trust, and Politics in a Chinese City*, Cambridge: Cambridge University Press.

72. Xuan Binglong, 2004, *Tansuo, Chuangxin: Kunshan Jingji Jishu Kaifaqu de Shijian* (Explorations and Innovations: The Experiences of KETDs), Beijing: Zhongguo Caizheng Jingji, p. 280.

73. Lanchih Po, and Ngai Pun, 2003, "*Kuajia Zhili: Taizhi Canyu Kunshan Zhidu Chuangxin de Ge'an Yanjiu*" (Making Trans-border Governance: A Case Study of the Role of Taiwanese Capital in Kunshan's Institutional Change), *Chengshi yu Sheji Xuebao*(Journal of Urban Design), Vol. 15/Vol. 16, pp. 73–74.

74. See Jean C. Oi, 1999, *Rural China Takes Off: Institutional Foundations of Economic Reforms*, Berkeley: University of California Press; Ding Lu, 1994, *Entrepreneurship in Suppressed Markets: Private-Sector Experience in China*, New York: Garland; Xiaobo Lu, 2000, "Booty Socialism, Bureau-preneurs, and the State in Transition," *Comparative Politics*, Vol. 32, No. 3, pp. 273–295.

75. Shousong Yang, 1995(1991/1992/2002), *Yang Shoushou Wenji Juan 10: Kunshan Zhilu I, Suzhou Laoxiang, Kunshan Zhilu II* (Collective Works of Yang Shousong Vol. 10: *The Kunshan's Way I, The Kunshan's Way II, Comrade from Suzhou*), Nanjing: Jiangsu Wenyi.

76. Susan H. Whiting, 2001, *Power and Wealth in Rural China: The Political Economy of Institutional Change*, Cambridge: Cambridge University Press.

77. Research Team of Suzhou CCP, 2006, *Suzhou zhi Lu: Liangge Shuaixian de Shijian yu Sikao* (The Suzhou Way: Practices and Reflections on the Two Pioneering), Suzhou: Suzhou Daxue, p. 82.

78. Among our interviewees, many of them, especially those who came to Kunshan in the early 1990s, were attracted by the land ownership and single ownership. However, some of our interviewees in Dongguan and Zhongshan also told us that they were attracted and were thus considering moving to Kunshan. However, Dongguan and Zhongshan quickly learned from "the experiences of the Yangtze River Delta" (it is in fact the case of Kunshan) and adjusted their property right arrangements. In other words, the experience of Kunshan has triggered a wave of "property right transformation," first in regions targeting foreign investors, and later all over the country.

79. You-tien Hsing, 2006, "Land and Territorial Politics in Urban China," *China Quarterly*, No. 187, pp. 575–591.

80. According to the "3-6-9 Project," for each mu of farming land a peasant lost, he would be given annual pension of 300 for "contracted land" (*chengbao di*), of 600 for "family reserved land" (*ziliu di*) and 900 for "grain rationed land" (*kouliang di*). The pension was later raised to 400, 800, and 1200, respectively.

81. Xuan Binglong, 2004, *Tansuo, Chuangxin: Kunshan Jingji Jishu Kaifaqu de Shijian* (Explorations and Innovations: The Experiences of KETDs), Beijing: Zhongguo Caizheng Jingji, p. 2.

82. Shucheng Zhang, 2004, *Kunshang Fumin Zhidao* (Kunshan's Approach to Make the People Rich), Nanjing: Jiangsu Jiaoyu, Section II.

83. TEEMA's ranking is based on a survey-based investigation. After witnessing the new measures of the Kunshan government, many Taiwanese, though without any coordination, became very angry with the Kunshan government and thus withdrew their endorsement of Kunshan as a "highly recommended Chinese city for Taiwanese investors."

84. Albert O. Hirschman, 1970, *Exit, Voice, and Loyalty: Responses to Decline in Firms, Organizations, and States*, Cambridge, Mass.: Harvard University Press.

85. Peter B. Evans, 1987, "Foreign Capital and the Third World State," in Myron Weiner and Samuel P. Huntington (eds.), *Understanding Political Development: An Analytic Study*, Boston: Little, Brown, p. 344.

86. Peter B. Evans, 1987, "Foreign Capital and the Third World State," in Myron Weiner and Samuel P. Huntington (eds.), *Understanding Political Development: An Analytic Study*, Boston: Little, Brown, pp. 319–352.

87. Peter B. Evans, 1997, "The Eclipse of the State? Reflections of Stateness in an Era of Globalization," *World Politics*, Vol. 50, No. 1, pp. 62–87; Linda Weiss, 1998, *The Myth of the Powerless State*, Ithaca, N.Y.: Cornell University Press; John L. Campbell, 2004, *Institutional Change and Globalization*, Princeton, N.J.: Princeton University Press; Yongnian Zheng, 2004, *Globalization and State Transformation in China*, Cambridge: Cambridge University Press.

88. Joel S. Migdal, 1988, *Strong Societies and Weak States: State-Society Relations and State Capabilities in the Third World*, Princeton, N.J.: Princeton University Press; Peter B. Evans, 1995, *Embedded Autonomy: States and Industrial Transformation*. Princeton, N.J.: Princeton University Press; Linda Weiss, and John M. Hobson, 1995, *States and Economic Development: A Comparative Historical Analysis*, Cambridge, Mass.: Polity; John M. Hobson, 1997, *The Wealth of States: A Comparative Sociology of International Economic and Political Change*, Cambridge: Cambridge University Press; Atul Kohli, 2004, *State Directed Development: Political Power and Industrialization in the Global Periphery*, Cambridge: Cambridge University Press.

89. Arend Lijphart, 1971, "Comparative Politics and the Comparative Method," *American Political Science Review*, Vol. 65, No. 3, pp. 682–693.

90. Jean C. Oi, 1999, *Rural China Takes Off: Institutional Foundations of Economic Reforms*, Berkeley: University of California Press.

91. David L. Wank, 1999, *Commodifying Communism: Business, Trust, and Politics in a Chinese City*, Cambridge: Cambridge University Press.

92. Arend Lijphart, 1971, "Comparative Politics and the Comparative Method," *American Political Science Review*, Vol. 65, No. 3, pp. 682–693.

93. For example, Peter B. Evans, 1995, *Embedded Autonomy: States and Industrial Transformation.* Princeton, N.J.: Princeton University Press; Linda Weiss, and John M. Hobson, 1995, *States and Economic Development: A Comparative Historical Analysis*, Cambridge, Mass.: Polity; Sylvia Maxfield, and Ben Ross Schneider, 1997, *Business and the State in Developing Countries*, Ithaca, N.Y.: Cornell University Press.

94. Eric A. Nordlinger, 1981, *On the Autonomy of the Democratic State*, Cambridge, Mass.: Harvard University Press, pp. 42–73; Joel S. Migdal, 1988, *Strong Societies and Weak States: State-society Relations and State Capabilities in the Third World*, Princeton, N.J.: Princeton University Press, pp. 3–41; Scott Prasser, H. K. Colebatch, and J. R. Nethercote, 1997, *Business-Government Relations: Concepts and Issues*, South Melbourne, Australia: Nelson, pp. 18–100.

95. For example, more implicitly like Andrew G. Walder, 1986, *Communist Neo-Traditionalism: Work and Authority in Chinese Industry*, Berkeley: University of California Press; Dorothy J. Solinger, 1984, *Chinese Business under Socialism: The Politics of Domestic Commerce, 1949–1980*, Berkeley: University of California Press; and more explicitly like Jean C. Oi, 1989, *State and Peasant in Contemporary China: The Political Economy of Village Government*, Berkeley: University of California Press; Edward Friedman, Paul Pickowicz, and Mark Selden, 1991, *Chinese Village, Socialist State*, New Haven, Conn.: Yale University Press.

96. Ying Du, and Nansheng Bai, 1997, *Zouchu Xiangcun: Zhongguo Nongcun Laodongli Liudong Shizheng Yanjiu* (Farewell to the Countryside: A Study of the Migrant Workers from Rural China), Beijing: Jingji Kexue; Fang Cai, 2007, *Zhongguo Liudong Renkou Wenti* (Issues of Floating Population in China), Beijing: Sheke Wenxian.

97. Jean C. Oi, 1992, "Fiscal Reform and the Economic Foundation of Local State Corporatism," *World Politics*, Vol. 45, No. 1, pp. 99–126.

98. Some under-the-table deals included purchasing a land-use quota from other cities in Jiangsu and the Joint-Development Project with Taicang, in order to relocate some of Kunshan's industries to Taicang, a neighboring county-level city in Suzhou.

Chapter Nine

Cross-boundary State-Society Interactions in South China

Peter T. Y. Cheung

INTRODUCTION

The phenomenal expansion of cross-boundary social and economic interactions has recast the political and economic landscape in the south China region comprising Guangdong, Hong Kong, and Macao. Many cross-boundary issues merit scholarly and governmental scrutiny. For instance, what is the pattern of cross-boundary social interactions since Hong Kong's reunion with the Mainland in 1997? Are the societies in both areas becoming more integrated or not? If so, what are the manifestations and implications of such a trend? What has been done by governments in both Hong Kong and the Mainland, especially the central authorities and Guangdong province, to cope with the consequences of such growing social interactions? Finally, what are the political and administrative implications of these governmental responses to the emerging social trends? This chapter aims to examine the challenges confronting the state authorities in managing cross-boundary social interactions between Hong Kong and Guangdong province.

This chapter is organized into four parts. First, I will provide an overview of the economic transformation of south China and briefly discuss its implications. Second, several key cross-boundary issues, such as the pattern of demographic flows, cross-boundary housing, public health, and other emerging social concerns, will be examined to illustrate the salient trends in the changing social interactions in south China. Third, the governmental responses to some of these developments, such as the establishment of intergovernmental mechanisms, the formulation of a population policy in Hong Kong, and the role of the central authorities in cross-boundary coordination will be examined. Finally, the conclusion will offer some preliminary observations on the implications of these governmental responses to cope with the growth in cross-boundary social and economic interactions. My discussion will focus more on Hong Kong's concerns and the interactions between Hong Kong and its Guangdong counterparts and the central authorities in Beijing.[1]

THE ECONOMIC TRANSFORMATION IN SOUTH CHINA: AN OVERVIEW

The economic and social transformation in contemporary south China can be traced to the reform and open policy adopted by Deng Xiaoping since late 1978. Most commentators characterize the transformation as a market-driven phenomenon built upon the economic synergy between Hong Kong and the neighboring Guangdong. However, this change also reflects a deliberate effort by the Chinese state to re-engage the world economy and to achieve national unification, especially given the huge social and economic gap between Hong Kong and the rest of China at that time. In order to fully utilize its social and economic links with neighboring Hong Kong and to jumpstart its economic reform, Guangdong, together with Fujian, was granted "special policies, flexible measures" in 1979.[2] The state authorities on both sides of the Hong Kong-Guangdong boundary continue to play key roles in regulating the cross-boundary social and economic interactions since 1997 under the "One Country, Two Systems" framework.

The intimate economic ties between Hong Kong and Guangdong are characterized by extensive Hong Kong investment in export-processing industries and other sectors in the province in the past thirty years. With the continuous inflow of Hong Kong and overseas investment, their transfer of management expertise and their access to foreign markets, Guangdong's economy has experienced unprecedented growth since 1978. After more than two decades of rapid economic development, the Pearl River Delta (PRD)—Guangdong's economic core—has already emerged as a key economic powerhouse in the mainland. The GDP of the PRD has grown from RMB 87 billion in 1990 to over RMB 836 billion in 2001. By 2001, the PRD already accounted for 8.7 percent of China's GDP, 34 percent of exports, and 29 percent of realized foreign capital.[3] Some economists hence characterize the Greater PRD comprising Guangdong, Hong Kong, and Macao as "the world's fastest-growing export-oriented manufacturing region."

The relocation and subsequent expansion of Hong Kong's manufacturing sector into the PRD where land and labor are both much cheaper has not only connected the south China region with the global economy, but also brought about increasing economic interdependence between Hong Kong and Guangdong. By 2006, a cumulative total of 92,500 enterprises from Hong

Kong have invested in Guangdong.[4] Hong Kong accounted for 66 percent of the cumulative US $112.2 billion of foreign investment actually utilized by Guangdong province.[5] In the latest survey by the Federation of Hong Kong Industries (FHKI) completed in 2006, an estimated 55,200 manufacturing enterprises and 57,500 factories hiring over 9.6 million employees in the PRD had been established by Hong Kong businessmen.[6]

This process also brings about a massive reduction of Hong Kong's industrial workforce from over a million in the 1980s to around 400,000 in 2001 and approximately 160,000 in 2006.[7] The share of the service sector in Hong Kong's GDP rose from 67.3 percent in 1980 to 91 percent in 2006, and its share in employment jumped from 42 percent to 86.1 percent in the same period.[8] The contribution of manufacturing to Hong Kong's GDP, however, shrank from 23.7 percent in 1980 to only 2.7 percent in 2006 and its provision of employment plunged from 45.9 percent to 5.1 percent in this period.[9] In other words, Hong Kong has developed into a service economy as it has extended its manufacturing to the PRD in the past thirty years. The Guangdong and Hong Kong economies are clearly interwined at the dawn of the twenty-first century.

The relocation of Hong Kong's service sectors into south China has also been happening since the mid-1990s. Services, such as banking and telecommunication, have already relocated their labor-intensive operations such as call centers and data processing units across the boundary. Others have expanded their role in the mainland because they are lured by the business opportunities after China's accession into the World Trade Organization (hereafter the WTO). The FHKI survey in 2003 suggests that this process may even speed up in the near future. According to the survey, there were some 83,000 Hong Kong employees working for Hong Kong–based firms on a close to full-time basis, but within five years, there might well be a loss of over 20,000 such jobs.[10] More than half of the companies surveyed indicated that they would enlarge their operations in Guangdong, except for functions in headquarters and financial management. Half of them have already replaced all the Hong Kong staff in engineering with mainland employees. About one quarter indicated that they have already replaced their research and development (R&D) and management staff from Hong Kong. What is even more significant is that about one quarter of the companies said they would replace all their Hong Kong staff in engineering, R&D, management, sales and marketing, and finance-accounting-legal functions with mainland staff within five years. In fact, more than half of the firms surveyed believed that they would eventually replace all their Hong Kong employees working in Guangdong. In other words, with the continuing huge gap in salary between Hong Kong and the mainland, the improvement of investment environment and the provision of qualified staff in Guangdong, Hong Kong–based firms in manufacturing and import-export will eventually expand the provision of producer services in south China and replace their Hong Kong staff with mainland workers.

Nonetheless, whether the Hong Kong staff to be displaced by the mainland workers can find employment elsewhere in the mainland or Hong Kong is hard to assess at this point. In fact, the conclusion of the Closer Economic Partnership Arrangement (hereafter CEPA) in June 2003—which opened China's service sectors to Hong Kong professionals and firms about one or two years ahead of the WTO schedule—may also be a new impetus for Hong Kong's managerial and professional staff to seek new career and business opportunities across the boundary. These cross-cutting trends aptly reveal the intricate social and economic trends in south China. The Government of the Hong Kong Special Administrative Region (hereafter the HKSAR) would nonetheless have to cope with the economic challenges and the social consequences engendered by the growing integration between the two areas.

CHANGING CROSS-BOUNDARY SOCIAL INTERACTIONS IN SOUTH CHINA

Paralleling the growing economic integration in south China is the amazing growth in cross-boundary social interactions. Many studies of border and border regions show that they have different forms and scales.[11] Aside from exhibiting the characteristics of most borders and border regions elsewhere, the Hong Kong-Guangdong case also has several unique features. First, the status of the Hong Kong-Guangdong boundary has changed from an international boundary, between the United Kingdom and the People's Republic of China, to an internal boundary inside China. Since the mid-19th century and up to June 1997, Hong Kong was governed as a British colony. Therefore, this area is different from other border and cross-border regions where they actually span the borders of different sovereign states. Nonetheless, the sharp growth in cross-boundary traffic and demographic flows has compelled both Hong Kong and the mainland to adopt measures to facilitate these flows. Second, the Basic Law has laid out the legal parameters for a material boundary because Hong Kong enjoys, among others, the privilege of a free port, its own currency, and a separate customs territory. The "One Country, Two Systems" framework has set the HKSAR apart from other mainland cities. Indeed, the boundary between Hong Kong and the mainland has to be "real." Otherwise, foreign countries may not treat Hong Kong as a separate entity and all other related privileges accorded to Hong Kong would be rolled back.[12]

Third, the political framework and the socioeconomic geography of cross-boundary interactions in south China do not entirely concur. The overwhelming majority of Hong Kong people are Cantonese, sharing extensive linguistic, cultural, and social affinities with Guangdong province. However, the two societies have radically different economic, political, and legal systems. Such dissimilarities are also exhibited in the strong local identity of the Hong Kong people. According to the surveys on the identity of the residents in Hong Kong conducted by the Chinese University of Hong Kong, more than half of the respondents regarded themselves simply as "Hong Kong people" (*Xianggan ren*) ever since the survey was conducted in 1985. When they were asked to choose among "Hong Kong people," "Chinese," "both Hong Kong people and Chinese," or "neither Hong Kong people nor Chinese," about 60 percent of the respondents regarded themselves as "Hong Kong people" in 1985. While this figure dropped somewhat to 56.5 percent in 1997, it stays at the range of 51 to 57 percent in surveys carried out between 2001 and 2006. The share of respondents who regarded themselves as "Chinese" (*Zhongguo ren*) alone has never reached 40 percent or more throughout the surveys before and after 1997. Their share in the total actually fell from 36 percent in 1985 to 33 percent in 1997, and the figure varies in the range of 31 to 37 percent between 2001 and 2006.[13] A clear regional identity or mindset in both Hong Kong and Guangdong, despite extensive cross-boundary social and economic interactions, has *not* emerged. In spite of the growing economic interdependence, calls for closer political and administrative convergence or integration, have rarely been articulated, since such integration is often perceived as the erosion of the "One Country, Two Systems" policy. The mass media, the business community, and the ordinary people in Hong Kong have in fact developed a rather negative impression of the governmental authorities in south China; they were often characterized as inefficient and arbitrary. After surveying the characteristics of the south China region, the following sections will examine the remarkable changes in several areas of social and demographic interactions and discuss their implications.

CHANGING PATTERNS OF CROSS-BOUNDARY TRAVEL AND DEMOGRAPHIC MOVEMENTS

The Hong Kong-Guangdong boundary is likely one of the world's busiest land boundaries because the cross-boundary movement of people, especially from Hong Kong to the mainland, has increased by leaps and bounds since 1997. First, reflecting the flourishing social and economic interactions, cross-boundary passenger and vehicle traffic flows have grown remarkably. The volume of vehicles moving between Hong Kong and Guangdong increased from about 8.5 million in 1997 and almost 15 million in 2006.[14] The average daily flow of cross-boundary vehicular traffic already rose from 26,000 in 1997 to 41,000 in 2006, an increase of 54 percent, but the average daily flow of cross-boundary passenger traffic at land control points more than doubled from 175,824 in 1997 to 477,700 in 2006.[15] The number of mainland visitor arrivals to Hong Kong also more than tripled from 2.3 million in 1997 to 6.8 million in 2002. While the total number of visitors fell in 2003 because of the Severe Acute Respiratory Syndrome (hereafter the SARS) epidemic, the number of mainland visitors to Hong Kong continued to rise and reached 8.4 million that year.[16] With the relaxation of entry for mainland tourists through the introduction of the Individual Visit Scheme in July 2003, the number of mainland visitors to Hong Kong further rose to 17.1 million in 2006, contributing more than half of the total number of tourists visiting Hong Kong![17] Tourists from the mainland have replaced overseas tourists as the primary source of visitors to Hong Kong. The share of tourists from overseas countries (excluding those from Macao, Taiwan, and the mainland) has significantly dropped from 55.7 percent of the total number of tourists in 1997 to 35 percent in 2006.[18] The rapid expansion of cross-boundary traffic and passenger flows aptly reveals the unfolding social and economic interactions between the two areas.

Second, the pattern and motivation of cross-boundary trips has clearly become much more varied. The four cross-boundary travel surveys conducted by the HKSAR Government, respectively in 1999, 2001, 2003, and 2006, provide the most systematic data for assessing such travel patterns.[19] The overall trend shows a steady growth in the frequency of cross-boundary travel. Owing to the restrictions imposed on mainland visitors coming to Hong Kong, which was only relaxed in mid-2003, the majority of trips were made by Hong Kong residents. In 2006, about 74 percent of cross-boundary trips were undertaken by Hong Kong residents and another 9 percent were made by Hong Kong residents living in the mainland. The number of trips made by mainlanders has nonetheless risen from 5 percent in 1999 to almost 15 percent in 2006. An overwhelming majority of the trips to the mainland made by Hong Kong people living in Hong Kong (e.g., about 92 percent in 2006) were to Guangdong province, with two-thirds visiting mainly Shenzhen. Comparing the results of these surveys, the key purpose of these trips by people living in Hong Kong is fairly consistent, that is, mainly for leisure (about 41–42 percent) and visiting relatives and friends (20–23 percent). The share of passenger trips for business has actually dropped from 29 percent in 1999 to 23 percent in 2006, but what merits particular attention is that the percentage of people going to work has jumped from a mere 2 percent to 7 percent during this period.

A group of frequent cross-boundary travelers is now clearly identifiable. There were already half a million frequent trip makers who usually travelled at least once a week between Hong Kong and the mainland, especially Guangdong, in 2001, yet this number further rose by 20 percent to 669,500 in 2006. Among them, about 33,100 travelled for work on a daily basis.[20] About 219,400 persons living in Hong Kong travelled to the mainland, most notably the PRD, for leisure weekly, and about 185,500 people living in Hong Kong crossed the boundary for business purposes at least once a week. In short, many people from Hong Kong now travel regularly across the boundary to Guangdong, and some do so frequently, whether to work, shop, or enjoy their leisure. Similarly, the number of mainland visitors to Hong Kong has also risen sharply since July 2003.

CROSS-BOUNDARY WORKING AND SHOPPING

Coupling these frequent cross-boundary trips is the conspicuous growth of cross-boundary consumption activities after 1997. The Asian Financial crisis and the onset of economic stagnation since 1998, together with the obvious improvement in the quality of consumer products and services in the mainland, have attracted many ordinary Hong Kong people to flock to Shenzhen and other parts of the PRD for cheap consumer products and other leisure activities.[21] While the amount of consumption by Hong Kong visitors in the mainland was roughly similar to that of the mainland visitors in Hong Kong (around HK $26 billion) in 2002, mainland tourists already spent more in Hong Kong (HK $37.8 billion) than their counterparts from Hong Kong in the mainland (HK $20.4 billion) by 2003.[22] But with the relaxation of travel for mainlanders, the total spending of Mainland tourists in Hong Kong already jumped to HK $47 billion in 2006, and its share of the total tourist spending shot up to 56 percent.[23] Further, the average expenditure per person-trip of the Mainland visitors (HK $4,705 for overnight visitors in 2006) was more than seven times that of the Hong Kong visitors (HK $610 in 2006) because mainland visitors tended to purchase jewellery, cosmetics, foreign-made electronic products, and brand name fashion while visiting Hong Kong, whereas Hong Kong visitors preferred purchasing cheap electronic products, herbal medicine, household items, and Chinese food in the Mainland.[24] Some Hong Kong people living close to the boundary can even take regular weekly trips to Shenzhen and nearby areas to shop for food and household items, often at a fraction of the prices in Hong Kong. Whereas Shenzhen and other nearby PRD cities have benefited tremendously from the regular inflow of Hong Kong consumers, Hong Kong's leading shopping districts now look forward to the inflow of mainland tourists. In fact, shopping is often considered more important than touring for many of these mainland tourists. In other words, the cross-boundary shopping route has now been reversed by allowing the inflow of mainland shoppers back into Hong Kong after the launching of the Individual Visit Scheme.

Another salient development is that an increasing number of Hong Kong residents are working in the mainland. One set of systematic household surveys carried out by the Census and Statistics Department of the HKSAR Government provides a glimpse of the trend of Hong Kong residents working in the mainland and their socioeconomic profile. The estimated number of Hong Kong residents working in the mainland had more than doubled from 64,200 in 1992 to 157,300 in 1998. Between 1998 and 2005, their number further increased sharply by 50 percent. According to the 2005 survey, some 237,500 Hong Kong residents, representing 7 percent of the workforce, had worked in the mainland.[25] About 66 percent of this group were males aged thirty to forty-nine, compared with 59 percent of the total workforce. Over 85 percent of the Hong Kong people surveyed worked in the mainland because of their work requirement; 20 percent cited "better career prospect" and a mere 6 percent cited "easier to seek jobs" as the reason. The overwhelming majority of these people worked in Guangdong (87 percent), especially Shenzhen (38 percent) and Dongguan (26 percent).

Both the education level and salary of the Hong Kong residents working in the mainland were higher than the general workforce in Hong Kong. About 42 percent of this group had tertiary education, compared with only 29 percent of the total working population, and more than 36 percent of these Hong Kong residents who worked in the mainland were managers and administrators, and another 45 percent were professionals or associate professionals. They were primarily serving in manufacturing (47 percent), and wholesale, retail, import and export trade, restaurants, and hotels (32 percent). The median monthly earnings of these Hong Kong people working in the mainland were HK $16,000, which was considerably higher than the median monthly earnings of the working population in Hong Kong, that is, HK $10,000 in 2005.[26] Nonetheless, the Hong Kong residents did not stay in the Mainland for long. Their average duration of each stay was three days, but the median frequency of their trips to work in the Mainland was thirty-six times during the twelve months before the survey.

As shown in the above review, a more integrated south China region is clearly in the making. The improvements in boundary crossing (e.g., the improvement of the Huanggang-Lok Ma Chau control point) and other transport links (e.g., the completion of the Western Corridor linking Hong Kong and Shenzhen) will further expedite more cross-boundary demographic movements. The conclusion of CEPA and China's gradual opening up after its WTO accession mean that more Hong Kong professionals may work and settle down in the mainland, either by taking advantage of the earlier opening up of the professional sectors, or by serving in foreign firms. With the pending construction of the Hong Kong-Macao-Zhuhai bridge linking Hong Kong and the western part of the PRD and the express rail link between Hong Kong and Guangzhou, such demographic movements will likely increase further in the coming decade.

CROSS-BOUNDARY HOUSING ISSUES

Hong Kong's real estate market has experienced a severe downturn with the onset of the Asian Financial Crisis and the introduction of a new housing policy by the HKSAR Government after 1997. By 2003, property prices have dropped 50 to 60 percent if compared with the heydays of 1996–1997. Nonetheless, Hong Kong's property prices are still very expensive if compared with those of the mainland. At the same time, real estate in the PRD experienced a new phase of development since the early 1990s. The attraction of property in the PRD for Hong Kong residents can be attributed to several important factors, including their low prices, their proximity, the gradual improvement of cross-boundary transport links, and the marked improvement in the living conditions of the PRD. However, if a growing number of Hong Kong residents buy property and perhaps reside in the PRD, this will have important impacts on Hong Kong's property market and other aspects of economy and society. Although the property markets in Hong Kong and Guangdong are not yet fully merged together, the developments in one market may influence the other in the future because the numbers of property ownership and renting by Hong Kong people in Guangdong have been on the rise. The reverse flow of mainland people purchasing property in Hong Kong has already happened, but given the high cost of real estate in Hong Kong, the transactions will likely be concentrated on the high-end segments of the real estate market.

Three major studies done by the HKSAR Government in 2001, 2003, and 2005 have provided some useful, even if still preliminary, data on the Hong Kong residents' experience of and aspirations for taking up residence in the mainland.[27] The results of the surveys are broadly similar: more and more Hong Kong residents are taking up residence in the mainland, and more and more households aspire to take residency in the mainland. The 2005 survey indicates that the number of Hong Kong residents who had taken up residence in the mainland had more than doubled from 41,300 in 2001 to 91,800 in 2005 (about 1.7 percent of all Hong Kong residents).[28] The number of residential properties in the mainland owned and rented by Hong Kong residents had decreased slightly by 2.6 percent from 218,000 in 2001 to 212,200 in 2005. Nearly 91 percent of the properties were located in Guangdong province, notably Shenzhen and Dongguan, both of which are very close to Hong Kong. In other words, these Hong Kong people have already taken up a substantial amount of resident property in south China. The majority of these Hong Kong residents were living in Guangdong, especially Shenzhen. They were predominantly male, married, and economically active. While the majority of these properties (68 percent) were used for self-use, such as second homes or vacation houses, the cross-boundary travel survey already shows an upward trend of people working in the mainland, and this may stimulate more desire for purchasing or renting property in the PRD in the near future.

The 2005 survey also shows an increase in the ownership and renting of mainland properties by Hong Kong residents. There is an increase of 4 percent and 13 percent respectively in the number of Hong Kong residents purchasing and renting property in the mainland respectively. In other words, some 221,600 and 36,600 persons, respectively, owned and rented residential properties in the mainland. The 2005 survey shows that the median monthly personal income of these residents who owned resident property in the mainland has increased slightly from HK $10,200 in 2001 to HK $10,400 in 2005. The profiles of the Hong Kong residents taking residency in 2005 were similar to those in 2001.

What is even more significant is that when the household heads were asked whether their entire household intended to take up residence in the mainland in the next ten years, some 32,200 households (about 1.4 percent of all households in Hong Kong) expressed such an interest, and 17,500 of them may consider moving within the next five years, which marked an increase of 26 percent and 33 percent, respectively, when compared with the 2001 survey, but the figures have dropped by about 19 percent and 13 percent between 2003 and 2005. The median monthly household income of those who intended to take up residence in the mainland was HK $17,500, which was 15 percent higher than the figure of HK $15,100 in 2001. Nonetheless, the number of individuals who had such an intention had somewhat dropped more than half from 172,000 in 2001 to 80,200 in 2005 (about 1.5 percent of all Hong Kong residents). Among the key reasons that those persons who intended to take up residence in the mainland in the next ten years are the following: lower cost of living (47 percent), better living environment (31 percent), and retirement (29 percent). The median monthly personal income of the individuals wishing to take up residency in the mainland had also fallen from HK $9,000 in 2001 to HK $8,500 in 2005. Nonetheless, similar to 2001, the 2005 survey shows that the remaining 97 percent of Hong Kong residents did not plan to take up residence in the mainland. Many of the key reasons cited include: difficulties in adapting to or lack of familiarity with the mainland environment (28 percent), having a job in Hong Kong (27 percent), and ownership of resident property in Hong Kong (27 percent). Actually, about 82 percent said they would not consider residing in the mainland under any circumstances, which is higher than the figure of 79 percent recorded in the 2001 survey.

There are no studies undertaken in the PRD or other mainland cities regarding the amount of property purchased by Hong Kong residents, hence the above data provide by far the most important indicators. However, according to the estimates by a leading real estate agency in Hong Kong, the estimated number of mainland flats purchased by Hong Kong residents has risen steadily from 12,700 to 14,100 units, involving RMB 6.9 billion in 2001, to 24,900 to 26,100 units, involving RMB 14.7 billion in 2006.[29] With the improvement of cross-boundary transport in the near future, it is conceivable that the number of Hong Kong residents taking up residence in the PRD will further increase. At this initial stage, it is likely that the properties purchased (or rented) are used as second homes or vacation houses. However, for areas like Shenzhen and Dongguan, the trend of commuting between these cities and Hong Kong (and perhaps purchase of property by Hong Kong residents) may become even more prevalent when boundary crossing and transportation improve further.

The preferred scenario in the minds of some top officials of the HKSAR Government and the private sector is that the high cost of living in Hong Kong will drive the lower classes to move to the PRD and hence reduce the demand for social services and health care, both of which are clearly more expensive in Hong Kong. Whether such a scenario, which was articulated most vocally when Antony Leung served as the Financial Secretary in 2001–2003, can materialize is unclear. For instance, the nonportability of education, medical care, and social services, and the absence of a large number of employment opportunities in the mainland for these low-income groups from Hong Kong, probably continue to be key constraints that inhibit them from moving to the PRD. The portability of Hong Kong's social services and health care benefits across the boundary is a complicated issue that is unlikely to be resolved comprehensively in the near term. The improvement of transport links actually make it easier for Hong Kong residents to return to the HKSAR for, say, important and expensive medical care and services, unless the Government can reduce the availability of these services to this group. Nonetheless, the trend of Hong Kong people taking up residence in south China has increased since 1997, and this may have a long term impact not only on Hong Kong's own property market, but also other aspects of social and economic life.

PUBLIC HEALTH HAZARDS

Given the geographical proximity between Hong Kong and Guangdong and the rising social interactions, health hazards have become a new cross-boundary issue. Viruses know no boundaries. The avian flu outbreak in 1997 already suggests the danger of cross-boundary health hazards, but the most devastating case is undoubtedly the SARS epidemic. The tragic outbreak of SARS in south China in early spring 2003 not only shows the perils of a cross-boundary epidemic, but also the immense difficulties of managing cross-boundary demographic flows. A notification system of infectious disease was set up before the SARS outbreak, yet the mechanism failed to curb the SARS outbreak in 2003. The lack of effective communication between health authorities on both sides and the unwillingness of Guangdong province to share its vital information about SARS with Hong Kong are important factors shaping the eventual outbreak in Hong Kong. Despite repeated calls from Hong Kong's health officials for information in the initial stage of outbreak, their Guangdong counterparts did not even respond.[30] Hong Kong's SARS crisis began to unfold after a "super-spreader" infected with the SARS virus from Guangzhou visited the HKSAR in late February 2003.[31] In mid February, only about 305 cases of SARS were reported in Guangdong. However, the epidemic soon haunted Hong Kong and the rest of China. It was not until mid-April that both sides could establish an exchange and notification mechanism so that they could further cooperate and share information directly without going through the central authorities. By late April, the cumulative number of SARS cases skyrocketed to almost 1,600 in Hong Kong and 3,460 in Guangdong and the rest of China, killing more than three hundred people in those areas.[32] By late June, there were over 1,500 infected cases and 56 deaths in Guangdong and about 1,755 cases in Hong Kong and almost 300 deaths. Medical experts investigating the outbreak aptly concluded that Hong Kong's health sector and professionals needed to enhance collaboration in data reporting, surveillance, and exchange with its counterparts in the PRD.[33]

OTHER EMERGING CROSS-BOUNDARY SOCIAL CONCERNS

With the growing volume of cross-boundary demographic movements and the introduction of the Mainland Individual Visit Scheme, many new social issues have emerged on the horizon. One concerns the delivery of babies by pregnant mainland women in Hong Kong. The number of pregnant women from mainland delivering their babies in Hong Kong has risen substantially in recent years, as it is now becoming easier for mainland people to visit Hong Kong. According to the past practices of the HKSAR Government, mainland women would not be refused entry even if they were pregnant. Hong Kong can only rely upon the assistance of mainland authorities in paying attention to this issue during their processing of applications for exit permits by mainland women. If the babies delivered in Hong Kong are Chinese nationals, they will then enjoy the right of abode in the territory. This has not only offered a loophole for mainland people to get the right of abode in Hong Kong, but also created pressure on the provision of obstetric care and paediatric services.[34] The number of babies born in Hong Kong from mainland women (including those whose spouse is a Hong Kong resident) has grown from 7,810 to 20,577 between 2001 and the first ten months of 2006.[35] Concerns loom at the growing number and proportion of births in Hong Kong in which both of the parents are not Hong Kong residents, as these births jumped from 620 in 2001 to 12,072 by the end of 2006.[36] The share of babies born in Hong Kong when both of their parents were mainland residents in the total number of babies born in Hong Kong from all pregnant mainland women (including those whose father are Hong Kong residents) has substantially increased from 7.9 percent to 61.6 percent during the same period.[37] The share of babies born from pregnant mainland women in the total number of births in Hong Kong has also significantly increased from 16.2 percent in 2001 to 39.3 percent in the first ten months of 2006.[38]

Further, many of these mothers failed to pay the nonresident medical fees when they delivered their babies in Hong Kong's public hospitals.[39] In fact, after the Audit Commission of the HKSAR Government revealed the nonpayment by nonlocal pregnant woman in public hospitals in November 2006, a number of local pregnant women protested on the inadequate facilities in public hospitals for them. Hong Kong legislators also demanded that the government contain the influx of mainland mothers at the immigration control points in late 2006. The HKSAR Government thus discussed the issue with the Ministry of Health and the Ministry of Public Security on formulating measures to curb the influx of mainland pregnant women to Hong Kong.[40] The Guangdong Public Security Bureau agreed in February 2007 that they would deny the applications of the two-way permit from pregnant women in Guangdong who were suspected of planning to give birth in Hong Kong as their sole purpose for visiting the city.[41] The HKSAR Government has also introduced a number of measures to stop mainland pregnant women from entering Hong Kong, such as requiring pregnant women from the mainland to show certificates of bookings of appointment in obstetrics wards in Hong Kong hospitals at the immigration counters and a substantial increase of the nonresident medical fees in public hospitals for all noneligible persons using the obstetrics wards since February 2007.[42]

Similarly, mainland visitors who overstayed and worked as illegal workers have become a new social concern.[43] Hong Kong's labor groups have long criticized the HKSAR Government for failing to take adequate action to deal with this problem. The number of illegal workers from the mainland caught, including both mainland visitors and illegal immigrants, rose only gradually from 1,927 in 1997 to 2,366 in 2001, but the figure more than doubled to 5,316 by 2004.[44] The actual situation may well be much worse because the illegal workers could work for their relatives in Hong Kong and hence could not be easily caught. The Hong Kong law enforcement agencies also could not devote most of their efforts to the raids on illegal workers.[45] Nonetheless, such numbers do not really threaten the livelihood of the majority of the existing working population, who are more concerned with the increasing relocation of jobs across the boundary. In response to the need to retrain unskilled workers, the HKSAR Government has injected more funding into the Employees Retraining Scheme, which was originally launched in 1992. Starting from 2000, an annual recurrent subvention of around HK $400 million has been allocated to this Scheme, whose main target is the group of displaced workers aged 30 or more, but with less than lower secondary education. In fact, the number of trainees in government-sponsored retraining programmes already doubled from 55,632 in 1997/98 to over 103,536 in 2002/03.[46] However, the high unemployment rate in Hong Kong since 1999 (in the range of 6 to 8 percent during the economic downtown) suggests that the process of economic restructuring will continue to have a major impact on the working people who cannot adapt to the changing circumstances, and such retraining schemes are unlikely to fully arrest these structural trends.

The increase of cross-boundary crimes has also attracted much community attention in Hong Kong, especially in view of the growth of mainland visitors. The total number of mainland people who have been arrested for having committed crimes in Hong Kong, including prostitution and illegal employment, has already doubled from 5,617 in 2000 to 11,717 in 2002 and 14,554 in 2004. The majority were arrested for prostitution (68 percent) and illegal employment (36 percent).[47] The number of mainland visitors arrested for suspected involvement in prostitution in fact more than tripled from 3,057 in 2001 to 9,916 in 2003.[48] Similarly, the number of mainland visitors convicted also nearly tripled from 4,136 in 2000 to 11,243 in 2003.[49] While the number of mainland people who have committed crimes in Hong Kong is still not large, especially given the huge increase in the number of mainland visitors since mid 2003, this problem has nonetheless loomed large in the minds of Hong Kong people. Another problem that attracted extensive media attention is that Hong Kong residents had become crime victims in the mainland. The popular Hong Kong newspapers often devote a great deal of coverage to news on these victims, such as Hong Kong people being held for ransom or tortured by the robbers. Hong Kong's legislators have already voiced concern over such issues because the HKSAR Government could not offer much assistance to these victims.[50]

STATE REPONSES TO THE GROWING SOCIAL INTERACTIONS IN SOUTH CHINA

Initial state responses to the rapidly developing cross-boundary social interactions are incremental and reactive. For instance, in response to the growing cross-boundary traffic flows, the operating hours of the control points have been extended, but only one of the land checkpoints in Hong Kong is open twenty-four hours for both goods and passengers. However, with the emergence of new cross-boundary issues and the articulation of a clearer strategy toward integration with the mainland by the HKSAR Government, both sides have proceeded to expedite cross-boundary governmental cooperation. The following section examines three salient developments addressing different state responses to the cross-boundary social interactions in south China: the growth of intergovernmental cooperation mechanisms, the formulation of a population policy, and the increasingly activist role of the central government in coordinating cross-boundary issues.

GROWTH OF INTERGOVERNMENTAL MECHANISMS

One of the most immediate responses to cross-boundary issues is the gradual establishment of intergovernmental mechanisms. Owing to the competing views and interests of the different governments involved and their concerns with the repercussions of such measures for "One Country, Two Systems," intergovernmental mechanisms have evolved in a gradual manner.[51] Both the chief executive (hereafter the CE) of the HKSAR Government and the governor of Guangdong emphasized the significance of cross-boundary cooperation as soon as the HKSAR was established in 1997. The high-level Hong Kong/Guangdong Cooperation Joint Conference (hereafter the HKGDCJC), to be headed respectively by Guangdong's Executive vice governor and HKSAR's chief secretary for administration (hereafter the CS), was established in 1998 to provide a strategic framework to foster closer cross-boundary cooperation.

Intergovernmental relations between Guangdong and Hong Kong engage many different policy sectors. Some of these sectors, such as customs, are the prerogative of the central government. Others, such as economic development and environmental protection, come mainly under the authority of the provincial and subprovincial authorities. In addition to the many direct contacts between individual government departments, there are three standing cross-boundary mechanisms: (a) the Cross-boundary Liaison System (established in 1982), which deals with boundary crossing; (b) the mainland/HKSAR Conference on the Coordination of Major Infrastructure Projects, and most importantly, (c) the Hong Kong/ Guangdong Cooperation Joint Conference (established in 1998), which has now become the umbrella framework for coordinating all key areas in cross-boundary cooperation.

In the 1998–2002 period, several alternatives on cross-boundary cooperation, especially over the environment, transportation, and tourism, were considered by the HKGDCJC. Nonetheless, perhaps with the exception of tourism and the gradual improvement in boundary crossing, these efforts were not particularly successful. Hence this mechanism has not fully achieved the original objectives as laid out by the CE, or the Guangdong governor in 1998. Despite the high-level status of the mechanism, the HKGDCJC has experienced various difficulties in its operation. For instance, the HKSAR government did not have a clear strategy for cross-boundary cooperation when this mechanism was established. The HKGDCJC is supposedly scheduled to meet twice a year. In practice, after the first two meetings, which respectively took place in March 1998 and September 1999, the HKGDCJC did not hold meetings for the third time until one year later in September 2000. This suggests that both sides could not agree on the agenda or there were no immediate issues that could be tabled for approval. The fourth and fifth meetings were later convened in July 2001 and March 2002. Key cross-boundary measures over issues such as environmental protection, boundary crossing, and tourism, all of which were key issues for Hong Kong, dominated the agenda of this mechanism until mid-2001. The Guangdong side was obviously disappointed at the initial operation of this mechanism because economic cooperation was not the focus. It was not until the fourth meeting held in July 2001 that more economic policy issues finally made it to the agenda. While this mechanism has resulted in agreements on some cross-boundary issues, it has nonetheless not enhanced cross-boundary cooperation to the more strategic level of policy coordination as anticipated.

The primary interest of the HKSAR government, especially during the first term of C. H. Tung, was to facilitate the flow of people and goods in the PRD, especially the improvement of boundary crossing and infrastructural links, and the management of environmental problems. Although both parties agreed that these issues should be addressed, the Guangdong authorities favored much more government initiative in supporting cross-boundary economic cooperation. Despite the initial momentum achieved in 1997–1998, few major concrete initiatives were launched in 1999 and 2000. With the appointment of Donald Tsang as the new CS in mid-2001, a host of initiatives on cross-boundary matters, such as the extension of boundary crossing hours, more coordination in infrastructural development, and facilitation of the inflow of mainland tourists, have been proposed. New topics were soon put on the HKSAR government's policy agenda, such as a new express rail link between Hong Kong and Guangzhou, the exploration of cross-boundary cooperation in logistics, and finally, the consideration of a bridge link between Hong Kong and the western part of the PRD. A small team, the Hong Kong Guangdong Cooperation Coordination Unit, was soon established under the office of the CS to help with many practical tasks in administrative coordination.[52]

C. H. Tung's Policy Address in January 2003, the first in his second term, finally considered economic integration between Hong Kong and Guangdong as a key policy initiative. In the sixth HKGDCJC held in August 2003, a number of vital institutional changes and policy endeavours were introduced. Both sides finally agreed on a general division of labor in economic development. Guangdong agreed to develop itself into one of the world's prime manufacturing bases whereas Hong Kong would work toward the goal of "an important service centre in finances, business, transportation, logistics and high-value-added services." The guiding principles for cooperation are defined as "forward-looking, comprehensive, pragmatic, and mutually beneficial." More privileged treatment of Hong Kong investors in Guangdong's service sectors, such as retail and transportation, would be provided under the CEPA framework.

The HKGDCJC framework was only reorganized in August 2003 in order to encourage more policy coordination over cross-boundary issues and to better manage the process of social and economic integration. The Joint Conference has now been upgraded to the level of the heads of administration, as they will be presided by Guangdong's Governor and the CE. More importantly, a permanent liaison office under the conference has been set up. An executive vice governor and the CS will be responsible for "steering and taking forward the co-operation items." Research organs on both sides will be tasked to undertake studies on Hong Kong-Guangdong cooperation. A total of twenty-two expert groups overseeing a dozen cooperation items were consolidated and established under the Joint Conference in order to achieve more coherence in intergovernmental cooperation over key priority areas, including economic and infrastructural development, tourism, education, infectious diseases, joint promotion, expanding economic cooperation to Guangdong's hinterland, and most recently, on informatization, the cooperation of the Pan-PRD and the provision of social welfare. Having learned from the bitter lessons of the SARS epidemic, the Conference has finally put the issue of infectious disease directly under the Hong Kong-Guangdong cooperation framework, and the province has promised to share the information on unexpected or new infectious diseases that it submits to the Ministry of Health with Hong Kong in future. An agreement of cooperation on contingency measures during public health emergencies between Guangdong, Hong Kong, and Macau was signed in June 2006.[53] In July 2007, Guangdong, Macao, and Hong Kong health authorities also agreed to strengthen mutual communication and cooperation in combating infectious diseases, including the prevention and control of dengue fever, AIDS, tuberculosis, and plague.[54] In September 2007, the health departments from Hong Kong and Guangdong further agreed to promote their exchanges and cooperation.[55]

Since the mainland has always been the largest provider of food to Hong Kong. There has also been growing concern over the monitoring of food safety after a number of food safety incidents in the mainland broke out in late 2005 and 2006. Hong Kong and Guangdong decided to establish a new mechanism on exchange and cooperation in food safety in April 2006.[56] After the food scares in 2006, it was agreed that a dedicated expert group on the quarantine of the agricultural products from Guangdong to Hong Kong will be established under the HKGDCJC, and the State Administration for Quarantine, Inspection and Quality Supervision (AQSIQ) will designate officers in the new expert group as well.[57]

Further, responding to the requests of Hong Kong's business community, the Greater Pearl River Delta Business Council, comprised of business leaders, representatives from major business associations, professional bodies, the Hong Kong Trade Development Council and the Hong Kong Productivity Council, and representatives of the relevant government departments, was launched in March 2004 to foster more exchanges between the government and business sectors and between them and their counterparts in Guangdong. While cross-boundary advisory commissions involving both governmental and nongovernmental actors are often found in other countries, this is the first major initiative in incorporating societal input into cross-boundary mechanisms in south China.[58] Since its establishment, six subgroups have been established under the Council, and several research studies have already been conducted.[59]

Last but not least, in order to enhance the coordination between Hong Kong and the mainland, the HKSAR Government established a mainland Affairs Liaison Office under the Constitutional Affairs Bureau in April 2006, and the Guangdong Cooperation Coordination Unit was merged into the Office.[60] Later, the Constitutional Affairs Bureau formally changed its name to the Constitutional and Mainland Affairs Bureau to reflect its growing portfolio in dealing with the mainland. In March 2006, the Guangdong Provincial Government also upgraded its Hong Kong and Macau Affairs Office, which was previously under the Foreign Affairs Office of Guangdong province, to an independent office under the direct supervision from the Provincial Government and led by its executive vice-governor.[61] In short, despite some initial hiccups in the 1997–2000 period, it is clear that the HKSAR government has taken firm steps to undertake various intergovernmental initiatives in order to manage cross-boundary issues and to promote better cross-boundary cooperation.

FORMULATION OF A POPULATION POLICY BY HONG KONG

The formulation of a population policy by Hong Kong is by far the most comprehensive attempt to address a social concern arising from cross-boundary social interactions. In view of the aging of Hong Kong society, the low fertility rate, and the prospect of the continuing inflow of a large number of mainland migrants who were spouses and children of Hong Kong residents, the HKSAR government decided to formulate a "population policy" in the aftermath of the controversy over the right of abode issue in 1999. The new immigrants from the mainland, that is, those who have stayed in Hong Kong for less than seven years, are mainly wives or children of Hong Kong residents and of those aged fifteen or above, their education level is lower than the total population.[62] But the daily quota of 150 is mainly offered to these immigrants coming for family reunion. After two years of study, the HKSAR Government finally released a report which proposed different initiatives on population policy in February 2003.[63]

Some of the policy measures do not have a major impact on cross-boundary demographic movements, for example, imposing a levy on Hong Kong residents hiring foreign domestic helpers and considering policy support for the elderly. But most others clearly have important bearings on cross-boundary demographic movements, such as improving the management of the admission of the children and spouses of Hong Kong residents in the mainland, providing more incentives to tertiary institutions to attract more mainland and overseas students, and reducing the restrictions for admission of mainland professionals. It was also proposed that the entitlement to the Comprehensive Social Security Assistance would only apply to those new immigrants who have resided in

Hong Kong for seven years. Nonetheless, other more controversial issues, such as the availability of subsidized public services for Hong Kong residents who are absent from the territory for a long period of time, and the portability of social services across the boundary and its implication for Hong Kong's public finance, are only raised as issues for further studies. The recommendations of this report have been largely introduced, but some achieved only limited success. For instance, the introduction of investment immigrants in Hong Kong under the "Capital Investment Entrant Scheme" only applies to residents from Macao, Taiwan, and overseas countries. Mainland investors are not included in the scheme, possibly out of concern that they would use Hong Kong as a means for channeling money out of the mainland. By the end of 2006, the total number of such applications only reached 1,910.[64]

The revamping of the policy on the admission of mainland professionals is perhaps the most important cross-boundary initiative in the population policy exercise. Hong Kong used to adopt a restrictive policy toward the admission of mainland people to work in the territory, although the policy toward other foreign nationals is more liberal. In order to promote a more knowledge-based economy and to enhance economic competitiveness, the HKSAR Government has adopted various schemes to attract mainland talents to work in the territory after 1997, but the effectiveness of such efforts is rather limited.[65] Such a process came only gradually because of the government's concern with the political sensitivity of admitting more outside job seekers during a time of economic downturn. After the intense lobbying effort by the private sector, the HKSAR Government first introduced two schemes to attract mainland talents and professionals to work in Hong Kong. One was introduced in mid-December 1999 to attract people with expertise and skills not available in Hong Kong, especially in "technology-based, knowledge-intensive and high-value added activities." Yet, by 2002, only 256 applications have been approved for applicants in IT, communication, multimedia technology, and engineering. Another scheme was introduced in June 2001 to attract mainland professionals in IT and financial services were introduced, but by 2002, only 268 applications were approved.[66] These two schemes demanded a high level of qualifications and the processing of these visas was slow; hence, both failed to attract a large number of such talents or professionals to Hong Kong. In addition, Hong Kong's business environment, which lacks a supportive infrastructure for promoting hi-tech or IT-related sectors, could hardly compete with the attraction of other booming mainland cities such as Beijing, Shanghai, or even Shenzhen.

Following the recommendations of the population policy, a less restrictive policy on admitting mainland talents and professionals was adopted in mid-2003. A combined scheme was introduced in mid-July 2003 to replace the two previous programs, and no more sectoral restrictions or quotas would be imposed under this new scheme. By the end of 2003, over 1,500 visas for such mainland talents and professionals had been processed. The Immigration Department received a cumulative total of 15,212 applications to the Scheme by September 2006, of which 12,857 applications were approved. However, out of the 3,228 approved applications between April and September 2006, 1,486 were related to academic research, 500 were related to commerce and industry, and about half of them were short-term employment.[67] As indicated in the statistics, the Scheme failed to tap mainland talents to work in the key sectors of Hong Kong such as finance and logistics, and they were not offered long-term employment. To further enhance the tapping of mainland talents, the HKSAR government introduced a "Quality Migrant Admission Scheme" in June 2006, allowing those who have not yet secured work contracts to stay temporarily in Hong Kong to find jobs. By the end of 2006, 587 applications have been received, and 66 applications were approved.[68] Starting from August 2001, students from Mainland China who have graduated from publicly funded higher educational institutions in Hong Kong since 1990 are allowed to find jobs in the territory, provided that they have skills or knowledge of value to, but not readily available in, Hong Kong. In 2001, only twenty-one such graduates received approval to work in Hong Kong. Although the number rose from 97 in 2002 to 236 in 2005 and 405 in 2006, the number of mainland graduates who will work in Hong Kong through this channel is likely to be small unless the number of mainland students recruited into Hong Kong's universities will further increase.[69]

In short, with the growing economic integration between Hong Kong and the mainland, Hong Kong realizes that it needs to adopt a more holistic approach in managing demographic flows. While maintaining the existing quota system of admitting Mainlanders for family reunions, the HKSAR government has completely reversed the policy toward attracting mainland talents to work and stay in Hong Kong. The trend is to further open up Hong Kong's job market to qualified mainland talents and graduates, as long as their skills or expertise are needed, but the data so far do not indicate that a really large number of qualified applicants have come, or will soon come, to Hong Kong. Hence, the immediate challenge for Hong Kong is actually to continue to attract more mainland or overseas talents. At the same time, various localities or government agencies from coastal cities such as Shanghai or Shenzhen have also held recruitment expos to lure Hong Kong professionals to work in the mainland. Nonetheless, given the relatively lower income offered by mainland units, it is unlikely that a large number of Hong Kong professionals would end up working for mainland firms or government offices, because the main trend for these Hong Kong people is still to operate their own business or firms, or to work for Hong Kong or other overseas companies stationed in the mainland.

AN INCREASINGLY ACTIVIST CENTRAL GOVERNMENT

In view of the lack of progress in Hong Kong-Guangdong cooperation in 1997–2000, the central government has stepped in and expedited regional cooperation since 2002, most importantly in facilitating the twenty-four-hour boundary crossing and coordinating infrastructural development such as the proposed Hong Kong-Zhuhai-Macao bridge. For instance, Guangdong no longer exhibited the same kind of enthusiasm in 2001–2002 when Hong Kong became much more concerned with the need to connect better with the western part of the PRD. The feasibility study led by the researchers from the National Development and Reform Commission generally supported the construction of a Hong Kong-Zhuhai-Macao bridge.[70] Nonetheless, the proposed Hong Kong-Zhuhai-Macao bridge linking Hong Kong with the western PRD conflicts with Guangzhou's plan to develop Nansha into a major port. Shenzhen is also not eager to see Hong Kong extending its logistic reach to the western delta. In fact, the improvement of their infrastructure and transportation services, such as Shenzhen's Yantian Port and Guangzhou's new airport, already suggests keener competition with Hong Kong. Hence, central government support is critical in a regional development project like this bridge.

Most importantly, the conclusion of the CEPA arrangement is widely considered as a means by the central authorities to help the HKSAR government to restructure the Hong Kong economy and to benefit from the economic integration with the mainland. This unprecedented free trade area arrangement was proposed by Hong Kong's business community, which soon gained government approval, as a response to reap benefits from China's accession to the WTO. After more than eighteen months of tough negotiation, the central government and the HKSAR government signed the CEPA on June 29, 2003. In fact, the conclusion of CEPA provides an important policy platform for both Hong Kong and Guangdong to forge closer links in the services sector. In order to relax the rigid control over the inflow of mainland visitors into Hong Kong and to boost tourism, personal visits to Hong Kong by residents from eight cities of Guangdong were further relaxed with the introduction of the Individual Visit Scheme. This relaxation was later applied to all residents from the province in mid-2004.[71] Other major coastal cities such as Beijing and Shanghai, also benefit from this scheme later. The scheme has been further extended to encompass forty-nine cities covering a total population of 220 million in China.[72] The importance of the Scheme is that the relaxation in travel will facilitate not only tourism, but also business and all other kinds of personal visits between Hong Kong and the mainland.

The CEPA constitutes a landmark in the economic integration between Hong Kong and the mainland, especially south China.[73] Starting from January 1, 2004, Hong Kong can export 374 types of goods to the mainland tariff-free, and seventeen of its service sectors can also enter the mainland market, especially Guangdong, earlier than overseas countries.[74] In late August 2004, the CEPA arrangement was further liberalized.[75] In the second and third supplement of the CEPA Agreement promulgated in January 2006 and January 2007, the zero tariff arrangements have been extended to cover all products of Hong Kong origin to the mainland, and the further extension of the scope and depth of concessions to the Hong Kong service sector operators in the twenty-seven service sectors covered in the CEPA and its first supplement was introduced.[76] These measures, if effectively utilized, might help Hong Kong professionals and firms to enjoy some time advantage and preferential treatment before China fully opens up in accordance with the schedule of the WTO. While mainly economic in nature, the framework will also encourage closer social connections between Hong Kong and the mainland.

CONCLUSION: SOME PRELIMINARY OBSERVATIONS ON THE CHANGING STATE-SOCIETY RELATIONS IN SOUTH CHINA

The above analysis clearly shows that the society and economy in Hong Kong and Mainland China are moving toward closer integration since 1997. Many discussions of the future Greater PRD suggest the development of a metropolitan area whereby the movement of people and goods can be smoother and regional economic development can benefit the entire region.[77] Aside from Guangzhou and Shenzhen, there will be half a dozen or so budding cities in the PRD, and this cluster of cities inside the PRD will be linked up by a light transit system to be built in the coming decade. Hong Kong and Macao should be closely linked with this booming region with improved infrastructural links and transport services. However, such discussions focus on urban planning, environmental management, and economic integration, rather than on complex social and political challenges resulting from such a process of deep integration.

Many Hong Kong people are still concerned that the economic and social consequences of growing integration between Hong Kong and Guangdong may seriously affect Hong Kong's public finance and society. For instance, the growth in cross-boundary consumption by Hong Kong residents may impact on the city's domestic consumption and government revenue, and the growing inflow of mainland visitors poses challenges to the urban infrastructure, public order, and public health in Hong Kong. The availability of affordable and good quality real estate in Shenzhen and other parts of the PRD may also depress the Hong Kong property market in the future. As examined above, state authorities in Hong Kong and the mainland have already spent an increasing amount of efforts in managing the social consequences of the growing economic integration between Hong Kong and Guangdong. Yet, the political and administrative implications of this emerging integration are far from clear and simple at this moment. Several developments merit particular attention.

First, with the extensive economic changes happening on both sides of the Hong Kong-Guangdong boundary and the emerging economic interdependence, governments in Hong Kong and the mainland have to respond to the community demands for further facilitation of traffic and demographic movements and to cope with the various problems arising from such interactions. Such state responses were initially often incremental and reactive, rather than strategic and proactive, because the volume of cross-boundary traffic and demographic flows has gone beyond their expectation. Further, the HKSAR government did not fully articulate a clear strategy and undertake concrete measures in expediting cross-boundary cooperation until around 2001, partly because of administrative inertia and party because of concerns over the political implications of closer social and economic integration between Hong Kong and south China. Especially in the 1997–2000 period, many in Hong Kong, including some senior officials and various segments of society, still capitalized on the importance of the "separateness" of Hong Kong under the "One Country, Two Systems" framework. For instance, the twenty-four-hour operation of the boundary for passenger traffic was introduced only in late January 2003. It is not until more discussion in the community and championing by senior government officials in promoting cross-boundary cooperation has been conducted that such concerns have finally been allayed. The political sensitivity concerning the solution of various regional issues (such as environmental protection), the competing interests of the different governments involved, and the implications of regional cooperation measures for "One Country, Two Systems" further complicate the articulation of solutions to the many political and administrative challenges resulting from the integration process. Nonetheless, what is increasingly clear is that the need to manage the cross-boundary social trends has increased the involvement of both the central and local states, since the resolution of cross-boundary problems and the removal of obstacles to such cross-boundary social interactions often call for some form of state action and better intergovernmental coordination.

Second, while much of the initial intergovernmental attention on cross-boundary cooperation since 1997 was on boundary management, economic cooperation, and infrastructural coordination, the scope of such intergovernmental interactions has expanded to encompass a much wider agenda including social, environmental, and public health issues. For instance, in the aftermath of SARS, top health officials from Hong Kong, Macao, and the Mainland recognized that the chances of people spreading infectious diseases across the boundary merits special attention.[78]

Third, Hong Kong's merit under "One Country, Two Systems" is highly privileged within the unitary Chinese state, but this special treatment has not necessarily entailed smooth inter-governmental cooperation between Hong Kong and the mainland. On the one hand, while other localities in south China expected Hong Kong to take the lead in pursuing closer economic and social integration, Hong Kong still encountered considerable difficulties in such an endeavour. Actually, successful examples of intergovernmental cooperation in managing cross-boundary social interactions are largely confined to areas where both Hong Kong and Guangdong share common interests, such as in fighting crimes. Crime is a direct threat to social and political stability in south China, so there is common interest among the local governments in the region to cope with such threats. Other more difficult issues, such as environmental pollution, are still hard to tackle. For instance, the deteriorating air quality in the PRD has compelled both sides to reach an agreement on improving air quality in April 2002. In fact, both Hong Kong and Guangdong agreed to draw up the PRD Regional Air Quality Management Plan to help meet the reduction levels of pollutants, and a regional air quality monitoring network has been set up.[79] Both sides also finally agreed to promulgate the Emission Trading Scheme for Thermal Power Plants in the PRD region in January 2007, after several years of discussion.[80] But Hong Kong's environment minister frankly admitted that there were things that Hong Kong could not do unilaterally, and Guangdong's cooperation was critical in order to overcome the many hurdles in tackling cross-boundary pollution.[81] As long as the pace of economic growth in the PRD continues to be fast, it is difficult for Guangdong's provincial authorities to impose some of the policy measures to clean up the environment on its localities.

Fourth, whether the newly formed intergovernmental mechanisms to manage cross-boundary affairs are able to address such complicated cross-boundary problems remains to be seen. With greater state involvement in managing cross-boundary affairs, cross-boundary issues have also become highly politicized matters on the policy agenda, especially in Hong Kong where there is a pluralistic and vibrant civil society and mass media. While these new state responses carry important symbolic, political meanings, as evidence of cooperation rather than conflict and confrontation, in order to ensure public confidence, they also generate more debates about the proper form of intergovernmental relations under the framework of "One Country, Two Systems," especially in Hong Kong. Hence, institutional adaptation and innovation will continue to be key features in the changing state-society relations in south China. For instance, the provision of "co-location" of customs and immigration services in the future Western Corridor road link between Hong Kong and Shenzhen is a good example. Moreover, the pattern of cross-boundary demographic movement may compel more provision of Hong Kong public services, either by the creation of public service agencies, the establishment of jointly managed agencies, or the contracting out of such services to service providers in Guangdong. Such scenarios may lead to different kinds of cross-boundary public-private partnership arrangements, which are not yet explored at the present moment.

Major changes may also happen inside the governmental structures of the state authorities in the region. For instance, the establishment of new government offices or reshuffling of bureaucratic functions to cope with cross-boundary issues has already taken place, and some form of regional governance structure should not be ruled out in the future. In fact, many people in the private sector have long called for the convening of a mayoral conference of key cities in the PRD as a means to facilitate intra-regional social and economic cooperation. What has been established so far are still mainly Hong Kong-Guangdong intergovernmental mechanisms.

Fifth, there are also signs that the central authorities in Beijing were increasingly asked by the HKSAR government (and perhaps by Guangdong as well) to play a role in balancing the different interests and governments in south China, such as in the case of CEPA, boundary crossing, infrastructural coordination, environmental protection, and infectious disease control. Nonetheless, it is not entirely clear what the implications of these developments may have for "One Country, Two Systems." Will this hamper the autonomy of the HKSAR as the central authorities become more involved in coordinating regional issues in south China? Or will the HKSAR better manage these cross-boundary problems if they could secure the support from the central government? What are the key challenges to Hong Kong's autonomy in view of the deepening social and economic integration with Guangdong? What is certain is that the consequences of social and economic integration between Hong Kong and south China, both extant and latent, will offer many new and difficult policy challenges to governments in both areas.

Last but not least, the management of cross-boundary social and economic flows will be a big challenge to the HKSAR government's capacity to govern effectively. On the one hand, the volume of traffic and demographic movements signify important economic and social processes at work. As the CEPA provides for closer economic integration between both areas, Hong Kong's services may further expand into the Mainland ,and the accompanying outflow of professionals and revenue may have implications for the economy and public finance, unless Hong Kong's schemes to attract the inflow of overseas and Mainland talents and investment work as well. Other challenges, such as the need for Hong Kong and Guangdong to work closely together to solve cross-boundary problems, like infrastructure development, environment or public health issues, will demand great political and administrative skills from the top echelons of the HKSAR Government. So far, there are clear indications that they often have to rely upon the good will and support from the central authorities in managing various cross-boundary problems. The HKSAR Government will soon find the management of cross-boundary social and economic issues one of their greatest challenges in governance.

NOTES

1. The author would like to acknowledge the support by the Hong Kong Research Grants Council for my project, "Managing the Guangdong-Hong Kong Interface" (Reference No.: HKU 7131/98H), which provides the data for this chapter. The intricate state-society relationship in south China involves interactions between different layers of governments and their respective communities on both sides of the boundary. However, this chapter cannot possibly cover all aspects of this multi-faceted relationship.

2. For an analysis of Guangdong's special policies, see my chapter, "Changing Relations between the Central Government and Guangdong," in Yeung Yueman and David Chu (ed.), 1998, *Guangdong: Survey of Province Undergoing Rapid Change*, 2nd ed., Hong Kong: Chinese University Press, pp. 23–61.

3. Michael Enright, et al., *Hong Kong and the Pearl River Delta: The Economic Interaction*, Hong Kong: The 2022 Foundation, p. 26.

4. *Wen Wei Po*, March 9, 2007, A2.

5. *Nanfang Ribao* (Southern Daily), 30 January 2007, A1.

6. Federation of Hong Kong Industries, "HK/PRD partnership key to continual prosperity of the Greater PRD region," *Press release of Federation of Hong Kong Industries* 2007, http://www.industryhk.org/english/news/news_press/pr_070419_023.php.

7. Census and Statistics Department, The Government of the Hong Kong Special Administrative Region (hereafter HKSAR), 2005, *Hong Kong in Figures: 2005 Edition*, Hong Kong: Census and Statistics Department, p. 12; and 2008, *Hong Kong Monthly Digest of Statistics February 2008,* Hong Kong: Census and Statistics Department, pp. 19; 234.

8. Chun Yang, 2006, "The Pearl River Delta and Hong Kong: an evolving cross-boundary region under 'one country, two systems,'" *Habitat International*, Vol. 30, No. 1, p. 70. Also see 2008, *Hong Kong Monthly Digest of Statistics February 2008*, Hong Kong: Census and Statistics Department, pp. 19; 234.

9. Chun Yang, 2006, "The Pearl River Delta and Hong Kong: an evolving cross-boundary region under 'one country, two systems,'" *Habitat International*, Vol. 30, No. 1, p. 70; the Government of HKSAR, 2006, *Hong Kong in Figures: 2006 Edition*, pp. 12, 15.

10. Federation of Hong Kong Industries, 2002, *Made in PRD: The Changing Face of Hong Kong Manufactures (Part II and Full Report: Executive Summary)*, Hong Kong: Federation of Hong Kong Industries.

11. James Anderson, and Liam O'Dowd, 1999, "Borders, Border Regions and Territoriality: Contradictory Meanings, Changing Significance," *Regional Studies*, Vol. 33, No. 7, pp. 593–604.

12. Foreign concerns over Hong Kong are both political and economic. Their concerns will serve as an incentive for Beijing to keep its promise of a high degree of autonomy as well as the "One Country, Two System" framework for Hong Kong. Further, a more porous boundary between Hong Kong and the mainland may facilitate even more illegal activities, such as smuggling of humans and goods, which would likely aggravate their concerns.

13. Timothy Wong Kar-ying, and Wan Po-shan, 2004, "Dui zhongguo de 'chongxin xiangxiang': huigui hou shenfen rentong de yanxu yu bianhua" ("'Re-imaging' of China: The Continuities and Changes in Identity after Reunification"), in Lau Shiu-kai, Timothy Wong Kar-ying, and Wan Po-shan (eds.), *Xianggang shehui Zhengzhi de yanxu yu bianqian (The Continuities and Changes of Hong Kong Society and Politics)*, Hong Kong: Hong Kong Institute of Asia-Pacific Studies, The Chinese University of Hong Kong, pp. 213–242; Wong Kar-ying, and Wan Po-shan, 2006, "Siyuefan xianggang shinin dui zhongguo dalu fazhan yijian diaocha jieguo zhaiyao"("Summary of the Results of the Survey on the Development of the Mainland of China from Hong Kong Residents in April,") *Hong Kong Institute of Asia-Pacific Studies, The Chinese University of Hong Kong*, http://www.cuhk.edu.hk/hkiaps/telpress/CHI_HK_17_PRESS.pdf (May 5, 2006).

14. Census and Statistics Department, HKSAR, PRC, 1998, *Hong Kong Annual Digest of Statistics 1998*, Hong Kong: Census and Statistics Department, p. 143; 2003, *Hong Kong Monthly Digest of Statistics, July 2003* (Hong Kong: Census and Statistics Department, pp. 100–101. Also see HKSAR Government Information Centre, 2004, "Hong Kong 2003–Population and Immigration Control," *HKSAR Government Information Center* 2004, http://www.info.gov.hk/yearbook/2003/english/chapter20/20_03.html; Census and Statistics Department, 2005, *Hong Kong Monthly Digest of Statistics, February 2005*, Hong Kong: Census and Statistics Department, pp. 115–116.

15. HKSAR Government Information Centre, *Hong Kong Yearbook* (Hong Kong: Government Printer, various years).

16. *Hong Kong in Figures: 2005 Edition*, p. 38; HKSAR Government Information Centre, "Hong Kong 2003–Population and Immigration Control," *HKSAR Government Information Center* 2004, www.info.gov.hk/yearbook/2003/english/chapter20/20_03.html.

17. In 2006, over 5.5 million travelled to Hong Kong under the Individual Visit Scheme. See Hong Kong Tourism Board, 2007, "Hong Kong Tourism Sees Steady

Growth in 2006," *Press Release of the Hong Kong Tourism Board* 2007, http://partnernet.hktourismboard.com/pnweb/jsp/doc/listDoc.jsp?doc_id=97018 (Jan. 22, 2007). In 2003, 1.64 million visas were issued under the Individual Visit Scheme and over 1 million have visited Hong Kong, *Wen Wei Po*, February 7, 2004, A3.

18. Hong Kong Tourism Board, *A Statistical Review of Hong Kong Tourism* (Hong Kong: Hong Kong Tourism Board, various years).

19. The data of the *Cross Boundary Travel Survey* can be found from the website of the Planning Department, HKSAR Government, see the Web page of the Planning Department of the HKSAR Government, http://www.info.gov.hk/planning/index_e.htm.

20. About 16,000 lived in the mainland and 17,000 lived in Hong Kong.

21. There are very few systematic studies of cross-boundary consumption behaviour in south China. The following analysis mainly uses primary data collected by the HKSAR Government. The 2002 data are from the Census and Statistics Department, quoted in Chun Yang, 2006, "The Pearl River Delta and Hong Kong: an evolving cross-boundary region under 'one country, two systems,'" *Habitat International*, Vol. 30, No. 1, p. 74.

22. Census and Statistics Department, 2004, "Consumption Expenditure of Hong Kong Residents Travelling to the Mainland of China, 2000–2003," in *Hong Kong Monthly Digest of Statistics, May 2004* (Hong Kong: Census and Statistics Department, FA1–FA12; Census and Statistics Department, 2004, *Hong Kong Annual Digest of Statistics 2004*, Hong Kong: Census and Statistics Department, p. 210; and Hong Kong Tourism Board, 2005, "Tourism Spending Jumps to HK $91.8 billion in 2004," *Press Release of the Hong Kong Tourism Board*, 2005, http://partnernet.hktourismboard.com/pnweb/jsp/doc/listDoc.jsp?doc_id=76032 (March 9, 2005).

23. Hong Kong Tourism Board, 2005, *A Statistical Review of Hong Kong Tourism 2006*, Hong Kong: Hong Kong Tourism Board.

24. Hong Kong Tourism Board, 2006, *A Statistical Review of Hong Kong Tourism 2005*, Hong Kong: Hong Kong Tourism Board, p. 16; Census and Statistics Department, 2006, "Consumption Expenditure of Hong Kong Residents Travelling to the Mainland of China, 2005," in Census and Statistics Department, The Government of the HKSAR, *Hong Kong Monthly Digest of Statistics May 2006*, Hong Kong: Census and Statistics Department, FA5.

25. *South China Morning Post*, May 9, 2003, A5; and Census and Statistics Department, 2005, *Hong Kong Residents Working in the Mainland of China: Special Topics Report No. 42, Social Data Collected via the General Household Survey*, Hong Kong: Census and Statistics Department.

26. This figure refers to the salary of the 228,900 employed persons who had worked in the mainland during the twelve months before enumeration and were still required to work there in their present job at the time of enumeration, but this figure should be similar to the 237,500 who had worked in the mainland during the twelve months before enumeration.

27. The summaries of these three surveys can be found in the website of the Planning Department, HKSAR Government, see the Web page of the Department at http://www.pland.gov.hk/planning. The 2003 survey was done between May and August,

so the impact of the CEPA arrangement could not be fully discerned. It should be noted that the HKSAR Government has not collected authoritative statistics of the number of Hong Kong residents who have resided permanently in the mainland, so it is unclear how many have actually moved across the boundary and decided not to return to Hong Kong.

28. These people had stayed in Hong Kong for at least one month but less than three months during the six-month period before or after the reference time-point. In other words, these Hong Kong residents have become "mobile residents." See also Planning Department, 2005, *Executive Summary of Hong Kong Residents' Experience of and Aspirations for Taking Up Residence in the Mainland of China in the Thematic Household Survey 2005*, Hong Kong: Planning Department.

29. *Wen Wei Po*, January 25, 2007, B12.

30. See para. 3.7 in "Gathering of information/intelligence about epidemic of infectious diseases in the Mainland and strategy/ contingency plan of the Hospital Authority for dealing with a large-scale outbreak of an infectious disease," in Select Committee of the Legislative Council of the Hong Kong Special Administrative Region, 2004, "Report of the Select Committee to inquire into the Handling of the Severe Acute Respiratory Syndrome Outbreak by the Government and the Hospital Authority," *Hong Kong: Legislative Council of the HKSAR*, 2004, http://www.legco.gov.hk/yr03-04/english/sc/sc_sars/reports/sars_rpt.htm, pp. 27–37.

31. I have addressed these and related issues in, "The SARS Outbreak and Cross-boundary Cooperation in South China," (paper presented at the Eighth Biennial Conference of the Chinese Studies Association of Australia held at the University of New South Wales, July 10–12, 2003).

32. World Health Organization, 2003, "WHO Severe Acute Respiratory Syndrome (SARS)- Multi-country outbreak–Update 43," *World Health Organization*, 2003, http://www.who.int/csr/don/2003_04_30/en/index.html (April 30, 2003).

33. See "Chapter 18: Main Recommendations of the Report of the SARS Expert Committee of the HKSAR Government," in the SARS Expert Committee, 2003, *Report in SARS in Hong Kong: from Experience to Action*, Hong Kong: HKSAR Government, pp. 165–172. The chapter in the report can also be downloaded from the internet at http://www.sarsexpertcom.gov.hk/textonly/english/reports/reports/files/e_chp18.pdf.

34. *Ming Pao*, October 9, 2004, A15.

35. See the paper presented to the Panel on Health Services of the Legislative Council of the HKSAR, 2007, "Impact of the Use of Obstetric Services by Mainland woman on Public Health Resources," *Legislaive Council of the HKSAR*, 2007, http://www.legco.gov.hk/yr06-07/english/panels/hs/papers/hs0108cb2-761-3-e.pdf, Appendix A.

36. The HKSAR Government, 2007, *Press Release from the Hong Kong Special Administration Region Government*, 2007, http://www.info.gov.hk/gia/general/200701/10/P200701100268.htm.

37. See the paper presented to the Panel on Health Services of the Legislative Council of the HKSAR, 2007, "Impact of the Use of Obstetric Services by Mainland woman on Public Health Resources," *Legislaive Council of the HKSAR*, 2007,

http://www.legco.gov.hk/yr06-07/english/panels/hs/papers/hs0108cb2-761-3-e.pdf, Appendix A.

38. Compiled from the data in Appendix A of the paper presented to the Panel on Health Services of the Legislative Council of the HKSAR, "Impact of the Use of Obstetric Services by Mainland woman on Public Health Resources."

39. A fee of HK $20,000 was charged to any non-eligible patient staying in the obstetrics wards in public hospitals from September 1, 2005. According to a report from the Audit Commission made in November 2006, the fees owed by Non-Eligible Person for using the facilities provided by the Hospital Authority amounted to HK $215.7 million. The noneligible persons were predominately pregnant woman using the obstetric services in the public hospitals in Hong Kong. (Audit Commission, "Hospital Authority: management of outstanding medical fees," *Audit Commission Hong Kong*, 2006, http://www.aud.gov.hk/pdf_e/e47ch05.pdf.

40. The HKSAR Government, 2006, "CE's transcript," *Press Release of the HKSAR Government* 2006, http://www.info.gov.hk/gia/general/200612/28/P200612280278 .htm.

41. *Ming Pao*, February 5, 2007, A18.

42. The HKSAR Government, 2007, "New measures on obstetric services and immigration control announced," *Press Release of the HKSAR Government* 2007, http://www.info.gov.hk/gia/general/200701/16/P200701160184.htm.

43. In fact, the number of employers convicted of employing illegal workers has increased from 264 in 2000 to 303 in 2002, and another 287 were convicted in the first nine months of 2003. The government statistics did not differentiate those employers who were convicted of employing illegal workers from the Mainland and from other areas. See Legislative Council, 2003, "LCQ8: Penalties for employing illegal workers," *Press Release of the HKSAR Government*, October 22, 2003, http://www.info.gov.hk/gia/general/200310/22/1022178.htm.

44. Data provided by the Immigration Department, HKSAR Government, May 23, 2005. The majority of these illegal workers are mainland visitors on various visa types, only less than 200 illegal immigrants were caught each year between 1999 and 2003.

45. There are also illegal workers with other nationalities, but those from the mainland accounted for 94 percent of the total in the first ten months of 2004.

46. See the statistics provided at the Employment Retraining Board of the HKSAR Government at http://www.erb.org/english/content5.shtml.

47. Data provided from an inquiry to the Security Bureau, HKSAR Government, May 12, 2005, and the Immigration Department, HKSAR Government, May 23, 2005.

48. Legislative Council, 2004, "LCQ11: Persons suspected of involving prostitution in Hong Kong," *Press Release of the HKSAR Government* 2004, http://www.info.gov.hk/gia/general/200407/07/0707183.htm. Data from an inquiry to the Security Bureau and the Immigration Department of the HKSAR Government, May 12, 2005 and May 23, 2005.

49. The latest figure available for 2002 only includes data for the first ten months. As of October 2003, there are 3,473 Mainland Chinese who are serving prison terms. See Legislative Council, 2003, "LCQ18: Mainlanders serving sentences in Hong

Kong," *Press Release of the HKSAR Government* 2003, http://www.info.gov.hk/gia/general/200310/08/1008173.htm. Information obtained from the Security Bureau and the Immigration Department of the HKSAR Government, May 12, 2005 and May 23, 2005.

50. Between April 2003 and May 2004, there was a total of 283 Hong Kong people being detained or held for ransom; see Legislative Council, 2004, "LCQ4: Hong Kong residents being crime victims in the Mainland," *Press Release of the HKSAR Government* 2004, http://www.info.gov.hk/gia/general/200406/23/0623238.htm.

51. The following discussion on intergovernmental mechanisms draws selectively from my unpublished manuscript, "Cross-boundary Cooperation in South China: Perspectives, Mechanisms, and Challenges."

52. In order to better coordinate the various government bureaus and departments in handling cross-boundary affairs, the Hong Kong Guangdong Cooperation Coordination Unit was established under the office of the chief secretary and financial secretary in August 2001 to help these top officials monitor the implementation of the initiatives endorsed at the Hong Kong-Guangdong Cooperation Joint Conference, to review existing policies and arrangements, especially in transportation and boundary crossing, and to tap input from the community to further cross-boundary cooperation. See "Hong Kong-Guangdong Joint Cooperation Unit," (paper submitted by the Hong Kong Guangdong Cooperation Coordination Unit of the HKSAR Government Submitted to the Panel on Commerce and Industry of the Legislative Council of the HKSAR, November 2001), http://www.legco.gov.hk/yr01-02/english/panels/ci/papers/ci-1112-cb1-220-1e.pdf.

53. The HKSAR Government, 2006, "Tripartite meeting on infectious diseases held in Dongguan," *Press Release of the HKSAR Government* 2006, http://www.info.gov.hk/gia/general/200606/29/P200606290161.htm.

54. The HKSAR Government, 2007, "Consensus reached at tripartite meeting on infectious diseases," *Press Release from the Hong Kong Special Administration Region Government*, 2007,http://www.info.gov.hk/gia/general/200707/27/P200707270198.htm.

55. The HKSAR Government, 2007, *Press Release from the Hong Kong Special Administration Region Government*, 2007, http://www.info.gov.hk/gia/general/200709/13/P200709130187.htm.

56. The HKSAR Government, 2006, "Framework Agreement on Exchanges and Co-operation in Food Safety signed," *Press Release of the HKSAR Government* 2006, http://www.info.gov.hk/gia/general/200604/11/P200604110145.htm.

57. The HKSAR Government, 2006, "CE's transcript (English portion)," *Press Release of the HKSAR Government* 2006, http://www.info.gov.hk/gia/general/200612/28/P200612280278.htm.

58. North American examples include the Great Lakes Commission, which engages state and provincial governments, experts, and other stakeholders in the United States and Canada to examine economic and environmental issues in the Great Lakes region.

59. The six subgroups are cross-boundary infrastructure planning subgroup; the services-implementation of CEPA subgroup; the sustainable development subgroup;

the joint investment and trade promotion subgroup; the technology, education, and human resources subgroup; and the tourist, culture, and sports subgroup.

60. Paper presented by the HKSAR Government on the Establishment of the Mainland Affairs Liaison Office to the Panel on Constitutional Affairs of the Legislative Council, para. 19.

61. *Hong Kong Economic Times*, February 25, 2006, A29.

62. For instance, only 30 percent of the immigrants have a secondary or above education, as compared with 52 percent of the total population. See The HKSAR Government, *Report of the Task Force on Population Policy*, http://www.info.gov.hk/info/population/eng/report_eng.pdf.

63. *Report of the Task Force on Population Policy*, http://www.info.gov.hk/info/population/eng/report_eng.pdf.

64. Five hundred fifty-three have been granted "Formal Approval" and ninety-eight have been granted "Approval in Principle." See the statistics in the Immigration Department website http://www.immd.gov.hk/ehtml/hkvisas_13_19.htm.

65. It should be noted that the following discussion does not take into account the number of mainland professionals or talents who have attained a foreign citizenship and then move to work in Hong Kong. Such data are not available. It is clear that in various service sectors, such as law, consulting, banking, and finance, quite a number of Mainland talents who have received advanced degrees from foreign countries have been working in Hong Kong. But their numbers probably will not change the overall picture that is described below.

66. Data comes from HKSAR Government Information Center, 2002, "Chapter 20: Population and Immigration Hong Kong Yearbook 2002," *HKSAR Government Information Center* 2003, http://www.info.gov.hk/yearbook/2002/ehtml/e20-07.htm.

67. All these three schemes allow the spouses and unmarried children of the person admitted to apply for entry to Hong Kong as dependants, and they all may apply for the right of abode after having resided in Hong Kong continuously for seven years. Immigration Department, "Statistics on Admission Scheme for Mainland Talents and Professionals," *Immigration Department, HKSAR Government* 2005, http://www.immd.gov.hk/ehtml/hkvisas3.5_12.htm; Immigration Department, "Progress Report on the Admission of Mainland Talents and Professionals," *Legislative Council* 2007, http://www.legco.gov.hk/yr07-08/english/panels/mp/papers/mpsecb2-133-1-e.pdf.

68. The HKSAR Government, 2007, "Immigration Department year-end briefing 2006," *Press Release of the HKSAR Government* 2007, http://www.info.gov.hk/gia/general/200702/08/P200702080211.htm.

69. The data here are compiled from the various *Hong Kong Yearbook*, 2001–2006.

70. *Hong Kong Commercial Daily*, July 26, 2003, A3. The National Development and Reform Commission stated that the feasibility report would be presented to the State Council for approval in July 2003, see *Wen Wei Po*, July 1, 2003, A15.

71. The data come from the secretary general of the Guangdong provincial government, *Wen Wei Po*, November 29, 2003.

72. See the discussion paper for the Professional Services, Information and Technology and Tourism Focus Group of the Economic Summit on "China 11th Five-

Year Plan and the Development of Hong Kong," http://www.info.gov.hk/info/econ_summit/eng/pdf/paper_10.pdf.

73. Presentation by Ms. Zhou Meng, a deputy bureau chief in trade promotion bureau of the Ministry of Commerce, and other speakers at the CEPA Economic Forum, CEPA SME EXPO, Hong Kong, December 2, 2003.

74. *South China Morning Post*, June 30, 2003, A1.

75. The HKSAR Government, 2004, "CEPA II provides further trade liberalization," *Press Release of the HKSAR Government* 2004, http://www.info.gov.hk/gia/general/200408/27/0827152.htm.

76. The HKSAR Government, 2005, "Mainland and Hong Kong sign legal text of CEPA III," *Press Release of Trade and Industry Department, HKSAR Government* 2005, http://www.tid.gov.hk/english/aboutus/presspeech/press/2005/20051018.html; The HKSAR Government, "Mainland and Hong Kong Closer Economic Partnership Arrangement (CEPA)," *Statistics and Research of Trade and Industry Department, HKSAR Government* 2008, http://www.tid.gov.hk/english/cepa/statistics/hkss_statistics.html.

77. See, for instance, Commission on Strategic Development, 2000, *Bringing the Vision to Life: Hong Kong's Long-term Development Needs and Goals*, Hong Kong: Commission on Strategic Development; and Michael Enright, et al., *Hong Kong and the Pearl River Delta: The Economic Interaction*, Hong Kong: The 2022 Foundation.

78. *South China Morning Post*, October 17, 2004, 2.

79. The HKSAR Government, 2006, "Regional Air Quality Monitoring Network: First report of monitoring results announced today," *Press Release of the HKSAR Government* 2006, http://www.info.gov.hk/gia/general/200610/31/P200610310205.htm.

80. The HKSAR Government, 2007, "Implementation framework of emission trading pilot scheme announced," *Press Release of the HKSAR Government* 2007, http://www.info.gov.hk/gia/general/200701/30/P200701300144.htm.

81. *South China Morning Post*, October 26, 2004, A3.

Index

www.ingramcontent.com/pod-product-compliance
Lightning Source LLC
LaVergne TN
LVHW102005210926
848483LV00009B/49